T0140545

ECSCW 2015: Proceedings of the 14th European Conference on Computer Supported Cooperative Work, 19–23 September 2015, Oslo, Norway

Nina Boulus-Rødje · Gunnar Ellingsen
Tone Bratteteig · Margunn Aanestad
Pernille Bjørn
Editors

ECSCW 2015: Proceedings of the 14th European Conference on Computer Supported Cooperative Work, 19–23 September 2015, Oslo, Norway

 Springer

Editors
Nina Boulus-Rødje
Department of Media, Cognition
  and Communication
The University of Copenhagen
Copenhagen
Denmark

Gunnar Ellingsen
Telemedicine and eHealth Research Group
The University of Tromsø—The Arctic
  University of Norway
Tromsø
Norway

Tone Bratteteig
Department of Informatics
University of Oslo
Oslo
Norway

Margunn Aanestad
Department of Informatics
University of Oslo
Oslo
Norway

Pernille Bjørn
Department of Computer Science
The University of Copenhagen
Copenhagen
Denmark

ISBN 978-3-319-36794-1   ISBN 978-3-319-20499-4   (eBook)
DOI 10.1007/978-3-319-20499-4

Springer Cham Heidelberg New York Dordrecht London
© Springer International Publishing Switzerland 2015
Softcover reprint of the hardcover 1st edition 2015

Printed on acid-free paper

Springer International Publishing AG Switzerland is part of Springer Science+Business Media
(www.springer.com)

ECSCW 2015 Conference Committee

General Chairs
Tone Bratteteig, University of Oslo, Norway
Margunn Aanestad, University of Oslo, Norway

Programme Chairs
Nina Boulus-Rødje, The University of Copenhagen, Denmark
Gunnar Ellingsen, The University of Tromsø—The Arctic
University of Norway, Norway

Exploratory Papers Chairs
Kari Kuutti, Oulu University, Finland
Kjeld Schmidt, Copenhagen Business School, Denmark

Workshops and Master Classes Co-chairs
Sisse Finken, Linnaeus University, Sweden
Lars Rune Christensen, IT University, Denmark

Posters, Demos and Videos Co-chairs
Mads Bødker, Copenhagen Business School, Denmark
Michael Prilla, Ruhr University of Bochum, Germany

Proceedings Chair
Pernille Bjørn, The University of Copenhagen, Denmark

Doctoral Colloquium Co-chairs
Ina Wagner, University of Oslo, Norway
Toni Robertson, Technical University of Sydney, Australia

ECSCW 2015 Program Committee

Margunn Aanestad, University of Oslo, Norway
Mark Ackerman, University of Michigan, USA
Alessandra Agostini, Università di Milano-Bicocca, Italy

Markus Rohde, University of Siegen, Germany
Mark Rouncefield, Lancaster University, UK
Pascal Salembier, Université de Technologie de Troyes, France
Kjeld Schmidt, Copenhagen Business School, Denmark
Carla Simone, Università di Milano-Bicocca, Italy
Gunnar Stevens, University of Siegen, Germany
Norman Su, Indiana University, Bloomington, USA
Hilda Tellioğlu, Vienna University of Technology, Austria
Ina Wagner, Vienna University of Technology, Austria, and University of Oslo, Norway
Volker Wulf, University of Siegen, Germany
Pär-Ola Zander, Aalborg University, Denmark

Additional Reviewers
Konstantin Aal, Helena Webb, Juri Dachtera, Angela Locoro, John Hutchinson

Preface

This volume represents the proceedings of ECSCW 2015, the 14th European Conference on Computer Supported Cooperative Work, held in Oslo, Norway, September 19–23, 2015.

ECSCW 2015 received 60 paper submissions. After extensive review, 14 were selected to form the core of the traditional single-track technical programme for the conference. They are published in these proceedings from the conference.

This year, exploratory papers have been introduced as a new peer-reviewed category of short papers. The exploratory papers should represent a more open and daring approach to topics and questions in CSCW and are not only short papers. In total, there were eleven exploratory papers submitted and three were accepted to the conference after extensive review. The three exploratory papers are also included in these proceedings. We gratefully acknowledge the work carried out by the exploratory papers co-chairs Kari Kuutti and Kjeld Schmidt to establish a fair review process for this new category of papers, valuing novelty, openness and a critical approach to CSCW research in Europe. We hope that the exploratory papers will spur reflection, discussion and development of our research field.

The papers published in this proceeding are supplemented by workshops, master classes, posters, demos, videos and doctoral colloquium, all of which cover a broad range of topics and allow for wider and more active participation.

The technical programme this year focuses on cooperative work in work settings as well as outside of work and on the challenges of involving citizens, patients, and others into collaborative settings. The papers embrace new theories and discuss known ones. They challenge the ways we think about and study work and contribute to the discussions of the blurring boundaries between home and work life. We have theoretical papers as well as papers offering detailed empirical studies. The papers introduce recent and emergent technologies, and study known social and collaborative technologies. Classical settings in computer-supported cooperative work are looked upon anew. With contributions from all over the world, the papers in interesting ways help focus on the European perspective in our community.

Many people have worked hard to ensure the success of this conference, and we wish to gratefully acknowledge their crucial contribution: all the authors who submitted high-quality full papers and exploratory papers; all those who contributed through taking part in workshops and master classes, demos and demonstrations, doctoral colloquium and posters; the 59-member global programme committee, who dedicated time and energy to reviewing and discussing individual contributions and shaping the programme; the people who helped organise the programme: the workshop and master class chairs, the chairs of demos, videos and posters, the chairs of exploratory papers and doctoral colloquium; and finally, the student volunteers who provided support throughout the event; we thank the sponsors and those who offered their support to the conference.

Nina Boulus-Rødje
Gunnar Ellingsen
Tone Bratteteig
Margunn Aanestad
Pernille Bjørn

Contents

Part I   Papers

**Human Data Interaction: Historical Lessons
from Social Studies and CSCW**   3
Andy Crabtree and Richard Mortier

Mining Programming Activity to Promote Help   23
Jason Carter and Prasun Dewan

**"*It's About Business not Politics*": Software Development
Between Palestinians and Israelis**   43
Nina Boulus-Rødje, Pernille Bjørn and Ahmad Ghazawneh

Social Media-Based Expertise Evidence   63
Arnon Yogev, Ido Guy, Inbal Ronen, Naama Zwerdling and Maya Barnea

**3D Printing with Marginalized Children—An Exploration
in a Palestinian Refugee Camp**   83
Oliver Stickel, Dominik Hornung, Konstantin Aal,
Markus Rohde and Volker Wulf

Intertext: On Connecting Text in the Building Process 103
Lars Rune Christensen

**Analyzing Collaborative Reflection Support:
A Content Analysis Approach** 123
Michael Prilla, Alexander Nolte, Oliver Blunk,
Dennis Liedtke and Bettina Renner

Keeping Distributed Care Together: Medical Summaries Reconsidered ... 143
Troels Mønsted

**Constructing Awareness Through Speech, Gesture, Gaze
and Movement During a Time-Critical Medical Task**................. 163
Zhan Zhang and Aleksandra Sarcevic

**Online Social Networks and Police in India—Understanding
the Perceptions, Behavior, Challenges**............................ 183
Niharika Sachdeva and Ponnurangam Kumaraguru

The Work of Infrastructuring: A Study of a National eHealth Project... 205
Miria Grisot and Polyxeni Vassilakopoulou

**How Do User Groups Cope with Delay in Real-Time
Collaborative Note Taking**...................................... 223
Claudia-Lavinia Ignat, Gérald Oster, Olivia Fox,
Valerie L. Shalin and François Charoy

Configuring Attention in the Multiscreen Living Room............... 243
John Rooksby, Timothy E. Smith, Alistair Morrison,
Mattias Rost and Matthew Chalmers

**Measures and Tools for Supporting ICT Appropriation by Elderly
and Non Tech-Savvy Persons in a Long-Term Perspective**............ 263
Claudia Müller, Dominik Hornung, Theodor Hamm and Volker Wulf

Part II   Exploratory Papers

CSCW and the Internet of Things.............................. 285
Toni Robertson and Ina Wagner

Ageing Well with CSCW 295
Ann Light, Tuck W. Leong and Toni Robertson

**Collaborative Visualization for Supporting the Analysis
of Mobile Device Data**... 305
Thomas Ludwig, Tino Hilbert and Volkmar Pipek

Part I
Papers

Human Data Interaction: Historical Lessons from Social Studies and CSCW

Andy Crabtree and Richard Mortier

Abstract Human Data Interaction (HDI) is an emerging field of research that seeks to support end-users in the day-to-day management of their personal digital data. This is a programmatic paper that seeks to elaborate foundational challenges that face HDI from an interactional perspective. It is rooted in and reflects foundational lessons from social studies of science that have had a formative impact on CSCW, and core challenges involved in supporting interaction/collaboration from within the field of CSCW itself. These are drawn upon to elaborate the inherently social and relational character of data and the challenges this poses for the ongoing development of HDI, particularly with respect to the 'articulation' of personal data. Our aim in doing this is not to present solutions to the challenges of HDI but to articulate core problems that confront this fledgling field as it moves from nascent concept to find a place in the interactional milieu of everyday life and particular research challenges that accompany it.

Introduction

> … what experience and history teach is this - that people … never have learned anything from history, or acted on principles deduced from it. Each period is involved in such peculiar circumstances, exhibits a condition of things so strictly idiosyncratic, that its conduct must be regulated by considerations connected with itself, and itself alone. (G. W. F. Hegel)

A. Crabtree (✉)
School of Computer Science, University of Nottingham, Nottingham, UK
e-mail: andy.crabtree@nottingham.ac.uk

R. Mortier
Computer Laboratory, University of Cambridge, Cambridge, UK
e-mail: richard.mortier@cl.cam.ac.uk

© Springer International Publishing Switzerland 2015
N. Boulus-Rødje et al. (eds.), *ECSCW 2015: Proceedings of the 14th European Conference on Computer Supported Cooperative Work, 19–23 September 2015, Oslo, Norway*, DOI 10.1007/978-3-319-20499-4_1

3

We write this paper in the sincere hope that Hegel got it wrong, and that something of value may be learnt from historical works to inform considerations in the current circumstances of inquiry. The current circumstances and considerations we refer to are, as the title of this paper suggests, to do with Human Data Interaction or HDI, an emerging field of computer science concerned with understanding and developing the underlying technologies required to support human interaction with digital data (algorithms, analytics, visualisations, etc.). This field of research is driven by the recognition that digital data has become what phenomenologists (Hegel included) might call an 'object-in-itself', a distinctive phenomenon worthy of treatment in its own right as reflected, for example, in widespread current interest in 'Big Data'. Whether the data is big or small is not of particular concern here, however. Rather, the issue is essentially one of developing some appreciation of what the 'I' means in HDI, and the challenges this raises for the development of computer support for human data interaction in the round.

Our aim in this paper is, first, to understand what HDI is about as a distinctive field of research and to unpack the ways in which human data interaction is construed of. We then reflect on social studies of human data interaction to highlight the contrast between technological and ethnographic conceptions, which suggest that data is not so much a thing-in-itself as a thing-embedded-in-human-relationships (Star and Griesemer 1989). The contrast draws attention to the interactional demands that may be placed on HDI as a socio-technical infrastructure (Star 1999), and the subsequent interactional challenges that accompany this, particularly the development of interaction mechanisms that support the 'articulation' of personal data between parties involved in sharing it (Schmidt and Bannon 1992). Our reflections draw attention to the need to develop social models and mechanisms of data sharing that enable users to play an active role in the process. We identify a number of core research challenges involved in bringing this about, which revolve around personal data discovery, data ownership and control, data legibility, and data tracking.

What is Human Data Interaction?

As per most academic ventures the reader might anticipate that answering the above question won't be straightforward, and indeed even a cursory glance at the literature makes it visible that different meanings already attach to the term; we discern at least 5 distinct 'versions' to date.

- HDI is about human manipulation, analysis, and sense-making of large, unstructured, and complex datasets (Elmqvist 2011).
- HDI is about delivering personalized, context-aware, and understandable data from big datasets (Cafor 2012).
- HDI is about providing access and understandings of data that is about individuals and how it affects them (Mashhadi et al., unpub. manu.).

- HDI is about federating disparate personal data sources and enabling user control over the use of 'my data' (McAuley et al. 2011).
- HDI is about processes of collaboration with data and the development of communication tools that enable interaction (Kee et al. 2012).

While distinct, there is a sense of continuum running through the different versions of HDI; a connecting thread as it were that suggests (a) that there is a great deal of digital data about, so much so that it might be seen as 'the next frontier' for computing and society alike (Pentland 2012); (b) that HDI is very much configured around large amounts of 'personal data' (whether in terms of delivering personalised experiences or in terms of it being about individuals); and (c) that interaction covers a range of interrelated topics from data analytics to data tailoring, and enabling access, control, and collaboration.

On reading the literature, such as it is (this is a fledgling field), we come to the view that HDI is not about data per se then, not even digital data, but is very much centred on digital data pertaining to people and digital data that may be considered to be 'personal' in nature. As McAuley et al. (2011) and Haddadi et al. (2013) put it respectively,

> Modern life involves each of us in the creation and management of data. Data about us is either created and managed by us (e.g., our address books, email accounts), or by others (e.g., our health records, bank transactions, loyalty card activity). Some may even be created by and about us, but be managed by others (e.g., government tax records).
> An ecosystem, often collaborative but sometimes combative, is forming around companies and individuals engaging in use of personal data.

We are not suggesting that everyone who has used the term HDI buys into this conception, only that it captures a distinct problematic: the management and use of personal data in society at large (Mortier et al. 2014, Haddadi et al. 2015). HDI is a distinctively socio-technical problematic, driven as much by a range of social concerns with the emerging personal data 'ecosystem' as it is by technological concerns, to develop digital technologies that support future practices of personal data interaction within it. It will come as no surprise then that HDI has opened its doors to interdisciplinary engagement. In this paper we seek to go beyond considerations of social context—i.e., of the ethical, political, economic, and legal considerations that frame HDI (as important as these are)—to understand how the social might actually *shape* interaction within HDI. To do that, we first need to unpack how interaction is construed of within the field.

How is Interaction Construed within HDI?

In begging the question of how interaction is construed within HDI we recognise the need to move beyond the vague generalities outlined above and say something concrete about how analytics, tailoring, access, control and collaboration (etc.) are to be supported so as to afford human data interaction within the personal data ecosystem. It is perhaps useful to first consider the posited nature of interaction in HDI.

> We are not dealing with explicit interactions but with more passive scenarios. In HDI we consider people interacting with apparently mundane infrastructure, which they generally do not understand and would rather ignore. (Haddadi et al. 2013)

HDI seeks to transform the current circumstances of interaction from a 'passive' situation in which personal data or more specifically 'data about you' is generated in your mundane interactions with digital infrastructure and is increasingly accessible to third party use, into an active situation in which 'my data' and its subsequent use is actively managed and controlled by the people who produce it. The interactional situation is further complicated by the recognition, as stated above, that 'data about you' may not be yours but may either be generated by you on behalf of a third party (e.g., the taxman) or by third parties (e.g., retailers) in your interactions with their services. This creates an interactional situation that negates 'data containment'— i.e., the idea that 'data about you' could be handed over to you and that third parties could be prohibited from distributing copies of it without your permission. That 'my data' can, in the current circumstances, be readily copied and distributed by third parties further compounds the problem of human data interaction.

So we have a current interactional situation in which 'data about you' is passively generated by you in your mundane interactions with digital infrastructure, and rather more actively by you on behalf of others or by others themselves in your interactions with their services, and that any of this data is, in principle and increasingly in practice, available to infinite replication and (re)distribution. The current situation underpins the very viability of the Big Data society, and the situation is on the verge of an exponential explosion as the Internet of Things locates a myriad data gathering objects in the fabric of everyday life. How, then, is the interactional situation now and in the foreseeable future to be addressed?

Mashhadi et al. (unpub. manu.) propose various models of human data interaction (ranging from the pay-per-use model to the data market and open data models), but provide little insight into how interaction would actually be provided for within them. By contrast McAuley et al. (2011) seek to provide computational means of supporting human data interaction through the development of 'dataware', which seeks to federate disparate sources of data 'about me' and to build digital infrastructure that enables people to exercise control over the use of data that belongs to them and/or is about them. Data federation seeks to enable people to become involved in third party processing of personal data without requiring that they take sole responsibility for the data. Data control complements data federation by focusing on who is gathering, processing and distributing 'my data', when and for what purposes, and the means by which an individual can enable processing services and applications to access the data on their behalf.

The Dataware Model

The dataware model does not capture all there is about HDI, but rather provides a particular instantiation of some core concepts. The model is based on three fundamental types of interacting entity: *the user*, by or about whom data is created;

the *data sources*, which generate and collate data; and the *data processors*, which wish to make use of the user's data in some way. To assist the user in managing the relationship between these entities, the model posits that the underlying technology will provide the user with a 'personal container' or 'databox', which will enable them to oversee and manage access to their data sources and processing of their data by various 'data consumers'. This is a logical entity formed as a distributed computing system, with the software envisaged to support it consisting of a set of APIs providing access to data held by data sources. Data processors would write code to use these APIs, and then distribute that code to the data sources which take responsibility for executing it and then return results as directed by the data processor. The final and key piece of infrastructure envisaged is a *catalogue*, within which a user would register all their data sources, and to which processors would submit requests for metadata about the sources available, as well as requests to process data in specified ways.

From a user's point of view, interaction with this model works as follows: processors desiring access to one or more datasets within the catalogue present a request for access along with information about the request (minimally a representation of the processing to be carried out); the user permits (or denies) the request, which is indicated by the catalogue returning some form of token to the processor representing granted permission; the processor subsequently presents the request (the processing to be carried out) and the token to the data sources it covers; finally, the data sources return the results of the processing as directed in the request to the data consumer. The model assumes that the catalogue and the data sources it references are governed by the user, including logging and auditing the uses made of data so that the user can retrospectively inspect what has been done, when, by whom and to what end.[1]

Dataware can be seen as an attempt to build a digital infrastructure that supports human data interaction by surfacing a user's personal data sources and what third parties would do with them or have done with them. It construes of the 'I' in HDI as an *accountable transaction* between the parties to it, configured in terms of request, permission, and audit. In this respect it potentially transforms the current situation of interaction, which is characterised by the largely unaccountable use of personal data by third parties, but it leaves untouched how any such transaction will, in practice, be accountably conducted. We do not mean by this how requests, permissions and audits will actually be carried out. Though these are important matters to be resolved, what have in mind here are the accountable matters that any such actions turn upon and would have to turn upon if they were actually to be brought about and be 'pulled off' in the real world. It is towards unpacking what we mean by 'accountable matters' of human data interaction that we now turn.

---

[1]The model also permits a user to operate multiple catalogues, independent of each other, thereby providing a means to control the problems of linking accounts across different sources. Interactions between such catalogues are not considered an explicit feature of the system.

Accountable Matters of Human Data Interaction

Human data, as any other data, might usefully be understood as a 'boundary object' (Star and Griesemer 1989), a common notion in CSCW where it has been used both to shape studies of cooperative activity and concepts of CSCW systems, particularly the notion of 'common information spaces' in which boundary objects are understood as 'containers and carriers' of information between actors and organisations (Bannon and Bødker 1997). It is not our intention here to provide a detailed review of Star and Griesemer's work, as this is a well-trodden path in CSCW, but rather to draw out some salient features of relevance to HDI. Although the concept of a boundary object originated in ethnographic studies of collaborative activity in science, it is possessed of features that are of broader relevance to understanding the nature of information or data in human interaction.

Star and Griesemer's original account of boundary objects can be read more generally to suggest that human data interaction turns upon 'a mutual modus operandi' involving 'communications' and 'translations' that order the 'flow' of information through 'networks' of participants. This, in turn, creates an 'ecology' of collaboration in which data interaction becomes stable. As stable entities boundary objects inhabit 'several intersecting worlds' (e.g., the individual's, the supermarket's, the bank's) and meet the information requirements of each. Your credit card receipt might be seen to be a boundary object—as well as detailing how much you spent on shopping at the supermarket, for example, it enables the supermarket to bill your bank, and your bank to clear payment for your goods. As Star and Griesemer put it,

> Boundary objects ... are both plastic enough to adapt to local needs and the constraints of the several parties employing them, yet robust enough to maintain a common identity across sites ... They have different meanings in different social worlds but their structure is common enough to more than one world to make them recognisable, a means of translation.

Thus, the credit card receipt is a proof of payment for you, proof that a request for payment from your bank to the supermarket is valid, and proof that a valid transaction has been made on your behalf by the bank to the supermarket. The receipt spans several intersecting social worlds, has different meanings in each, and yet maintains a common identity across sites: it is a record of a financial transaction that coheres across social worlds.

The 'coherence' of boundary objects is something that needs a little unpacking. That boundary objects can cohere across social worlds, that they are *recognisable* and thus accountable to multiple parties, turns upon 'invisible work' (Star 2010) or action and interaction that largely goes unrecognised, is taken for granted and ignored. This invisible work is, nonetheless, consequential for the design of computational systems, as we have seen in other areas of systems development (Suchman 1995). The upshot is that when we turn to boundary objects we are not just turning to a 'container' or 'carrier' of informational material then, but to the interactional grounds upon which the 'containing' and 'carrying' of such material gets done. This means that boundary objects are 'the stuff of action' and are, as such, embedded in some underlying 'arrangement' of collaborative work (Star 2010). Boundary objects are inherently social then, cohering *in* action and interaction that inevitably reaches 'beyond a single site'. In this respect boundary objects are also spatially and temporally distributed, which points to their 'processual' character as well.

> The object (remember, to read this as a set of work arrangements that are at once material and processual) resides between social worlds ... where it is ill structured. (ibid.)

The 'ill-structured' nature of boundary objects points to their inherent malleability, though what is interesting here is how, over the course of being translated across social worlds and in 'tacking back-and-forth' between the local needs of parties to their collaborative production and use, boundary objects become 'well-structured' and stable. As Star (ibid.) puts it,

> ... when the movement between the two forms either scales up or becomes standardised, then boundary objects begin to move and change into infrastructure, into standards (particularly methodological standards), and into things and yet other processes, which have not yet been fully studied as such.

The coherence of boundary objects ultimately turns upon their standardisation, which is provided for 'methodologically'—i.e., through the development of methods for communicating data and coordinating data sharing. As these methods become standardised they become part and parcel of the mundane 'infrastructures' that permeate everyday life.

Here we touch upon another major concept to emerge from Star's ethnographic work, and something that has 'not yet been fully studied as such'—infrastructure, or the study of 'boring things' (Star 1999). What she means is unremarkable things, taken for granted things, things that are invisible-in-use. Infrastructure is a familiar feature of everyday life:

> People commonly envision infrastructure as a system of substrates – railroad lines, pipes and plumbing, electrical power plants, and wires ... This image holds up well enough for many purposes – turn on the faucet for a drink of water and you use a vast infrastructure of plumbing and water regulation without usually thinking much about it. (ibid.)

Star suggests that there is more to infrastructure than the configuration of technology, of pipes and wires and power plants, etc. She suggests that it is also, and essentially, 'relational', and that it is by virtue of this that infrastructure comes to be embedded in the 'organised practices' of everyday life.

> So, within a given cultural context, the cook considers the water system as working infrastructure integral to making dinner ... Analytically, infrastructure appears only as a relational property, not as a thing stripped of use. (ibid)

The notion of boundary objects makes it clear that there is a great deal more to data, and the development of infrastructures to support interaction with it, than meets the eye. It makes it clear that data is, as Star puts it, an 'n-dimensional' social object, containing (1) informational material that is (2) distributed spatially and temporally across (3) participating sites through (4) processual arrangements of collaborative work that are (5) coordinated through standardised methods of communication, elaborating (6) particular contextual relationships that embed data (7) in organised practices of everyday life and (8) thereby constitute infrastructure. So what?

Boundary Objects, HDI and CSCW

The infrastructural view on boundary objects suggests that data is not so much an object-in-itself as it is an object-embedded-in-human-relationships, and that data transactions within those relationships are possessed of particular account-able properties or 'dimensions' that provide for the coherence of human data interaction. We might ask the question then, is the interactional arrangement request-permission-audit *sufficient* to make HDI into a mundane infrastructure? When considered from a socio-technical viewpoint on infrastructure, the data-ware model, while marking a necessary step-change, would seem to lack overall coherence.

Take, for starters, the basic principle of human data interaction as elaborated by the notion of boundary objects: that it turns upon a 'a mutual modus operandi', which involves 'communications' and 'translations' that order the 'flow' of infor-mation through 'networks' of participants. At first glance it might appear that HDI within the dataware ecology reflects this principle, but in what sense is interaction mutual? Communications are driven by third parties, not by the people whose data is being transacted and translated. That you or I are implicated in the interaction through requests and permissions does not make it a mutual modus operandi. The 'user' (though this seems a strange term in this context, the 'used' seems more apposite) is essentially on the receiving end of interaction; it is something done to them, not by them. Even if they do have the ability to refuse or remove permis-sions, the user is dealing with one-way traffic. The dataware modus operandi is asymmetrical and begs the question of what a symmetrical relationship might look like, e.g., how might users drive data sharing by (for example) actively seeking out data processors?

Complicating the situation is the inherently cognitive character of the dataware model. It is a model based on 'my data' and on data 'about me'. It is, as such, an individuated model that ignores the n-dimensional character of human data. What we mean by this is that much of the data that 'I' generate is produced in 'my' inter-actions *with others*. Data is relational and it often relates not so much to 'me' or 'you' but to 'us', and with this the coherence of the 'my data' model starts to break down and break down in challenging ways. It is not just a matter of handling what, for example, 'you' posted on 'my' Facebook page, but of handling the media we produce and consume together. Thus, the unit of data is not always 'mine' but fre-quently 'ours'. How is 'our data' to be handled? How is social data to be cata-logued and governed?

The social character of human data in turn raises serious issues of data own-ership and control. The individuated model makes 'me' the owner and con-troller of data, but as this model breaks down in the face of the social, how is ownership and control of 'our' data to be provided for? It's not 'simply' a matter of enabling ownership and control over data that cannot be disambiguated and assigned to individuals, or enabling a self-defined cohort to pool or aggregate its members' data, such that, for example, one person in the home could 'house keep' personal data for all householders, much as we see with respect to the day to day management of the home network (Tolmie et al. 2007). A host of relational issues are wrapped up in any such endeavour: the age of members of 'our' cohort will shape ownership and control, as will the personal situations that members find themselves in. Who, for example, will own and control 'our' children's personal data? And what about elderly, infirm or temporally incapacitated members of 'our' cohort? Situated within a lively social context, and accompanied by differing relational rights and obligations, ownership and control cannot be permanently fixed and tied to an individual, as the dataware model presumes, but will instead change over time with respect to a host of evolving relationships and contingencies.

The inherent rub between 'my data' and 'our data' will need to be managed too. Even were users able to manage a pool of 'our' data, there persists a tension between members with regard to what should be pooled and what should remain 'mine'. This raises problems both of ownership and control. Take, for example, a young child's personal data—who owns it and who controls it? It cannot be assumed that the same person exercises ownership *and* control. Ownership may well reside with the person to whom the data applies as it were, but control in such a situation may well be delegated to another (e.g., a parent) thereby reflecting current organised practices of personal data handling (take, for example, a young child's health records or bank details). The same does not apply to a teenager, however. As they develop their independence we might well expect, again in line with current organised practices of human data interaction, that they will assume control over their own data along with a great many other aspects of their life, though this may be a phased rather than a sharp transition. The same may apply in reverse to an elderly member of the cohort who wishes to hand over the running of their affairs to someone else.

The subtleties of human data interaction in the social world make ownership and control into complex matters in which 'my data' must co-exist alongside 'our data', and mechanisms must exist to enable translations between the two. There is, then, a need to develop a much more encompassing and dynamic model of human data interaction, including the possibility for users not only to refuse or remove permissions but also, to redact data, both internally within a cohort (whether it be a family or some other grouping of people) and externally in our interactions with third parties. In the real world data sharing is 'recipient designed'—i.e., shaped by people with respect to the relationship they have with the parties implicated in the act of sharing. What you tell people of how much you smoke or drink or what kinds of foodstuff you eat and how much you weigh, for example, very much depends upon who you are doing the telling to. It is well known by doctors, for example, that such matters are grossly underestimated when they are told to them. The same applies more generally; not that we grossly underestimate things but that we are selective in what we divulge about our personal lives, with the 'selectivity' being done with respect to our relationship to the other parties involved.[2]

These problems, which are be no means exhaustive of the challenges confronting efforts to build digital infrastructures supporting human data interaction, suggest that there is a strong sense in which we need to factor 'articulation work' into HDI. Like the notion of boundary objects, articulation work is a familiar concept in CSCW (Schmidt and Bannon 1992), where it typically refers to an important feature in the design of cooperative information systems for the workplace. While some may be inclined to argue that the workplace is all that it applies to, we think it may also usefully extend to human data interaction in the round insofar as there is a *necessary interdependence* between users, both as individuals in their own right and as potential members of self-defined cohorts, and third parties who would purpose their data. Wittingly or not the dataware model makes users part of a division of labour whose work involves the organised harvesting of personal data, whatever its purpose (whether to drive the delivery of personalised digital services to users, or for financial reasons by users, or by all parties involved for the social good, etc.).

This may be a contentious claim to make and it is worth briefly reviewing what is distinct about cooperative work to substantiate it, as it may be tempting to see the dataware user as someone engaged in individual activity rather than cooperative work. As Schmidt and Bannon argued many years ago, cooperative work is a distinct category of work having certain fundamental features irrespective of technology past, present or future.

> ... the conception of cooperative work ... does not assume or entail specific forms of interaction such as mode and frequency of communication, comradely feelings, equality of status, formation of a distinct group identity, etc. or even specific organisational settings. (ibid.)

Indeed, Schmidt and Bannon go on to argue that cooperative work is not 'necessarily congruent' with the boundaries of formal organisations or legal definitions of work relations.

> Cooperative work is constituted by interdependence in work, that is, by work activities that are related as to content in the sense that they pertain to the production of a specific product or service. (ibid.)

The necessary interdependence of actors defines cooperative work, without presupposition as to the formal or legal status of the relationship between the parties to it. Schmidt and Bannon thus suggest that the term cooperative work should be taken as a 'general and neutral designation' of multiple persons working together

---

[2]HDI construes of the recipient as *the processor*, which presents a particular request for computation to be carried out to the data source after it has been granted permission. While this hold true, the issue is to enable *the user* to design permission with respect to just what of the data is available to the processor, and to others within a particular cohort too. Recipient design draws our attention for the need to support human judgement, decision-making and intervention in the course of human data interaction.

to produce a product or service. People may then be said to be engaged in cooperative work if they are mutually dependent upon one another in the production of a product or service. While essentially individuated, the dataware model nevertheless configures a relationship of mutual dependence between users and third parties who would purpose their data. The dataware user may not be employed by third parties in a formal or legal sense, and thus be deemed to be part of an organisation, but they are inevitably enmeshed in cooperative work.

A core feature of cooperative work is 'articulation work'—i.e., the meshing together of distributed individual activities (Strauss 1985). Drawing off Strauss, Schmidt and Bannon tell us that articulation work is a 'supra-type of work', an unavoidable 'overhead' implicated in the doing of any activity that is bound up with others. Someone taking a walk has to mesh the business of walking with those around them, for example, has to coordinate their individual actions with the other people whose paths they cross. Articulation work speaks to the coordinate character of human action, to the *gearing in* of individual courses of action with one another. It is done in innumerable and manifold ways, though Schmidt (1994), drawing off a range of ethnographic studies, highlights several generic features of action and interaction that coordination turns upon. These include 'maintaining reciprocal awareness' of salient activities within a cooperative ensemble; 'directing attention' towards the current state of cooperative activities; 'assigning tasks' to members of the ensemble; and 'handing over' aspects of the work for others to pick up and work on themselves. These general properties of coordinate action are manifest concretely in situated practices that create and sustain a 'common field of work', whether coordinating 'walking' in the company of others or the 'sharing' of personal data with processors.

The common field of work in HDI is the catalogue of data sources that users generate. Data 'sharing' is organised around the catalogue and is ostensibly coordinated through the interactional arrangement request-permission-audit. This is an insufficient arrangement when seen from the perspective of cooperative work, however, for reasons that Schmidt points out.

> ... in order to be able to conceptualise and specify the support requirements of cooperative work we need to make a fundamental analytical distinction between (a) cooperative work activities in relation to the state of the field of work and mediated by changes to the state of the field of work, and (b) activities that arise from the fact that the work requires and involves multiple agents whose individual activities need to be coordinated, scheduled, meshed, integrated, etc. — in short: *articulated*. (ibid.)

Requests, permissions and audit logs are mechanisms of coordination within the field of work itself, but they do not articulate the field of work. They *order the flow* of information between users and third parties, but the flow itself stands in need of articulation. What, for example, occasions a request being made and being made in such a way for it to seem 'reasonable' to a user? Consider the expectations we might ordinarily entertain and the potential responses that might attach to requests from strangers, for example. Add to the mix how we might ordinarily react to requests regarding our personal data from strangers and it soon becomes clear that making a request is a nontrivial matter; that it requires *articulation*. As Bannon and Schmidt remind us,

Building computer systems where work is seen as simply being concerned with 'information flow,' and neglecting the articulation work needed to make the 'flow' possible, can
lead to serious problems. (Schmidt and Bannon 992)

Thus, a key design challenge in HDI is not only one of developing appropriate
mechanisms to coordinate the flow of information within the field of work, but of
articulating and thus coordinating *the work that makes flow possible* as well.

What does this entail? Schmidt (1994) highlights several generic features of
'social mechanisms of interaction' to support articulation work—'salient dimensions' of cooperative work arrangements, such as who, what, where, when, how,
etc. Schmidt suggests that these salient dimensions constitute 'elemental objects'
implicated in the articulation of cooperative work arrangements (in contrast to the
field of work itself) and that they provide a conceptual foundation for constructing computational mechanisms of interaction that support articulation work. Their
elaboration geos beyond the 'minimal' representations of purpose wrapped up in
requests in HDI to include *actors* (e.g., the particular parties involved in data processing); *roles* (e.g., the responsibilities that the particular parties involved processing data have); *activities* (e.g., the sequence of discrete 'jobs' implicated in
processing the data and their status); *tasks* (the specific jobs being performed and
their outputs).

There is more to Schmidt's elaboration of salient features of articulation work,
and whether or not they constitute an adequate stipulation for articulation work
in HDI or not is besides the point. The point is that no such stipulation currently
exists in HDI. Neither the request or audit function provide adequate support and
with it insight into the cooperative arrangement of work between users and third
parties or the status of data processing *within that arrangement*. Cooperative
work in HDI effectively occurs within a black box. A user cannot tell then from
either the request or the audit such things as where in the arrangement of work the
processing of data has reached, who is doing what with it, what's going to happen next, if there are problems or issues of concern, and so on. The articulation
of work is limited to who wants the data for what purposes and reviewing such
information. There is then very little support within HDI as it stands for the *ongoing management of relationships* between the various actors implicated in personal
data sharing. Again, it is hard to see on what basis HDI could become a stable
socio-technical infrastructure in everyday life without such mechanisms.

A key challenge thus becomes one of creating computational mechanisms of
interaction that build the 'elemental objects' of articulation work into HDI to *make*
'salient dimensions' of distributed action *accountable* to users, thereby enabling
them to manage and coordinate interaction. In saying this, we are not saying that
we should blindly follow prior stipulations of salient features (though it does seem
that some will hold), but that we need to develop a much better understanding of
what needs to be articulated with respect to personal data sharing and the cooperative work arrangements implicated in it.

The same applies to the field of work itself. Schmidt points out that the distributed activities of a cooperative work arrangement are articulated *with respect to*
objects within the field of work itself (e.g., data sources within the catalogue).

A key issue here revolves around the 'conceptual structures and resources' that order the field of work, which enable members of a cooperative ensemble to make sense of it and act upon it. Again the question of interactional adequacy arises when we ask what conceptual structures HDI provides? It's not that it doesn't provide any, but the terms in which it does so are problematic from an interactional perspective. Take, for example, the dataware catalogue. It is conceptually ordered in terms of 'tables' that render data sources intelligible in terms of accounts, applications, installs, and services, etc. The problem in this is that the conceptual structure of HDI as instantiated in dataware is rendered in terms of the underlying technology, rather than in terms of what is being done through that technology, such as the processing of biological data as part of a healthcare regime. The problem thus involves ordering the field of work such that it *reflects* the work-being-done, or the work-to-be-done, rather than the underlying technical components of that work. It is hard to see then how users can articulate their distributed activities with respect to objects in the field of work when those objects (data sources) lack legibility or intelligibility to the broader populace in contrast to computer scientists and software engineers. Other, more 'user friendly' (and more pointedly) data-relevant, service-specific conceptual structures and resources are required.[3]

Gaining Traction: Interactional Challenges for HDI

Before we address the interactional challenges that confront HDI it is worth reviewing the problems that occasion them. We have seen in our treatment of personal data as a boundary object that data is not an object-in-itself, but an object possessed of various accountable social characteristics or 'dimensions', which ultimately embed it in mundane infrastructures. We have seen from a socio-technical perspective on infrastructure that human relationships are essential to the production and use of data, and that these relationships turn upon standardised methods of communication and coordination, which embed infrastructure in the organised practice of everyday life. We have seen too that mutual dependence is built into data sharing and that this occasions articulation work and the need to build computational mechanisms of interaction to support it. Our purpose in reviewing salient work in social studies of science and CSCW has not been to define what a boundary object, infrastructure or articulation work is (by which measure this paper will no doubt be found wanting). Rather, our intention in selectively invoking certain features of salient texts has been to make it perspicuous

---

[3]The requirement is reflected in the Article 29 Data Protection Working Party report on the IoT (14/EN WP 223 2014) and the recommendation that end-users be able to "locally read, edit and modify the data before they are transferred to any data controller … Therefore, device manufacturers should provide a user-friendly interface for users who want to obtain both aggregated data and/or raw data." The challenge, of course, is bring this about in practice, particularly as personal data sources expand and diversify with the advent of the IoT.

how HDI becomes problematic when seen through a social or collaborative lens. Thus, we can see now that two key challenges confront HDI: one revolves around articulating the field of work in HDI, the other around articulating the cooperative arrangements of work implicated in HDI. We treat each in turn below.

Articulating the Field of Work in HDI

In working our way through social studies of science and foundational CSCW texts we have seen how they occasion particular kinds of problem for HDI. We have seen that a mutual modus operandi is not in place and that the user whose data is being purposed by others does not have reciprocal opportunities for discovery. We have seen that data is not only 'mine' but 'ours' and thus social in character. We have seen that ownership and control are not isomorphic and that the life world drives the dynamics of these aspects of interaction. We have seen that data sharing is recipient designed. And we have seen that the conceptual structures and resources ordering the field of work lack legibility, intelligibility, and accountability in short. Each of the problems we have picked up on during our historical journey is an inherent feature of the field of work in HDI and presents challenges to its ongoing articulation.

User-Driven Discovery

There are various aspects to the 'discoverability' problem, though of particular issue is what exactly should be made discoverable, and what kinds of control can users exercise over the process of discovery? These issues prospectively turn upon the articulation of *metadata* about a user's personal data sources, ranging (for example) from nothing more than articulating where a user's catalogue or catalogues can be contacted to more detailed information concerning catalogue contents. The demands of articulation work place further requirements on this process however, for even if users are willing to *publish* metadata about their data some means of understanding who is interested in discovering it may well be needed to build trust into the process—e.g., providing rich *analytics* into which processors are interested, when, how often, etc. Such analytics might provide users with resources that enable them to decide what of their data to expose or hide, though discovery may also turn in important respects upon other aspects of access control (e.g., defining pre-specified policies on who can and can't discover their data).[4]

---

[4]All of this, as with so many interactions within the dataware model, trades on reliable identity mechanisms. The general problem of authentication in networked systems has been long studied and several solutions exist: TLS certificates (both server and client) or PGP-based web-of-trust seem feasible initial approaches, though both have weaknesses and would require careful engineering with respect to HDI.

The issue of how users might drive the discovery process (finding data processors for themselves, whether for personal, financial or social purposes) is, however, more problematic and not something that has been addressed within HDI to date. Nonetheless, we would suggest that the discovery of data processors might be much like discovering new apps, and that the *'app store' model* may be a promising one to explore. Users are familiar with and make a conscious choice to visit app stores, where they are provided with rich metadata about apps and app authors that shapes their decision-making. Not only could data processors be 'vetted', much like apps in the iTunes Store, and detailed information about processing be provided, much like app 'permissions' in the Google Play Store, the social aspects of app stores also play an important role in the discovery process. User ratings and social networking links are important ingredients in the mix and help build the trust between users and service providers that is essential in the discovery and adoption of new technologies.

From My Data to Our Data

It is clear that the individuated model of ownership and control is not sufficient for real world applications of HDI. The social challenges of data ownership and control make it necessary to consider how individual and collective data sources can be collated and collaboratively managed by users. Individuals will not only need resources that enable them to control their own personal data sources, but will also need resources that allow them to *delegate* control of data sources and catalogues to others such that (for example) 'I' can assign control of 'my' data sources to 'you'. How ownership and control relationships are represented within and between catalogues, and what mechanisms will be needed to provide adequate support for their ongoing articulation, is an open matter, though transparency/awareness will be an important matter to consider along with rights management.

The creation and curation of collective data sources is an equally challenging matter. In one sense this may appear trivial. We can readily imagine, for example, that energy consumption data might relate as it does now to the household rather than specific individuals and that no complex identity and management issues are involved in such circumstances. Purposing such data is anything but a trivial matter, however. Who has the right to view and share such data? Who can edit it or revoke its use? Who actually owns and controls it? One view might be to default to the bill payer, but not all collective data sources are necessarily premised on contractual relationships. Add to the mix a world in which personal data harvesting becomes increasingly associated with the things that we mundanely interact with, and the possibility of opening up both collective and individual behaviours to unprecedented scrutiny through data analytics becomes a real and problematic prospect. The inherent tension between individual and collective data will require the development of *group management* mechanisms that support *negotiated* data collection, analysis and sharing amongst a cohort.

The Legibility of Data Sources

Both the individual and negotiated production, analysis and sharing of personal data turn upon data sources being legible or intelligible to users. If users are to have the ability to exercise agency within an HDI system in any meaningful way, data sources must provide a minimum level of legibility as to what data they contain, what inferences might be drawn from that data, how that data can be linked to other data, and so on. Without some means to present this critical information, preferably in some form that can be standardised, it will be difficult for users to even begin to understand the implications of decisions they may make and permissions the give for processing of their data. As part of this it is key that users are not only able to *visualise* and inspect the data held by a source, but that they can also visualise and thus understand just what a data processor wants to take from a source or collection of sources and why—that just what is being 'shared' is transparently accountable to users, which may also involve making external data sources (e.g., consumer trends data) visible so that users understand just what is being handed over. Coupled to this is the need to enable *recipient design* by users. There are two distinct aspects to this. One revolves around enabling users to *edit* data, redacting aspects of the data they do not wish to make available to others both within a cohort and outside of it. The other revolves around *controlling the presentation of data* to processors when the accuracy of data needs to be guaranteed (e.g., energy consumption readings).[5]

Articulating Cooperative Arrangements of Work in HDI

Our selective trawl through the past has also made it perspicuous that HDI provides limited support to a key area of interaction: the articulation of cooperative arrangements of work implicated in personal data harvesting. This, in turn, raises the need to develop computational mechanisms of interaction that *surface* and *make visible* 'salient dimensions' of the cooperative work arrangements implicated in HDI to users. This goes beyond the interactional arrangement of request-permission-audit that orders the flow of information within the field of work itself to focus attention on enabling parties to the work to *manage* the flow of information between them, including data interactions between internal members of a cohort and not only external parties.

Salient Dimensions of Collaboration in HDI

While it is clear that users will need to know who wants their data and for what purposes, our reflections have suggested that there is more to the articulation of

---

[5]Controlling presentation of your meter readings may seem odd, but in a near future world where metering could be done on an appliance or device level, enabling users to control the granularity of energy consumption data (for example) becomes a much more coherent proposition.

data sharing than that. Requirements here are also admittedly vague—just what will users need to know about the cooperative arrangement of work in HDI to make the process work? Understanding this issue is a core research challenge and while our understanding is vague at this point in time it is clear that HDI will need to move beyond retrospective interrogation of audit logs to *real time* articulations that reflect the data sharing process itself. We might expect that the processing of data sources is an ongoing matter (as, for example, in the case of energy monitoring) and that this is something that users may want to monitor. Understanding the amassed body of outputs of ongoing data processing and the implications of this is something that users may well be interested in too. Ditto subsequent processing that might be applied by data consumers (e.g., the aggregation of personal data into big data sets). It is also clear that data consumers pass personal data on to third parties. *Tracking* what is being done with 'my data' and/or 'our data' becomes an important matter to consider then, articulating the *treatment* of personal data by data consumers, along with the development of mechanisms of that support this (e.g., preserving the provenance of data to enable tracking, notifying users of data reuse and transfer, and opening up such events to inspection and intervention).

The Incomplete and Open Status of Articulation Challenges in HDI

The challenges of articulating personal data within HDI are not settled matters. Rather, they open a number of *thematic* areas for further investigation, elaboration and support:

- *Personal data discovery*, including meta-data publication, consumer analytics, discoverability policies, identity mechanisms, and app store models supporting discovery of data processors.
- *Personal data ownership and control*, including group management of data sources, negotiation, delegation and transparency/awareness mechanisms, and rights management.
- *Personal data legibility*, including visualisation of what processors would take from data sources and visualisations that help users make sense of data usage, and recipient design to support data editing and data presentation.
- *Personal data tracking*, including real time articulation of data sharing processes (e.g., current status reports and aggregated outputs), and data tracking (e.g., subsequent consumer processing or data transfer).

Each of these themes stand in need of *interdisciplinary* investigation and elaboration, including ethnographic studies of current practices of individuals and groups around personal data creation and curation, co-designed interventions to understand future possibilities, and the engineering of appropriate models, tools and techniques to deliver the required technologies to support the complex processes involved in HDI and mesh the articulation of personal data with the organised practices of everyday life. What this amounts to in many respects is a call to the broader CSCW community to engage with the study and design of boring things—infrastructures—for personal data is embedded within them: in health infrastructures, communication infrastructures, financial infrastructures, consumption infrastructures, energy infrastructures, media infrastructures, etc. It is a call to study and build HDI around the unremarkable ways in which personal data is produced and used within the manifold infrastructures of everyday life, so that we might understand how personal data is accountably traded within human relationships and thereby develop actionable insights into what is involved in articulating those relationships in the future.

Conclusion

This paper set out to understand how interaction is configured within the field of Human Data Interaction, taking the Dataware infrastructure as an exemplar, and how this 'fits' with existing social viewpoints on personal data interaction. Seen from a social perspective, data interaction appears to be as much about *human relationships* as it is about data itself. Data, as Star makes visible, is always embedded in human relationships, and efforts to create infrastructure turn upon stabilising those relationships through appropriate methods of communication and coordination. CSCW orients us to key issues involved in creating such methods, particularly the need to devise mechanisms of interaction that *articulate* (a) the field of work and flow of information between parties, and (b) the arrangements of collaboration that make the flow possible. Historical insights drawn from social studies of science and CSCW have allowed us to identify a range of problems that affect HDI and a number of distinct thematic challenges they occasion. The broad challenge now is to address these problems and themes and shape the articulation of HDI around the accountable social nature of personal data interaction in order to drive a real and significant step-change in everyday life.

Acknowledgment   The research on which this article is based was funded by RCUK research grants EP/M001636/1 and EP/K003569/1.

References

14/EN WP223. (2014). Opinion 8/2014 on recent developments on the internet of things. *Article 29 Data Protection Working Party*, http://ec.europa.eu/justice/data-protection/article-29/documentation/opinion-recommendation/files/2014/wp223_en.pdf.

Bannon, L. & Bødker, S. (1997). Constructing common information spaces. *Proceedings of ECSCW '97*, pp. 81–96, Lancaster, Kluwer.

Cafaro, F. (2012). Using embodied allegories to design gesture suites for human-data interaction. *Proceedings of UbiComp'12*, pp. 560–563, Pittsburgh, ACM.

Elmqvist, N. (2011). Embodied human-data interaction. *Proceedings of the SIGCHI Conference on Human Factors in Computing Systems*. Workshop on Embodied Interaction: Theory and Practice in HCI. Vancouver: ACM. Retrieved July 9, 2015 from http://www.antle.iat.sfu.ca/chi2011_EmbodiedWorkshop/Papers/NiklasElmqvist_CHI11EIWkshp_EmbodiedHuman-DataInteraction.pdf.

Haddadi, H., Mortier, R., MaAuley, D. & Crowcroft, J. (2013). *Human data interaction*. Cambridge: Cambridge Computer Laboratory. www.cl.cam.ac.uk/techreports/UCAM-CL-TR-837.pdf.

Haddadi, H. et al. (2015). Personal data: Thinking inside the box, *Computing research repository*, http://arxiv.org/abs/1501.04737.

Kee, K., Browning, L., Ballard, D., & Cicchini, E. (2012). *Sociomaterial processes … towards effective collaboration and collaboration tools for visual and data analytics*. Austin, NSF: Science of Interaction for Data and Visual Analytics Workshop.

McAuley, D., Mortier, R. & Goulding, J. (2011). The dataware manifesto. *Proceedings of the 3rd International Conference on Communication Systems and Networks*, pp. 1–6, Bangalore: IEEE.

Mashhadi, A., Kawsar, F. & Acer, U. (unpub. manu.). *Human data interaction in the IoT*. Bell Laboratories. www.fahim-kawsar.net/papers/Mashhadi.WF-IoT2014-Camera.pdf.

Mortier, R., Haddadi, H., Henderson, T., McAuley, D., & Crowcroft, J. (2014). Human-data interaction: The human face of the data-driven society. *Social Science Research Network*, doi: 10.2139/ssrn.2508051.

Pentland, A. (2012). Reinventing society in the wake of big data. *Edge*, August 30 2012. http://edge.org/conversation/reinventing-society-in-the-wake-of-big-data.

Schmidt, K., & Bannon, L. (1992). Taking CSCW seriously. *Computer Supported Cooperative Work: The Journal of Collaborative Computing, 1*(1), 7–40.

Schmidt, K. (1994). *COMIC deliverable 3.2 social mechanisms of interaction*. Esprit Basic Research Action 6225, ISBN 0-901800-55-4.

Star, S. L. & Griesemer, J. (1989). Institutional ecology, 'translations' and boundary objects. *Social Studies of Science 19*(3), 387–420.

Star, S. L. (1999). The ethnography of infrastructure. *American Behavioral Scientist, 43*(3), 377–391.

Star, S. L. (2010). This is not a boundary object: Reflections on the origin of a concept. *Science, Technology and Human Values, 35*(5), 601–617.

Strauss, A. (1985). Work and the division of labor. *The Sociological Quarterly, 26*(1), 1–19.

Suchman, L. (1995). Making work visible. *Communications of the ACM, 38*(9), 56–64.

Tolmie, P., Crabtree, A., Rodden, T., Greenhalgh, C. & Benford, S. (2007). Making the home network at home: Digital housekeeping. *Proceedings of ECSCW '07*, pp. 331–350. Limerick: Springer.

Mining Programming Activity
to Promote Help

Jason Carter and Prasun Dewan

Abstract We have investigated techniques for mining programming activity to offer help to programmers in difficulty. We have developed a (a) difficulty-detection mechanism based on the notion of command ratios; (b) difficulty-classification mechanism that uses both command ratios and rates; and (c) collaboration mechanism that provides both workspace and difficulty awareness. Our studies involve interviews and lab and field experiments, and indicate that (a) it is possible to mine programming activity to reliably detect and classify difficulties, (b) it is possible to build a collaborative environment to offer opportunistic help, (c) programmers are not unnerved by and find it useful to receive unsolicited help arriving in response to automatically detected difficulties, (d) the acceptable level of privacy in a help-promotion tool depends on whether the developers in difficulty are student or industrial programmers, and whether they have been exposed earlier to a help promotion tool, and (e) difficulty detection can filter out spurious help requests and reduce the need for meetings required to poll for rare difficulty events.

Introduction

Imagine a tool that provides automatic detection, classification and communication of the difficulty faced by programmers and allows them to opportunistically receive help from remote observers in response to communicated difficulties. We

J. Carter · P. Dewan (✉)
University of North Carolina at Chapel Hill, Chapel Hill, USA
e-mail: dewan@cs.unc.edu

J. Carter
e-mail: carterjl@cs.unc.edu

© Springer International Publishing Switzerland 2015
N. Boulus-Rødje et al. (eds.), *ECSCW 2015: Proceedings of the 14th European Conference on Computer Supported Cooperative Work, 19–23 September 2015, Oslo, Norway*, DOI 10.1007/978-3-319-20499-4_2

refer to this mechanism as a help-promotion tool. The idea of such a tool raises several design, implementation, privacy, usability, and usefulness questions:

1. Inference: How should automatic detection and classification of difficulties be done: what should be the input; how should the input be mined; and what is the relationship between the detection and classification techniques?
2. Collaboration and privacy: How should the difficulty status and context of the programmer in difficulty be communicated to potential helpers; and what are the privacy and effectiveness implications of alternative sharing mechanisms?
3. Evaluation: How should the inference and sharing mechanisms be evaluated; and what conclusions can be drawn from this work?

In this paper, we address the questions above. We use an issue-based paper organization wherein both previous and new results are presented as responses to a series of questions raised by the idea of a help promotion tool.

Help Promotion

When people give help, they are prevented from making progress on their subtask, and thus the overall concurrency of a group reduces. This brings up our first major issue: What is the relationship between the productivity of a group of software engineers and the amount of help they give each other?

In a study comparing co-located and distributed software development teams, (Herbsleb et al. 2000) found that the productivity of co-located teams was significantly higher than that of distributed teams primarily because co-located developers were more apt to help each other finish their tasks. In a related study, (Teasley et al. 2000) found that the productivity of a team radically co-located in a single "war-room" was much higher than that of one spread out in different cubicles. A major reason was that if someone was having difficulty with some aspect of code, another developer in the war-room "walking by and seeing the activity over their shoulders, would stop to provide help". (Cockburn and Williams 2001) report that pairs sitting next to each other often find that seemingly "impossible problems become easy or even quick, or at least possible, to solve when they work together," and report that such help increases programmer productivity.

Regardless of the positive effect on group productivity, is there any incentive to offer help? Previous work by Dabbish and Kraut (2004) and Smith and Shumar (2004) has shown that a suitable reward structure can promote help. Our assumption, and the studies on which it is based, implies that such a structure exists, at least in some cases—arguably, a mentor/manager is rewarded by progress of an intern/employee—and that research on improving this structure is orthogonal to the nature of a help promotion tool. The mentor-intern and manager-employee relationship corresponds to the instructor-student relationship in education settings; and when instructors are willing to and have the time to provide help, a help-promotion mechanism allows them to discover more opportunities to help.

Passive Awareness of Difficulty

Assuming help promotion is beneficial to both help givers and receivers, the next question is: how is the difficulty status of programmers communicated to their collaborators? They can actively ask for help using a variety of mechanisms including forums, social media, email, progress meetings, and stream of consciousness "tweets" (Fitzpatrick et al. 2006). The other alternative is for observers of programmers to passively notice the need for help. This is an important alternative as actively asking for help can result in too few and, in some cases, too many help requests. (Herbsleb and Grinter 1999) found that distributed developers are less comfortable asking each other for help because they interact with each other less than co-located developers. Similarly, (Begel and Simon 2008) found that students and new programmers are late to ask for help; and (LaToza et al. 2006) established that programmers often exhaust other forms of help before contacting a teammate. As we see later in our results, lightweight active mechanisms during scheduled help sessions can lead to the opposite effect in which student programmers over-ask for help. In these situations, passive awareness can improve how resources are allocated to provide help by allowing the helper to triage.

Today, passive awareness is provided mainly through face- to-face interaction. Certain programming environments such as CollabVS (Hegde and Dewan 2008) provide distributed awareness of certain team members activities such as the current files being edited and if they are currently debugging or editing code. The paper on CollabVS explicitly hypothesizes the ability of such awareness to promote help, giving a scenario in which Bob, on seeing Alice stuck on debugging a particular class, deduces she could use help, and offers it. There are two problems with this hypothesis. First, it is not clear if the awareness provided by these tools is sufficient to determine if developers are indeed in difficulty. Second, having difficulty, by definition, is a rare event, if programmers are given problems they have the skills to solve. Thus, polling collaborators state to deduce this status can lead to wasted effort in trying to find "needles in haystacks." This problem can be addressed by automatically detecting and communicating information about difficulties of programmers that can be used to offer help to them.

Difficulty Detection

One part of this information is whether the programmers are facing difficulty, raising the question: Can a task-independent mechanism, not requiring special equipment, be built to detect programming difficulties as they occur?

At first glance, a difficulty detection mechanism seems impossible as it is trying to sense and detect something that is even hard to define. This problem is not unique to difficulty detection and arises in mechanisms for detecting other human emotions such as if users are engaged (McDuff et al. 2012) can be interrupted (Fogarty et al. 2005; Iqbal and Bailey 2007), or are frustrated (Kapoor et al.

2007). In all of these cases, the predictions of machine learning algorithms have worked well in comparison to those of humans, and there is reason to believe such algorithms will pass the Turing test also in this line of research. More important, there has been previous work demonstrating the feasibility of difficulty detection. Intelligent tutoring systems such as the Lisp Tutor (Anderson and Reiser 1985) detect difficulties using problem-specific rules. (Piech et al. 2012) detected difficulty of students in a CS 1 course after they had occurred, based on assignment submissions of the entire class.

Our previous work (Carter and Dewan 2010a, b) is designed to satisfy these requirements. To meet the goal of (a) not requiring special equipment, we processed software operations; (b) a problem-independent solution for detecting programming difficulties, we mined operations provided by a general-purpose programming environment to create code; and (c) making immediate inferences during code creation, we looked only at the log of the programmer whose status is being predicted—we did not look at the actions of others, who might not have even started their work.

The key intuition in this work is that programmers can be expected to change their interaction with the computer when they are in difficulty, and this information can be used to predict difficulties. Previous studies seem to indicate that programmer interaction does change when programmers are facing difficulty. In particular, when they are they are tracking bugs, their productivity reduces (Humphrey 1997; Cockburn and Williams 2001). A simple-minded approach based on this intuition is to use the interaction rate, edit rate, or code-growth rate as measures of progress, and if it falls below a certain threshold, assume the developer is in difficulty. This approach cannot distinguish between a person taking a break and a person in difficulty, though it may be possible to use thresholds for maximum think time, as in (Murphy et al. 2009).

In our previous work, we used a time-independent approach in which we looked, not at command rates, but at command ratios. The intuition behind this approach is that when facing difficulty, developers would enter relatively fewer edits and more of the other commands. In particular, they would increase debug commands to isolate problems; switch from the programming environment to another tool (to change tasks or lookup information), thereby increasing focus commands; and/or navigate to different parts of the source code to understand the source of difficulty. We divided the raw log into 50-command segments, and calculated, for different segments of the log, the ratio of the occurrences of each category of commands in that segment to the total number of commands in the segment, and used these ratios as features. Based on the intuition above, we looked at four command categories: edit, navigation, debug, and focus. We fed these features to the decision tree algorithm implemented in Weka (Witten and Frank 1999) to get raw predictions. In the training set, we used the Weka SMOTE filter to boost the members of the minority class (difficulty). Assuming that a status does not change instantaneously, we aggregated the raw predictions for adjacent segments to create the final prediction, reporting the dominant status in the last five segments. In addition, we made no predictions from the first 100 events to ignore the extra compilation, navigation and focus events in the startup phase and account for the fact that not enough events had been accumulated to make the prediction. Our laboratory results with a group model showed that this mechanism had low false positives but high false negatives.

This approach, and its implementation, was the starting point for this research. Our first goal was to determine if we could reduce false negatives while keeping false positives also low. To gather data for this part of our research, we conducted a lab study, which tried to ensure developers faced difficulty in the small amount of time available for a lab study, and yet did not find the problems impossible. After piloting, we settled on a task that required participants to use the AWT/SWT toolkit to implement a GUI. The main subtask was to create a program that draws a "bus" as a red rectangle, representing the body, with two black circles, representing the tires. The subjects were also asked to implement arrow keys to move the vehicle up, forward, left, and right by a fixed number of pixels. Another subtask allowed the end-user to make the bus a "double-decker" by clicking anywhere on the screen. Such a bus had an extra rectangle positioned directly on top of the previous rectangle and moved with the body below. The subjects were also asked to convert a double-decker bus to a single-decker bus if the user pressed an associated key. Two other subtasks involved allowing the end-user to double or half the size of the single/double-decker bus each time they press an associated key. Two additional subtasks required them to draw a transparent square with yellow borders around the single/double-decker bus and ensure that the bus could not be moved outside the square.

Seventeen graduate/undergraduate student programmers, many of whom had interned in industry, have so far participated in the study. Each participant was asked to complete as many subtasks as possible in about one had a half hours and was free to use the Internet. We used our earlier difficulty detection mechanism to log participants' programming activities and predict whether the subjects were having difficulty or making progress during the study. Participants were instructed to correct an incorrect prediction by the system using status-correction buttons. Additionally, they could ask for help, by pressing a help button, which was also considered an indication of difficulty. After participants pressed this button, they were instructed to discuss their issue with the first author. Help was given in the form of URLs to API documentation or code examples. By measuring how often the developers corrected their status and asked for help, we could derive the true difficulty points, as perceived by the developers.

We fed the four features identified by use previously to the Weka decision tree classification algorithm. To evaluate our results, we used a standard technique, known as 10-fold cross validation, which executes 10 trials of model construction, and splits the logged data so that 90 % of the data are used to train the algorithm and 10 % of the data are used to test it. The confusion matrix, shown in Table 1, compares the ground truth against the predictions, using data from ten initial participants.

Consistent with our previous results, the false positive rate is low but the false negative rate is high. Only a small fraction of the difficulties were classified correctly through all non-difficulty points were classified correctly.

Table 1 Confusion matrix with edit, navigation, focus, debug ratio

	Predicted difficulty	Predicted progress
Actual difficulty	11 (True positives)	44 (False negatives)
Actual progress	0 (False positives)	759 (True negatives)

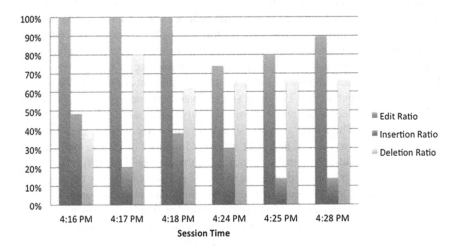

Fig. 1 Example edit, insert, and delete ratios during a difficulty

Not satisfied with the high false negatives, we observed programmer recordings to understand the reason why we missed so many difficulties. These observations showed that participants having difficulty made a significant number of edits, which were considered an indication of progress by the algorithm. They also indicated that these edits were dominated by deletions. To illustrate, consider Fig. 1, which shows the graph of the ratios for one participant in difficulty. In this graph, the x-axis is the session time and the y-axis are the edit, insertion, and deletion ratios. The figure shows that participant 1's edit ratio is high even though he is having difficulty; and when the edit ratio is split into insertion and deletion ratios, deletions make up the majority of the edit ratio.

Therefore we modified our previous mechanism by splitting the edit ratio into insertion and deletion ratios. Table 2 shows the results of this split. In comparison to the previous algorithm, the false negative rate decreased from 80 to 27 % and the false positive rate increased slightly from 0 to 3 %. Thus, modulo the slight increase in false positives, the new approach is an improvement over our previous one. Let us also evaluate the modified algorithm on an absolute basis by considering the influence it can have on the state of the art. It seems that if a choice has to be made between low false positives and negatives, the former is more desirable,

Table 2 Confusion matrix with insert, delete, navigation, focus, debug ratio

	Predicted difficulty	Predicted progress
Actual difficulty	40 (True positives)	15 (False negatives)
Actual progress	20 (False positives)	739 (True negatives)

as it does not unnecessarily waste the time of the developers and those who offer help. Missing 27 % of the "having difficulty" statuses is no worse than the current practice of not having any automatic predictions. Thus, if it is considered desirable to automatically let others know about developers' difficulties—an assumption of this research based on previous work and the field experiments described later—then it seems better to use the difficulty-detection tool than not use it. An implication of the significant false negative rate is that the difficulty mechanism augments but does not replace existing avenues for help such as forums and help sessions.

We extended this analysis by considering all seventeen subjects who have participated so far. This time, the initial (modified) scheme gave 44 % (23 %) false negatives and 8 % (8 %) false positives. Thus, the larger data set improved the false negative rates in both schemes and reduced the difference in these rates at the cost of a higher false positive rate. Both evaluations indicate that separating insert and delete events greatly reduces false negatives but slightly increases false positives.

As in numerous other academic studies involving software engineering and other topics, participants in this study were students. This is also the case in our field studies. This subject choice could limit the findings to education, as developers with industry experience may perform different programming actions when they are having difficulty. Our previous work did do a lab study in which five of the fourteen subjects were industrial developers, and the results in Table 1 are consistent with the previous study. In the previous work, we had better accuracy with industrial developers and more senior students, as they tended to make more use of debugging commands. In addition, our previous mechanism was used by one industrial programmer doing field work and several elements of it such as prediction aggregation were added in response to the feedback from this work. The results of our modification, thus, may apply as well or even better to industrial developers—a conjecture we leave for future work.

In this study, developers implemented programs from scratch, which could mean that our results may not apply as well to maintenance tasks, which can be expected to have more navigation for the same difficulty degree. On the other hand, navigation ratio is only of the five features used—so this work may apply to a large extent to maintenance tasks. This conjecture is supported to some extent by the field study described later.

Our experience with help promotion in lab studies and the field study described later shows that there are three phases in a process that involves a help offer: (1) Difficulty discovery: Potential helpers discover that a developer is facing difficulty. (2) Contextualization: They determine if they can or should offer help based on the nature of the difficulty. (3) Synchronous collaboration: They actually help the developer. So far we have addressed step (1). Let us consider step (2) next.

Barrier Detection

One kind of programming context that may be useful to potential helpers is the barrier that caused a developer to have difficulty. (Ko et al. 2004) categorized barriers student programmers faced based on explicit help requests. The ones they found were inability to: (a) design algorithms, (b) combine Application Programming Interfaces (APIs), (c) understand compiler or runtime errors, (d) find documentation for APIs, and (e) find tools within the programming environment. These barriers can allow potential helpers to decide if they can and should offer help. For example, a professor/senior teammate may want to help only with design barriers and TAs/junior teammates may wish to address only debugging barriers. So the next question we explored was, to what extent can these barriers be automatically detected?

Our answer to this question was based on data gathered doing real homework rather than lab assignments. As part of his Ph.D. requirement, the first author taught a course on object-oriented programming, which was taken by 35 students. We made use of this opportunity to gather data about barriers.

In this course, students could use the regular channels of office hours and asynchronous electronic communication (email) to receive help. In addition, to gather data for this work, for two weeks, they were offered the alternative of help sessions. Help sessions were different from office hours in that students could receive help in a small group (3 people) as opposed to a potentially large group in office hours. Help was given only after students attempted to solve problems and failed to solve them. A little less than half (17 out of 35) of the class attended help sessions. The help sessions were popular because (a) some students did not feel comfortable asking questions during office hours or class, (b) a few of these students sent the instructor emails asking for one-on-one help, and (c) students could receive help with problems as they occurred. The popularity of help sessions shows the importance of providing help synchronously, at least in an educational setting.

Our data suggested a simpler classification scheme than that of (Ko et al. 2004): algorithm design issues and difficulty with correcting incorrect output. No API barriers were found. The students did use a non-standard API—a GUI generation tool developed by the second author. However, by the time the difficulty studies were done in the course, issues with using this tool had been ironed out. For the same reason, compiler errors were no longer an issue. Therefore, we decided to determine if it was possible to automatically distinguish between design and incorrect-output barriers.

Our recordings of the help sessions provided us with the data required to make this distinction. We used two coders to derive this information. To enable this process, we developed a tool that shows all segments where participants asked for help, and allows observers to identify the barriers the participants faced. The coders agreed on 44 out of 50 difficulty points (k = 0.79). Only these 44 points were considered true barriers. 66 % of these were classified as design barriers and 34 % as incorrect output by both coders.

Now that we had ground truth, we had to identify appropriate features to automatically detect the barriers. Based on our observations of the recordings around difficulty points, we found the following: When programmers had incorrect output, the frequency of debug commands increased and the frequency of edit commands decreased. When they had design problems, they spent a large amount of time outside of the programming environment.

The feature set of our difficulty detection tool had been deliberately chosen to ignore wall time. The reason was that we wanted to prevent our mechanism from classifying idle phases as difficult ones. Based on the observations above, it seemed we now had to consider the passage of time. We envisioned a two-phase prediction approach in which, first our previous time-independent detection features are used to determine difficulties, and then a new set of classification features is used to identify the barriers. The second phase could follow explicit requests for help—it was not tied to difficulty detection.

We included all of the previous detection features (the five ratios) in the classification set as we knew they had something to say about difficulties. In addition, we added features measuring the rate of interaction with the programming environment, which are given below:

1. Mean time between events = total time/# of total events.
2. Mean insertion time = total insertion time/# of insertion events.
3. Mean deletion time = total deletion time/# of deletion events.
4. Mean focus time = total focus time/# of focus events.
5. Mean navigation time = total navigation time/# of navigation events.
6. Mean debug time = total debug time/# of debug events.

All of these times were measured in milliseconds. As before, we divided a log into 50-command segments, and computed these features independently for each segment.

To determine how indicative the detection and classification features are of programmers' behavior, we graphed the programming behavior of 6 programmers. In each graph, the x-axis is session time and y-axis is the percent or time (in milliseconds) for each feature. Figure 2a, b show portions of the graphs created for participant 1 and 2, respectively, illustrating commonalities in the behavior of the programmers when they are having difficulty correcting incorrect output. In both cases, participants' debug ratios increased, and the edit (insertion and deletion) ratios decreased. Figure 3a, b shows commonalities in the behavior of participant 2 and 4 when they are having algorithm design issues. In both cases, the participants spent a large amount of time outside of the programming environment, which is indicated by the high mean focus time. In particular, participant 3 (4) spent 120 (350) s outside of the programming environment. Thus, the four graphs justify our feature choice.

We fed to the Weka decision tree algorithm the features of (a) each segment during which the programmer had explicitly indicated difficulty, which we refer to as an explicit segment, and (b) each segment that preceded an explicit segment and occurred within 2 min of the explicit segment, which we refer to as an implicit segment. The reason for (b) is that, on average, coders took 2 min to determine the barrier, and we assumed an algorithm would need the same amount of information.

As before, we used a group model, the decision tree algorithm, and 10-fold cross validation. The confusion matrix of Table 3 shows the results. It correctly

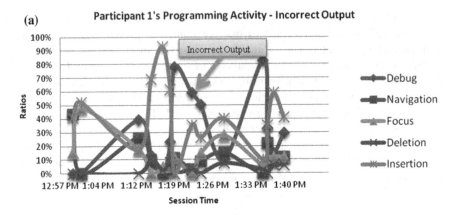

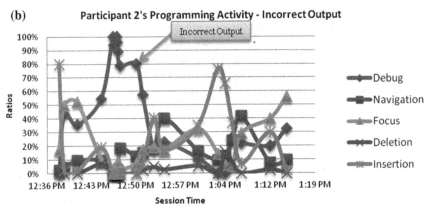

Fig. 2 Ratios change for incorrect-output barriers

classified 25 of the 29 (86 %) design barriers, and 11 of the 15 (73 %) incorrect—
output barriers.

In this case, we do not have a previous version of our approach to compare
these results. Therefore, we use three standard baselines, all of which make
a binary choice between two labels (in this case, design and incorrect output): (a) randomized approach, which predicts each label 50 % of the time, (b)
modal approach, which always predicts the label that occurs most often, and (c)
data distribution approach, which makes predictions based on the distribution of

Table 3 Barrier confusion matrix

	Predicted incorrect output	Predicted design
Actual incorrect output	11(True pos.)	4 (False neg.)
Actual design	4 (False pos.)	25 (True neg.)

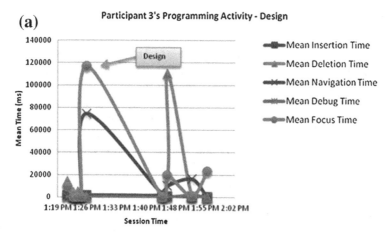

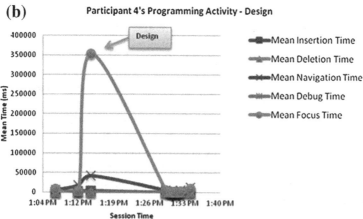

Fig. 3 Rates change for design barriers

labels. The random/modal/data-distribution baselines gave a true positive rate of 53/0/33 % and true negative rate of 52/100/66 %. The binomial test showed that there is a significant statistical difference between each baseline and the results of our decision tree algorithm.

In comparison to our previous study, these subjects interacted over a much larger time span (two weeks), and did real work. However, the group was still homogeneous, and thus, these results may not apply to more experienced programmers.

The previous two sections have addressed detection and contextualization of difficulties. We now consider the last step—a distributed collaborative environment to actually offer help in response to difficulty references.

Collaboration Environment

The environment we first envisioned was based on Community Bar (Tee et al. 2006). In this tool, an awareness sidebar contains the thumbnail of a remote user's screens, which can be expanded to show the full screen. Users can use peripheral vision/polling to monitor the thumbnail, and when a thumbnail change indicates a potentially interesting event, can expand it to further investigate, and possibly modify their own work or transition to synchronous collaboration.

Experience with the Community Bar found that observers used the tool to determine remote users' availability, and to monitor, using track changes, how much progress co-authors were making on shared documents. In particular, the degree of progress of a user was determined by how much tracked text in the document had the color of the user.

Arguably, screen awareness, alone, cannot promote help. It is not clear if the fact that a developer is in difficulty is manifested visually in a thumbnail. More important, as mentioned before, by definition, making slow(er than normal) progress is a rare event. Therefore, with pure screen awareness, observers would have to continually monitor remote developers' screens looking for the rare difficulty events.

Integrating screen awareness with difficulty detection and communication, on the other hand, can create a more effective help-promotion mechanism—observers can expand a programmers' thumbnail only when they are informed by the difficulty-detection system that the programmers are in difficulty.

Therefore, we decided to test this idea in the first author's class. At that point we were gathering data about barriers from his students, we did not have barrier detection in place. Also at that point, we were using our previous detection mechanism (without the insert event adaptation, which gave better results in the lab). We combined this older mechanism with a custom screen-sharing component.

We expected that most students would install the screen-sharing help tool for two reasons. First, students would receive extra help. Second, participants who used the screen sharing feature in Community Bar were comfortable with allowing co-workers to view their complete screen. Surprisingly, none of the 35 students was willing to use a tool that shared their screens. When the instructor asked for the reason, most of them stated that they perform activities other than programming, and would not want that information to be shared. For example, one student remarked: *"I don't want you looking at my Facebook page."* In response, we changed our tool to record only the Eclipse window. Even after the instructor mentioned this new feature, students were hesitant and would not install it.

This experience forced us to take a step back and consider the ways in which a programming context can be shared between two users. It can be shared at multiple levels of abstraction such as the frame-buffer, windows, toolkit widget, and model; and the level of the ideal shared abstraction goes down with the desired coupling or divergence between the actions of the collaborators (Dewan 1998). Our screen-sharing help tool essentially provided window sharing. Based on the privacy concerns of the students, we decided to replace window sharing with Eclipse model sharing. We refer to this version of the tool as Eclipse Helper.

Figure 4 shows the student and instructor views of the tool. Students could hide their real names and university IDs (called onyens), as anonymous IDs were generated by the tool. Buttons were provided to correct the predicted status. After some user testing, we used the term "slow progress" for having difficulty and "making progress" for not having difficulty, and "Indeterminate" for not having accumulated enough events to make the prediction. For each online student, the instructor view showed a status widget, which changed from green to red when a student had difficulty (predicted automatically or indicated manually by the student) and back to green when the student was making progress. The view also displayed a notification when a student had difficulty. It also offered a View Project

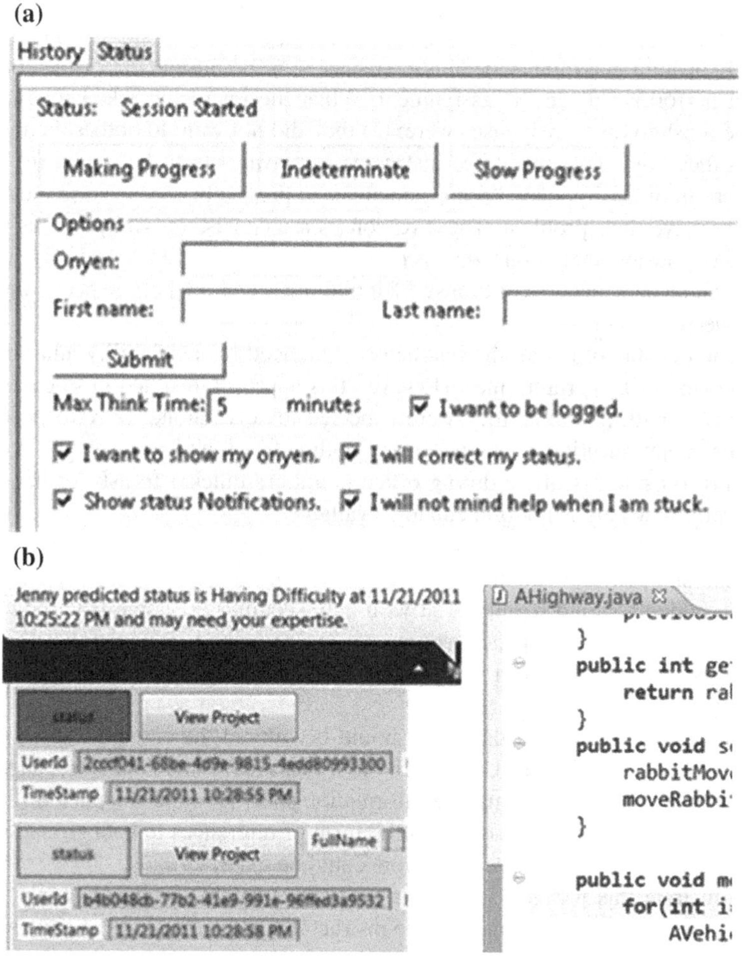

Fig. 4 Student view and instructor view of Eclipse Helper, a student view, b instructor view

button that opened up the instructors' programming environment and displayed students' edits, in real-time, in an editor window. The instructor could view these edits before deciding to help.

This time we had much more success with adoption—the majority of students (30 out of 35) installed Eclipse Helper. Thus, our work shows that the level of sharing is a function of not only the coupling between the tasks of the collaborators but also the perceived privacy risks of the users.

As mentioned earlier, students in the class could receive help through office visits, email, and special help sessions. Eclipse Helper gave students a fourth avenue for receiving help—they could now receive distributed synchronous assistance when they were facing difficulty. This tool was made available for the last four of the nine assignments in the class.

For the first monitored assignment, students were required to manually indicate their status to ask for help because the instructor was not sure about the reliability of the tool in field use. However, only one student pressed the "slow progress" button to indicate a need for help. This was surprising because some of the students did not perform well on the assignment. When the instructor asked for the reason, the most common responses were: (a) they did not want to bother the instructor, (b) they were not sure if the instructor was available to help, and (c) when they were in difficulty, they did not remember to press a button because they were trying to solve their problem. These responses are consistent with previous work, mentioned earlier, that found that people are late or hesitant to ask for help—which in our case occurred because of inhibitions, lack of help expectation, and being overwhelmed.

To counter this problem, the instructor announced his availability and willingness to help during certain times. However, this approach resulted in students asking for help with problems they were expected to solve alone. In retrospect, this behavior is not surprising, as the second author has found that several students who work outside his office during office hours are quicker to ask for help than those who know help is not immediately available.

Therefore, we turned on automatic difficulty detection in the tool, and the instructor stopped announcing when he would be available for help. We wondered if students would be unnerved with help seeming to "come from nowhere" at unanticipated times, but the students who were helped indicated that this was not a problem as they knew it was possible to receive help when they were having difficulty.

If the instructor decided that help should be offered, he entered into an email discussion with the student. Usually, the first message in the email exchange had the subject of "Help" and contained information specific to the students' difficulty. The type of help offered was either in the form of references to background material or a description of how specific errors could be fixed.

To illustrate this process, in one case, after watching a student attempt to fix compiler errors for several minutes, the instructor sent an email to the student asking if she needed help. Several minutes later the student responded saying, *"Yes! I am having a few problems. I'm getting an error message and it won't recognize that I'm using methods from the AVehicle class*". The instructor sent an email asking her to: "*review how to write a method that takes parameters and how to call a method with parameters.*" The student emailed back a few minutes later saying: "*thanks that fixed my problem. I struggled with that for over an hour.*"

Several students were appreciative of not only the specific help offered but also the instructor's willingness to help and a tool that allowed such help to be offered, as illustrated by the following response to a help inquiry: "*Cool to see that the helper is working! Thanks for asking me what is wrong!*" This comment seems to imply that even if a help inquiry does not result in immediate benefits, it could help the two users bond, which could address the issue (Herbsleb and Grinter 1999) found in distributed software development that employees were less comfortable asking remote rather than co-located teammates for help.

Even though the students had a positive experience and appreciated the help, there was one case where a student, having trouble with conditionals, could not overcome the difficulty. To help the student, the instructor sent the following message: "*Are you having issues with your if statements in your while loop and the while loop as well?*" The student responded to the email two hours later saying, "*I am having issues with my while loop and if statements. I'm not exactly sure what I am doing wrong. It only lets me enter commands once and after that it doesn't print anything.*" After several email exchanges, the student did not solve the problem. One reason was that she had difficulty explaining her problem, and would have preferred if the instructor would have been able to see her screen so that she could point to it and explain the problem. Nonetheless, she still appreciated the attempt to help her.

Before the last assignment of the semester, we surveyed students to see if they would be more willing to install the screen sharing tool. About half (20 out of 35) of the students in the class were now willing to install the tool. The students gave two reasons for changing their minds. First, they said that they trusted the instructor more now than at the beginning of the semester. Second, students who were helped with Eclipse Helper indicated that it should be much easier to point at something on their screen to explain their problem than trying to explain it through email. After the last assignment, the most difficult one, we surveyed students again to see if they would be more willing to install the screen sharing tool. Almost all (31 out of 35) of the students in the class were now willing, which provides some evidence for our initial intuition that screen sharing is a useful abstraction in a help session.

The instructor was able to offer help 9 times to 8 different students over the last three assignments. There were some instances where Eclipse Helper did not predict that students had difficulty, but the next day students came to office hours for help. However, each time the tool predicted a student was in difficulty and the student was asked if they needed help, the student answered in the affirmative. This result is consistent with our lab studies of the tool mentioned earlier with our previous implementation, which also showed the lack of false positives but the presence of false negatives. The result shows that a tool trained by several iterations of lab studies can, without extra training, be used in a field study. In this class, the later assignments built on the earlier ones. Thus, in the last few assignments monitored by Eclipse Helper, students were essentially "maintaining" code implemented by them. This result shows that our fear that in maintenance extra navigation would result in false positives did not materialize in this case.

Again, this part of our work applies to a homogeneous population of students. However, it shows that in at least one respect, a help promotion tool may be more applicable to a work rather than educational environment. As mentioned earlier, experience with Community Bar showed that workers were comfortable sharing screens, while students in the first author's class were not, at least at first. On the other hand, it is possible that a new employee would have the same concerns as the students. Thus, this part of our work motivates the need to support workspace sharing through both screen and model sharing.

The whole idea of a help promotion tool was motivated by industrial studies showing the positive influence of help on productivity. Therefore we were interested in also finding some validation of such a tool in an industrial setting. One of the industrial participants in our studies asked his manager if his team could use our tools for communicating difficulties in daily work, but understandably, his company did not want to use an untested technology. To gather some industrial data, we performed semi-structured interviews about the usefulness of a help promotion tool that integrates workspace and difficulty awareness.

We focused on the intern/mentor scenario and interviewed eight subjects—four actual mentor/intern pairs—in a large organization. The subjects had professional experience ranging from 3 months to 20 years. Some of the subjects were not employed as programmers, but programming played a major part of their job role. We asked them the usefulness of integrated workspace and difficulty awareness. Specifically, we asked participants if they could give examples of when this combination would have been useful in previous help-giving interactions. All subjects liked the general idea of this combination and gave motivating examples. For instance, one intern reported that he liked that his mentor would be able to watch over his shoulder when he needed help. Similarly, one mentor reported that the tool would eliminate the overhead of scheduling multiple project status meetings with interns. This last statement has an interesting implication regarding the overhead on helpers of inferred difficulty. A scheme such as ours that has low false positives can, in fact, reduce the overhead as the helpers do not have to use meetings to "poll" developers for rare difficulty events—they can instead be notified automatically.

Conclusions and Future Work

Given the state of the art in the practice and teaching of software engineering, the notion of an environment that automatically detects and classifies programmer difficulties, communicates this information to potential helpers, and allows the developer to receive opportunistic help seems like science fiction. The overall contribution of this paper is a systematic study that shows that such an environment is realistic, at least in certain scenarios. The insights in the design and evaluation of such an environment seem "intuitively obvious," at least in retrospect.

The main design insights are: (a) when programmers are in difficulty, their insertion ratio decreases (as they make less progress) and other ratios increase (as they try to find solutions); (b) design and incorrect-output barriers can be distinguished by the fact that the former result in the focus rates becoming higher (as the developers constantly try to find solutions outside the programming environment) and the other rates becoming lower; and (c) triggering workspace sharing in response to difficulty detection can allow help to be opportunistically offered to developers in difficulty.

The main evaluation insights are that: (a) student programmers are not unnerved by and find it useful to receive unsolicited help arriving in response to automatically detected difficulties, (b) the acceptable level of privacy in a help-promotion tool depends on whether the developers in difficulty are student or industrial programmers, and whether they have been exposed earlier to a help promotion tool, and (c) difficulty detection can filter out spurious help requests and reduce the need for meetings required to poll for rare difficulty events.

The first author's dissertation (Carter 2014) and other papers addresses several related issues not covered here such as (a) to what extent can mining postures of programmers reduce the significant number of false negatives in the mechanism described here, (b) what is the relationship between student grades and the amount of help they receive through various means (Carter et al. 2015), (c) how can we define and distinguish between surmountable and insurmountable difficulties (Carter et al. 2015), (d) to what extent is the time needed to solve a surmountable difficulty reduced by providing help, (e) is it useful to replay the actions of a programmer in difficulty to a helper, and (f) what design patterns and architectures can allow code to be shared among mechanisms provided by different programming environments such as Eclipse and Visual Studio (Carter and Dewan 2010b)?

Of course, our research leaves numerous unresolved issues. There are questions regarding its applicability to large programs and maintenance, and its performance in industrial field studies. Large programs cannot be created in small lab studies, and require academic field studies of advanced programming courses or industrial studies. Industrial field studies are a difficult goal as our tool is a rough prototype and involves adoption by multiple people—a classical problem in research of collaborative tools. If conducted, field studies can help determine if a difficulty-based collaboration environment does provide benefits of radical-colocation found in (Teasley et al. 2000). Maintenance is tricky because it is ill defined. As mentioned above, arguably, the students in our class study were doing maintenance as they were building on and modifying code written weeks ago. On the other hand, it can be argued that maintenance should involve a large code base written by others that has not been visited recently by the developers modifying it. In this first cut effort at a help promotion tool, we did not have the resources to play with varying the size of the foreign code base and the time between code visits.

As mentioned above, there has been work in automatic detection of emotions other than difficulty such as interruptibility, engagement, and frustration.

It is attractive to consider the detection and communication of these emotions in an integrated fashion and create a common toolkit for supporting multiple emotions, as discussed in (Dewan 2015). Another future direction is multiple degrees of difficulty awareness—in particular both screen and workspace awareness, depending on the privacy concerns and needs of the collaborators in difficulty. See Ellwanger et al. (2015) for preliminary work towards this goal. Yet another direction is expanding the set of barriers automatically detected to include, for instance, API barriers. In this work, the input of a programming environment was mined to determine difficulty. It would be useful to mine input of other applications such as word processors and spreadsheets to infer non-programming difficulties. A related direction is to mine the input of multiple applications together. For instance, mining the input of Web browser and programming environment could help better infer certain kinds of difficulties, especially API barriers. Here, we have provided awareness of difficulty of specific individuals so that they can be helped. It would be useful to provide awareness of group difficulty (by aggregating individual difficulties) to determine problems that are inherently difficult. Moreover, collaborative filtering could be used to predict the difficulty programmers will face on a problem based on the difficulties faced by others like them on similar problems.

Our detection model defines a design space of prediction schemes in which the classification algorithm, mapping from specific commands to attributes, attribute set, and prediction aggregation scheme can vary. It will be useful to systematically explore this space to improve prediction. Such an exploration can be eased by interactively visualizing the inference algorithm and performing what-if analyses correlating current and past logs with predictions. See Dewan (2015), Long et al. (2015) for preliminary work towards such a test-bed. The cross validation technique used here, in which data of all programmers are used in both the training and test set, is not realistic in a practical environment in which inferences for new programmers are made based on the training provided by previous programmers. It would be useful to perform "leave one out" analysis in which inferences for a particular participant are based on the training provided by other participants. The insights, features, mechanisms, tools and evaluations presented here provide motivation for and a basis to address these future directions.

Acknowledgment   This research was supported in part by the NSF IIS 1250702 award.

References

Anderson, J. R., & Reiser, B. J. (1985). The LISP tutor: It approaches the effectiveness of a human tutor. *Lecture Notes in Computer Science 10*(4).

Begel, A., & Simon, B. (2008). Novice software developers, all over again. In *International Computing Education Research Workshop*.

Carter, J. (2014). Automatic difficulty detection. Ph.D., Chapel Hill: University of North Carolina.

Carter, J., & Dewan, P. (2010a). Are you having difficulty. In *Proceedings of CSCW*. Atlanta: ACM.

Carter, J., & Dewan P. (2010b). Design, implementation, and evaluation of an approach for determining when programmers are having difficulty. In *Proceedings Group 2010*, ACM.

Carter, J., Dewan P., & Pichilinani M. (2015). Towards incremental separation of surmountable and insurmountable programming difficulties. In *Proceedings SIGCSE*, ACM.

Cockburn, A., & Williams L. (2001). The costs and benefits of pair programming. Boston: Addison Wesley.

Dabbish, L., & Kraut R. E. (2004). Controlling interruptions: awareness displays and social motivation for coordination. In *Proceedings of CSCW* (pp. 182–191), New York: ACM Press.

Dewan, P. (1998). Architectures for collaborative applications. *Trends in Software: Computer Supported Co-operative Work, 7,* 165–194.

Dewan, P. (2015). Towards emotion-based collaborative software engineering. In *Proceedings of ICSE CHASE Workshop*, IEEE.

Ellwanger, D., Dillon, N., Wu, T., Carter J., & Dewan, P. (2015). Scalable mixed-focus collaborative difficulty resolution: A demonstration. In *CSCW Companion Proceedings ACM*.

Fitzpatrick, G., Marshall, P., & Phillips, A. (2006). CVS integration with notification and chat: Lightweight software team collaboration. In *Proceedings of CSCW* (pp. 49–58). New York: ACM Press.

Fogarty, J., Hudson, S. E., Atkeson, C. G., Avrahami, D., Forlizzi, J., Kiesler, S., Lee, J. C., & Yang, J. (2005). Predicting human interruptibility with sensors. *ACM Transactions on Computer-Human Interaction 12*(1), 119–146.

Hegde, R., & Dewan, P. (2008). Connecting programming environments to support Ad-Hoc collaboration. In *Proceedings of 23rd IEEE/ACM Conference on Automated Software Engineering*, L'Aquila Italy, IEEE/ACM.

Herbsleb, J., & Grinter, R. E. (1999). Splitting the organization and integrating the code: Conway's law revisited. In *Proceedings of International Conference on Software Engineering*.

Herbsleb, J. D., Mockus, A., Finholt, T. A., & Grinter, R. E. (2000). Distance, dependencies, and delay in a global collaboration. In *Proceedings of CSCW*.

Humphrey, W. (1997). *A discipline for software engineering*. Boston: Addison Wesley.

Iqbal, S., & Bailey, B. (2007). Understanding and developing models for detecting and differentiating breakpoints during interactive tasks. In *Proceedings of CHI*, ACM.

Kapoor, A., Burlesonc, W., & Picard, R. W. (2007). Automatic prediction of frustration. *International Journal of Human-Computer Studies 65*(8).

Ko, A., Myers, B. A., & Aung, H. H. (2004). Six learning barriers in end-user programming systems. In *Proceedings of IEEE Symposium on Visual Languages—Human Centric Computing*.

LaToza, T. D., Venolia, G., & Deline, R. (2006). Maintaining mental models: A study of developer work habits. In *Proceedings of ICSE*, IEEE.

Long, D., Dillon, N., Wang, K., Carter, J., & Dewan, P. (2015). Interactive control and visualization of difficulty inferences from user-interface commands. In *IUI Companion Proceedings* (pp. 25–28), Atlanta: ACM.

McDuff, D., Karlson, A., Kapoor, A., Roseway, A., & Czerwinski, M. (2012). AffectAura: An intelligent system for emotional memory. In *Proceedings of CHI*.

Murphy, C., Kaiser, G. E., Loveland, K., & Hasan, S. (2009). Retina: Helping students and instructors based on observed programming activities. In *Proceedings of ACM SIGCSE*.

Piech, C., Sahami, M., Koller, D., Cooper, S., & Blikstein, P. A. (2012). Modeling how students learn to program. In *Proceedings of the 43rd ACM Technical Symposium on Computer Science Education*.

Smith, M., & Shumar, W. (2004). *Using netscan to study identity and interaction in a virtual community*. In *Proceedings of ASA*.

Teasley, S., Covi, L., Krishnan, M. S., & Olson, J. S. (2000). How does radical collocation help a team succeed? In *Proceedings of CSCW*.

Tee, K., Greenberg, S., & Gutwin, C. (2006). Providing artifact awareness to a distributed group through screen sharing. In *Proceedings of ACM CSCW* (Computer Supported Cooperative Work).

Witten, I. H., & Frank, E. (1999). *Data mining: Practical machine learning tools and techniques with java implementations*. Burlington: Morgan Kaufmann.

"It's About Business not Politics": Software Development Between Palestinians and Israelis

Nina Boulus-Rødje, Pernille Bjørn and Ahmad Ghazawneh

Abstract This paper focuses on the collaboration in an Israeli-Palestinian tech start-up company. We investigate the strategies enacted by the IT developers for managing the political dynamics and making collaboration possible under the highly challenging political conditions. We found that one of the key strategies was explicitly separating the work domain of software development from the domain of politics. We argue that the IT developers manage to collaborate by displacing the political conflict through strategies of non-confrontation instead of engaging in translating conflicting agendas against each other. By insisting on keeping politics outside of the workspace, the IT developers adopt a strategy of keeping the collaboration *together* by keeping politics and work *apart*. However, we found that despite the attempts to manage the sub-group dynamics, politics constantly invade the workspace and challenge the collaboration. Significant resources are invested into managing the regimes of differentiated identity cards, permits, and checkpoints, all of which have consequences on the employees' freedom or restriction of mobility. Thus, we argue that the IT development domain is inseparable from and deeply dependent upon the political domain.

Introduction

Politics, power, and conflict in collaborative work have always been of interest to CSCW researchers (Suchman 1994). In 2014, we had the unique opportunity to study collaboration in a tech start-up company located in the geographical region

N. Boulus-Rødje (✉) · P. Bjørn
The University of Copenhagen, Copenhagen, Denmark
e-mail: nina.boulusrodje@hum.ku.dk

P. Bjørn
e-mail: pernille.bjorn@di.ku.dk

A. Ghazawneh
IT University of Copenhagen, Copenhagen, Denmark
e-mail: agha@itu.dk

© Springer International Publishing Switzerland 2015   43
N. Boulus-Rødje et al. (eds.), *ECSCW 2015: Proceedings of the 14th European Conference on Computer Supported Cooperative Work, 19–23 September 2015, Oslo, Norway*, DOI 10.1007/978-3-319-20499-4_3

where the political conflict between Israel and Palestine is pertinent. The company, Alpha Corporation (a pseudonym) was the first joint Israeli-Palestinian venture tech start-up founded in 2006 by two entrepreneurs: An Israeli and a Palestinian. While Alpha no longer exists as a company, its former employees continue to work in new constellations. In our ethnographic work, we focus on the Palestinian IT developers and on their experiences of collaboration in Alpha.

Alpha received a considerable amount of attention in local and international media, as well as investments from international organizations. The aim of the company was to develop a virtual operating system, an innovative idea introduced before the cloud-computing era. The company had two teams located in two cities 13 miles away from each other. Getting from one office to the other is a mere 20-min ride; however, the two cities—one in Palestine and one in Israel—are separated by an 800-km wall and several checkpoints. According to B'Tselem—the Israeli Information Center for Human Rights in the Occupied Territories—there are 96 fixed checkpoints, 57 internal checkpoints, and 361 flying checkpoints in the West Bank (B'Tselem 2015). Thus, movement between these two offices is challenging, and so is the task of finding a meeting place that permits entry to staff from both teams. Alpha employees encountered challenging circumstances created by various discontinuities (Watson-Manheim et al. 2002), such as ethnicity, religion, history, geography, language, etc. However, we found that despite the challenging conditions, Alpha employees managed to preserve a meaningful collaboration and develop an innovative web solution.

We set out to investigate how Alpha employees manage the collaboration despite the alignment in participants' demographic attributes (e.g., discontinuities in ethnicity, geography, religion, etc.), which typically increases the risk of subgroup dynamics across sub-groups counterproductive to collaboration (Cramton and Hinds 2005). This led to the formulation of the following research question: What strategies do the employees enact to reduce the risk of sub-group dynamics, making collaboration possible even under the highly challenging political conditions? This investigation was made possible by the access we had to Ramallah and to the Palestinian IT developers from Alpha. In addition, the strong press coverage about Alpha allowed us to trace the challenges of the organizational setup in this politicized context. In contrast to other ethnographies that focus solely on work practices, our study focuses on the wider socio-political matters and the underlying beliefs through which work practice is mediated.

We found that the political dynamics in Alpha are managed in practice through the IT developers' resilience to the political situation and the determination to make the collaboration work despite the demographic differences and discontinuities. This determination is articulated in the motto that working at Alpha "*is about business, and not politics*"—a view repeatedly emphasized by the Palestinian IT developers. However, despite the various attempts of the IT developers to separate politics from business, politics constantly invade the workspace and utterly challenge the collaboration. These challenges necessitate workarounds, which have become a normal natural troubles encountered when running a business in that region, particularly when a company has offices and employees spread across two different jurisdictions and authorities, and where the one authority maintains de facto military control over the other. In prior research where discontinuities are strongly embedded within the collaborative effort, we have seen how the basic nature of articulation work was transformed (Matthiesen et al. 2014). Understanding the complex organizational setup and the impact on articulation work raises a number of questions. First, what motivated the co-founders to establish a start-up with such a complex organizational setup? Second, what motivated the IT developers to invest so much effort into dealing with the challenges resulting from the longstanding political conflict? We argue that the driving force for making this collaboration work is the sincere thirst that the Palestinian IT developers have for acquiring international experience and working with global businesses. Due to the Palestinian industry's financial dependency on Israel (Tawil-Souri 2011), Palestinian IT developers who want to obtain experience working *globally* need to collaborate *locally* with Israeli entrepreneurs. However, in the eyes of the Palestinian developers, *collaborating (working) with* Israel is not equivalent to *supporting* Israel (i.e., its policies and the occupation), but rather it is a *necessity* if they wish to develop further the IT sector in Palestine and build global relations.

This paper is structured as follows: We lay out the theoretical foundation for the paper by drawing from literature on discontinuities and sub-group dynamics within geographically dispersed teams, and from literature about the political situation in Israel and Palestine. We then introduce the case and the political context surrounding it, followed by a section about the method and the multi-sited ethnographic approach we apply. We present our results unpacking strategies, identity, and mobility. This is followed by a discussion and a conclusion.

Discontinuities and Dynamics

Investigating the strategies deployed by Alpha employees for managing the political dynamics, we draw upon one set of literature containing concepts related to the complexities of the collaborative work practice, and another set which introduces literature related to the political situation in Israel and Palestine.

Discontinuities, Sub-groups, and Common Ground

Collaborating within complex organizational setups, for example, across different geography, time zones, and languages, is often referred to as collaboration across discontinuities. Discontinuities are gaps or lack of coherence in work (Cramton and Hinds 2005) often arising in situations where participants must collaborate despite differences in, for example, age, organizational culture, and professions. The purpose of theorizing about collaborative setups in terms of discontinuities is to move beyond the dichotomous perspective that contrasts collocated and distributed work to a more nuanced hybrid conceptualization of what makes the collaboration difficult (Cramton and Hinds 2014). We bring the discontinuity framework to our case to better understand and identify what may otherwise seem like paradoxical differences in how team members respond to boundaries created by the local political circumstances present in our case.

However, before we can look into the strategies by which the participants manage the paradoxical and complex collaboration, we need to identify the boundaries that are produced, as well as the types of discontinuities that are pertinent in the collaboration between the Alpha employees. Unpacking the possible discontinuities points to the demographic attributes of the different IT developers, including for example, geographic location, language, ethnicity, age, religion, etc. All these demographic attributes are fundamental parts of the identity of the employees, and these can be viewed as possible sources of discontinuities that arise and which employees need to address, negotiating boundaries to make the collaboration function in practice. Alignment of demographic attributes risks introducing sub-group dynamics (Cramton and Hinds 2005), especially in situations where communication breakdowns experienced in practice are not grounded in the work practices but rather related to the fundamental value schemes and beliefs of the participants (Bjørn and Ngwenyama 2009). Earlier work on conflicts in teams with participants from diverse cultures identified a tendency to use 'culture' as a rhetoric move, covering up coordination or communication challenges (Jensen and Nardi 2014). Clearly it is far more difficult to cross boundaries produced by fundamental societal structures, which are socialized to the public through constant rehearsing of history and the past (Pilecki and Hammack 2014). Thus, to understand the strategies applied by Alpha employees to manage the political dynamics, we identify the pertinent discontinuities serving as boundaries, which participants negotiate and cross in order to make the collaboration work.

Crossing boundaries across cultural discontinuities is difficult (Boden et al. 2009), and organizations risk forgetting cultural circumstances and other boundaries in attempts to focus on the remote and the foreign culture. When collaborating across discontinuities, we forget how we are to adjust ourselves, not only in terms of trying to change the "other," but also in terms of taking into account our cultural blind spots (Matthiesen et al. 2014). We need language to articulate the changes in our own work practices and in the collaborative relations with the other in order to have common ground. Establishing common ground is critical for collaborative practice (Olson and Olson 2014), as we need to know the knowledge we have in common, and know we have in common (Olson and Olson 2000). Two aspects of common ground have been identified as problematic in collaborative situations of software development, namely, common ground related to process (Bjørn et al. 2014) and common ground related to domain-specific language (Jensen and Bjørn 2012). When investigating the strategies for managing the political dynamics in our cases, we will look into the kinds of common ground practices that emerge to determine whether we can apply existing conceptualizations or whether these need to be revisited.

Political Situation Between Israel and Palestine

Within CSCW there is an increased interest in the role that different technologies might play in the context of Palestine. In a study by Aal et al. (2014), the concept of computer clubs—used in German neighbourhoods with migrant populations to foster social learning and integration—is introduced to a Palestinian refugee camp. Comparing the two settings allows the authors to identify fundamental cultural, social, and political differences (*ibid.*). Another central study by Wulf et al. (2013) analyzes the use of social media by activists in a Palestinian village. They explain how these activists do not make any effort to distinguish between the personal and the political, because the political activities are an integral part of the personal life. Thus, the two are deeply interwoven and cannot be kept apart. Recently, there have been a few studies that focus on the influence of the political situation on the Palestinian IT industry. For instance, Grace C. Koury, of Birzeit University, has written extensively about the topic from a business management and organizational behavior approach (Khoury and Khoury 2014), and has, among others, studied Palestinian business leaders (Muna and Khoury 2012). Both studies unpack the harsh economic realities and challenging conditions that Palestinian entrepreneurs and industry confront with resilience.

Key topics across the literature about Palestine centered around negotiated spaces and practices of political resistance and resilience that Palestinians deploy as a mechanism to live with the occupation (Hass 2002; Tawil-Souri 2011). For instance, Hage (2013) describes the "practices of resilience" that Palestinians exercise to "preserve their own being" within the existing colonial order of domination. The endurance becomes a "strategic foreclosure" because it is "something that the body has been trained to do unconsciously but at appropriate times and for appropriate durations" (*ibid*, p. 5). Resilience as strategic foreclosure takes a paradoxical form, as it is both necessary and impossible. Foreclosure, Hage (2013) explains, should not be understood as a permanent state of being, but rather as a socially and historically acquired capacity to deploy and produce strategies efficient to deal with particular circumstances. "The colonized cannot permanently forget, they have to negotiate the difficulty of both needing to forget (resilience) and needing not to forget (resistance)" (*ibid*, p. 6).

The Palestinian high-tech industry exists under very specific sociopolitical and economic conditions. After the Oslo Accords, the occupied territories were divided into zones of Palestinian and Israeli control, and this was viewed as a demographic separation without meaningful political separation (Hass 2002). Furthermore, the telecommunications sector was handed over to the Palestinian Authority (PA). However, just like Palestine is still seeking national independence and sovereignty while Israel maintains de facto military control in the territories, Palestinian economic dependence on Israel has been deepening throughout the years. Palestinians are faced with ongoing limitations on the telecommunications sector and Internet infrastructure, resulting in what has been labeled "digital occupation" (Tawil-Souri 2012). This marks a shift from a traditional military occupation toward a high-tech one, characterized by increasing surveillance and control enabling new enclosure mechanisms. These mechanisms are added on top of existing *visible* bordering mechanisms (e.g., borders, walls, gates, fences, and checkpoints) by forming *less visible* mechanisms for regulation of telephones, TV channels, and other forms of low-tech restrictions, such as the ID card (Tawil-Souri 2011). Similar to other infra-structures in Palestine (e.g., sewage, population registries, water, transportation), the high-tech industry has been subjected to various constraints imposed by Israeli policies and hampered in its ability to build an independent system (Tawil-Souri 2011). Thus, geographic mobility, economic growth, and digital flows are contained and controlled by Israeli politics. In addition, these infrastructures are unstable, as they are constantly exposed to new policies and political conditions. These are the political conditions surrounding the Alpha project, where the Israeli and Palestinian developers need to collaborate in order to develop their cloud-computing software.

Case Description and the Political Context

In 2006, an Israeli and a Palestinian entrepreneur founded Alpha, which built the first virtual web operating system, providing users with a working environment over the Internet that mimics the classic desktop operating systems. As the Israeli CEO explained it in a presentation at the Web 2.0 Summit, the idea was "*Getting rid of walls, allowing you to free your data*". The company had two offices. The first was located in the Palestinian city of Ramallah, with more than 35 (80 at the peak period) Palestinian software developers and designers responsible for research, development, and programming. Ramallah is central city in the West Bank, hosting almost all governmental headquarters of the PA and Beir Zeit University (the oldest university in Palestine). It is known for being liberal yet politically conscious city. The Israeli team (5 staff) was located in an office in the Israeli town of Modiin, only 21 km away from Ramallah. Modiin is a very young city, formed in 2003 and located in Israel's 1967 borders. There are several check-points between the two Alpha offices. Qalandiya is the main route out of the West Bank for Palestinians and is known for its humiliating and lengthy security screen-ing (B'Tselem 2014), and Hizma (located a few kilometers to the south) which typically has a little more friendly screening and less traffic jams.

Alpha received a lot of media attention and press coverage because of its tech-nology, but primarily because of its political set up. The technology was unique enough to attract investors and venture capitalists. The political dimension was unique as it was the first joint web start-up between Palestinians and Israelis. This was emphasized when Alpha had their official launch in 2009, near the wall in the West Bank. The launch was attended by former UK Prime Minister Tony Blair and other key political players in the Middle East (e.g., Ahmad Tibi, a key Arab-Israeli politician and member of the Israeli Parliament). In March 2010, Alpha announced that it would be closing its services to all users. The company cited "changes in the marketplace" as the main reason behind its closure.

Multi-sited Ethnography

To investigate the strategies deployed by the IT developers at Alpha, we applied multi-sited ethnography (Marcus 1995). Multi-sited ethnography is an emergent ethnographic approach in CSCW (Blomberg and Karasti 2013), and is particularly relevant when investigating contemporary local changes in culture and society. In multi-sited ethnography there are no local-global distinctions; instead, the "global" is an emergent dimension of following connections and associations across sites relevant for the domain in question. Thus, in studying Alpha a key part of our work is to identify the relevant sites for investigation. We started in the office, but it quickly became apparent to us that to understand the collaboration in Alpha, we must follow the associations from Alpha outside of the office, including politics, news, economics, history, etc., and investigate their relationship while paying particular attention to the ways in which cultural logics are multiply produced (Marcus 1995). Connections and relationships form the basic building blocks of multi-sited ethnography, and the aim becomes the actual mapping of new objects of study, which emerge during the work. Comparison emerges from formulating questions to an emergent object of study, and through this practice the researchers' unpacking of the new relationships becomes core and the descriptions of the relations are by themselves contributions.

Applying a multi-sited ethnography enabled us to follow connections and associations from the very practices we encounter in the empirical work to news, histories, online content, and other data sources that make up our empirical case. Thus, analyzing the various news stories on the Alpha project found in Israeli, Palestinian, and international media (e.g., *Haaretz*, the *New York Times*), written in Hebrew, Arabic, and English became pertinent for our ethnographic investigations. We read these articles carefully, as well as the many comments that were written by the readers. We also gained access to the Facebook group made by and for Alpha members. Since two of the authors speak and read both Hebrew and Arabic, we were able to follow Alpha from the different perspectives. We also collected video material (about Alpha) publically available on the Internet and transcribed two video clips from which particular quotes where used in this paper (an interview in Hebrew with the Israeli CEO to the Israeli Channel 10 and a presentation of Alpha by the Israeli CEO to Web 2.0 Summit). The first author travelled twice to Ramallah (June and December, 2014), visiting the city, crossing the checkpoints from Israel, and conducting interviews with former Palestinian Alpha employees. All interviews were conducted in the native language of the interviewee, audio recorded, and partially transcribed and/or summarized, as well as translated by the first and third author.[1] In total, 7 Palestinian developers[2] were interviewed

---

[1]The interviews were conducted in July 2014, when the political situation was relatively calm as there were negotiations with Israel about releasing Palestinian prisoners and negotiations within Palestine for a unity government between Hamas and Fatah. A few days after the researcher left Ramallah, three settlers were kidnapped and this lead to a military crackdown on the West Bank and to an invasion on the Gaza Strip.

[2]The names of all the informants are pseudonyms in order to preserve their anonymity.

(30–120 min); this includes software developers, designers, marketing managers, project managers, and business analysts. The age of the developers interviewed varied; some were young and began working in Alpha right after graduation, while others were seniors and had more years of experience. Observations were carried out in the offices of the new company established in Ramallah with a similar organizational set up and some of the same people. Finally, in each of the fieldtrips, the first author passed from Tel-Aviv to Ramallah using different checkpoints, thus subjecting herself to the experience of crossing at Qalandiya versus Hizma.

Strategies, Identity, and Mobility

Investigating how the IT developers managed the political dynamics influencing their collaboration, we found that a critical part of this effort was linked to a wide range of strategies for leaving politics outside the office space. The Palestinian IT developers repeatedly portrayed politics as a domain that can be separated from the work domain of IT development. Politics were portrayed as a jacket, which could be taken off whenever appropriate and hung temporarily outside the office. This was puzzling, since the Alpha project was portrayed in the local and international media as a political project. How could the IT developers working on such a highly political project situated in a conflict zone label their collaboration as "apolitical"? When the developers refer to their offices as "politically-free-space," they do not mean that politics were forgotten or accepted. On the contrary, politics are *not* simplified nor made unproblematic, but they are temporarily put aside in the Alpha office. As Tawfik explains, he neither forgets, nor is at peace with, the political situation. Rather, the IT developers deploy various strategies for placing politics temporarily aside.

Shutting off any political discussion that occurs in the office is one way in which politics are put aside. When working and living in societies with a deep and longstanding political conflict, countless incidents take place outside of the office (e.g., siege on Gaza, losing a family member), leading inevitably to adversities and tensions among the employees, who may be unable to avoid discussing these incidents in the office space. However, in the effort to keep politics outside of the workspace, it was necessary for the IT developers to shut down any heated, emotional, or controversial discussions. Thus, stopping others from opening such discussions was an "obvious" yet unwritten rule that employees subscribe to, willingly or unwillingly. This practice was a pragmatic necessity required to enable the collaboration between the IT developers situated within a longstanding historical, religious, and political conflict.

Balancing the language is important to enable the collaboration, and one approach is to avoid political categories and apply neutral ones in everyday interactions. For example, the Israeli CEO is often referred to as British, as he carries British citizenship. The IT developers strived to avoid the political categories, which were present and constant reminders of the political situation. The Israeli colonization and the ongoing conflict make it somewhat "easier" for the Palestinian developers to relate to a British entrepreneur than to relate to an Israeli CEO—even though both categories refer to the same person. Furthermore, when referring to the different offices, the IT developers consciously avoid mentioning Israel or Palestine. Instead, they refer to the "Modiin office" and the "Ramallah office," using the names of the cities. As explained by Ibrahim, *We don't mention Israel. We try to avoid these things. We look at it as one team.*" Introducing these politically neutral categories removes, to a certain extent, the political tensions that other labels may connote. The professionalism that results from stripping away political dimensions from people and locations is emphasized in the collaboration, and in this shift, politics become linked to private and personal matters, which do not belong to the professional business context. As explained by Tawfik:

It is personal. It's not that I don't care, but this is business. [...] I can't pretend that I'm friendly with Israelis. We each stand on our own side. When there were discussions, these would be closed down. It damages the relationships...It's not that I cancel my identity or forget it, but I need to continue with my life and do something for my city. Life goes on in the end.

Similarly, Mustafa, another young Palestinian developer, explains that he cannot blame the Israeli team for the political situation.

When I used to go to my aunt's house in Israel, I used to see Jews. I then I realized that I'm seeing the other party, and I don't think of them as monsters. I have the ability—when looking at Jews—not to imagine the Palestinian kid that was killed by them. I know that killing him was not right and it's not forgiven. At the same time, I can't go to Noam [the Israeli CEO] and ask why his people killed that Palestinian kid. Similarly, Noam can't blame me for my previous classmate who killed Jews in a settlement.

In the above quote, the IT developer explains how he sees the human in his Israeli colleagues; he sees them as individual people who cannot be (directly) responsible for the consequences of the military occupation and the ongoing war (e.g., the killing of a Palestinian kid or Israeli settlers). He explains how neither him, nor the Israeli team, can blame each other for these events grounded in the 70-year colonial history of the region and the contemporary political conflict. By separating politics and the contemporary adverse events that take place outside the workplace from the activities that take place inside the office, they enact a mechanism of survival that allows them to cope with the current situation.

Separate but Mixed Identities

To a certain extent, the organizational structure of Alpha is similar to an outsourcing software project, except that all participants are geographically located within the same region, with only 13 miles of distance between the offices. Still, the IT developers live and work under different conditions and salaries. However, Israelis and Palestinians have been living side by side for many generations. Thus, there are many similarities across the cultures located within the same geographical area. Examining what it means to have two distinctly separate *yet already mixed* cultures creates certain conditions for the collaboration not seen elsewhere in outsourcing setups.

The mixture of cultures within the same geographical area is especially applicable to those living in Jerusalem, as it is known for being a mixed city, with Israelis and Palestinians living side by side. George, who lives in Jerusalem, points out, *"We're living in the same 10-mile radius."* Similarly, Tawfik explains: *"I live in Jerusalem so I interact with them … although Jerusalem is divided, we still meet."* Due to the financial dependency of Palestinians on Israel, many Palestinians grew up either working in Israel or having their families work in Israel. They would travel on a daily basis from Palestine to work in Israel, and are therefore familiar with the Israeli culture. However, this situation has changed after the second intifada (in 2000), as the number of permits issued to allow Palestinians to work in Israel has decreased dramatically (B'Tselem 2015). Therefore, in the eyes of the Palestinian IT developers, Palestinians and Israelis are very similar.

> They [the Israelis] are not totally 'fremd' [in german; foreigner]. We are not starting from scratch, like working with the Indians, whom we don't know anything about. We know a lot of things [about them]. There is a strong interaction between us and them. [...] We know for instance their holidays [...] we know...that Saturday is a sacred day.

George explains above how the cultural differences between Israelis and Indians are larger than between Israelis and Palestinians. Similarly, Elias explains that prior to Alpha he worked for Siemens in Ramallah and collaborated with IT developers in Germany. While he experienced this collaboration as very formal and highly structured, collaborating with Israelis, he explains, is much more casual and informal. "Our accent in English is close, and we understand each other very well," he says. Furthermore, several developers emphasize how the two cultures are similar and exposed to the same things. George clarifies: *"there are many similarities between the two cultures. There is great resemblance between the two languages. We almost look alike. [...] We dress the same and you can't tell us apart".* Several IT developers emphasize how the two cultures are exposed to the same things, wearing the same cloths, and eating the same food. After all, *"we both like Houmous"* said George while laughing.

We found that depicting the collaboration in Alpha as constitutive of two distinct cultures is rather imprecise and simplistic. The Alpha team constitutes a wide variety of nationalities, including British, American, Jordanian, Kuwaiti, Salvadorian, Egyptian, Israeli, and Palestinian. While the Israeli team lives in Israel, the Palestinian team is scattered across both Israel (mostly Jerusalem) and Palestine. Furthermore, the team includes a rich variety of different religions, including both religious and secular Jews, Muslims, Christians, humanists, atheists, and some who view themselves as being part of the geek community.

Still, important differences exist and these have a major impact on the collaboration. The Israeli team does not speak Arabic, and most of the Palestinian team does not speak Hebrew. They depend on English as the common language. Thus, although they know about each other's culture, the familiarity is still limited due the highly politicized circumstance. As explained by George:

We know a lot of things; there is a strong interaction between us and them. Still, on the personal level we don't know anything about them. We watch them on TV in the news, we pass by them in the Machsom [checkpoint in Hebrew]; that's it. And they- what do they hear? They have their own news; they don't enter Ramallah and the only interaction that we have is through the soldiers in the Machsom.

Most interaction between Palestinians and Israelis is with soldiers at the checkpoints. The knowledge about each other is mediated by the local news in different languages, where each party is depicted in a negative manner. It can be said that the mediascape within the region is differentiated by audience, language, and political agendas, keeping the two cultures alienated. Alpha has given the IT developers the opportunity to get to know each other on an individual level. This is true particularly for the Israeli team. In one of the interviews for the Israeli Channel 10, the Israeli CEO admits that Alpha gave him the opportunity to meet Palestinians for the *first* time. The opportunity to meet each other influences the knowledge they gradually acquire about each other.

Complex Identities and Work Relationships

Maintaining the separation between politics and work is not easy. Politics keep sneaking in despite the repetitive attempts to block them and keep them out of the office. Mustafa tells about a barbeque gathering at the home of the Israeli CEO, saying: *"We don't feel anything special when we are at [Noam's] home. But we feel awkward when we are walking together in the streets."* There have been several situations where politics constantly clashed with business. Ibrahim recalls when there were resignations from the Palestinian team during one of the sieges on Gaza when the political situation was particularly tense. He explains: *"One girl came and said I can't continue."* When approached by her team leader, she said *"she could no longer work with Jews. It was enough."* This incident illustrates how the strategy of separating politics from business is challenging, as it is impossible to completely detach politics from the professional work domain.

> I don't know if I can articulate that…but sometimes I feel that what I'm doing [working with Israelis] is wrong. But again, I repeat and tell you that we never felt that what we're doing is going the wrong direction. But sometimes…one feels ah…perhaps, for example, [I wonder] if I worked in a different place, if it would have been different. But there were no other opportunities. This was a very good [job] opportunity, both financially and experience wise. At that time, there weren't so many companies working with these things [software development]…now the situation might be different. (Shadi)

As can be seen from above, the Palestinian IT developers face perplexing and conflicting positions. On the one hand, they feel they need to *work with* Israel if they wish to develop further the IT sector in Palestine and build global relations. On the other hand, they fear that *working with* Israel would be confused with *supporting* Israel and its policies, as there have been situations where they were accused for subscribing to normalization discourse (عيبطت), thus accepting the

Israeli occupation and various forms of discrimination and oppression against the Palestinians (Palestinian Campaign for the Academic and Cultural Boycott of Israel 2007[3]). While feeling uncomfortable with the current political situation, they still must work, be professional, and treat work as "pure business." This introduces paradoxical situations, as the below incident illustrates:

> There was a Jewish employee called Yaki at the company that I have worked with for several months. Once, I went with Noam [the Israeli CEO] to our office in Jerusalem. That time, Yaki wasn't working as he was called for a military service. During the working day, Yaki dropped by the office wearing his military uniform. Here, I was shocked; this guy that I know and worked with is entering the office with that uniform. I worked with him a lot and…I didn't care about his religion…When we used to go to work together, we talked about a lot of human things. But, when he entered [the office] with the uniform, I couldn't accept it. Here, you feel those people who we see at checkpoints and humiliate us, they have the same uniform.

When the Israeli employee enters the office wearing the military uniform, this contradicts the unwritten yet agreed upon norms of keeping politics outside the workspace. While most of the employees adhere to this unwritten norm, the particular societal circumstances (i.e., the ongoing war resulting in enlisting Israeli employees to the military) impose certain contradictory conditions affecting the common ground for work.

Freedom and Restriction of Mobility

In a TV interview to the Israeli Channel 10, the Israeli CEO explains how "Israelis are not permitted entry [into Ramallah]" and "how he is maybe the only CEO in the world who cannot visit his main office". Indeed, the Israeli government bans Israelis from entering Palestinian areas (so-called Areas A, according to the Oslo agreements). But, when the topic of mobility was raised during our interviews, most informants viewed themselves as free to move across geographical locations and viewed this topic initially as non-problematic. Ibrahim explained how the Israeli CEO can visit the Ramallah office whenever is needed.

> No, it's not easy [for the Israeli CEO to enter Palestine]. You [the researcher] don't know everything [about the political situation]. But we know and understand the subject. He can actually drive with any car [with an Israeli yellow plate]; he can get in; no one will speak to him. So it's soooo easy. And then, it was Ibrahim [a Palestinian developer] who went to pick him up [with his Palestinian green-plated car], so it's not a problem.

Thus, what might seem as problematic from the outside, the politics of movement, is worked around and managed differently in practice. Most informants tell repeatedly that entering Israel is not a problem. For example, Tawfik explains that *"the only problem is the checkpoint; Qalandiya. But I don't pass through it that*

---

[3]http://www.pacbi.org/atemplate.php?id=100.

often...I go through Hizma instead...After a while it becomes a routine. You get used to it." The 96 fixed checkpoints in the West Bank and 57 internal checkpoints (B'Tselem 2015) are an integral part of the everyday practices, and so is the practice of applying various workarounds to manage the political contextual situation of the day. What from the outside seems an exception is seen from the perspective of the Palestinian IT developers as part of the normal natural troubles encountered when working at Alpha.

These workaround practices include, for example, calculating additional time to pass through checkpoints. Driving between Jerusalem and Ramallah takes merely 30 min, but the Palestinian developers always estimate additional time, typically amounting to an hour, depending on who is in the car. For example, driving with Palestinians from the West Bank makes it more difficult, since they are not permitted to pass through Hizma—the checkpoint with less traffic and smoother screening. In the daily planning of the work, precision is not required and a 30-min delay is tolerated to accommodate mobility challenges. If the Palestinian IT developers on particular days are not given permits to travel to Israel, they can "*always Skype*" explains Tawfik.

Permits are essential, as they determine the mobility of the IT developers. While the Palestinian developers who hold Jerusalem IDs can choose to pass through Hizma, the majority of Palestinian developers do not have this choice. George explains, "*to get the whole team to the other side, it might take a couple of hours [...] once the event is done, you have to hurry up and leave because there is a time limit on the permits.*" Different Palestinian employees have different time limits to their permits, which reduces their flexibility, especially when most of the time is spent on waiting at the checkpoint. These mobility restrictions impose high overhead costs for Alpha. Managing the Palestinian IT developers' movement requires good contact with the Israeli authorities issuing permits. One of the informants mentioned that the Israeli CEO has internal contacts with the Israeli authorities, making the process of issuing permits a little smoother.

Mobility is also complicated by the sophisticated regimes of differentiated colorful identify cards and permits. Each color of an ID card permits the residents particular mobility to limited geographical locations, often for a limited time period. There are three colors of ID cards. A blue ID card is given to Jewish residents granting them freedom of movement. A blue ID card is also given to Palestinians residing in Israel (such as the one carried by the first author); and although it officially has no limitations, it has constantly been subject to threats of being withdrawn (Tawil-Souri 2011). The green ID card is given to Palestinians residing in the West Bank, and the orange ID card is given to those residing in the Gaza Strip. Each of these ID cards permits movement to particular areas. For instance, residents of East Jerusalem typically carry either an Israeli travel permit or a temporary Jordanian passport/travel permit, which must be renewed if leaving the city for an extended period of time. Residents of parts of the West Bank typically carry a PA passport, a Jordanian temporary passport, or a travel document. The Palestinian developers in Alpha reside in many different places on both sides of the wall. Thus, there are different restrictions on movement and various types of permits that need to be issued each time the two teams need to meet face-to-face. Consequently, it is utterly challenging for the Ramallah office to meet the Modiin office. One challenge is related to the element of unpredictability when issuing permits. Not knowing if an employee may attend the event or not makes it difficult to plan events. Getting a permit is done through faxing information to the Israeli authorities. There have been several situations at Alpha where Palestinian developers were rejected permits, and there is one employee who never gets a permit because he is banned from entering Israel, allegedly for political reasons. When the teams need to meet face-to-face, they travel to a gas station located near Jericho, a neutral geographical place, which permits entry to both teams. Some of the job interviews conducted by the Israeli CEO with the Palestinian developers took place at this remote gas station.

When it comes to freedom of movement outside of the Territories, the Palestinian IT developers adopt similar non-problematic attitudes. Tawfik explains that when he needs to travel outside the country, he simply passes through Jordan, instead of Israel. The extra effort required for travelling is experienced as a regular routine, as part of the normal natural troubles encountered when being a Palestinian and living in the region. Elias explains that if he has to travel to Europe, he will normally pass through Jordan. Since he cannot predict exactly how much time it will take to pass the check-point, he will normally arrive in Jordan a day before his flight to Europe. He points out how this unavoidably ends up being very costly for the company, because one needs to factor in an extra day before and after the travel. There is a certain irony for some of the Palestinian employees, as the restrictions imposed on their mobility change when they leave their country. Consider the following story by George:

> I have a Salvadorian passport. The last trip I did we had an urgent business meeting. I booked a flight the second day. I arrived there and I booked a car while on my way. I did 8 trips in five days…I travelled England from Manchester to London by car. Communicating with my wife, via Facetime, she is asking me where are you now. I was in Manchester; then I had lunch in Birmingham, I slept the night in London [and] I woke up in Stansted […] every time I got hungry I drop in a gas station. Every time I spoke to my wife I was in a different location. She then told me, apparently you can go wherever you wish, drive wherever you want, but you can't drive to your own home in Jerusalem. This is because, I have a Palestinian ID and my wife has an Israeli ID and we both live in Jerusalem. My Palestinian driving license isn't valid there and I can't drive to my own home. I feel free in the whole world but not in my own city.

As can be seen from above, George sees himself as a free man outside of his own country, where his Salvadorian passport gives him the possibility to travel and drive freely. Paradoxically, his native Palestinian ID prohibits him from travelling to certain areas and restricts his movement in his own country.

Strategies for Managing Political Dynamics

What are the strategies enacted by Alpha employees to manage political dynamics and enable a meaningful collaboration in such complex political conditions? We found that the political dynamics in Alpha are managed in practice through the employees' dedicated effort to making the collaboration function despite the demographic differences and discontinuities (Watson-Manheim et al. 2012; Cramton and Hinds 2014). The most pertinent boundaries we identified relate to the ways in which *identity and mobility were produced*. Unpacking the demographic differences it is clear that the distinction between "Israeli" and "Palestinian" as separate classifications exists but is not nuanced enough to capture the complex collaborative situations. The two *distinct* and *separate* classifications are not clear-cut entities, as they are *similar* in some ways and are already somewhat *mixed*. It was clear from our data that even if the employees within Alpha wanted to put these categories aside and concentrate on software development, this was not always possible. Working at Alpha required utmost attention to the complex classifications of citizens in the region. It includes the enormous efforts required for transporting Alpha employees through the checkpoints between the offices and managing the regime of colourful ID cards restricting the movement of the Palestinian IT developers. The nuances in the categories of Israeli and Palestinian only serve as a first type of descriptive category of movement, and then the distinct attributes (e.g., place of birth, home town, etc.) serve as modifiers determining which checkpoints can legally be crossed, when, how, and for how long. Thus, while the demographic attributes of location and ethnicity are aligned within the sub-group of Palestinian, it does not mean that the Palestinian developers share religion or ID cards. The production of the Palestinian or Israeli identity thus becomes pertinent in the collaborative work, as it determines the mobility of the employees across the two offices. When employees were prohibited from passing a checkpoint due to a certain classification, workarounds were developed to accommodate these challenges.

Moving away from the streets and checkpoints and into the Alpha offices, the main strategy applied by employees was to keep politics out. Previous CSCW work in Palestine found out that it was impossible for political activists to separate between their political lives and their personal lives. Politics were such a dominant part of their lives that they could not keep the two apart (Wulf et al. 2013). In our case, however, the IT developers insisted on keeping politics outside of the work, and in this way applied a strategy of keeping things together (the collaboration across discontinuities) by keeping things apart (politics and work as separated). Thus, in the Palestinian developers' view, their collaboration through Alpha is *about business, and not politics*. This does not mean that they accept the political situation. On the contrary, several Palestinian developers resist the occupation, and have reflected upon the perplexing, paradoxical, and conflicting position they encounter when working with Israelis. To understand this paradox it is important to remember that most of the IT developers have never lived under different circumstances (without occupation). The occupation is a forming force of the lives and work of the Palestinians (Hage 2013). Thus, we see the strategies of collaborating with the Israelis at Alpha as an attempt to construct a form of normality by carving out a space—preserving a sense of existence—that is not governed by colonialism or by resistance to it. For this to happen, practices of resilience are crucial; that is, practices of forgetting and "of absenting the occupation and any preoccupation with the occupation" (Hage p. 5).

Earlier work on conflicts in cross-cultural teams with power imbalance (as is typically found in outsourcing companies purchasing cheaper services) found the use of rhetoric moves to reframe experienced coordination and communication challenges as 'clashes among cultures' (Jensen and Nardi 2014). The case in Alpha was different. Instead of using culture to reframe coordination challenges, Alpha employees dedicated major efforts to create a 'new common culture'—the 'Alpha culture'—one that does not refer to ethnic categories but rather refers to the profession of software development and provides space for all categories. We illustrated the different strategies used by the IT developers for managing the political dynamics by creating politically neutral categories when referring to the collaborative situations. This was manifested in the way they referred to the Israeli CEO as British rather than Israeli/Jewish, and to the offices as Modiin or Ramallah rather than referring to the countries hosting the offices. The production of politically neutral language developed to separate the politics from the work practices can be seen as an approach for creating common ground (Olson and Olson 200). The IT developers construct a language they share and know they share consisting of politically neutral categories. However, this language is not only about the work practices (Jensen and Bjørn 2012), it is *common ground characterized by a different nature*. The IT developers implicitly (through strategies of silence, putting politics aside, and avoiding discussing politics) and explicitly (by shutting down political discussions) *avoid applying political language* and only use the politically neutral language. The process of grounding in communication is usually seen as a process where participants develop a shared language through interaction and engagement (Clark and Brennan 1991). However, we found that the grounding process in our highly politicized collaborative setting was dedicated to developing a revised shared language of politically neutral categories. The grounding process included redefining shared concepts as well as negotiating which concepts to avoid even though they were already shared. Reframing a collaborative situation by redefining concepts is an effective strategy in conflict situations (Jensen and Nardi 2014; Bjørn and Ngwenyama 2009). In this way, the common ground, which existed prior to the project in Alpha as a result of the years of living side-by-side, was re-negotiated. Similar strategies have been reported in studies of post-conflict societies, for example, Rwanda (Yoo et al. 2013); however, in our case, the colonial context and the conflict still exist, and the tech start-up community that started at Alpha continues to exist under contemporary political conditions.

In this way, Alpha employees manage to work within a paradoxical context. They mix what *cannot* be mixed—like oil and water—by displacing the inner paradox through strategies of non-confrontation instead of engaging in translating conflicting agendas. However, despite the sincere attempts to keep politics out of the office, the political conflict continues to impact the workplace. At times, these politics of exclusion (e.g., prohibiting an employee to enter Israel) are worked around by finding politically neutral ground (e.g., the gas station). Other times, the political situation becomes too unbearable, leading to resignations. Thus, although the employees do not actively engage in political discussion, they are constantly reminded of the political conflict.

Our data demonstrate that collaboration within Alpha requires additional efforts outside what CSCW researchers normally would refer to as articulation work in software development (Boden et al. 2014). We know that working across geographical boundaries changes the nature of work for IT developers, requiring them to engage in additional articulation work when compared to collocated work (Matthiesen et al. 2014). The Alpha project challenges the ways we in CSCW think about articulation work. The justification for incurring the overhead cost of articulation work and thus the reason for the emergence of cooperative work formations is that participants could not accomplish their tasks if they were to do them individually (Schmidt and Bannon 1992, p. 14). However, the complex organizational setup in Alpha requires a new category of articulation work addressing the emergent obstacles and the workarounds imposed by the political conflict. This raises the question of what motivates the two teams to invest so much effort into dealing with obstacles imposed by the longstanding political conflict.

From the Israeli perspective, the financial benefit is one explanation. Employing Palestinian IT developers based in Ramallah results in considerable saving on wages. As for the Palestinian employees, they view working with Israel as a necessity due to the limited alternative options within the high-tech industry in Palestine. Thus, geographic mobility and economic growth are contained and controlled by Israeli politics (Tawil-Souri 2011), leading to a demographic separation without meaningful political separation (Hass 2002) and financial independence. This financial dependency results in few options for Palestinian IT developers. To achieve international work experience they must collaborate locally with Israeli entrepreneurs. Thus, working at Alpha has given the Palestinian developers an opportunity to acquire experience in global business. It is the thirst for these unique and international experiences, for technological progress and innovation, that was the driving force for making this collaboration work. After all, these unique experiences turned the Palestinian developers who used to work at Alpha into highly attractive and competitive hires after the company was shut down. Thus, in spite of the challenges imposed by the different political dynamics (e.g., being accused of subscribing to normalization discourse), the Palestinian IT developers did manage to create and apply strategies reducing the risk of sub-group dynamics while supporting meaningful collaboration.

Conclusion

We found that the political dynamics at Alpha are managed in practice by the employees dedicated efforts to making the collaboration work despite the demographic discontinuities. Strategies include cautious consideration of using politically neutral categories when referring to the offices and the collaborative situations, putting politics temporarily aside, shutting down political discussion, and, finally, insisting that politics are personal and therefore should not interfere with the business domain. We argue that Alpha employees manage to work in a paradoxical context by displacing the inner paradox through strategies of non-confrontation instead of engaging in translating conflicting agendas. Thus, the IT developers applied a strategy of keeping the collaboration across discontinuities together, by keeping politics and work apart. Tony Blair, who attended the official launch of Alpha, called for more partnerships across the Israeli-Palestinian divide, while emphasizing that *"we need a political solution, but we also know it's not just about politics. It's about business"* (Associated Press 2009). However, we argue that the business domain is deeply dependent upon the political domain. Thus, despite the sincere efforts invested by the IT developers, politics keep sneaking into the office, utterly challenging the possibility of getting access to politically neutral ground.

Acknowledgments We would like to thank the Palestinian developers from Alpha for welcoming us so warmly to Ramallah and for taking the time to kindly and generously share with us their honest reflections and critical experiences. This work was supported by The Danish Agency for Science, Technology and Innovation: International Network Programme grant #4070-00010B.

References

Aal, K., Yerousis, G., et al. (2014). Come_in@ Palestine: Adapting a german computer club concept to a Palestinian refugee camp. In *Proceedings of the 5th ACM International Conference on Collaboration Across Boundaries: Culture, Distance and Technology* (pp. 111–120).

Associated Press (2009). Israeli-Palestinian partnership launches startup. http://www.ynetnews.com/articles/0,7340,L-3746717,00.html

B'Tselem. (2014). Qalandiya checkpoint, March 2014: An obstacle to normal life. http://www.btselem.org/photoblog/201404_qalandiya_checkpoint.

B'Tselem (2015). Checkpoint, physical obstructions, and forbidden roads. http://www.btselem.org/freedom_of_movement/checkpoints_and_forbidden_roads

Blomberg, J., and Karasti, H., (2013). Reflections on 25 years of ethnography in CSCW. *Computer supported cooperative Work*, 22(4–6), 373–423.

Bjørn, P., & Ngwenyama, O. (2009). Virtual team collaboration: Building shared meaning, resolving breakdowns and creating translucence. *Information Systems Journal*, 19(3), 227–253.

Bjørn, P., Esbensen, M., Jensen, R. E., Matthiesen, S. (2014). Does distance still matter? Revisiting the CSCW fundamentals on distributed collaboration. *ACM Transaction Computer Human Interaction (ToChi)*, 21(5), 1–27.

Boden, A., Avram, G., et al. (2009). Knowledge management in distributed software development teams: Does culture matter? In *International Conference on Global Software Engineering (ICGSE)* (pp. 18–27). Limerick, Ireland: IEEE Press.

Boden, A., Rosswog, F., et al. (2014). Articulation spaces: Bridging the gab between formal and informal coordination. In *Computer Supported Cooperative Work (CSCW)*. Baltimore, USA: ACM.

Clark, H., & Brennan, S. (1991). Grounding in communication: Perspectives on social shared cognition. In L. Resnick, J. Levine & S. Teasley (Eds.), (xiii, 429 pp). Washington, DC, US: American Psychological Association.

Cramton, C. D., & Hinds, P. (2005). Subgroup dynamics in internationally distributed teams: Ethnocenterism or cross-national learning. *Research in Organizational Behavior*, 26, 231–263.

Cramton, C. D., & Hinds, P. (2014). An embedded model of cultural adaptation in global teams. *Organization Science, 25*(4), 1056–1081.

Hage, G. (2013). *In unoccupied Palestine: Keynote delivered at the 'between dependence and independence: What future for Palestine?' conference*. Ramallah, Palestine: Ibrahim Abu-Lughod Institute of International Studies, Birzeit University.

Hass, A. (2002). Israels closure policy: An ineffective strategy of containment and repression. *Journal of Palestine Studies, 31*(3), 5–20.

Jensen, R. E., & Bjørn, P. (2012). Divergence and convergence in global software development: Cultural complexities as societal structures. *COOP: Design of cooperative systems* (pp. 123–136). France: Springer.

Jensen, R. E., & Nardi, B. (2014). The rhetoric of culture as an act of closure in cross-national software development department. *European conference of information system (ECIS)*. Tel Aviv: AIS.

Khoury, G., & Khoury, M. (Eds.). (2014). *Cases on management and organizational behaviour in an Arab context*. USA: Business Science Reference IGI Global.

Marcus, G. (1995). Ethnography in/of the world system: The emergence of multi-sited ethnography. *Annual Review Anthropology, 24*, 95–117.

Matthiesen, S., Bjørn, P., et al. (2014). Figure out how to code with the hands of others: Recognizing cultural blind spots in global software development. *Computer supported cooperative work (CSCW)*. Baltimore, USA: ACM.

Muna, F. A., & Khoury, G. (2012). *The Palestinian executive: Leadership under challenging conditions*. London: Gower Publishing, Ltd.

Olson, G. M., & Olson, J. S. (2000). Distance matters. *Human-Computer Interaction, 15*(2), 139–178.

Olson, J., & Olson, G. (2014). *Working together apart: Collaboration over the internet*. California, US: Morgan & Claypool Publishers.

Pilecki, A., & Hammack, P. (2014). Negotiating the past, imagining the future: Israeli and Palestinian narratives in intergroup dialog. *International Journal of Intercultural Relations, 43*, 100–113.

Schmidt, K., & Bannon, L. (1992). Taking CSCW seriously: Supporting articulation work. *Computer Supported Cooperative Work (CSCW) An International Journal, 1*(1–2), 7–40.

Suchman, L. (1994). Do categories have politics? The language/action perspective reconsidered. *Computer Supported Cooperative Work (CSCW) An International Journal, 2*(3), 177–190.

Tawil-Souri, H. (2011). Colored identity: The politics and materiality of ID cards in Palestine/Israel. *Social Text, 29*(2), 67–97.

Tawil-Souri, H. (2012). Digital occupation: Gaza's high-tech enclosure. *Journal of Palestine Studies, 41*(2), 27–43.

Watson-Manheim, M. B., Chudoba, K., et al. (2002). Discontinuities and continuities: A new way to understand virtual work. *Information Technology and People, 15*(3), 191–209.

Watson-Manheim, M. B., Chudoba, K., et al. (2012). Perceived discontinuities and constructed continuities in virtual work. *Information Systems Journal, 22*(1), 29–52.

Wulf, V., Aal, K., et al. (2013). Fighting against the wall: Social media use by political activist in a Palestinian village. *Human factors in computing systems CHI*. Paris, France: ACM.

Yoo, D., Lake, M., et al. (2013). Envisioning across generations: A multi-lifespan information system for international justice in Rwanda. *Human factors in computing systems CHI*. Paris, France: ACM.

Social Media-Based Expertise Evidence

**Arnon Yogev, Ido Guy, Inbal Ronen, Naama Zwerdling
and Maya Barnea**

Abstract Social media provides a fertile ground for expertise location. The public nature of the data supports expertise inference with little privacy infringement and, in addition, presentation of direct and detailed evidence for an expert's skillfulness in the queried topic. In this work, we study the use of social media for expertise evidence. We conducted two user surveys of enterprise social media users within a large global organization, in which participants were asked to rate anonymous experts based on artificial and real evidence originating from different types of social media data. Our results indicate that the social media data types perceived most convincing as evidence are not necessarily the ones from which expertise can be inferred most precisely or effectively. We describe these results in detail and discuss implications for designers and architects of expertise location systems.

Part of the research was conducted while working at IBM Research.

A. Yogev (✉) · I. Ronen · N. Zwerdling · M. Barnea
IBM Research-Haifa, Haifa, Israel
e-mail: arnony@il.ibm.com

I. Ronen
e-mail: inbal@il.ibm.com

N. Zwerdling
e-mail: naamaz@il.ibm.com

M. Barnea
e-mail: mayab@il.ibm.com

I. Guy
Yahoo Labs, Haifa, Israel
e-mail: idoguy@acm.org

© Springer International Publishing Switzerland 2015
N. Boulus-Rødje et al. (eds.), *ECSCW 2015: Proceedings of the 14th European Conference on Computer Supported Cooperative Work, 19–23 September 2015, Oslo, Norway*, DOI 10.1007/978-3-319-20499-4_4

Introduction

Social media is becoming more and more prevalent on the web and also inside enterprises. Enterprise social media platforms, such as Jive,[1] Yammer[2] and IBM Connections,[3] enable employees to share and collaborate through blogs, wikis, communities, and other social media applications. Employees engage on these platforms by describing their projects and solutions, problems they have encountered, customers they have met, ideas they want to promote, and more (DiMicco et al. 2008).

While traditionally expertise used to be mined through explicit organizational skill sources such as CVs and project databases, as well as private sources, such as email and local file systems (Becerra-Fernandez 2000; Reichling and Wulf 2009), social media enables expertise identification by implicit means with little privacy infringement. Through their public contributions to social media, employees leave traces of their areas of interest and knowledge, which enables effective expertise mining. The dynamic and up-to-date nature of contributions facilitates the constant update of an employee's expertise, whereas organizational databases are often not updated on a regular basis and thus do not provide accurate information.

Evidence has been shown to be highly important in search and recommendation systems for explaining the reasoning behind retrieved search results or recommended items. For example, search engines highlight matching terms in their returned results and recommender systems add explanations such as "We recommend you this movie because you watched another movie with the same actors". We believe that evidence may play a key role in expertise location systems too, yet the topic has hardly received any attention in the literature thus far. Evidence provides transparency for why a recommendation has been made and therefore increases the confidence of a user in the system (Tintarev and Masthoff 2007; Sinha and Swearingen 2002). In particular, for expertise location systems (Macdonald et al. 2008; Balog et al. 2006), evidence enables users to understand why a person is suggested as an expert, which can increase their likelihood to approach the recommended individual.

The rich and public nature of social media data allows for providing high quality evidence for expertise, which is otherwise often hidden and inaccessible. As social media evolves, more content types emerge, such as blogs, microblogs, wikis, communities, shared files, and bookmarks. In addition, in social media users may be associated with content not just as its authors, but also as commenters, taggers, 'likers', or members. A previous study has shown that these other types of user-content relationships are highly useful for expertise mining and inference (Guy et al. 2013). It was speculated that with social media, experts often engage not necessarily as the authors, but rather as feedback providers or

---

[1]https://www.jivesoftware.com/.

[2]https://www.yammer.com/.

[3]http://www-03.ibm.com/software/products/en/conn.

annotators through commenting, tagging, and liking. Due to the diversity of content types and possible user associations with content, a large variety of expertise evidence types may be exposed through social media contributions. For example, a person can be identified as an expert in a topic because s/he authored blog posts on the topic, commented on wiki pages, uploaded files, answered related questions, participated in related communities, and more.

In this paper, we examine which types of social media-based evidence users perceive as strongest indicators of expertise. As already mentioned, previous research has mined these different contribution types to identify experts (Guy et al. 2013). Different social media activities were weighted according to how much they reflect expertise in a topic. However, activities that provide strong evidence from an analytics perspective are not necessarily the best indicators from a user's perspective. Due to the variety and richness of data sources, there are many potential expertise indicators and a need arises to decide which of them to display in the application's user interface. This is especially true for mobile devices where real estate for display is small. Using this research, user interface designers can more sophistically decide which evidence types to highlight and on which to put less focus.

We examined the perception of evidence through two unique user surveys within a large global enterprise. In each of the surveys, participants rated anonymous experts presented to them along with evidence items. In the first survey, we sought to understand how enterprise social media users perceive potential evidence types with synthetically composed evidence, while in the second survey we examined the users' perception through the presentation of real evidence related to topics extracted from a deployed expertise location system within the studied organization. Participants were asked to rate the experts based on the presented evidence. We then compared results from both surveys.

The rest of this paper is organized as follows. The next section discusses related work. Following, we describe our experimental setup and the two surveys we conducted. We then present our results, which indicate that there is a substantial difference with regards to social media evidence presentation as compared to expertise mining. The paper concludes by summarizing these differences and their implications for expertise location system builders.

Related Work

Expertise location, in particular within organizations, has been widely studied (Yiman-Seid et al. 2003; Reichling and Wulf 2009). With the growth of social media usage within and outside the firewall, social media-based expertise location emerged. Examples outside the firewall exist for social applications, such as question and answering (Adamic et al. 2008), forums (Kardan et al. 2010), microblogs (Xu 2014), and collaborative tagging (Noll et al. 2009). Chi (2012) provides a good overview of the challenges of such applications. Li et al. (2013)

describe a system that returns a ranked list of experts for a given query built over the LinkedIn social graph. Within the enterprise, social media applications such as corporate blogs (Kolari et al. 2008), communities (Zhang et al. 2007), and people tagging (Farrell et al. 2007) were explored. A combined approach was conducted by Serdyukov and Hiemstra (2008) who concluded that expertise derived from sources outside the organization such as Yahoo and Google and their combinations with organizational data are often of higher quality than organizational data only. Varshney et al. (2014) used social media to infer skills within the enterprise by mining enterprise and social data. They developed a classification methodology to predict expertise based on features derived from the digital footprints of employees with the label set coming from the organization's expertise taxonomy. Guy et al. (2013) conducted a comprehensive study of expertise location based on social media data through a user survey in which participants provided self-evaluations for their areas of expertise and interest. The analysis focused on which data sources provided better basis for expertise inference, to most effectively predict the self-evaluation ground truth.

The importance of the display of evidence (often referred to as explanations) has been widely highlighted in the broad domain of recommender systems. Tintarev and Masthoff (2007) defined seven aims of evidence, transparency, scrutability, trust, effectiveness, persuasiveness, efficiency and satisfaction. They compared various academic and commercial systems according to these criteria. Sinha and Swearingen (2002) found that transparency in the form of explanations led users to have more confidence in the recommendations, as they could understand the justification for the system's choices. Herlocker et al. (2000) explained the challenge of generating explanations for collaborative filtering systems. They suggested that the black-box image of recommender systems might be one of the reasons for why they have gained much less acceptance in high-risk domains, such as holiday packages or investment portfolios than in low-risk domains, such as music or movies. Guy et al. (2009) showed the positive effect of evidence on employees' trust in a people recommendation system and their willingness to invite those people into their enterprise social network. Vig et al. (2009) used tag-based explanations to recommend movies. They concluded that tag relevance and tag preference play a key role for justification, effectiveness, and compatibility with the user's mood of recommendations.

Expertise location has been sometimes associated with the recommender system domain, referred to as "expert recommendation" (McDonald and Ackerman 2000; Reichling and Wulf 2009). Yet, since it is usually triggered by an explicit user query, expertise location more naturally belongs to the search domain. Pu and Chen (2006) investigated different explanation interfaces for recommender systems and compared their contribution to trust formation. They found that what they call organization-based explanations were most effective and increased the user's intention to return to their application as it assisted them in the comparison of products. Organization-based explanations adhere to five principles they defined such as categorization and diversity.

To the best of our knowledge, almost no publication has focused on the presentation of evidence for expertise location. Macdonald et al. (2008) built an expert search system that suggested people with relevant expertise to a topic of interest. Similarly to the approach taken in our paper, they used a document-based method for computing an expertise score. They proposed five techniques to predict the quality of documents (which they call evidence) within a candidate's profile in the expert search task. Those techniques were tested over three TREC topic sets. Balog et al. (2006) showed that the document-based approach outperformed a candidate-based approach for expert identification. Both papers did not address the issue of the presentation of expertise evidence to the user, but rather referred to the identified documents as evidence during score computation.

Experimental Setup

Social Media Applications

Our experiments were based on an enterprise social software application suite, which has been commonly used in the studied organization (a large global enterprise) for over eight years. The suite includes eight types of social media applications:

- A blogging system that allows users to write blog posts, comment on posts, and 'like' posts.
- A social bookmarking system that allows users to share bookmarks of both intranet and internet pages.
- A file sharing system that allows users to upload files and read files uploaded by other users.
- A forum system that allows users to start new topics and comment on their own or other topics.
- A microblogging system that allows users to write short messages (status updates) of up to 500 characters on their profile wall, comment on their own or other messages, and 'like' other messages.
- A wiki system that allows multiple users to co-author wiki pages.
- A tagging system that allows users to tag each other, or to tag content items, such as blog posts or wiki pages.
- A communities system that allows users to create (and own) new communities of interest, or become members of existing communities. A community can include content items such as blogs, bookmarks, files, forums, and wikis.

Each application has its own entity type(s), and users can have different associations to the entities. For example, for the blogging application, the corresponding entity type is a blog post, and a user can be associated with the blog post as an author, a commenter or a liker. We refer to a combination of an entity type and an association (e.g., blog post liker, wiki page author) as an "expertise indicator" or, in short, an "indicator".

Table 1 Social media applications, entity types, and associations

Application	Entity type	Associations	#People
Blogs	Post (386,851)	Author (386,851) Commenter (301,975) Liker (375,544)	55,377
Bookmarks	Bookmark (1,459,510)	Bookmarker (1,459,510)	34,138
Communities	Community (149,152)	Owner (149,152) Member (2,855,139)	402,434
Files	File (384,527)	Author (384,527) Reader (1,382,610)	54,851
Forums	Topic (548,832)	Author (548,832) Commenter (1,391,417)	142,853
Microblogs	Message (1,021,927)	Author (1,021,927) Commenter (280,812) Liker (145,109)	97,891
Tags	Content tag (357,553)	Tagger (3,226,711)	115,279
	Profile tag (96,628)	Tagged-with (1,248,972)	186,381
Wikis	Page (1,240,834)	Author (1,240,834)	112,619

Table 1 details the applications we experimented with, their related entity types, and the set of associations by which users can relate to the entities. The table also provides an overview of the usage level of the different applications in the studied organization: the numbers in parentheses indicate the amount of social entities and associations of each type. The rightmost column indicates, per application, the number of unique people who are "covered" by it, i.e., the number of employees who are associated with at least one entity. Overall, it can be seen that each application contains a large number of entities and associations, and covers at least 30,000 individuals.

Expertise Location System

The social applications mentioned in the previous section form the basis of the Expertise Locator (EL) system used in the studied organization. To the best of our knowledge, the EL system is the first to use social media-based expertise evidence, thus our study's results can potentially be of significant value for it and for similar systems to come. The EL system enables web and mobile users to search for experts on a certain topic, using a document-centric approach where each social entity, such as a blog entry, wiki page, or tag, is stored as a document in an index. The experts are retrieved based on their social activity in the context of the provided topic. First, documents related to the queried topic are retrieved. Then, the people associated with these documents (entities) are scored based on weights assigned to combinations of document types and associations to the document, as in Guy et al. (2013). The association of a person with a social media entity in the result is returned as evidence. Figure 1 shows a top expert for the query "graph",

Lucille Suarez

DE & CTO, Open Technology
Software Group, Strategy | AUSTIN, TX United States | Local time: 03:35AM

I check e-mail very regularly. I am not at the office number very often. I am usually easy to reach on my cell phone.

1st degree

▼ Why Lucille?

Profile   Microblogs(11)   Forum Topics(27)   Files(3)   Wiki Pages(3)   Community(1)   Bookmarks(49)

Tags

graph (5) graph-analytics (1) graph-databases (2) property+graph (1)

Fig. 1 A "graph" expert returned by the expertise locator web application

as displayed in the EL web application. The EL evidence presentation is divided into different tabs according to the originating social media application. The heading of each tab includes the number of evidence items of the corresponding evidence type; only tabs of evidence types with nonzero items are presented. The tab selected by default is the "Profile" tab. This design choice might not be optimal, since (1) it is not clear that profiles are indeed the strongest evidence and (2) by default the user sees a single type of evidence rather than a mixture. Better understanding the value of the various evidence types can help designers improve expertise presentation for the end user.

Figure 2a shows the same top expert for the query "graph", as well as the evidence, as displayed by the mobile application of the EL system. Since the screen is smaller, the approach taken was showing a summary of the evidence first and upon the user tapping on a specific summary line, showing the corresponding details. Figure 2b illustrates the list of bookmarks, triggered when the user taps "49 related bookmarks" on the screen shown in Fig. 2a. The only exception to this is the display of tags, which are presented inline as in Fig. 2a and are not attached to any additional content. Users are not exposed to any direct evidence aside from tags, unless they explicitly choose to tap one of the summary lines. In addition, there is no indication of the strongest evidence item (e.g., a specific blog post or file) when a multitude of evidence exits, as in Fig. 2a. Overall, the smaller screen of mobile devices makes it even more important to understand social media-based expertise evidence. As we will detail in the following section, the design of our two surveys mimics evidence presentation in the EL applications: the first survey focuses on evidence summary of multiple types and the second survey focuses on specific evidence types, with real content.

User Surveys

In this work, we examine the different expertise indicators and how strongly each indicator supports one's expertise when presented as evidence. To this end, we

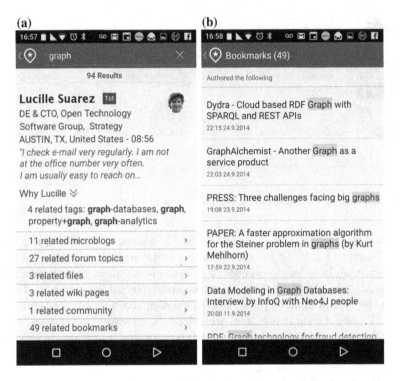

Fig. 2 a A "graph" expert as presented in the EL mobile application. **b** Bookmark evidence of the "graph" expert in the mobile application

conducted two separate user surveys, with different sets of participants, where each survey focused on evidence in a different manner. In the first survey, the most active users of the organization's social software application suite were asked to rate experts, basing their decision solely on the type and the count of the expert-related activity. In the second survey, users of the EL system were asked to rate experts, basing their decision on the actual content of the expertise evidence, i.e., specific evidence examples collected from real data of the studied organization's EL system.

User Survey I

In the first user survey, we focused on the types and counts of expertise indicators, without referring to their actual content. The goal was to identify the most significant indicators, as perceived by the users, without referring to specific evidence items. Each participant was presented with a list of 10 anonymous experts, whose data was synthetically composed. For each expert it included a list of three related indicators, which explained why they were recommended as experts. Each

Fig. 3 An anonymous expert as presented in Survey I

indicator included the type and count of the entities related to the expert (e.g., "Authored 5 blog posts", "Read 2 files"). For indicator types, we experimented with all available entity types and associations as detailed in Table 1 (16 in total). For counts, we opted to experiment with two values—2 and 5. These values were selected by examining real data from the EL system: we calculated the number of evidence items per indicator in a large collection of results for different topics and found 2 to be the median and 5 to be the 75 percentile. We did not include other count values in the survey, as this would have resulted in investigating too many combinations of indicators and counts.

Figure 3 illustrates an anonymous expert as presented in the survey. The three evidence items are presented on the left. Based on the displayed indicators, the participant was asked to rate each expert's expertise level on a 5-point Likert scale, where 1 indicated "Not an expert" and 5 indicated "Definitely an expert". Participants were also asked to select which of the three indicators was the 'best' one, i.e., the one they found the most significant. Finally, participants had an option to add a comment about a specific expert and a general comment to express their thoughts and give feedback at the end of the survey.

One of the goals of the survey was to retrieve an average rating score for each indicator. Since each expert's evidence included 3 different indicators, there was a need to balance the effect of indicators on one another, e.g., avoid a case where 'blog liker' received higher average ratings because it often appeared together with 'wiki author'. To this end, we referred to an 'evidence configuration' as a combination of 3 different indicators (out of the 16), where each indicator's count value was either 2 or 5. An example for an evidence configuration could be: "authored 5 wiki pages, commented on 2 blog posts, read 2 files". The survey was designed such that each configuration was scored by exactly one participant, thus making sure each indicator appeared alongside all the possible combinations of indicators and enabling a "fair competition" among all indicators and their counts. The total number of configurations was $(16 \cdot 2) \cdot (15 \cdot 2) \cdot (14 \cdot 2)/(3!) = 4480$.

As each participant was asked to score 10 experts and exactly 4480 configurations had to be scored, we needed 448 participants for the survey. We invited the 3000 most active users of the social software suite to participate in the survey. Invitations were sent via email and 617 participants responded (20.5 %). We then selected the first 448 responses so that each evidence configuration was covered exactly once. The rest of the responses were discarded, as the number of total responses did not reach the next multiplication of 448.

Many of the participants who submitted the survey chose to add comments (either on a specific expert or general ones) in order to express their thoughts on an expert, an indicator, or the expertise location system in general.

User Survey II

The second user survey focused on the content of the indicators. The goal was to present the user with real and detailed evidence extracted from the EL system and compare the results with those of the first survey.

In this survey, participants were presented with a real topic of expertise, which they had previously queried for in the EL system (e.g. "Big Data", "Java", "Gamification"). We selected the 30 most popular topics, i.e., those issued as a query to the EL system by the largest number of users. An invitee list was then generated by selecting users who had issued a query on one or more of the 30 topics at least once, in order to increase the likelihood that a participant had knowledge about the topic and could assess the quality of the evidence items. Each participant was asked to rate the expertise level of 5 anonymous experts on a 5-point Likert scale. The evidence list for each expert was comprised of either 2 or 5 evidence items associated with the expert, all of the same type. Each item included a title (e.g., 'Project Breadcrumbs Overview') and a link to its page within the social software suite, allowing participants to access the actual blog post, wiki page, community, etc. Tag indicators (*tagger* and *tagged-with*) were an exception, as they have no associated content other than the tag itself. In order to avoid biased decisions, the experts were fully anonymized and their identity was removed both from the survey page and from the corresponding evidence pages to which the links pointed. Figure 4 illustrates two anonymous "banking" experts as presented in the second survey.

In order to have sufficient information to compute an average score for each of the 32 indicator-count combinations (16 indicator types, 2 possible count values),

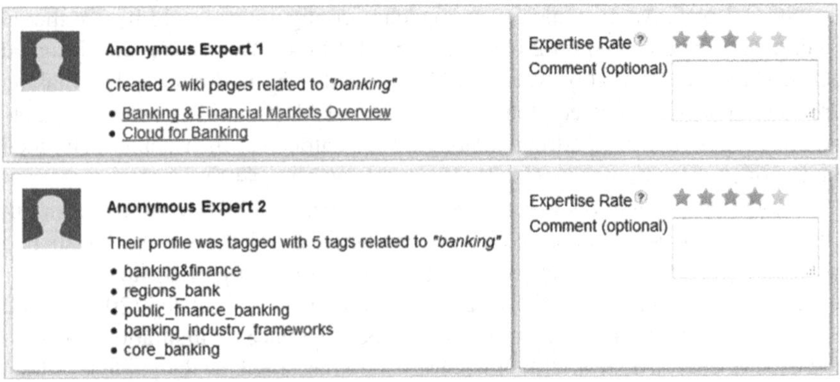

Fig. 4 Two anonymous experts as presented in Survey II

we used a round-robin method such that each indicator was scored by the same number of participants.

Overall, the survey was sent to 3000 users who had used the EL system to perform one of the 30 queries, out of which 579 users responded (19.3 %). Each of the 16 indicator types was rated by 180 participants, half with count 2 and half with count 5. Similarly to the first survey, many of the users added comments, either on a specific expert or general ones.

Experimental Results

User Survey I

In this section, we analyze the results of the first survey. We examine which indicators were found to be stronger than others, considering both the average scores and the proportion each indicator was voted as "best". Recall that each evidence configuration was rated exactly once, such that each indicator symmetrically appeared with all other indicators. We first analyze the ratings given to each of the 16 indicator types, and at the end of the section we inspect the ratings while also considering the count values.

The first analysis focuses on the average rating per indicator, as shown in Fig. 5a. The error bars indicate 95 % confidence intervals for the rating averages. We observe a division of the indicators into three groups: the first group, which received the highest scores (indicators ranked 1–6), consists of indicators that show significant contribution of content, such as authorship and community ownership. The second group (ranks 7–9, 11) consists of indicators that show light contribution of content, such as commenting and microblogging. In the third

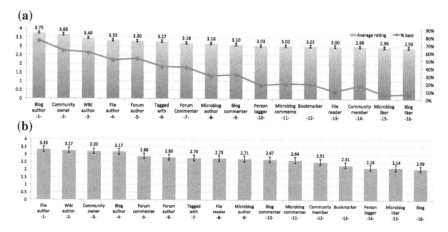

Fig. 5 **a** User survey I: average ratings (primary y axis) and 'best' proportions (secondary y axis). **b** User survey II: average ratings

group, which received the lowest scores (ranks 10, 12–16), we find indicators that show "minimal" activity, without any contribution of content, such as tagging, liking and reading. We now focus on each of these three groups.

The top scored group of indicators consists of 4 authorship indicators (blog, wiki, file, and forum), community owning, and profile tagging. In Guy et al. (2013), it was found that authorship is not a stronger indicator for expertise than commenting and liking, when it comes to social media. Here we see that in terms of evidence, authorship still prevails, with all authorship types (aside from microblogs) leading the list. Even in forums, where authorship is often about asking a question, it is still perceived higher than commenting, which in many cases contains an answer. The two top authorship indicators were blogs, ranked 1st with an average score of 3.75 and wikis, ranked 3rd with 3.46. These two social entities typically contain rich content, as one participant noted: "*Authoring multiple blogs is a sign of someone who has something worthwhile to say*". Community ownership (2nd with 3.55) is also perceived as a strong evidence for expertise, as owning a community related to some topic suggests a strong involvement in it (Ronen et al. 2014). Community ownership was also considered a type of "authorship" by some users, since the owners manage the community. One participant explained: "The *owner is the one who really manages the communities and edits all the relevant content on the communities*." The last indicator in this group (6th with 3.27) is *tagged-with*, which is a kind of an outlier, as a person whose profile was tagged with a topic did not contribute content, but was indicated as related to the topic by other users. One participant commented: "*The tags indicate others recognize and accentuate the expertise shared*." In Guy et al. (2013), people tagging was found to be the most precise data source. It is also the most direct indicator of expertise and reflects the "wisdom of the crowd" rather than the person's own activity. In spite of all that, *tagged-with* is ranked below all authorship forms, except for microblogs.

In the second group, we find indicators that represent light contribution of content. These indicators received medium scores and were ranked between the authorship indicators and the reading\tagging\liking indicators. Leading the list is *forum commenter* with an average score of 3.18. This is the strongest indicator of all commenting evidence, since a forum comment is often an answer to a question, as one participant noted: "*Forum topics are generally discussing issues where an expert is being sought. Adding comments could mean you are offering your expertise on the forum topic or question*." The next commenting indicator is for blogs, which also topped the authorship indicators.

The only authorship indicator included in the second group is *microblog author*. Microblogs had the best combination of precision and recall in Guy et al. (2013). This concise form of text expression was shown to be very effective for expertise mining in the enterprise. Here we see that despite its effectiveness for expertise inference, it is perceived as particularly weak evidence by users. It is the weakest authorship indicator and is lower than *tagged-with* and *forum commenter*. The reason may be that microblogs are limited to 500 characters and are typically used for sharing short messages, rather than contributing "heavy" authoritative content. The difference between authoring a microblog and authoring a blog was expressed in several comments made by participants, for example: *"Blogs are typically lengthy and inform on a particular area of expertise versus microblogs which tend to be a quick/short update"*.

In the third group, we find indicators that reflect more passive feedback, with no contribution of new content by the potential expert. These indicators received the lowest scores and were mentioned by many participants as weak or even meaningless. This list of indicators includes tagging, reading, or being a member of a community. At the bottom of the list are the two liking indicators—*blog liker* and *microblog liker*. Blogs and microblogs are similar in many characteristics, with the former having richer content. As we have seen this difference leads to a big gap in ranks between the two in terms of authorship and commenting evidence. When it comes to liking, however, there is no such difference and both are at the bottom of the list. One of the more surprising yet very consistent findings of the study by Guy et al. (2013) was that expertise inference from a user's liking activity is as effective as inference from their authorship or commenting activity. It was speculated that with social media, experts may engage in feedback providing as much, and sometimes more frequently, as they do by authoring content. Our survey reveals that expertise location users still do not "buy" liking and other weaker forms of feedback as strong expertise evidence. Our participants' comments imply that liking evidence shows a person's interest in the topic, rather than knowledge or expertise, e.g., *"[…] liking only indicates some level of interest."* Guy et al. (2013) compared inferring expertise and interest from social media data sources and found that in practice liking equally reflects expertise as it reflects interest in a topic.

The selection of 'best' evidence, also drawn in Fig. 5a, is generally consistent with the average rating and also supports the partitioning into the three above-mentioned groups: substantial content contribution, light content contribution, and no content contribution. The differences among the groups are even more clearly reflected through the proportion of 'best indicator' selection, i.e., the ratio between the number of times an indicator was selected as 'best' and the number of configurations it appeared in. The 'best' proportion of heavy-content indicators is the highest. *Blog author*, the top ranked indicator, was also the evidence that was chosen as best most often, exactly 75 % of the configurations it appeared in. Similarly to the average ranking, the light content contribution indicators are placed in the middle. Closing the list, once again, are the two liking indicators, voted as best in only about 5 % of their configuration occurrences. One difference between the average rating results and the 'best indicator' results is for *forum author*, which received a lower average score than *file author*, but was selected as 'best' more often. Another difference is for *community member*, which was lower than *file reader* on average rating, but higher in terms of 'best' selection. Despite these differences, the fact that the ranking of indicators based on 'best' selection is generally in agreement with the ranking of indicators based on their average rating, increases our confidence in these results.

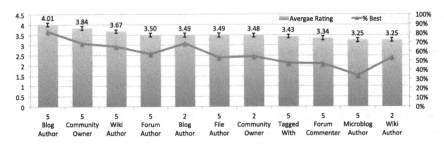

Fig. 6 User survey I: top average ratings and 'best' proportion for type-count combinations

We further inspected the comparison among all indicators, considering the number of evidence items (2 or 5) that were presented to the participants. Figure 6 shows the top of the list of indicators when distinguishing between the two counts (2 and 5). Generally, we see that the combination of quantity and quality of the evidence determines its ultimate ranking. It appears that the type (quality) plays a more central role, and stronger types are perceived as better evidence even if their quantity is lower. We sought to identify indicators at the top of the list with a count of 2, which are strong enough to outrank other indicators with a count of 5. It can be seen that blog authorship, the top evidence type, is also high when only including two items, lower only than 5 community ownerships, forum and wiki authorships. Another example is 2 owned communities, which are also lower than 5 authored files, but higher than all other 5's, including tagged-with and microblog authorship. As can also be seen in Fig. 6, the selection of 'best' indicator is even more favorable of strong types with a lower count.

As mentioned above, the participants of the first user survey were asked to rank the experts based on evidence type and counts only, without referring to the content itself. Many of them expressed a concern, finding it difficult to evaluate expertise based on this information only, as one participant commented: *"In all cases I would also review the content that [the expert] authored or commented on to try and get a better understanding of their knowledge on the subject ..."*. This lays the ground for our second survey.

User Survey II

In this section, we analyze the results of the second survey. We examine which indicators received better ratings than others and compare the results to those of the first survey. Note that the most significant difference between the two surveys is the content of each indicator. In survey II, participants were presented with 5 experts for the same topic (which they had searched for in the past), and a list of 2 or 5 evidence items per expert. The participants were able to click the title of each item and access its (anonymized) page, allowing them to view the community, read the blog, download the file, etc.

At high level, the results of survey II are similar to survey I: Authorship indicators are at the top along with community ownership. Liking is at the bottom, and commenting (as well as weak authorship indicators—forums and microblogs) are in the middle. There are, however, a few prominent differences between the results of the two surveys, which we discuss in the following paragraphs. One important thing to note is that the average ratings of the two surveys are not comparable—in the first survey participants rated experts according to combinations of evidence types, whereas in the second each expert had evidence of one type. For that reason, we see that survey I's average ratings are generally higher than survey II's, as the participants perceived evidence with combinations of 3 indicators as more convincing than evidence that included single indicators. Therefore, when analyzing the results of both surveys, we compare the rank of each indicator, rather than the rating it received.

As can be seen in Fig. 5b, at the top of survey II's ratings list we find the same four indicators as in survey I. Three strong authorship indicators (blog, wiki, file), along with community ownership, are at the top, by a relatively large margin. The order of the four, however, is different between the surveys: *blog author*, the top indicator of survey I, moved down to number 4, whereas wiki and file authorship moved from ranks 3 and 4 to the top 2 spots. Authoring a blog on some topic sounds like a solid indication of a person's expertise. On the other hand, many blogs describing a product or a technology are written for publicity, rather than for providing technical details. They also tend to reflect a personal viewpoint of the author towards a topic, with many socializing aspects, rather than objective authoritative content. This may be the reason why this indicator was ranked lower when the users actually viewed the content of the blog. On the same note, wiki pages often contain technical information (e.g. APIs, step-by-step guidelines, etc.), and so do shared files. Wikis and files typically contain collaboration data used for working together and sharing content, which can explain the two indicators being ranked higher when including the content. One participant explained: *"files generally indicate more 'hands on' expertise."*

Forum commenter, which was ranked 7th in the first survey, moved up to 4th in the second survey, outranking *forum author* and *tagged-with*. Forum is the only type of social application where the commenting association was ranked higher than the authorship association. As mentioned before, commenting on a forum topic often provides an answer to a question posted by the author. Survey II participants could see the content of the entire forum thread and realize that the author is the one seeking for an expert, while the commenter is the knowledgeable individual.

As in survey I, authoring and commenting on microblogs were substantially weaker than other content types, indicating that the intuition of participants in survey I, who perceived microblogs as a way to share short messages rather than contribute content, was reinforced when they saw the actual evidence on survey II. Microblogs, shown to be very effective for expertise mining by Guy et al. (2013), were ranked even lower in survey II than in survey I.

The indicator with the largest rank difference between the two surveys is *file reader*, which moved up 5 spots from 13th in survey I to 8th in survey II. When the survey participants viewed the content of the files, the technical and detailed nature of the files might have compensated for the fact that the expert was not the author, but merely a reader. One participant, who gave a rating of 4 to a "security" expert who read 2 related files, commented: *"Great shared information on the topics. May not be his own, but the topics strike at the heart of security"*. Other participants who rated file reading experts seem to have considered the fact that the expert made the effort to read the file, as one participant noted: *"Maybe not a top expert, but has taken the time to read on the topic"*. Although ranked below average in the context of expertise mining in Guy et al. (2013), file related indicators were rated high by survey II participants, who perceived writing and reading files as a strong indication of expertise.

Another indicator that moved up is *community member*, ranked 14th in survey I and 12th in survey II. After viewing the communities' content, many participants appreciated the fact that the person is part of the community, in spite the fact that they did not own it. A participant who gave a rating of 5 to a "retail" expert, who is a member of 5 communities, commented: *"This member has great access to 'retail' information that can be very beneficial for the end user!"*.

At the bottom of the list are the two 'liking' indicators, which received the lowest ratings on both surveys. Liking a content item is perceived as a very poor evidence of a person's expertise, regardless of the quality of the liked content. Several participants commented on this issue, e.g., *"Liking is not promoting nor is it necessarily social, it may be just someone 'checking a box' cause everyone else is doing it"* or *"Shows interest but not expertise"*.

Differences in the results of the two surveys also emerge when examining how the count values affected the average scores. Figure 7 shows the top indicators when distinguishing between the two counts (2 and 5). Counts seem to play a stronger role in the second survey than in the first. The first 8 indicators (out of $16 \times 2 = 32$) in survey II are of count 5, compared to only the first 4 in survey I. A suggested explanation for this result is the fact that an expertise evidence item in survey I was comprised of three indicators, thus the count of each indicator was less significant. On the other hand, an evidence item in survey II included a single indicator, giving more weight to its count.

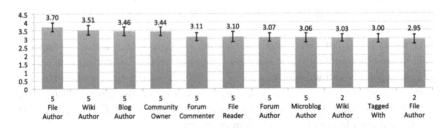

Fig. 7 User survey II: top average ratings for type-count combinations

The results of the two surveys portrait a coherent picture, where heavy content contribution is perceived as a strong indicator of expertise, followed by light and minimal contribution of content. These findings are also consistent with regards to both metrics applied in the first survey (average rating and 'best' selection). The internal order within the three groups, however, was different between the surveys, as a close examination of the content provided participants with additional information and different insights.

Discussion and Future Work

Our results indicate a substantial difference between social media data used for evidence presentation as compared to expertise mining: for evidence, authorship of "heavy" content is most productive, while more concise indicators, which involve less content, are perceived as weaker evidence. In this section, we summarize the differences, discuss the implications and limitations of our study, and suggest future directions.

In a previous study it was shown, based on self-evaluation ground truth, that when it comes to social media, authorship is not a stronger indicator than content feedback signals, such as commenting, tagging, or liking (Guy et al. 2013). This result, while may seem counter-intuitive, was shown consistent across a variety of social media data sources and for various types of feedback signals. Our own study, by contrast, shows that when it comes to social media-based evidence, users still possess the basic intuition that authorship and management of heavy content are most meaningful. Other forms of feedback are perceived as weaker evidence and the less content they involve, the less convincing they are. Commenting is perceived stronger than tagging, which is typically stronger than reading, liking, or being a member. 'Liking' of content, which was found valuable for expertise mining, was particularly perceived as a weak expertise indicator, even when the number of evidence items was higher.

In the expertise mining study by Guy et al. (2013), profile tagging was identified as the most precise data source for expertise. This was explained by the fact that profile tags are the most direct means for indicating a person's expertise and reflect the perception of a person by others, rather than their own associated content. The profile tagging data source had lower recall, however, since it was not as commonly used as some of the other data sources. The data source with the best combination of precision and recall was microblogs. It was speculated that a person's expertise areas are well propagated through this fast-pace, real-time, concise form of expression. Our experiments for evidence reveal a very different picture: profile tags were perceived weaker evidence than almost all authorship types, such as blogs, wikis, files, and even forums, where authorship often expresses a question rather than an answer. The one authorship type that did not outrank profile tags was microblogs, which had the lowest scores among all authorship indicators. It appears that while profile tags and microblogs serve as good data sources for expert mining and ranking, they are less convincing as evidence items.

These results have various practical implications. Expertise locator designers often need to carefully consider how much and which evidence to present alongside an expert that was found matching the user's query. As demonstrated in our studied organization's EL system, since the user is presented with a list of experts and for each there is a need to show evidence, the real estate for evidence presentation might not be large and require smart selections. This may even be a bigger challenge on mobile devices, which have less user interface space. For example, even if the user interface shows multiple tabs with different evidence types, as in the EL system's web application, the tab order, and particularly the default tab to be presented, play a key role in evidence presentation. Our results indicate that the default choice made in the studied organization to show profile tags may not be ideal; showing authorship of rich-content documents, such as blogs, wikis, or files, may be more desirable.

From a backend/analytics perspective, our results indicate that expertise evidence may require its own calculation. While this may entail further computational cost, our findings suggest that using the scores from the expert ranking algorithms to calculate the top evidence to be presented might not be the best choice: while expertise inference can often be achieved by aggregating many signals such as liked blog posts and "tweets", for evidence it is important to include the most authoritative pieces, if such exist.

We experimented with two different user surveys: the first included synthesized evidence types and counts, without real data, allowing us to artificially compose evidence lists and compare users' perception of them; the second survey delved into presentation of specific evidence item types with actual titles and content pages, originating from a real social media-based expertise location system. The two surveys enabled us to examine users' perception more thoroughly and provided a broader picture. We believe that the results' consistency across the two survey grants more validity to our findings.

Our experiments were conducted in one organization and are naturally influenced by this organization's characteristics and particular way of enterprise social media use. Social media in our organization is used mainly for collaborative work and information sharing, which might explain why employees view authorship of new content as critical. It could be that other organizations, which use such systems mainly for socializing and networking, would see more value in the tagging or liking operations. We hope to see more research on the topic in other environments, which would further validate and extend the results reported here. We note, however, that our study included the most common types of social media applications, each with a large user base of tens of thousands of employees. In addition, both of our surveys were based on responses from hundreds of employees. We therefore believe that our fundamental results regarding authorship, commenting, and liking, and massive versus concise content, are likely to be valid in other organizations as well.

Our evaluation in this paper was based on user surveys. As mentioned, we conducted two different surveys to examine evidence perception from different aspects and validate our results. Yet, both surveys presented anonymous experts and asked participants to assess the level of confidence they have in their expertise based on the presented evidence. We did not use a field study of a live system such as the studied organization's EL system, since it is in early stages of deployment, and its usage level is not broad enough to allow appropriate evaluation. As social media-based expertise locators continue to evolve, future research should apply techniques such as A/B testing, to examine the effect of evidence presentation on real users as they search for experts.

References

Adamic, L. A., Zhang J., Bakshy, E., & Ackerman, M. S. (2008). Knowledge sharing and yahoo answers: Everyone knows something. In *Proceedings of the WWW'08* (pp. 665–674).

Balog, K., Azzopardi, L., & De Rijke, M. (2006). Formal models for expert finding in enterprise corpora. In *Proceedings of the SIGIR'06* (pp. 43–50).

Becerra-Fernandez, I. (2000). Facilitating the online search of experts at NASA using expert seeker people-finder. In *Proceedings of the PAKM'00*.

Chi, E. H. (2012). Who knows? Searching for expertise on the social web: Technical perspective. *Communications of the ACM, 55*(4), 110–110.

DiMicco, J., Millen, D. R., Geyer, W., Dugan, C., Brownholtz, B., & Muller, M. (2008). Motivations for social networking at work. In *Proceedings of the CSCW'08* (pp. 711–720).

Farrell, S., Lau, T., Nusser, S., Wilcox, E., & Muller, M. (2007). Socially augmenting employee profiles with people-tagging. In *Proceedings of the UIST'07* (pp. 91–100).

Guy, I., Avraham, U., Carmel, D., Ur, S., Jacovi, M., & Ronen, I. (2013). Mining expertise and interests from social media. In *Proceedings of the WWW'13* (pp. 515–526).

Guy, I., Ronen, I., & Wilcox, E. (2009). Do you know? Recommending people to invite into your social network. In *Proceedings of the IUI'09* (pp. 77–86).

Herlocker, J. L., Konstan, J. A., & Riedl, J. (2000). Explaining collaborative filtering recommendations. In *Proceedings of the CSCW'00* (pp. 241–250).

Kardan, A., Garakani, M., & Bahrani, B. (2010). A method to automatically construct a user knowledge model in a forum environment. In *Proceedings of the SIGIR'10* (pp. 717–718).

Kolari, P., Finin, T., Lyons, K., & Yesha, Y. (2008). Expert search using internal corporate blogs. In *Workshop on Future Challenges in Expertise Retrieval, SIGIR'08* (pp. 2–5).

Li, C. T., & Shan, M. K. (2013). X2-search: Contextual expert search in social networks'. In *Conference on Technologies and Applications of Artificial Intelligence (TAAI)* (pp. 176–181).

Macdonald, C., Hannah, D., & Ounis, I. (2008). High quality expertise evidence for expert search. In *Advances in Information Retrieval* (pp. 283–295).

McDonald, D. W., & Ackerman, M. S. (2000). Expertise recommender: A flexible recommendation system and architecture. In *Proceedings of the CSCW'00* (pp. 231–240).

Noll, M. G., Yeung, A. C., Gibbins, N., Meinel, C., & Shadbolt, N. (2009). Telling experts from spammers: Expertise ranking in folksonomies. In *Proceedings of the SIGIR'09* (pp. 612–619).

Pu, P., & Chen, L. (2006, January). Trust building with explanation interfaces. In *Proceedings of the 11th International Conference on Intelligent User Interfaces* (pp. 93–100).

Reichling, T., & Wulf, V. (2009). Expert recommender systems in practice: Evaluating semi-automatic profile generation. In *Proceedings of the CHI'09* (pp. 59–68).

Ronen, I., Guy, I., Kravi, E., & Barnea, M. (2014). Recommending social media content to community owners. In *Proceedings of the SIGIR'14* (pp. 243–252).

Serdyukov, P., & Hiemstra, D. (2008). Being omnipresent to be almighty: The importance of global web evidence for organizational expert finding. In *Workshop on Future Challenges in Expertise Retrieval, SIGIR'08* (pp. 17–24).

Sinha, R., & Swearingen, K. (2002). The role of transparency in recommender systems. In *CHI'02 extended abstracts on human factors in computing systems* (pp. 830–831).

Tintarev, N., & Masthoff, J. (2007). A survey of explanations in recommender systems. In *23rd International Conference on Data Engineering Workshop* (pp. 801–810).

Varshney, K. R., Chenthamarakshan, V., Fancher, S. W., Wang, J., Fang, D., & Mojsilovic, A. (2014). Predicting employee expertise for talent management in the enterprise. In *Proceedings of the KDD'14* (pp. 1729–1738).

Vig, J., Sen, S., & Riedl, J. (2009). Tagsplanations: Explaining recommendations using tags. In *Proceedings of the 14th International Conference on Intelligent User Interfaces* (pp. 47–56).

Xu, Z. (2014). Expertise retrieval in enterprise microblogs with enhanced models and brokers (Doctoral dissertation, The Ohio State University).

Yiman-Seid, D., & Kobsa, A. (2003). Expert-finding systems for organizations: Problem and domain analysis and the DEMOIR approach. *JOCEC, 13*(1), 1–24.

Zhang, J., Ackerman, M. S., & Adamic, L. (2007). Expertise networks in online communities: Structure and algorithms. In *Proceedings of the WWW'07* (pp. 221–230).

3D Printing with Marginalized Children—An Exploration in a Palestinian Refugee Camp

Oliver Stickel, Dominik Hornung, Konstantin Aal,
Markus Rohde and Volker Wulf

Abstract We work with a multi-national network of computer clubs for families and children called *come_IN*. In two such clubs (located in Palestinian refugee camps in the West Bank), we worked with children on playful approaches concerning 3D modeling and 3D printing within a five-week, qualitative field study. Based on this study, we report on the achievements as well as on the difficulties of digital fabrication and of "Making" in developmental and educational contexts. The benefits are related to an overarching theme of *self-expression* where the main focus was on dimensions as *playfulness, approachable complexity, individualization, immediacy and physicality* and *collaboration* as well as *motivation*. The problematic aspects were mostly related to socio-technical limitations concerning the themes of *orientation and camera control*, the *lack of coordination and collaboration features, usability and UX issues* as well as *the construction and limitations of current 3D printers*. Based on those findings, we have derived implications for the design and the appropriation of future systems for digital fabrication with children, especially in developmental/educational settings, such as improvements of their collaboration support or better feedback mechanisms regarding the system status towards the end user.

O. Stickel (✉) · D. Hornung · K. Aal · M. Rohde · V. Wulf
University of Siegen, Siegen, Germany
e-mail: oliver.stickel@uni-siegen.de

D. Hornung
e-mail: dominik.hornung@uni-siegen.de

K. Aal
e-mail: konstantin.aal@uni-siegen.de

M. Rohde
e-mail: markus.rohde@uni-siegen.de

V. Wulf
e-mail: volker.wulf@uni-siegen.de

O. Stickel · M. Rohde
International Institute for Socio-informatics, Bonn, Germany

© Springer International Publishing Switzerland 2015
N. Boulus-Rødje et al. (eds.), *ECSCW 2015: Proceedings of the 14th European Conference on Computer Supported Cooperative Work, 19–23 September 2015, Oslo, Norway*, DOI 10.1007/978-3-319-20499-4_5

83

Introduction

The access to digital fabrication technologies like 3D printers has become a more and more widespread in recent years. It is no longer limited to professional organizations but also to smaller businesses and especially to end users and hobbyist *Maker* communities. Bottom-up communities and associated Makerspaces or Fabrication Laboratories (Fab Labs) are flourishing world-wide. These socio-technical phenomena represent an evolving field whose values, challenges, practices and socio-cultural significance are emerging rapidly and in a huge variety of domains, and make them to a fascinating field of research. Digital fabrication and the socio-technical movements like the Maker culture increasingly blur the lines between professional and voluntary work. CSCW is called to investigate those trends and help to shape future developments—which already start to happen all over the world. An area where Making might show distinct potential is in ICT4D-related settings. Less privileged and education-focused settings might benefit from its potentials regarding empowerment and socio-economical change. This is why we decided to empirically investigate into such case: We focus on marginalized Palestinian refugees in the West Bank within the framework of our global network of constructionist computer clubs for children called come_IN (Aal et al. 2014). Come_IN is a long-term venture encompassing many projects ranging from playful programming up to film projects—a sensible setting for a deeper investigation into Making. Two of our researchers spent five weeks in two come_IN clubs in the West Bank, brought a 3D printer and worked with several groups of children regarding playful and also collaborative approaches to 3D modeling and 3D printing. The study was exploratory, qualitative and led by the field. This approach is grounded in the belief that the socio-technical CSCW and ICT4D issues we are interested in are highly complex and inextricably embedded in a local context and interrelated to complex communal, societal and other structures, values and practices. This position necessitates a deeper, situated and qualitative approach (cf. Adams et al. 2008).

As a central focus of our study, we found that 3D printing seems to harbor quite a lot of potential for developmental, educational contexts (especially regarding to individual self-expression), yet still faces many socio-technical problems that CSCW and HCI are called to solve. Thus, we will first introduce the related work before elaborating on the research setting. Subsequently, we will report on our results, structured along the overarching themes of benefits and problems. Finally, we will discuss our results with a focus on implications for design.

Related Work

Making, Do-It-Yourself (DIY) and hacking, backed by digital fabrication technologies have seen a significant upwind in recent years. This is facilitated through advancements in technological capabilities for sharing and collaboration (Tanenbaum et al. 2013) and, of course, through cheaper and more approachable digital fabrication machinery.[1] These developments were also responsible for the formation of an increasing number of related communities, which build physical spaces to pursue Making. The number of Fabrication Laboratories (Fab Labs), Hacker- or Makerspaces (Gershenfeld 2005) is steadily growing.[2] This *Maker movement* is a world-wide phenomenon and finds applications for its DIY-spirit in a huge variety of projects which range from the manufacturing of personal electronic devices (Mellis and Buechley 2012) through the deployment of digital fabrication technologies in educational settings with children (Blikstein 2013) up to Fab Labs as venues for bottom-up efforts in ICT for Development or ICT4D (Krassenstein 2014; Mikhak et al. 2002). There have been investigations into bringing together DIY electronics with other crafts (e.g. Buechley and Perner-Wilson 2012; Weibert et al. 2014) or even into DIY biology (Kuznetsov et al. 2012). It has been noted that communities of Makers often have certain entrance hurdles for newcomers, be it through a preconception as "nerdy", domain specific knowledge and vocabulary or the complexity of the machines (cf. Ludwig et al. 2014a). Understanding and treating Fab Labs and Makerspaces as boundary (negotiating) objects (Star and Griesemer 1989; Lee 2007) has been indicated as potentially helpful for such issues (Ludwig et al. 2014b). In a more macro sense, Kuznetsov and Paulos (2010) look at the "Rise of the Expert Amateur" and argue for more engagement between HCI practitioners and DIY expert amateurs while Lindtner et al. (2014) make a strong case for the relevance of Maker practices and -sites for innovation and pose that HCI has a key position in Making. Furthermore, the Maker movement often has aspects of a counterculture to mass-production and consumption (Tanenbaum et al. 2013; Moilanen and Vadén 2013) in that it utilizes and develops technologies but also places great value in doing so in open, democratic community spaces. Values such as sharing, learning and teaching, playful and collaborative exploration, mutual support and socio-economic change are emphasized (Hatch 2013). Digital fabrication is even hailed as the next stage in the digital revolution (Gershenfeld 2012), opening up production of physical goods in a similar fashion as the PC did for the digital domain, potentially disrupting existing socio-economic patterns (Troxler 2013).

The central learning theory the come_IN clubs (which frame our research) are based on is *Constructionism* (Harel and Papert 1991). It focuses on experiential learning and holds that learning does not happen through instructions but rather through active learning facilitated via the construction of individually meaningful artifacts through ICT. There are long-running and successful related projects such as Scratch (Resnick et al. 2009) centering on constructionist approaches to programming. This obviously fits very well with digital fabrication and Making (cf. Gershenfeld 2005) with many successful educational Maker projects based on constructionist approaches, cf. Blikstein (2013) for an extended overview.

---

[1]The Printrbot Simple, a compact 3D printer we used for this study costs 349 USD as a kit, just to give an example. The printer works with Fused Filament Modeling—basically similar to the working principle of a hot glue gun, however, computer controlled and extruding harder plastic.

[2]See http://fablabs.io for a global overview.

The concept of appropriation (Pipek 2005) is also relevant for our project and related to learning: It is the discovery and sense-making of a specific artifact such as an ICT-system *while using it*. It is related to such work of Dourish (2003) which is about how users fit ICT in their practices by adoption and adaption. Appropriation entails end user customization of ICT but is more encompassing. It can also relate to changes in practice and possibilities of changing the system in ways not anticipated or intended by its designer. Again, community aspects are relevant since appropriation is often associated with social networks of users, sharing and exchange (cf. Pipek and Kahler 2006; Wulf et al. 2015). The relevance of scaffolding appropriation for 3D printing has been emphasized in Ludwig et al. (2014a).

As already indicated, Making might offer significant potential for developmental aid, empowerment and help in marginalized settings (Mikhak et al. 2002). Projects such as DIY prosthesis, which are very cheap and which can be manufactured by amateurs in the field (Krassenstein 2014) or 3D printable tools to support personal hygiene in disease-ridden areas (Gardner 2014) are already being deployed. There has been increasing interest in development issues in HCI in recent years (Ho et al. 2009) and there are arguments for this interest to be expanded to Making in order to develop better, affordable, human centered tools and machines (von Rekowski et al. 2014; Willis and Gross 2011). Furthermore, ICT4D aspects are connected to teaching and learning in that bottom-up constructionist education. Empowerment via Making and digital fabrication can help to bridge the digital divide that is prevalent in developing countries (Kafai et al. 2009; Aal et al. 2014).

Research Gap: As the related literature shows, Making and digital fabrication seem to have relevance for a broad variety of areas. However, those areas are essentially linked through a form of work—the *Making* itself—as well as new forms of collaboration, sharing and learning which potentially result in socio-economic change on a grassroots level. One of the prevalent areas where Making already seems to show such impact is ICT4D—however, there is a lack of empiric, situated fieldwork around the potentials of Making in such settings, especially when looking at changes emerging from a *bottom-up* fashion. At the same time, there are indications that current ICT for Making is often less than optimal from an usability perspective. Understanding the two come_IN clubs in Palestine as an educational, bottom-up initiative in a developmental setting, we have access to an apt research field to help fill this research gap.

Research Setting

During the 1948 Arab-Israeli war and the 1967 war, many Palestinians were expelled or fled from their homes in what is now a part of Israel. This led to the establishment of refugee camps on the Palestinian territories and surrounding countries. Originally intended to be short-term, those camps still exist today and face unsustainably growing population, makeshift infrastructure and insecure socio-economic structures. Some camps have 40 % unemployment rates and a population of up to 60 % under the age of 17, packing more than 10,000 people into an area of less than one square kilometer.[3] The camps have a highly sensitive role in Palestinian society in that they symbolize the perceived *"right to return"* to the pre-1948 land. So, their existence is a political reminder of the populations' lost homes and a complete social integration within the mainstream population is politically problematic. Yet, at the same time, camp inhabitants are often treated as second class citizens and there is a notable gap in social standing between mainstream Palestinians and inhabitants of the camps (cf. Aal et al., 2014; Wulf et al., 2013). Education in the camps is basic and provided by the UN relief organization (UNRWA) in gender-separated camp schools.

Over the last decade, our research group has built a network of "come_IN" computer clubs for children and adults with different cultural and ethnic backgrounds where they can meet, work, play, learn and collaborate as well as express themselves through projects based on ICT. Today, the come_IN network consists of multiple clubs in Germany, one in the US as well as two in Palestine, both located in refugee camps. come_IN is based on the computer clubhouse project in the United States (Kafai et al. 2009) but expands its focus on ICT4D through aiming at social integration (cf. Stevens et al. 2005; Schubert et al. 2011). Our clubs mainly target areas with a significant migrant population where integration is a problem. For example, in Germany, the clubs try to engage the German-Turkish community, while in the Palestinian clubs, issues are even more manifold, ranging from the regional conflicts and instabilities over gender inequalities up to the marginalized state of the refugees in their own society. Furthermore, come_IN is grassroots-oriented: Each club is established in a bottom-up fashion together with local actors. Over the years, a successful model has emerged, consisting of coupling the clubs with institutions like elementary schools in Germany or youth centers in Palestine that help to provide continuity, space and situatedness. Collaboration with a local Palestinian university has also proved to be very valuable and can provide (student) volunteers as acting tutors, bring in innovation in the form of new ICT or project ideas and facilitate meaningful collaboration between children, adults, parents and students/researchers (Aal et al. 2014).

We describe the come_IN structure as well as the complexity of the Palestinian clubs in Yerousis et al. (2015). However, it has to be said that the Israeli-Palestinian conflict is a matter of daily life in the camps. An example are the frequent raids of the Israeli Defense Forces which often involve violence and in some cases death. Getting access to ICT and the Internet at home is problematic and further hampered by the fact that many refugees do not have the skills to use such technologies. At this point, the come_IN approach offers opportunities to bridge this digital divide, especially regarding the gap between the in-camp and the out-camp society. The two come_IN clubs in the West Bank are located in the refugee camps Al-Am'ari and Jalazone which are both located in/near the city of Ramallah. In both camps, the clubs are housed in central community

---

[3]The numbers relate to the camp of Jalazone as estimated by the camp administration.

Fig. 1 Come_IN sessions in Palestine

buildings and offer about 12 computer workstations, internet access, a printer and basic office supplies. Weekly sessions are run by student volunteers from the local Birzeit University in cooperation with the camp administration (Aal et al. 2014). Participants gather at the come_IN clubs voluntarily once a week for joint sessions and individual projects which are usually related in a meaningful way to their situation, values or experiences (see Fig. 1). Up until mid-2014, the ICT used in the come_IN clubhouses focused mainly on entirely digital representations such as programming, for instance with Scratch (cf. Weibert and Schubert 2010). However, we are aiming to expand all our clubs towards the digital-physical intersection. Therefore, we started to explore the video game Minecraft tentatively as a playful, collaborative 3D modeling tool in one of our German come_IN clubs. Multi-medial self-expression and storytelling via ICT are also important aspects of all come_IN clubs (Weibert and Schubert 2010)—see also Sawhney (2009) for a study on the power of such approaches in ICT4D.

Research Methods

Given the nature of Making which, as already implied, is evolving and developing quite rapidly and our goal of exploring the potential of digital fabrication within the constructionist come_IN setting, we favored a Participatory Action Research (PAR) motivated approach (cf. McTaggart 1991) where we went into the field, implementing a change by means of introducing the 3D printer. Generally speaking, PAR is about researching community structures and effects utilizing the instruments of change and action. The researcher actively takes part in the studied community and the community itself also actively takes part in the research. We knew that we necessarily would implement change and action by introducing 3D printing. Given the importance of trust and personal contact in sensitive, marginalized refugee settings, it was also clear that we had to actively take part in the sessions as tutors, support staff, or whatever would become necessary. We also knew that our participants should have the power to decide about what to make, to work in groups or individually and other similar decisions that might be pre-determined

Fig. 2 CubeTeam (l), 3D modeling (m) and printing (r) in Palestine

by researchers in other settings. Given such a constellation, PAR offers an honest and practical framework.

In 2014, two researchers from our research group in Germany (the founding institution for the come_IN network) visited the two Palestinian clubs. Members of our research group visit the Palestinian clubs quite regularly when doing field studies. We had already done exploratory work with children and 3D printing in Germany. This led us to the idea that our Palestinian colleagues might be interested in this relatively new technology and its digital-physical alignment. They subsequently confirmed their interest, so we decided not just to send a 3D printer but also ourselves to support and study the appropriation of the new technology within the very special settings of the refugee camps. While we were in the field, we moderated the club sessions: First, we introduced 3D-modeling and printing live by printing a demo-object and demonstrating basic modeling interactions such as moving the viewport. As a 3D modeling tool, we used CubeTeam[4] (see Fig. 2, left). It is similar to the video game Minecraft: 3D models are assembled from small cubes in a "Lego"-like fashion. CubeTeam is also collaborative as multiple actors can work in the same world. Unlike Minecraft, CubeTeam offers a default camera control mode inspired by regular CAD-tools, i.e. by clicking and dragging the canvas instead of ego-perspective "WASD"-keyboard movement (which, however, can be enabled, too). The children were free to create their own projects in CubeTeam with us and the volunteers always available to help. Finished projects were then 3D printed by us in situ. We used a Printrbot Simple 3D printer which is compact, has a build volume of 15 cm³, prints with PLA (a cheap and easy to handle plastic) and is easy to fix due to its simple design and many off-the-shelf parts.

Our participants were between the ages of 8 and 14 and usually worked in groups of 2–4. In total, we worked with about 20 children for about 12 h during 6 sessions. The participation was somewhat fluctuating—there is, according to the local coordinator, a lack of a culture of attendance and punctuality in the camps which also affects other institutions, such as the schools (cf. Yerousis et al. 2015; Aal et al. 2014). We observed the sessions, took extensive field notes (about 60 pages) as well as photos and talked to the children and the volunteers throughout

[4]www.cubteteam.io.

the process. Our activities had to deal with the language barrier and we were mainly depending on volunteers for translation. These conversations were ad hoc and a bit chaotic most times as the course of the club sessions were often unstructured, the environment in the camp chaotic, the language barrier problematic and the fact that we had to fulfill many roles at the same time (researcher, tutor, operator of the 3D printer, IT-troubleshooter,) very difficult. Hence, our analysis mainly relates to our observations and field notes. All names were anonymized due to privacy and security concerns. Analysis was done using Thematic Analysis or TA (Braun and Clarke 2006). This was deliberately started quickly in the field to bring up questions and sharpen the research lens through daily exchange and discussion of the notes and memos between the field researchers, interspersed by occasional Skype calls with senior researchers at home to ensure inter-coder reliability. The analysis was then finalized at home together with researchers not involved in the field work. Furthermore, the 3D printing infrastructure was left in Palestine to remotely study the more long-term appropriation and projects. This paper draws on both our fieldwork as well as the remote observations conducted from Siegen.

Opportunities in 3D Printing

As a general theme, we observed that the playful, collaborative approach to the introduction of 3D printing was well received by the children and that they were able to create their first printable models quite quickly—sometimes in considerably less than one hour. This is especially remarkable since none of the children ever had anything to do with 3D modeling, let alone 3D printing. In the initial sessions, they quickly started to explore the interface of CubeTeam and figured out its workings on a basic level with on-request help by ourselves and the local volunteers. After some exploration, testing the functions, and some random cube placement in the world, the groups usually started a verbal negotiation process about what to build before actually doing so. For example, we observed a group of three children who, after some discussion, settled on modeling the initials of their names. They then sat in front of one computer with one child taking charge and executing the modeling while the others gave suggestions, pointed at interface or model elements and this way influencing the executing child. The three most frequent categories of projects the children chose were: Names or initials, buildings such as a tower with a Palestinian flag on top (inspired by the flag monument in Ramallah's city center) as well as creatures inspired by fantasy, their representation in other media or the real world (usually a favorite animal). The artifacts displayed a high level of the children's **self-expression**: All 3D models had personal meaning, expressed a story, a fantasy or a wish such as the mosque-inspired building in Fig. 3 (top middle) made by Rabi (10) as a *"new house for her family"*—motivated by the poor and cramped living conditions she grows up in.

We generally could observe projects getting more ambitious over time, especially regarding usage of all dimensions. At the beginning, the children treated

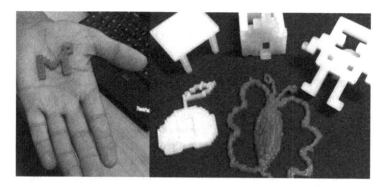

Fig. 3 Some sample 3D prints from the field

the building space rather like a 2D canvas, creating merely "brushing" models such as their name with no real complexity in the z-axis, after some time, they started to attempt building more complex structures. Some examples can be found in Fig. 3—the house-like structure (top middle) was built in a later session and includes complexity in all axes while the apple at the bottom left is, essentially, flat. Not only the models themselves but also the negotiation process became more complex and started to include sketches made with pen and paper and more elaborate planning (see Fig. 2, middle where a sketch can be seen in front of the computer. The following aspects stood out as beneficial for the success of our project.

Playfulness: Playfulness is deeply rooted in constructionism itself as well as the approach taken by game-inspired tools such as CubeTeam: Freely building things *you want* from Lego-like cubes while zooming around in a virtual world with your friends is *fun* and actually seeing your creations taking shape in a whirring, whizzing machine is even more fun. This sense of ludic exploration also seemed to be inherent in the 3D printer itself, which is not a new insight in itself but it was especially salient in the dire straits of the children's daily lives with limited access to toys and hardly any play areas. Aafia, a student volunteer, emphasized "*you have seen, there is no room to play for the children, they have to play on the streets*". The collaborative and playful tinkering and Making resulted in laughing, joy and beaming faces. There was a group of boys who treated CubeTeam like a video game, running around and building an artifact similar to a game level—a building with a path leading through it and a central chamber with stairs and windows. At the beginning, they had great fun shaping and interacting with the object but later on, when they saw other kids getting their printouts, they became curious and when we printed out their "*level*", they were amazed, compared it to the digital version on the screen and all three group members wanted a printout.

Approachable Complexity: The children suddenly had the means to create shapes which would have required significant skills, resources and equipment to be made by hand. There was a new degree of freedom regarding self-expression and storytelling through artifacts. An example can be found in the butterfly depicted in Fig. 3. This model was built by Nahid, 9 years old, who attended all of our sessions in the camp and was very motivated and curious. She really liked butterflies but was only able to draw them previously, what she frequently did. Through digital fabrication, she is now also able to make her own physical butterfly models that she wants to incorporate in her playing. Furthermore, her butterfly now has depth and a shape, e.g. a curved body, which would have been impossible to create by drawing and quite hard if not impossible with other available tools and the skill-set of a young child. Nahid was very happy with what she had achieved and proudly took her creation home. This aspect proved to be especially powerful in the camp setting because of the children's usually limited access to tinkering material such as Lego, coping saws, or other tools. Wasimah, another volunteer put it this way: "*We now can make things we normally can't*". At this point, however, we have to emphasize that not the whole 3D printing process proved to be approachable and suitable for children—we will report on the caveats in detail later.

Individualization: It is notable that the children quickly realized that they could not only make things but also customize and individualize them. A group of three boys, for example, figured out that they could model eyelets attached to the already finished models of their names' initials in order to make their creations wearable (see Fig. 3, left side). This discovery happened in both camps we worked with independently and each time, it spread quickly by word of mouth as well as over-the-shoulder learning. The children expressed great satisfaction about being able to carry around *their* creations on their bodies and some of them showed off their brand-new bracelets or necklaces fashioned from string and the 3D prints in the next sessions. Nahid, the girl who likes butterflies was especially proud, approached us and showed a bracelet with her initials while smiling broadly. Individualization of models through inscriptions or favorite motives became quickly popular, too (transmitted through word of mouth and over-the-shoulder learning). Incidentally, this led the children to discover basic 3D modeling operations on their own in an observably intuitive fashion. They had to apply boolean subtractions in order to cut out their names from other solids. Hadil, a girl of 10, discovered this cutting process first and modeled an apple (depicted in Fig. 2, middle) which she later on decided to individualize by adding her name. Notably, all inscriptions were done in Latin letters.

Immediacy and Physicality: We could observe a similar effect in almost every session (always when new children were present). At the beginning, when we demonstrated the 3D printer, the children were rather interested but not really fascinated yet. We then told them that they can make things and that we can print them right now, right here. However, this did never really become an imaginable reality until the first kid tentatively and usually a bit nervously showed us her or his model to be printed. After we initialized the print and the children saw that what we promised was actually possible and one of their peers was *really making something*, eyes widened, interest turned into fascination and efforts to build 3D models were redoubled. A short time later, we usually were buried in models to print. The children surrounded us and the printer, observing the prints—especially if they recognized the model in the printer as their own, which heightened the excitement in the room even more. Another central aspect which is related to the theme of individualization is that the children really liked being able to *take their prints home*, to show them to their friends and parents and explain how they had created the artifacts and what they meant to them. This led to *conversations* between children and their parents about their activities. These conversations often dealt with the individual artifacts. The 3D printing allowed to bring the individual project results home. In previous projects, e.g. with Scratch, the children simply were not able to show their parents what they had done due to a missing computer and no internet at home. To say it with Aafia's words: *"They do not have internet and the parents do not know how to use a computer. It is bad because if we make Scratch projects they [the children] can't show them [to the parents]"*.

Collaboration: As explained, CubeTeam is inherently collaborative in that users can work in the same virtual world at the same models. Most children expressed curiosity about what their friends did and were able to check on their projects directly in CubeTeam. This opportunity generated a certain awareness and had beneficial effects, for instance, starting the popularity of eyelets started as described above. However, as already indicated, most of the actual exchange happened by word of mouth and over-the-shoulder learning with the virtual world only providing the initial spark. Real time collaboration on the same model in the virtual world did not happen. Instead, the children rather changed or expanded their team structure depending on current interest. For instance, Ruhi (12) changed groups because he did not want to build names anymore but rather wanted to join a group working on a building-like structure. Notably, Gulshan and Nakia, two girls from different camps figured out how to copy models. So, one child would start a model and another would remix it according to their tastes and fantasies. Figure 4 (r) shows variations of such a Spongebob-inspired model. In this case, things even went so far that the initial model was created in one camp by Gulshan and later found, copied and modified in the second camp by Nakia. Her modifications seemed to be experimental in nature and artistically inverted the figure or attached a frame around it. There were also inter-generational collaborations: The older student volunteers were rather fascinated by the technology, too. Some of them started not just to supervise and help but to actually work together with the children. A very powerful and expressive example of such a project (which was

Fig. 4 Rocket on a truck (l), Spongebob variations (r)

built after we departed) can be seen in Fig. 4 (l). The 3D model itself was downloaded from the Internet but its coloring and the way it was put together was done in collaboration between children and older volunteers. It was inspired by the 2014 escalation of the Gaza conflict and is a testimony to the local conditions.

Motivation (to Come Back): The camp children often exhibited *"lack of motivation and distracting behavior"* (Zahid, local coordinator) and *"attend infrequently"* (Aafia). The 3D printing project aroused motivation to come back for the next session, to explore more challenging models and to learn more. For instance, Masun, a boy of 10 or 11 was generally rather unruly, unfocused and did not really do anything but disturb other children during most of his first sessions. However, after he saw another group of children admiring their own physical creations, Masun suddenly went back to his computer and tried to model his initials. He still needed some tutoring and occasional quieting-down but finally managed to successfully make a printable model (and he came back in the next sessions).

Caveats in 3D Printing

As already indicated, we also encountered some caveats when introducing 3D printing to the refugee camps. The most notable ones were the following.

Orientation and Camera Control: The orientation in 3D space for the intended task seems to be very difficult for children. We repeatedly observed attempts of children placing a building block at locations partially occluded by other structures. The tasks would have been made easy by moving the camera to a different angle but this usually only happened after multiple failed attempts or through tutor support. To give an example: Hadil, the girl who made the apple, was quite adept with CubeTeam's interface and knew exactly what she wanted to make. However, she needed continuous help from one of the volunteers (see Fig. 2, middle for a scene) to figure out perspective and camera control. However, as a counter-example, the group of boys we described above moved with the "WASD"-keys, quite adeptly. This mode is inspired by common controls in ego shooter video games and indeed, when we asked them, they reported quite a lot of experience with such games. Orientation in 3D space was, all in all, quite heterogeneous.

Lack of Collaboration and Coordination Support: As indicated above, collaboration was proved to be a beneficial factor. However, on the tool level, we observed problems with actually supporting negotiation and coordination among the children. It was often unclear who owns or works on which structure. Wasil (13) wanted, for instance, to extend the video-game level-like structure we described previously. However, the original authors did not attend the session which (after figuring out who the authors actually were from memory since there is no way to find this out in CubeTeam) led to uncertainty if the modification would be acceptable for them. The only real means for collaboration support inside CubeTeam is a single chat channel which did not get used at all by the children. Another factor that came up was mischief. Masun started to randomly place huge amounts of cubes all over the world. He even added these cubes int structures on which other kids currently worked on. This led to frustration, especially by Nahid who was working on an intricate model of a human face which got disturbed by the troublemaker. We had to intervene and manually use the undo-function at the boy's computer.

Construction and Limits of Current 3D Printers: The currently prevalent plastic 3D printers have certain limitations regarding overhangs, printing in color, resolution, or floating structures. Those limitations can be complex, vary from printer to printer and are highly relevant to the outcome of a 3D print. Since the children cannot reasonably be expected to know or understand such those issues quickly, we frequently observed attempts at building structures with problematic elements. An example would be the letter "i" in a model of Nima's (11) name: In the virtual world, it does not matter if the dot of the "i" is not connected to the lower part—it stays where it has been placed, unlike in the physical printout. We usually resolved such issues by explaining the basic problem (often hard to understand for the children) and, in many cases, applying small fixes ourselves before printing. Color also was problematic—some children understood the fact that we could print with only one color at the same time (e.g. Nahid the girl with the butterfly) while others such as Nakia with her Spongebob-variations tried to use multiple colors which got lost in the printout. Another problem is caused by the fact that many current 3D printers are constructed openly. So, we had to take care to keep prying fingers away from dangerous parts. Masun in particular was very curious and repeatedly tried to touch the hot end (about 210) of our printer despite being told equally often that this would hurt quite a lot. Therefore, at least one of us or the volunteers had to stay near the printer at all times.

Usability and UX issues: We frequently observed problems with the interface for the 3D modeling tool where icons and concepts for certain operations were not understood. Random clicking on the UI until something happened was a regular interaction pattern. More advanced functions, like options to add helper planes, were not used at all. Furthermore, in some instances, children left the world, usually by accident, and got lost in the tool, sometimes even creating a new virtual world containing only themselves from the main menu. These problems were, however, probably reinforced by the language barrier in our case. The later steps in the 3D printing process were even more problematic. Actually printing something out requires work steps such as calibrating the printer or handling advanced tools such as *Slicer* software.[5] Such software requires many technical parameters to transform a 3D model into instructions for the 3D printer. Hence, we had to carry out the printing ourselves. In some cases, we tried to explain what we did to some interested children. However, they quickly lost interest due to the high

---

[5]We used Repetier Host with the Slic3r option, see http://repetier.com.

degree of complexity involved and the very technical nature of the tools. This turned our former approach into lectures which did not fit well with the constructionist tone of the project.

Discussion

Apart from hopefully delighting and helping a few children, we were able to find some new aspects on the appropriation of 3D printing in a very particularly structured ICT4D environment. Making as a tool for self expression in marginalized settings seems to be promising and we were able to identify at least some of the aspects which appear to be responsible for this success. Relatedly, we could extrapolate some design implications for future tools for digital fabrication which we will discuss in the following.

The Promises

We think it is safe to state that 3D printing and, more generally, digital fabrication constitute powerful and innovative tools for ICT4D, mainly along a broad theme of self-expression.

Playfulness seems immanent to Making and digital fabrication in general which is also confirmed in corresponding literature (cf. Blikstein 2013; Gershenfeld 2012). However, this aspect really shines in ICT4D settings where there is a sore lack of ludic engagement. In such settings, we have seen that an emphasis on playfulness helps to work towards continuity in participation and motivation which is otherwise often missing. However, the modeling tools used need to be understandable in their complexity by the envisioned audience. Despite functional shortcomings when compared to more powerful CAD tools, the choice of a toned-down and especially playful tool like CubeTeam works well to help building an appropriation infrastructure (Stevens et al. 2009) in which the children could progress on quickly and iteratively. The aspects of *immediacy and physicality* may be among the most important and lasting ones. Apart from the general social dynamic of learning 3D modeling and printing (slow start, huge motivational boost when seeing your *own* creations being printed), the most central aspect is: *taking things home*. When we are talking about ICT4D, we often think of purely digital projects given the fact that everyone of us usually has access to (multiple) computers and the internet whenever desired. This is not true in settings such as the refugee camps. Making storytelling and self-expression transcend the come_IN club is difficult for the children. 3D printing interconnects the digital with the physical, the printouts taking the role of boundary negotiating artifacts (Lee 2007). In previous work with older Makers, we found that digital fabrication frequently seems to take on such a role (Ludwig et al. 2014b) which leads us to the speculation that immediacy and physicality might be generalizable factors influencing the motivation to put work and perseverance in the process of Making as well as in spreading the word.

Another central theme for self-expression is *individualization* through inscriptions or the attachment of eyelets to make creations wearable. This also proved to be a significant motivational factor. The aspect of wearability nicely relates and compliments the previous work in Weibert et al. (2014) and other Maker-related contributions such as Kuznetsov and Paulos (2010) who focus on wearables. Individualization also helped the children to show off and talk about their creations as well as the stories behind them and to engage friends and family members in joint activities such as manufacturing bracelets to attach the 3D prints. If we try to look at this theme in a more general sense, we see relations to the Maker movement as sort of an antithesis to mass production and consumption. The value behind creating individual and innovative products through one's own work seems to be highly relevant in a spectrum of settings ranging from our refugee camps up to highly industrialized countries where the market relevance of end user innovation has long been announced (von Hippel 1988) and where we currently see experimentation with related shifts towards a more peer-based idea of production (Moilanen and Vadén 2013). Aspects of *collaboration* are highly relevant for ideas such as peer production and the Maker movement in general—and indeed, we also found them to relate to self-expression in ICT4D-settings. Curiosity about the activities of others in the group as well as sharing of ideas and even whole 3D models happened frequently and proved to be a motivational factor. Cases such as the remixing of a model across camps illustrate the power of distributed digital fabrication in changing bits to atoms and vice versa (Gershenfeld 2005). A child can build on the work of others virtually, and subsequently, they can make physical items resulting from their virtual collaboration. This effect of collaborative work that breaks the digital physical boundaries in non- or semi-professional settings also has the potential to scale to much bigger projects such as DIY prosthesis (Krassenstein 2014).The collaboration aspect of working in the same virtual world in itself quickly proved to have potential with children learning and copying from each other, confirming previous work with similar tools such as Minecraft (e.g. Duncan 2011). However, it was notable that, for the most part, there was a significant element of face to face interaction in the collaboration we could observe. This might have been due to the convenience and social conventions when participants were in the same room, but we suspect that the limitations of the available tools and interfaces to support cooperative work are also relevant factors (more on this below). If we look at collaborations among Makers in a more general sense, we see a significant element of face-to-face collaboration while there are also virtual collaborations which are important for the successes of the movement (Tanenbaum et al. 2013) but there is also: The Maker culture places great emphasis on real-world events such as Maker Faires, the FAB series of conferences and the social meeting and collaboration aspects of Makerspaces and Fab Labs. So, a balance between physical and virtual collaborative work seems to be essential. However, there are shortcomings in the currently available ICT for collaboration (Ludwig et al. 2014a). In the following, we would now like to turn towards those tools we worked with in more depth. These toolsets are one of the pillars supporting the work which can be done by Makers and their often problematic design emerged as a central aspect in our analysis.

The Obstacles (and What We Can Do to Avoid Them)

In a general sense, it is possible to achieve a notably quick learning and understanding process by using available, playful and collaborative tools such as Minecraft or CubeTeam, see e.g. Short and Short (2012). However, there are obstacles and significant gaps in the learning and appropriation processes due to the limitations of those tools as well as the current 3D printer ecosystems. At this point, we confirm and support previous works calling for novel tools and interfaces, such as as Willis and Gross (2011). This part of our discussion will focus on implications for design.

Orientation and camera control relates to movement in the 3D space and executing tasks in conjunction with appropriate camera position which is crucial for successful modeling. Therefore, we argue for the inclusion and exploration of alternative ways of navigation: e.g. utilizing 3D mice, which would map directly to three axes, or even game controllers to support familiar appropriation patterns. We saw indications that game-inspired camera and/or movement control might be useful. Some of the children were quite clever in using the "WASD" movement control mode in CubeTeam. Furthermore, the exploration of virtual reality with higher degrees of immersion in the 3D-space (e.g. utilizing virtual reality glasses such as the Oculus Rift) might be an option. Switches between navigational modes, as employed by CubeTeam, either should be avoided or introduced especially carefully and with appropriation support in mind.

While in Palestine most of the *coordination and collaboration* work happened face-to-face, we see in more long-term projects in Germany that there is a need for advanced coordination mechanisms beyond what is currently available in most playful tools for digital fabrication. Ownership signifiers (such as color or signs) would be worth to be explored. If we turn to the success of voice chat in online multiplayer gaming (e.g. Teamspeak), this line of thought might also be one that could be integrated into collaborative 3D modeling. An interesting option might be to constrain (voice) chat channels geographically, meaning a conversation could only be heard or read if in close proximity to the relating structure.

Usability and UX issues are a problem, especially when supporting novices in their work with complex technologies. It is not surprising that we found many issues, for example relating to modal navigation or less-than-optimal icons in the tools we utilized. Future tools should support a centrally configurable interface in which, for instance, leaving a project could be remotely disabled, or, at the very least, there should be a very simple "bring me to my group" feature. The actual modeling UI should be as minimalistic as possible and also configurable, offering only basic operations (e.g. placing and deleting a building block) at first and subsequently getting more complex (undo, copying blocks, etc.).

The construction and limitations of current 3D printers can result in problems when trying to print something that works in the virtual but not the physical world. Future tools should be aware of those device-specific limitations. They should not only attempt to correct them automatically or simply do not allow certain operations. However, we would suggest to provide a more gentler mode to support the appropriation by making the user aware of why something like a significant overhang probably will not print well. Automated notifications and animations (such as a printing process simulation) might also be ways to supplement this. Similar results and ideas have been proposed in Ludwig et al. (2014a). With other, less restricted, 3D printing technologies which are more affordable (such as laser sintering), this problem might be solved in the medium-term. Furthermore, there is a gap between the ease with which children are able to pick up basic 3D modeling capabilities and the fact that the 3D printing itself necessitates a lot of previous technical knowledge. This leads to a certain "black box" perception of the 3D printer, as phrased by Ludwig et al. (2014a). Hence, future educational tools should integrate the the printer, modeling tools, control software and print material to a denser ecosystem. Speaking overly simplified: Offering a *Print-now* button. Actual printers for educational purposes should be designed safer, more encapsulated and should offer basic *it-just-works* settings, based on which exploration can be initiated. Such an approach would positively contrast to the current state of affairs where a significant amount of configuration and knowledge has to be done/acquired *before* the first print. A printing simulation could serve as an intermediate step in such a process.

Conclusions and Outlook

We were able to show that 3D printing can be a powerful tool in an educational ICT4D environment. Furthermore, we identified key factors like physical immediacy. Based on our experiences as well as on other Maker projects, we think that our findings are transferable to a certain extent—factors such as playfulness certainly hold true as important for the success of non-professional digital fabrication in other settings (cf. Ludwig et al. 2014a). However, aspects of immediate physicality and the ability to take home printed artifacts have a particular deep meaning and potentially beneficial consequences for settings with marginalized populations. These aspects place Making and digital fabrication into an important position for developmental and educational work with ICT (cf. Mikhak et al. 2002). However, we also saw many shortcomings and caveats such as deficits with tools and interfaces as well as lacking coordination support. These problems hamper (but do not prevent) current efforts with digital fabrication. However, we assume that none of the issues we found was insurmountable or systematic—instead, they represent problems that can be solved by careful and participatory refining and the co-development of tools for digital fabrication (cf. Willis and Gross, 2011). This is a challenge especially geared towards CSCW and HCI researchers and a field we believe to be sustainable and important. While 3D printing is a sensible and currently booming entry point into digital fabrication, other means of Making such as laser cutting or CNC milling (which are all available in more and more Fab Labs and Makerspaces all around the world) should be used and researched in a similar practice-oriented manner. This is a challenge we are currently working on.

In a more macro sense, we discovered that the mediation of physical-digital boundaries was crucially important. It was scaffolded through digital fabrication technologies and moderated by factors such as the culture and value set developed by the Maker movement. These values seem to remain valid and scale for quite different social settings and markets. They prove to be relevant for the work in Palestinian refugee camps but may also be a factor for socio-economic change towards a common- and peer-production based society in other parts of the world—as envisioned by Gershenfeld (2012). In our opinion, investigations into the dynamics of collaborative practices in Making communities and opportunities for their technological support offer a valuable research agenda for CSCW.

Acknowledgments We are indebted to the volunteers and participants in Palestine, especially George Yerousis, Birzeit University.

References

Aal, K., Yerousis, G., Schubert, K., Hornung, D., Stickel, O., & Wulf, V. (2014). Come_in@ Palestine: Adapting a German computer club concept to a Palestinian refugee camp. In *Proceedings of CABS* (pp. 111–120).

Adams, A., Lunt, P., & Cairns, P. (2008). A qualitative approach to HCI research. In P. Cairns & A. Cox (Eds.), *Research methods for human-computer interaction* (pp. 138–157). Cambridge: CU Press.

Blikstein, P. (2013). Digital fabrication and 'making' in education: The democratization of invention. In J. Walter-Herrmann & C. Büching (Eds.), *FabLabs: Of machines, makers and inventors*. Transcript Verlag.

Braun, V., & Clarke, V. (2006). Using thematic analysis in psychology. *Qualitative Research in Psychology, 3*, 77–101.

Buechley, L., & Perner-Wilson, H. (2012). Crafting technology: Reimagining the processes, materials, and cultures of electronics. *ACM TOCHI, 19*, 21:1–21:21.

Dourish, P. (2003). The appropriation of interactive technologies: Some lessons from placeless documents. *Journal Computer Supported Cooperative Work, 12*(4), 465–490.

Duncan, S. C. (2011). Minecraft, beyond construction and survival. *Well Played, 1*, 1–22.

Gardner, A. (2014). *Oxfam teams with MyMiniFactory to provide humanitarian aid in Syria, using 3D printing.* http://3dprint.com/3400/syrian-crisis-oxfam. Accessed January 10, 2015.

Gershenfeld, N. (2005). *Fab: The coming revolution on your desktop—from personal computers to personal fabrication*. New York: Basic Books.

Gershenfeld, N. (2012). How to make almost anything the digital fabrication revolution. *Foreign Affairs, 91*, 42–57.

Harel, I., & Papert, S. (1991). *Constructionism*. New York: Ablex Publishing.

Hatch, M. (2013). *The maker movement manifesto*. New York: McGraw Hill Education.

Ho, M. R., Smyth, T. N., Kam, M., & Dearden, A. (2009). Human-computer interaction for development: The past, present, and future. *Information Technologies and International Development, 5*, 1–18.

Kafai, Y. B., Peppler, K. A., & Chapman, R. N. (2009). *The computer clubhouse: Constructionism and creativity in youth communities, technology, education-connections.* New York: Teachers College.

Krassenstein, E. (2014). *Man compares his $42k prosthetic hand to a $50 3D printed cyborg beast.* http://3dprint.com/2438/50-prosthetic-3d-printed-hand. Accessed January 10, 2015.

Kuznetsov, S., & Paulos, E. (2010). Rise of the expert amateur: DIY projects, communities, and cultures. In *Proceedings of NordiCHI* (pp. 295–304).

Kuznetsov, S., Taylor, A. S., Regan, T., Villar, N., & Paulos, E. (2012). At the seams: DIYbio and opportunities for HCI. In *Proceedings of DIS* (pp. 258–267).

Lee, C. P. (2007). Boundary negotiating artifacts: Unbinding the routine of boundary objects and embracing chaos in collaborative work. In *Proceedings of CSCW* (Vol. 16, pp. 307–339).

Lindtner, S., Hertz, G., & Dourish, P. (2014). Emerging sites of HCI innovation: Hackerspaces, hardware startups and incubators. In *Proceedings of CHI* (pp. 1–10).

Ludwig, T., Stickel, O., & V. Pipek (2014b). 3D Printers as potential boundary negotiating artifacts for third places. In *2nd WS on HCI for 3rd Places at DIS'14*. Canada: Vancouver.

Ludwig, T., Stickel, O., Boden, A., & Pipek, V. (2014a). Towards sociable technologies: An empirical study on designing appropriation infrastructures for 3D printing. In *Proceedings of DIS* (pp. 835–844).

McTaggart, R. (1991). Principles for participatory action research. *Adult Education Quarterly, 41*(3), 168–187.

Mellis, D. A., Buechley, L. (2012). Case studies in the personal fabrication of electronic products. In *Proceedings of DIS* (pp. 268–277). New York: ACM.

Mikhak, B., Lyon, C., Gorton, T., Gershenfeld, N., Mcennis, C., & Taylor, J. (2002). Fab lab: An alternate model of ICT for development. In *Development by Design (DYD02)* (pp. 1–7).

Moilanen, J., & T. Vadén (2013). 3D printing community and emerging practices of peer production. *First Monday*, 18(5).

Pipek, V. (2005). From tailoring to appropriation support: Negotiating groupware usage (Doctoral dissertation, University of Oulu, 2005).

Pipek, V., & Kahler, H. (2006). Supporting collaborative tailoring. In *EUD* (pp. 315–345).

Resnick, M., Maloney, J., Monroy-Hernández, A., Rusk, N., Eastmond, E., Brennan, K., et al. (2009). Scratch: Programming for all. *CACM, 52*, 60–67.

Sawhney, N. (2009). Voices beyond walls: The role of digital storytelling for empowering marginalized youth in refugee camps. *Voices* (pp. 3–6).

Schubert, K., Weibert, A., & Wulf, V. (2011). Locating computer clubs in multicultural neighborhoods: How collaborative project work fosters integration processes. *IJHCS, 69*, 669–678.

Short, D., & Short, B. D. (2012). Teaching scientific concepts using a virtual world—Minecraft. *Teaching Science: The Journal of the Australian Science Teachers Association, 58*, 55–58.

Star, S. L., & Griesemer, J. R. (1989). Institutional ecology, 'Translations' and boundary objects: Amateurs and professionals in Berkeley's museum of vertebrate zoology, 1907-39. *Social studies of science, 19*(3), 387–420.

Stevens, G., Pipek, V., & Wulf, V. (2009). Appropriation infrastructure: Supporting the design of usages. In *Proceedings of 2nd International Symposium on EUD* (pp. 50–69).

Stevens, G., Veith, M., & Wulf, V. (2005). Bridging among ethnic communities by cross-cultural communities of practice. In *Proceedings of C&T* (pp. 377–396).

Tanenbaum, J. J. G., Williams, A. M., Desjardins, A., & Tanenbaum, K. (2013). Democratizing technology: pleasure, utility and expressiveness in DIY and maker practice. In *Proceedings of CHI* (pp. 2603–2612).

Troxler, P. (2013). Making the third industrial revolution—the struggle for polycentric structures and a new peer-production commons in the FabLab community. In J. Walter-Herrmann & C. Büching (Eds.), *FabLabs: Of machines, makers and inventors*.

von Hippel, E. (1988). *Users as innovators*. Oxford: Oxford University Press.

von Rekowski, T., Boden, A., Stickel, O., Hornung, D., & Stevens, G. (2014). Playful, collaborative approaches to 3D modeling and 3D printing. In *Proceedings of Mensch und Computer* (pp. 363–366).

Weibert, A., Marshall, A., Aal, K., Schubert, K., & Rode, J. (2014). Sewing interest in E-textiles: Analyzing making from a gendered perspective. In *Proceedings of DIS* (pp. 15–24). New York: ACM.

Weibert, A., & Schubert, K. (2010). How the social structure of intercultural computer clubs fosters interactive storytelling. In *Proceedings of IDC* (pp. 368–371).

Willis, K. D. D., & Gross, M. D. (2011). Interactive fabrication: New interfaces for digital fabrication. In *Proceedings of TEI* (pp. 69–72).

Wulf, V., Aal, K., Abu Kteish, I., Atam, M., Schubert, K., Rohde, M., Yerousis, G. P., & Randall, D. (2013). Fighting against the wall. In *Proceedings of CHI* (pp. 1979–1988).

Wulf, V., Müller, C., Pipek, V., Randall, D., & Rohde, M. (2015). Practice-based computing. In V. Wulf, K. Schmidt, & D. Randall (Eds.), *Designing socially embedded technologies in the real world*. London: Springer.

Yerousis, G., Aal, K., Rekowski, T. V., Randall, D. W., Rohde, M., & Wulf, V. (2015). Computer-enabled project spaces: Connecting with Palestinian refugees across camp boundaries. In *Proceedings of CHI* (pp. 1979–1988).

Intertext: On Connecting Text in the Building Process

Lars Rune Christensen

Abstract Actors in the building process are critically dependent on a corpus of written text that draws the distributed work tasks together. This paper introduces, on the basis of a field study, the concepts of corpus, intertext and intertextuality to the analysis of text in cooperative work practice. This paper shows that actors in the building process create intertext (connections) between complementary texts, in a particular situation and for a particular task. This has an integrating effect on the building process. Several types of intertextuality, including the complementary type, the intratextual type and the mediated type, may constitute the intertext of a particular task. By employing the concepts of corpus, intertext and intertextuality with respect to the study of the building process, this paper outlines an approach to the investigation of text in cooperative work.

Introduction

In this article, we attempt to achieve a better understanding of how cooperative work is accomplished by collaborative actors through the creation and use of mutually constituted texts in document-centric work practices. Previous studies have focused on single documents (e.g. Luff et al. 1992; Xiao et al. 2001), and on collections of documents (e.g. Cabitza and Simone 2007; Christensen and Bjorn 2014; Schmidt and Wagner 2004). Buiding on this work, we explore how written artifacts partly constitute cooperative work practice. Inspired by work within semiotics (Riffaterre 1980), we introduce the concepts of *corpus, intertext, and intertextuality* as analytical devices to unpack how text may be said to influence human action. The study argues that an ensemble of documents used and produced in the building process may form a *corpus* of written texts. On the basis of the corpus,

L.R. Christensen (✉)
IT-University of Copenhagen, Copenhagen, Denmark
e-mail: Lrc@itu.dk

© Springer International Publishing Switzerland 2015
N. Boulus-Rødje et al. (eds.), *ECSCW 2015: Proceedings of the 14th European Conference on Computer Supported Cooperative Work, 19–23 September 2015, Oslo, Norway*, DOI 10.1007/978-3-319-20499-4_6

or subsections hereof, the actors may create *intertext* between relevant (complementary) texts in a particular situation, for a particular purpose. The intertext of a
particular situation can be constituted by several kinds of *intertextuality*, including
the complementary type, the intratextual type, and the mediated type. This has an
integrating effect on the cooperative work practice.

The paper echoes Strauss et al. (1997), specifically the analysis of the complex and contingent nature of practice. Underscoring the fact that practitioners must establish a connection between the particular situation at hand and the
formal nature of text at work. According to the present study, these connections
are (partly) made when practitioners create intertext between select documents at
work according to the situation at hand. In this manner this study offers insights
into the making of connections in practice between the formal corpus of text and
the arising contingent situations of practice. That is, it addresses the core issue of
the interplay between structure and agency in work practice, where the corpus of
texts provides structure to practice and the individual actors creation of intertext
displays agency.

The empirical data originate from a study of the building process, more precisely, the planning and construction of a large commercial and residential complex in a suburb of Copenhagen. In the process of the building process, architects,
building engineers, general contractors, subcontractors, vendors, craftsmen and
builders continuously create and use documents such as for example architectural
plans, engineering plans, schedules, calculations, permits and meeting agendas,
and more. As such, a building process is a highly document-heavy practice and an
excellent vantage point for the study of documents in cooperative work. An understanding of these practices is key to improving computer support of actors working with multiple texts in complex cooperative work settings.

The article is structured in the following manner. First, we will describe related
research and introduce the main analytical concepts of the study. Second, we will
describe the research setting and methods. Third, we will consider the corpus
of written text internal to the practice. Fourth, we will consider the achievement
of intertext as well as three types of intertextuality pertinent to the construction of
intertext. Finally, some concluding remarks will be provided.

Related Research

The study of text in cooperative work has become a central research topic within
CSCW. Documents are used extensively in cooperative work for the execution of
individual tasks, as well as for the coordination of multiple tasks (Hertzum 1999),
and they may be said to manage 'the flow of information' (Cabitza and Simone
2007). For this reason, researchers have long been studying the manner in which
documents are used and produced in cooperative work practices. It is evident from
this research that documents are woven into cooperative work activities as intrinsic
components of those activities, rather than as secondary tools where information is

passively stored and retrieved (Malone 1983). Recent studies have pointed out that documents are not to be regarded as isolated artefacts, but rather as being intertwined within heterogeneous networks of actors, activities, and other artefacts, inherent to cooperative work practice (Bardram and Bossen 2005; Cabitza and Simone 2007; Christensen and Bjorn 2014; Harper 1998; Schmidt and Wagner 2004).

The fact that multiple texts used in conjunction can act as key constitutive elements of cooperative work, implies that actors must align and combine several texts as part of their everyday activities. For example, in the context of healthcare, Schmidt et al. (2007) found that multiple written artefacts are to be aligned and read together in order to give an adequate picture of a given patient's trajectory and to support workflow. Texts are often arranged in a systematic manner. This is what Schmidt and Wagner (2004), in the context of architectural work, call "ordering systems", i.e. complexes of interrelated practices and artifacts. Relatedly, Bardram and Bossen (2005) discuss how cooperative actors achieve coordination through the use of a wide range of interrelated non-digital artefacts, such as whiteboards, work schedules, examination sheets, care records, post-it notes and etc. Zhou et al. (2011) cast collections of artefacts in terms of 'assemblages', i.e. "*a complex system that includes boundary objects, the practices around these objects (including organizational policies), work processes and coordination mechanisms within these objects, and special functions for designated groups.*" (Zhou et al. 2011, p. 3354). Relatedly, Christensen and Bjorn (2014) have also studied how collections of documents shape work practice in their study of 'documentscapes' in global interactions. According to their study, documents may be said to form a documentscape, when each document depends upon the wider ensemble for meaning, as well as utility. Documents in the documentscape take their meaning from their position in an ensemble of documents, used or produced in series or in parallel. The concept of documentscape highlights how intertextuality may draw the distributed use of documents together and provide structure and integration to highly distributed cooperative work practice.

In sum, previous studies have established that documents may be key constitute elements of cooperative work practice, and that in many instances actors combine and align heterogeneous yet complementary texts as part of their practice. Very important contributions have been made in this area. However, few CSCW studies draw explicit inspiration from literary theory (an exception is Christensen and Bjorn 2014), and very few use concepts originating in that field. This is quite a conundrum. Given the fact that literary theory (and semiotics in general) is potentially well placed to give a new view and new insights into exactly how documents become such powerful instigators and are constitutive of cooperative work practice (Harper 1998). In his seminal work on documents in organizational life Harper (1998, p. 25) draws attention to this fact by stating that: "*Literary theory may appear well removed from our concern with documents in organizational life. But in fact it does have a lot to say on this topic. The semiotic view emphasises that there is no such thing as a 'free standing text' [...] rather each text is linked in one way or another to each and every other text in a system [...].*" The introduction of Riffaterre's literary theory concepts to CSCW may be said to follow Harper's suggestion (although he does not directly point to Riffaterre's work).

The notion of documents related to one another in systematic ways is important, and there is good reason for considering semiotics and literary theory in CSCW. We will now turn to presenting the proposed analytical concepts.

Analytical Concepts

As mentioned, we will rely on the influential French scholar of literary theory and semiotics Michael Riffaterre in an attempt to invigorate a CSCW analysis of documents in cooperative work. His work is part of the tradition of semiotics where names such as Saussure, Bakhtin, Volosinov, and Kristeva loom large. In the seminal work of Saussure (1974), followed by Bakhtin and Volosinov (1986) and, subsequently, Kristeva (1986), texts or documents are to be treated semiotically; that is, language is a system of signs in which one sign implies the presence or absence of another sign (Saussure 1974). This means that no document is "isolated". Rather, each document is linked to each and every other document through intertextuality, that is, through a practice of "presence and anticipated presence (absence)." The most crucial aspect of language, from this perspective, is that all language responds to previous utterances and to existing patterns of meaning and criteria of evaluation, but it also anticipates and seeks to promote future responses (Harper 1998). One cannot create or even understand an utterance or a written work, such as a document, as if it was detached in meaning, unconnected to previous or future utterances or written works (Bakhtin and Volosinov 1986, p. 72). This is the legacy that Riffaterre builds on and is a part of.

Before we venture any further, it should be made clear that Riffaterre was concerned with building a theory of literature focusing on the semiotics of, for example, novels, short stories and poems. He was not a scholar of cooperative work and interested in documents in the building process. Nevertheless, his work may turn out to be very useful to us in CSCW, if used carefully.

According to Riffaterre (1980), the reader routinely establishes *intertext* between texts, in order to make them meaningful. A text may be almost meaningless, unless connected to other texts by the actor, during his or her process of reading or writing. This presupposes a *corpus* of known texts (i.e. a body of texts familiar to the reader), as well as various forms of *intertextuality*, by which intertext may be created.

The concepts of *corpus, intertext* and *intertextuality* in a CSCW context are described here:

- *Corpus* refers to the ensemble of texts available to the collaborative actors—central to their work practice.
- *Intertext* is the meaning achieved by the actor by combining several texts from the corpus in accord with the demands of a given situation. Intertext may be said to be a 'situational property' as it is always created as part of performing a task in a given situation with specific circumstances. The concept of intertext is central to the analysis.

- *Intertextuality* refers to the various ways that intertext may be achieved. That is, the meaningful combination of several heterogeneous documents from the corpus in relation to a particular work task. There are, at least, three different kinds of intertextuality, namely, the complementary type, the mediated type, and the intratextual type.

By introducing the concept of *corpus* to the study of cooperative work, we become analytically sensitive to the body of text distributed among the many different actors involved in cooperative work. The concept of *intertext* allows us to consider how the individual actors achieve meaning by integrating and combining several texts in a particular situation, and the concept of *intertextuality* draws attention to the various ways intertext can be achieved.[1]

Note that, the concepts are interconnected in a systematic manner (e.g. the concept of *intertext* relies on the concepts of *corpus* and *intertextuality* as auxiliary concepts, and vice versa). This, in effect, potentially allows the empirical analysis to also have these same systematic virtues. That is, this set of concepts originating in the field of semiotics may help us conceptualise the individual's act of creating meaning using documents, and the system or structure of the documents influencing this act, in one and the same analysis.

Methods

The empirical material was generated through fieldwork, including interviews and observations of work practice. During the course of nine months, fieldwork at two building sites, as well as architectural offices, was carried out. Additionally, and central to the study, texts such as, for example, architectural plans, engineering plans, schedules, calculations, permits and meeting agendas, and minutes were collected and studied. The entire corpus of text used in the performance of a specific construction task was collected and studied. Written artefacts where studied by, for example, following their lifecycle (Harper 2000) with an optic on how individual texts where used in conjunction.

Twelve in-depth interviews on the practices of e.g. combining text with text in the building process were carried out. In general, during data generation and analysis, particular attention was paid to how different actors involved in the building process use the many texts in conjunction with each other, rather than one text at a time. One of the building projects studied was the development of a commercial and residential complex, a multi-storey project, in concrete, brick, glass and steel, situated in a suburb of Copenhagen, Denmark. It was a, relatively, large project totalling 7700 m^2 (82,882 ft^2), 4900 m^2 (52,743 ft^2), was distributed across

---

[1]There are, of course, more relationships to work practice than the textual relationships focused on in this article (e.g. relationships of materiality, equipment, technologies). However, accounting for these in detail, are outside the scope of this paper.

Fig. 1 A building engineer studying a construction plan during the erection of a concrete carcass of an apartment building

45 apartments in seven buildings (see Fig. 1), and 2800 m^2 (30,139 ft^2) was designated as commercial space. In this paper the focus is on the construction stage, more precisely, on the work done by the building engineer and craftsmen of the subcontractor at the stage of erecting the concrete carcass of the apartment buildings on the site. We will now turn to introducing the building process including the network of actors involved in order to provide some context for our analysis.

The Network of Actors and the Building Process

The building process studied here involves the creation of a unique structure, rather than mass-produced entity. Such projects almost always start with a client approaching an architect with the intent to acquire a new building. Briefly put, the building project that follows is planned and worked out step-by-step, phase-by-phase. Gradually the project takes shape, the requirements (e.g. size, materials, functions etc.) of the proposed building are put down on paper as written text and the first conceptual design sketches are drawn up. The number of people involved increases, sketches become scale drawings, and architectural plans become the basis for applications to the authorities. After an initial building permit has been

Table 1 The ensemble of actors involved in a large building project

Client	Architects	General contractor	Authorities
Initiates the process	Responsible for overall design	Moderates the design of the working plans	Building permit and regulations
Contracts architect and general contractor	Coordinates the design process	Plans the construction process	Environmental assessments
Formulates building program with architect	Formulates building program with client	Hires subcontractors and retains architect	

Users	Consultants	Subcontractors	Vendors
Contributes to requirements	Specialists for statics, lightning, building services and more	Retain the craftsmen that actually con-struct the building	Provides building material and fabricate components
			Design building components

issued, tenders are invited from contractors, and commission is awarded to a general contractor. The general contractor then hires the various subcontractors and the aim of putting up the building is within reach once the final architectural plans have been made and the subcontractors with their craftsmen, builders and workers has been coordinated on the building site.

For each new building project a network of actors is created or configured. The network is a diverse ensemble from many different professions, working for many different companies (see Table 1). Some such as the client and the main architects are with the project from start to finish, while others such as the various subcontractors are associated with the project only for the duration of their allotted tasks.

We may interject that large building projects are performed in a fast-track manner, which implies that design and construction overlap in a temporal sense (Sabbagh 1989). For example, the physical construction of a building's foundation may be well underway before the design of the buildings roof is finalised. That is to say that much design work is very much concurrent with the construction of the building.[2] However, the design of a specific building element generally precedes its construction. For example, the design of a roof is most often finalised before it is physically constructed.

The networks of actors found in the building process differ from other organizations of work such as manufacturing or services that may enjoy far more extended longevity. That is, the concrete configuration of actors (i.e. client, architects, general contractor, subcontractors, vendors etc.) is specific to the particular building project and dissolves as the project ends. However, a number of

---

[2]This is mainly grounded in a desire to save time by virtue of *not* having to wait until the whole building has been designed before commencing with its construction (Sabbagh 1989).

arrangements counteract these 'transient' tendencies of the network. First of all, the major players in the business may have worked together on various projects in the past. For instance the architect and the general contractors may be familiar with one another from prior engagements. Furthermore, it is not uncommon that for example the general contractor relies on a small group of trusted subcontractors when recruiting for a project. For example, in the project studied here the general contractors and a large part of the group of subcontractors had worked together on a previous project. Secondly, the various actors are all part of the construction industry at large, and although they may meet as strangers in relation to a specific project, they bring with them rather precise expectations of the manner in which the project ought to be carried out (Kreiner 1976, p. 83). The actors, then, are part of the same work domain, i.e. the building process, and as such they are familiar with the norms and practices that are part and parcel of it. Consequently, roles and responsibilities for example may merely have to be aligned anew for every project, rather than 'invented' from a clean slate.

Moreover, the norms and practices of the building process are 'inscribed' into the written artifacts used and produced by the actors, and it is up to the individual actors to use these written artifacts (often in conjunction with one another) according to the situation at hand. This is the focus in this paper.

We shall now turn to describe the body of text available to the cooperative work ensemble, and subsequently we will turn to the creation of intertext.

The Corpus of Text in the Building Process

As mentioned above, in the building process architects, contractors, craftsmen, vendors, and consultants continuously create, use, and revise texts and documents, such as architectural plans, engineering plans, schedules, calculations, permits and meeting agendas and minutes. In this respect, the building process is a highly document-heavy practice. As individual texts and documents are created, they may undergo integration with past, present and, potential future documents, each document being authored, co-authored, read, commented, embellished and altered by the various members of the network across time, place and organizations.

It may be argued, that the relations between the texts are a part of what brings the grand endeavourer of the building process together, by enabling connections between what was, otherwise, disparate actors, times and places.[3]

What we, employing a concept from Riffaterre (1980), dub 'the corpus of text' is in this context the body of written texts available to the cooperative network of actors. The texts of the corpus are related in multiple ways with criss-crossing

---

[3]Note that, coordination through the material field of work also plays an important role, by facilitating integration of the cooperative work tasks. This mode of coordination has been dubbed *stigmergy* (Christensen 2014).

references and integrations across temporal, spatial, and organizational divides and boundaries. Furthermore, the corpus is dynamic in nature, as the body of text develops and accumulates, over time, during the course of the building process. For example, at the start of a building process, the corpus may consist of, relatively, few documents, such as a building programme created by the client and the architect, i.e. some initial design sketches, descriptions of the desired nature and scope of the building, and associated calculations. As the building project proceeds to the tendering stage, the corpus grows in volume as more descriptions, architectural plans, engineering plans, permits, meeting agendas and minutes, offers, correspondence, contracts and time schedules are added. As the project enters the construction phase, the volume of the corpus increases ten-fold, as highly detailed architectural plans and engineering plans, to be used by the men and women constructing the building, are introduced in great numbers, as are many more time schedules, meeting agenda and minutes, further permits, calculations, environmental assessments, and more. Finally, as the building project draws to a close, architectural plans and descriptions of the building 'as built' are added to the corpus. In this manner, the volume of the corpus expands, over time (Christensen 2013).

The Corpus of Text for a Specific Construction Task

As mentioned above, the focus in this paper is on the construction stage, more precisely, on the building engineer and craftsmen practice of erecting the concrete carcass of a building (see Fig. 1). This is as indicated a practice that involves the use of multiple written artifacts that must be interconnected by the actors as part of the practice of constructing a building. We will take a closer look at this specific corpus now.

When relating to the text corpus, in general, in relation to the building process, we are referring to the accumulated body of texts, available to the whole range of actors involved. However, we may also consider the corpus in a more limited sense, that is, as related (with fuzzy boundaries) to a select subsection of the building process.

For example, consider the text corpus integral to the task of constructing the concrete carcass of a large building. In brief, the execution of this task, primarily, involves architects creating plans of the building in various projections and scales, a vendor creating plans for the montage and fabrication of the building elements, and engineers and a crew of workmen hoisting the building elements in place with cranes and binding them together with irons while guided by various plans, lists and time schedules. In this process, then, a set of interrelated texts (forming a corpus) is part of what integrates the distributed actions of the cooperative actors.

In the preparation of the actual construction work, the architects forward their architectural plans of the building to an offsite manufacturing facility, endowed with the responsibility of manufacturing the building elements, primarily concrete elements, such as decks and walls.

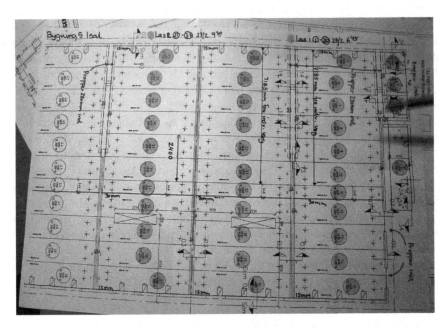

Fig. 2 Plan of deck element layout made by engineers at an offsite facility. The architect's original plan of the building is broken up into entities, which may be produced at the offsite facility. The plan is later colour coded to indicate which truckload the various building elements belong too

Fabrication in a factory environment enables the elements to have a consistent quality of strength, durability, and finish, and eliminates the need for onsite formwork. The external wall elements provide the building with horizontal stability and make up the horizontal part of the buildings concrete carcass. As far as the decks are concerned, these horizontal surfaces serve to support the structural loads of the building's mass, as well as the anticipated loads created by people, furniture and equipment. On the basis of the architectural plans, the actors who are responsible for casting the elements at the offsite plant create their own set of plans, depicting each building element and its placement (see Fig. 2).

Each element, then, is given a unique identity (ID) number. After the manufacturing, each concrete element is spray painted with the ID number and loaded onto trucks by factory workers, according to a loading list (see Fig. 3), to be transported to the building site. The load order is also indicated by colour coding of the deck layout plan. For example, orange for load No. 1 to arrive on February 2nd at 6:45 a.m., and blue for load No. 2 to arrive on February 2nd at 9:30 a.m. Also visible are the ID numbers of individual building elements (see Fig. 2).

The ID number is present, then, on the engineering plans, the concrete elements and the loading list. This cross-reference serves the purpose of ensuring that the building elements arrive at the site in the exact order that they are to be used during the construction efforts. As the elements arrive on site (see Fig. 4), the crew starts to offload the elements and hoist them into position. In this process, the

Element ID   Height   Length   Square metre   Weight   Truckload no.

Tinglev Elementfabrik A/S   **Læsseliste 1**

Sag nr . 133199
Sag ...: STTOAGERGRUNDEN BYGN.7
Kunde .: MT HØJGAARD A/S
     SDR. STATIONSVEJ 28F, 2. TV.
     SLAGELSE 4200 SLAGELSE SLAGELSE

Dato 23/11-07 12:.. , side 1
Etage ....: 2.SAL BYGNING 7
Sagsbehandler .: BJO

Element Nr.	Type	Dim. mm	Højde mm	Længde mm	Brutto Kvm	Netto Kvm	VOB Kvm	TE Kvm	Vægt kg	Akk.vægt kg	Læs Nr.
1	B25/2400	180	2.725	228	0,60	0,60	0,60	0,60	262	262	1
2	B25/2400	180	2.740	2.172	6,00	5,90	6,00	6,00	2.563	2825	1
2A	B25/2400	180	2.740	4.640	12,70	12,20	12,70	12,70	5.270	8095	1
3	B25/2400	180	2.740	2.328	6,40	6,40	6,40	6,40	2.742	10837	1
4	B25/2400	180	2.740	393	1,10	1,10	1,10	1,10	458	11295	1
5	B25/2400	180	2.740	2.028	5,60	5,60	5,60	5,60	2.394	13689	1
6	B25/2400	180	2.740	1.844	5,10	5,10	5,10	5,10	2.176	15865	1
7	B25/2400	180	2.740	2.068	5,70	5,70	5,70	5,70	2.440	18305	1
8	B25/2400	180	2.740	2.448	6,70	6,70	6,70	6,70	2.895	21200	1
9	B25/2400	180	2.740	1.120	3,10	3,10	3,10	3,10	1.324	22524	1
10	B25/2400	180	2.725	352	1,00	1,00	1,00	1,00	708	23232	1

Ant.elem ......: 11
Rejects Element: 2740

Fig. 3 Excerpt of loading list with element ID number, type, dimensions, weight, and designated truckload

Fig. 4 Building elements arrive on site. Note the spray-painted ID numbers on the concrete elements

engineering plans, the building element ID number, and the loading list are used. In addition, a set of detail drawings is used, depicting the details of the binding irons that secure the building elements to each other. Furthermore, the process is guided by descriptions, stipulating construction techniques, the overall time schedule and the plan for the layout of the building site, according to several rules, regulations, ordnances, recommendations, and industry standards.

In this manner a subset of the large document corpus, what we may call a task specific corpus (with fuzzy boundaries), may be identified as supporting the cooperative work ensembles efforts of designing, manufacturing, transporting and installing building elements for a particular part of a building.

As aforementioned, making the relations between the texts are a part of what brings the distributed endeavourer of the building process together, by enabling connections between what would, otherwise, be disparate actors, times and places. However, accounting for the document corpus is only half of the story, it denotes the distributions of documents among cooperative actors and suggests interrelations. But, how do the relevant relations occur? This is where the other half of the story becomes relevant. The other half of the story pertains to semantics. This perspective helps explain how the document corpus becomes meaningful as a corpus or, more precisely, as intertext. It allows us to shift focus from considering the totality of documents among members of a cooperative work ensemble, or subset thereof, towards considering the perspective of the individual actor making sense of what is read. Let us elaborate. We will start by taking a look at a useful distinction, namely, that between *corpus* and *intertext*.

Intertext

We must be careful to avoid confusion between the *corpus* and the *intertext*. As mentioned above, the *intertext* is the meaning achieved by the actor by combining several texts from the corpus in accordance with the demands of a given situation. Intertext is an activity concept. In reading the individual document at hand the situated actor is attentive to the wordings, phrasings, illustrations, and categories that are (only) meaningful in unison with other texts. This intertext has loose and flexible limits, as it is partly a situational property, a modality of perception associated with the situation of the reader. In reading the individual document the actor is perceptible to the wordings, phrasings, illustrations that the document at hand will not suffice to explain. It is partly in creating the intertext between relevant texts (i.e. assessing what the other relevant texts are) that the actor displays his competences and skills as an accomplished actor in the building process.

Consider, for example, the foreman on the building site, reading an engineering plan for the layout of the deck elements (e.g. Fig. 2). Directing the mounting of these building elements requires the creation of an intertext, including the layout of the decks, the loading list and the spray-painted ID codes on the concrete building elements. These texts complement each other. Each text cannot stand alone. It is by virtue of the complementary intertext between these texts that they become useful in this situation. The layout speaks of the spatial placement of the uniquely identifiable building elements, the loading list reveals the order in which they will arrive onsite, and the spray-painted ID numbers on the concrete slabs afford the identification of the individual building elements. This intertext is part of what the foreman needs to create, in order to be able to direct the crew and to mount the building elements in the correct order and in a timely manner. In addition to this immediate intertext, a property of the work task, a larger intertext might be created, that also includes the time schedule for the construction work, as well as, building technique standards, safety standards and more. However, the economy of practice suggests that no more intertext is created than the immediate situation calls for. That is, the intertext need not be more complete, extensive or consistent than required by the practical demands of the situation. This general phenomenon relates to what Schutz (1970) refers to as 'the problem of relevance', and what Bourdieu (1992) has called the 'economy of logic'.

We may say that the intertext is a situational property. That is, related to a particular actor, performing a particular task, for a particular purpose, in a particular context. In contrast, the text corpus of the building process, merely, refers to a collection of texts. Note that realising a workable intertext, based on the corpus of written text pertinent to the situation, is *not* a given, rather it is an achievement on the part of the competent actor. Occasionally texts are misread, misaligned or misjudged or simply incoherent, according to criteria internal to the construction process. For example, for the construction purpose at hand, there may be a lack of correspondence on some aspects between the descriptions of the materials to be used, what is depicted on the architectural plans, and the descriptions of construction techniques called for. This is not uncommon.

Part of the competences of an accomplished actor in the building process is to be able to create intertext, achieve adequate coherence, based on the (imperfect) corpus for the purposes of the situation at hand. The actors are striving for usefulness or adequacy in relation to a particular situation or context. It is important to emphasis that when we are talking of intertext between documents central to the building process we are aware that these creations need not be more complete, extensive or consistent than required by the practical demands of the situation.

In sum, for the competent cooperative actor creating intertext is a practical endeavour, for practical purposes, with constrains and possibilities associated with the situation and the corpus at hand. No more logic or consistency across documents, than are required by the needs of the practice, are mobilized as the foreman creates the intertext between what he deems to be the corpus of relevant documents for the construction task at hand. The foreman created intertext between the plan for the layout of the deck, the loading list, and the ID numbers that are spray-painted onto concrete slabs. He did so, in order to 'know what to do next'. Creating intertext is a question of making intertextual relations between texts for a specific purpose while employing various types of intertextuality. Various types of intertextuality will be more closely reviewed, in what follows.

Intertextuality

There are, at least, three types of intertextuality at play in forming intertext, namely, the complementary type, the intratextual type, and the mediated type.

The complementary type of intertextuality is, perhaps, the most intuitively recognizable one of the three types, as it refers to how documents complement each other in order to make up the syntagm, i.e. the meaningful whole (Riffaterre 1980). As indicated above, in reading the individual document, the foreman is perceptible to the wordings, phrasings, illustrations that the document at hand will not suffice to explain. What to the layman reader of the document may appear as obscurities or incompleteness and even ungrammaticalities are, to the competent actor, traces left by the absent intertext, completeness to be completed elsewhere, by virtue of, for example, the complementary type of intertextuality.

As indicated, in reading a document, such as for example in Fig. 2, in the course of construction work the competent actors *complements* the document at hand with other relevant texts, hence, the complementary type of intertextuality. However, there are other types of intertextuality creating intertext between the various documents of the corpus as they are read in various circumstances and situations.

The intratextual type of intertextuality is, perhaps, less evident in our example above. The intratextual type refers to instances where a text is superimposed upon another text. Perhaps, the most clear example of this is to be found in building services engineering, where the plans for the building services shafts, ventilation, sanitation, and electrical wiring are superimposed upon each other and onto a plan of the building, in order to bring about a collective overview (see Fig. 5). This intratextual assembly is the pivotal point of several coordination meetings, where specialists responsible, respectively, for the ventilation, electrical installations, and sanitation meet and coordinate their respective tasks. One objective of these meetings is to ensure that there are no 'collisions' between the various building services and that they, in fact, will fit into the designated service shafts designed for the purpose.

In this manner, intratextual constructs may be very useful in the building process. We have now described two types of intertextuality, common to the building process. A third remains to be described.

Imagine a situation where establishing intertextuality between two texts requires, or is mediated by, the shadowy presence of a third text—this is the mediated type of intertextuality. In the building process the shadowy presence of laws, regulations and industry standards may play the mediating role of inducing a meaningful intertextual relationship between two texts. We may argue that, for instance, intertextuality between architectural plans, on the one hand, and a layout for a construction site, on the other hand, is mediated by the shadowy presence of several laws, regulations and ordinances. For example, during winter, the layout of the building site and the plan for what is to be built are mediated by the "Directions on Construction During Winter" published by The National Housing and Building Agency, as well as other regulations, such as for example DS 409, "DIF standard for safe construction". DS 410, "DIF standard for loads on structures". DS 411, "DIF standard for concrete structures", DS 482, "Execution of

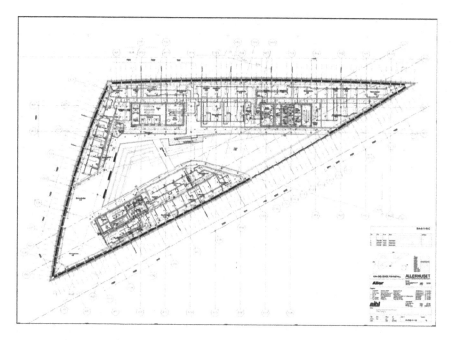

Fig. 5 This document was created by superimposing several plans for building services onto an architectural plan of a building under construction. Note that, this plan belongs to a project which is different from the one previously described

concrete structures". DS/EN 206-1 and EN 2426, "Concrete Technology". AT Announcement No. 25, "Protection of concrete against overturning during and after installation". BSR 2, "Building & Construction: Industry Guidance on installation of concrete". Precast Association: "Transport and installation of concrete".

These three distinctions should help check any tendency, perhaps all to common, to settle for unfocused notions of influence from text to text. Influence from text to text, as in inheritance, is best understood as a 'vertical' phenomenon often between texts of the same kind—think of an old version of a given text influencing the subsequent creation of a new version. In contrast, the creation of intertext by various techniques of intertextuality is best described as a 'lateral' phenomenon, in the sense that, there is simultaneity, a mutual solidarity between texts, so that in certain situations the text can function as an artefact by its engagement with other texts—each text contributing by its comparable otherness. It is diverse texts, rather than uniform ones, that allow for the creation of intertext, in our case.

Concluding Remarks

In this study we have found that an ensemble of documents used and produced in the building process, may form a *corpus* of written texts. On the basis of the corpus, or subsections hereof, the actors may create *intertext* between relevant (complementary) texts in a particular situation, for a particular purpose. The intertext of a particular situation can be constituted by several kinds of *intertextuality*, including the complementary type, the intratextual type, and the mediated type. In this manner the building process is (partly) organized through written text.

As noted, the study addresses the core CSCW challenge of characterizing how written artifacts party exert pressure on human action. It is (partly) at the movement of the creation of intertext that a corpus of texts imprints its norms on the cooperative actor. It is the movement where the (combined) meaning of the texts is produced and influence action. There is nothing mysterious about this. But we need to be able to account for this emergence of combined textual meaning in action. The concept of intertext allows us to pinpoint this moment. For example, recall how the foreman created intertext between the plan for the layout of the deck, the loading list, and the ID numbers that are spray-painted onto concrete slabs. He did so, in order to 'know what to do next'. Garfinkel (1967), points out that the question of "what to do next?", is the practical problem of organizational life par excellence.

Relatedly, the 'routine' of practice may, partly, stem from the systematic interweaving of text. At one level of abstraction practice within, for example, the building process, is contingent as lines of action vary from one instance to the next—tasks will have a different locations, durations, scope, and etc. Furthermore, the nature of the building-in-the-making will differ from one day to the next, as construction work progresses and the building changes. However, on another level of abstraction, these variations may be considered everyday or normal, and there is nothing ad hoc in the way they are handled. On the contrary, they are dealt with consistently, relying on a tested and tried corpus of text as the basis for the creation of intertext, according to the situation at hand. It is no surprise that the next instance of constructing a concrete deck (on another building) may follow the same modus operandi as we have already seen above, employing the same types of text (i.e. deck plan, loading list, and ID tags). The use of text may create regularity and routine across specific instances of action. The corpus of text or variations of it is repeated across situations and even building projects.

The term 'routine' as it is employed here, is not used in an effort to create a deterministic impression of the actors' actions in the building process. Of course, individual judgment and choice play significant roles. Practitioners must wield and apply a wide repertoire of skills and routines to work with widely varying circumstances. In light of this, we may suggest that practitioners in, for example, the building process do not 'standardise' the application of their routines so much as they standardise the 'toolkit' (e.g. texts), from which they draw. The particular concrete application of a toolkit (e.g. a corpus of text) requires an on-the-spot professional judgment, a capability that may be thought as essential in any situation with a measure of uncertainty. In the building process, judgment is a skill that is cultivated in education, training and apprenticeship (Christensen 2013).

While there are always actions that are not in accord with the norms of a given practice, the effects of norms inscribed in written artifacts such as forms, templates and guidelines is to nudge most activity towards a generally homogeneous set. More generally, the view of documents in cooperative work presented in this study shows the interplay between structure and agency, between written artifacts and human action. Of course there is individual judgement in relation to the use of the documents, but there is also a set of norms for their use, and not following the norm would be considered a 'mistake' something that may be excused in the novice but expected by the master practitioner (Williams 1999).

In regard to this papers place in the CSCW literature we may say that it is obvious that other studies have also focused on the interweaving of multiple text in cooperative work. As mentioned above, for example Schmidt and Wagner (2004) have coined the concept of *ordering systems*, Zhou et al. (2011) have worked with *assemblies*, and recently Christensen and Bjorn (2014) have introduced the notion of *documentscapes*. These are significant studies. One might ask: What is the value of yet another way of talking about texts and their interrelations?

First, the study explicitly address the interplay between structure and agency in work practice i.e. the case shows that the corpus of texts provides structure[4] to practice and the individual actors creation of intertext displays agency. Again, this echoes Strauss et al. (1997), specifically the analysis of the complex and contingent nature of practice. Underscoring the fact that practitioners must establish a connection between the formal nature of texts at work on the one hand and on the other hand the particular situation at hand. Second, the study opens up the possibility of explicitly designing and evaluating computer support for the creation of intertext by cooperative actors. Let us elaborate a little on the latter.

Briefly told computers have no situational awareness, at least not in terms of a sophisticated contextual understanding, they cannot create intertext proper. Recall that intertext is party a modality of perception, a situational property, associated with the situation of the reader (Riffaterre 1980). It is by no means given what constitutes relevant texts in a particular situation (Ellingsen and Monteiro 2003). Furthermore, it is by no means given how to define a situation in the process of creating intertext. We are fully attentive to the fact that some classes of computer technology are referred to in terms of 'context aware computing' or 'location based computing'. The literature is bursting with interesting contributions of this order (Bricon-Souf and Newman 2007). However, the kind of context awareness that for example sensors in computational devices can produce does not amount to the kind of complex assessment of situations that for example a trained building engineer can achieve.

In principle, then, computers cannot create intertext per se. That is, computers and their sensors are only able to produce 'thin descriptions' of a situation and consequently have no, for the purposes of creating intertext, useful situational awareness. Intertext is as mentioned a situational property and without the faculties to create a 'thick' situational understanding computational technology falls short of having the ability to create intertext.

---

[4]The corpus of text or variations of it is repeated across situations and even building projects.

Fortunately, this realization is not in vain or unproductive. It leaves us with the opportunity to clearly focus on the achievement of an orderly corpus of written text, by computational or other means, designed to support the actor's achievement of intertext by various types of intertextuality. The rationale being that the purpose of an orderly corpus, an ordering that computers may be part of, is (partly) to support the actor's creation of intertext by various types of intertextuality.

In terms of future workplace studies, the concepts of *corpus, intertext and intertextuality* may be employed to analyse the use of text in other cases. For example, if we leave the building process and change the domain to health care, and zoom in on the work of physicians in hospitals. One hypothesis could be that when physicians in a hospital write a patients discharge letter, they are creating intertext based on a corpus of written text, that includes the various parts of the patients record as well as the nurses' reports. The discharge letter is from this perspective the product of the physician's creation of intertext. This view may be pursued and empirically verified in future studies. At least that is an option now open by virtue of the concepts introduced in this study. The rationale for doing additional studies in other domains along the lines of this study would be to highlight and in turn inform the design of computer support for the creation of intertext.

Acknowledgments I am indebted to the people of MT Højgaard A/S and PHIL & Søn A/S for letting me take up so much of their time.

References

Bakhtin, M. M., & Volosinov, V. N. (1986). *Marxism and the philosophy of language.* Cambridge, MA: Harvard University Press.

Bardram, J., & Bossen, C. (2005). *A web of coordinative artefacts: Collaborative work in a hospital ward* (pp. 168–176). Sanible Island: GROUP.

Bourdieu, P. (1992). *The logic of practice.* Cambridge: Polity Press.

Bricon-Souf, N., & Newman, C. R. (2007). Context awareness in health care: A review. *International Journal of Medical Informatics, 76,* 2–12.

Cabitza, F., & Simone, C. (2007). "…and do it the usual way": Fostering awareness of work conventions in document-mediated collaboration. In *ECSCW* (pp. 119–138). Limerick, Ireland: Springer.

Christensen, L. R. (2013). *Coordinative practices in the building process: an ethnographic perspective.* London: Springer.

Christensen, L. (2014). Practices of stigmergy in the building process. *Computer Supported Cooperative Work (CSCW), 23,* 1–19.

Christensen, L. R., & Bjorn, P. (2014). Documentscape: Intertextuality, sequentiality, and autonomy at work. In *Proceedings of the 32nd Annual ACM Conference on Human Factors in Computing Systems* (pp. 2451–2460). Toronto, Ontario, Canada: ACM.

de Saussure, F. (1974). *Course in general linguistics.* London: Fontana.

Ellingsen, G., & Monteiro, E. (2003). Mechanisms for producing a working knowledge: Enacting, orchestrating and organizing. *Information and Organization, 13,* 203–229.

Garfinkel, H. (1967). *Studies in ethnomethodology.* New York: Englewood Cliffs.

Harper, R. (1998). *Inside The IMF: An ethnography of documents, technology and organizational action.* San Diego: Academic Press.

Harper, R. H. R. (2000). The organisation in ethnography—A discussion of ethnographic fieldwork programs in CSCW. *Computer Supported Cooperative Work, 9*, 239–264.

Hertzum, M. (1999). Six roles of documents in professionals' work. In *Sixth European Conference on Computer Supported Cooperative Work; Copenhagen, Denmark,* September 12–16, 1999 (pp. 41–60).

Kreiner, K. (1976). *The site organization—A study of social relationships on construction sites.* The Technical University of Denmark.

Kristeva, J. (1986). *The Kristeva reader.* Oxford: Blackwell.

Luff, P., Heath, C., & Greatbatch, D. (1992). Tasks-in-interaction: Paper and screen based documentation in collaborative activity. In *Proceedings of the Conference on Computer Supported Cooperative Work.* ACM.

Malone, T. (1983). How do people organize their desks? Implications for the design of office information systems. *ACM Transactioins on Information Systems, 1*, 99–112.

Riffaterre, M. (1980). Syllepsis. *Critical Inquiry, 6*, 625–638.

Sabbagh, K. (1989). *Skyscraper: The making of a building.* London: Macmillan.

Schmidt, K., & Wagner, I. (2004). Ordering systems: Coordinative practices and artifacts in architectural design and planning. *Computer Supported Cooperative Work (CSCW): The Journal of Collaborative Computing, 13*, 349–408.

Schmidt, K., Wagner, I., & Tolar, M. (2007). *Permutations of cooperative work practices: A study of two oncology clinics.* Sanibel Island, FL: GROUP. 2007.

Schutz, A. (1970). *Reflections on the problem of relevance.* New York: Pegasus.

Strauss, A. L., Fagerhaugh, S., Suczek, B., & Wiener, C. (1997). *Social organization of medical work.* London: Transaction Publishers.

Williams, M. (1999). *Wittgenstein, mind and meaning: Towards a social conception of mind.* London: Routledge.

Xiao, Y., Lasome, C., Moss, J., Mackenzie, C., & Faraj, S. (2001). Cognitive properties of a whiteboard: A case study in a trauma centre. In *Seventh European Conference on Computer Supported Cooperative work, Bonn, Germany, 2001* (pp. 259–278).

Zhou, X., Ackerman, M., & Zheng, K. (2011). CPOE workarounds, boundary objects, and assemblages. In *Proceedings of the SIGCHI Conference on Human Factors in Computing Systems* (pp. 3353–3362). Vancouver, Canada: ACM.

Analyzing Collaborative Reflection Support: A Content Analysis Approach

Michael Prilla, Alexander Nolte, Oliver Blunk, Dennis Liedtke and Bettina Renner

Abstract Collaborative reflection helps groups to learn from work experiences for future work. Although its potential has been recognized and initial work is available, insights on how tools support people in collaborative reflection at work are scarce. We present an approach to analyze collaborative reflection support based on content analysis and an initial study in which it was applied to four cases of using a tool for collaborative reflection. From this we derive design suggestions such as levels of support for different groups and support for the creation of results from collaborative reflection. Our work contributes to CSCW by showing how tools can foster collaborative reflection at work.

Introduction

Reflection is a process of going back to experiences, re-assessing them in the current context and learning from this for the future (Boud 1985). Outcomes of this process include new ideas for work, new perspectives on own experiences and changes in behavior. Reflection is a typical and desirable activity at work (Kolb 1984; Schön

M. Prilla (✉) · A. Nolte · O. Blunk · D. Liedtke
Ruhr-University of Bochum, Bochum, Germany
e-mail: Prilla@iaw.rub.de; prilla@iaw.ruhr-uni-bochum.de

A. Nolte
e-mail: Nolte@iaw.rub.de

O. Blunk
e-mail: Blunk@iaw.rub.de

D. Liedtke
e-mail: Liedtke@iaw.rub.de

B. Renner
Leibniz-Institut für Wissensmedien, Tübingen, Germany
e-mail: b.renner@iwm-tuebingen.de

© Springer International Publishing Switzerland 2015
N. Boulus-Rødje et al. (eds.), *ECSCW 2015: Proceedings of the 14th European Conference on Computer Supported Cooperative Work, 19–23 September 2015, Oslo, Norway*, DOI 10.1007/978-3-319-20499-4_7

1983), e.g. when workers think about how to improve individual or common work, and when peers help each other to understand and change practice. It has been described as a necessary attitude for nowadays' professional practice (Schön 1983) and as a *mind-set* to be cultivated and spread in organizations (Reynolds 1999). While this takes a look at reflection as an individual, cognitive activity a lot of reflection happens in groups and has implications on cooperative work (Boud et al. 2006; Daudelin 1996; Hoyrup 2004; Prilla et al. 2013). Despite this potential there is little work available on tool support for such **collaborative reflection** at work (see below).

In this paper we describe a research approach to analyze the content of reflection threads in a tool used to support collaborative reflection. The contribution stemming from this is the analysis of a study with 48 participants in four cases, in which we analyzed *how* the tool was used, *what* it was used for, and how support for collaborative reflection *leads to reflection results*. For the study we developed a content coding scheme for (collaborative) reflection content, which helped answering these questions. From the analysis we derive implications for the design and improvement of collaborative reflection support.

Collaborative Reflection Support: State of the Art

The potential of supporting collaborative reflection has been recognized recently (Baumer et al. 2014; Marcu et al. 2014; Porges et al. 2014), but the term is interpreted differently: While it is used for processes of data pooling and decision making (Marcu et al. 2014), most work (including this paper) understands it as collaboratively reviewing experiences and learning from them (Baumer et al. 2014; Boud 1985). Despite these differences, it is common understanding that collaborative reflection needs communication to share experiences, critically discuss them and draw conclusions together (Daudelin 1996; Scott 2010), especially if there is no time or possibility to meet in person. Therefore, in the same way as articulations provide "a set of activities required to manage the distributed nature of cooperative work" (Bannon and Schmidt 1992), collaborative reflection needs support for the articulation of experiences, of perspectives on these experiences and of ideas for change.

Supporting collaborative reflection at work faces different **challenges**: Time pressure makes it hard to step back and reflect (e.g., in meetings), and reflection is a secondary process at work, which is not implied by most work tasks. To cope with this, there is a need to establish reflective practices such as regular exchange of experiences (Vince 2002) and a need for facilitation (Daudelin 1996). Questions by a facilitator in face-to-face settings help facilitate collaborative reflection and create results from it (ibid). This may also help to overcome differences in people's ability to articulate problems and assumptions (Bjørn and Boulus 2011) or to address others' contributions (de Groot et al. 2013). Whether and how it translates into tools for collaborative reflection remains open.

As reflection depends on memories of experiences, which may be incomplete or get blurred over time, and on the continuation of reflection across single occurrences, **tools** can support it by providing data to reconstruct and sustain experiences or by reminding people periodically to reflect (Isaacs et al. 2013; Scott 2010). Tools investigated for reflection include learning portfolios or journals (Scott 2010), which contain write-ups of learning, and images captured during a certain event and later used for reflection (Fleck and Fitzpatrick 2010). Such tools capture data enabling and supporting reflection and help to diminish memory loss or deviations in perceptions over time, but they usually do not support reflection explicitly but expect it to happen, e.g. in group meetings. Another area of individual reflection support is **prompting** users to reflect (Davis 2000). In approaches as reported by Isaacs et al. (2013) tools prompt users to reassess experiences regularly, which helps them to stay aware of reflection, to structure the re-assessment and to gain insights from reflection over time.

Despite its value existing work focuses on individual reflection or education settings, in which reflection can be made an integral part of learning. Insights on how support for collaborative reflection creates impact at work are missing.

Related Streams of Work

There are certain overlaps of collaborative reflection with existing concepts, but it also differs from them in decisive aspects: Sensemaking and collective mind (Crowston and Kammerer 1998; Weick 1995) need people to collaboratively reach an understanding of past events, but sensemaking processes described in the literature usually do not have a clear focus on deriving insights for future work, which is a necessary step in reflection (to lead to change). Group decision support systems (Dennis et al. 1988) are about exchanging perspectives and arriving at decisions in teams, but focus on gathering data to reach a decision rather than creating new or alternative solutions (Power and Sharda 2009). Approaches of collaborative problem solving (Roschelle and Teasley 1995) use joint spaces to solve problems, but have to deal with the "shared information bias" (Baker 2010), in which information known to all collaborators from the start tends to be followed more than information held by individuals. Collaborative reflection, in contrast, needs experience exchange and critical discourse among all participants.

Analyzing Collaborative Reflection Content

Articulation support was described above as a central need for collaborative reflection: Reflection participants need to make their experiences, understanding and ideas explicit in order to reflect together. Therefore, in our work we used *content analysis* as a tool to analyze the articulations made by reflection participants in order to understand the course and output of collaborative reflection in tools. This, in turn, can create insights for the analysis and design for collaborative reflection support.

Content analysis is key to understanding how tools support communication processes (Lockhorst et al. 2003; Suchman 1987), and it enables a better understanding of them (Wever et al. 2006). It is a common method of understanding group communication in CSCW (e.g., Newman et al. 1995; Prinz and Zaman 2005) and regarded as the preferred method of analyzing communication if manual coding is possible (Introne and Drescher 2013). Differences in content, however, can only be understood by looking at further information such as the background and context of users and constraints of usage in the cases. Therefore, we complement content analysis by feedback from users, which is described to further extent in Prilla (2014) and Prilla and Renner (2014). Our analysis also cannot be used to make statements about reflection in general, as reflection also happens in face-to-face interaction among users of tools. Therefore we use our approach to explain how and why the app was used in the different cases and what led to reflection results being described in the app.

What Is Collaborative Reflection? A Model

Analyzing content needs a model of what is analyzed, that is, a "theoretical base and operational translation" (Wever et al. 2006) of collaborative reflection. De Groot et al. (2013) provide such an operationalization differentiating describing problems, critical reasoning and critical reflection dialogues. Moon (1999) proposes a nine-stage model including the expression of experiences, the clarification of issues in the experience, reviewing experiences and emotions together and transforming ideas into possible actions. Fleck and Fitzpatrick (2010) describe six activities in reflection such as returning to experiences, providing, sharing thoughts, offering alternative interpretations and the intent to create results. Others add steps such as inquiry to identify new practices (Raelin 2002), asking for feedback (van Woerkom and Croon 2008) and detecting patterns from experiences (Boud 1985). From these approaches we distilled core steps of collaborative reflection and created an initial model of it. The model contains **three levels** of activities and corresponding articulations in reflection (Table 1).

Table 1 Levels of (articulations in) reflection

Level	Description
1	**Describing experiences**, emotions and rationales for action (Boud 1985; Fleck and Fitzpatrick 2010; Moon 1999; Tigelaar et al. 2008)
2a	**Referring to experiences** by commenting and engaging in reflection (de Groot et al. 2013; Fleck and Fitzpatrick 2010; Raelin 2002; Tigelaar et al. 2008; Zhu 1996)
2b	**Referring to experiences** and triggering interaction by asking for information or feedback (van Woerkom and Croon 2008; Zhu 1996)
3	**Creating results** from reflection through drawing from experiences and transforming insights into practice (Boud 1985; de Groot et al. 2013; Fleck and Fitzpatrick 2010; Moon 1999)

Besides differentiating levels of reflection and thus allowing for a characterization of progress in reflection processes this model helps to recognize successful reflection: Along our understanding of reflection we regard reflection as successful when the process reaches level 3, that is, if it creates results.

A Content Scheme for Collaborative Reflection

When we started our work there was no scheme for analyzing collaborative reflection content available: Literature contains schemes for the analysis of computer-mediated communication (Lockhorst et al. 2003; Wever et al. 2006), and there is work describing reflection activities (see above). Based on literature analysis and the model presented above, we created a scheme for the analysis of collaborative reflection (Table 2). It includes 15 codes related to the levels shown in Table 1. There is **no sequence of codes implied** in the scheme: For example, users may have mentioned learning (code 9) without any traces of codes 6, 7 or 8.

Coding Level 1: Articulations Used to Describe Experiences

The **description and sharing of experiences**, which forms the basis for reflection, is represented by mentioning issues or good practices (code 1 in Table 2). When shared a description may trigger reflection (Tigelaar et al. 2008) and enable users to return to the experience reported (Boud 1985; Fleck and Fitzpatrick 2010). If descriptions include **emotions** (code 2), this may influence collaborative reflection positively, as others are more likely to react (Ellsworth and Scherer 2003). Concerning emotions we differentiate between emotions of the author of a report (code 2a) and reported emotions of others (2b) to distinguish between personal feelings during the event and contextual description. Reports may also include **initial interpretations of actions** (code 3) by the author of the report, which can help others to understand the experience better (Raelin 2002). A statement from one of the cases analyzed below includes codes 1, 2a and 3:

> So it's been quite a tough week, one of those where I haven't wanted to talk to anyone or immerse myself in any meetings. Sadly, I've had a few meetings! But I did make a couple of mistakes which I feel really bad about. [codes 1, 2a and 3]
>
> Has anyone else been in such a situation? How did you overcome your mental slump? [code Q2]

From our literature analysis we assume that both **emotions and initial interpretations in experience reports positively influence reflection** by improving the understandability of the report and triggering others to refer to it.

Table 2 Coding scheme for the analysis of content in (collaborative) reflection support tools

Code	Description and example(s) from the study	Level
1	**Mentioning issues or good practice** based on experiences, e.g. "I had a rude person on the phone. She […]"	1
2a	**Mentioning own emotions** in an experience (e.g., "Was not fun man" or "this made me angry")	1
2b	**Mentioning emotions of others** in an experience (e.g., "[resident] said he is unhappy living here")	1
3	**Interpretation or justification** of actions and situations (e.g., "As far as I am aware I had done nothing to deserve this"	1
4	**Linking an experience to other experiences** (e.g., "I made a similar experience", "X told me he was through this before …")	2a
5	**Linking an experience to knowledge, rules or values** (e.g., "never accept blame for another's mistake")	2a
6a	Responding to interpretation of the action by *challenging* **existing interpretation(s)/suggestions or adding perspectives** (e.g., "Hmmm. Is this really different from …"	2a
6b	Responding to interpretation of the action by *supporting* **interpretation(s) and suggestions** (e.g., "Agreed!")	2a
7	**Giving advice** without a reason or reference to experiences (e.g., "Never accept blame for another's mistake")	3
8	**Proposing solutions** with a reason and/or link to experiences, without suggesting how to set them in practice, including a reason (e.g., "from my experience a list of FAQ's is useful")	3
9a	Insights from reflection **as single-loop learning: Different or better understanding of experiences**. Expressed by reporting insights ("I realised that I shouldn't have …")	3
9b	Insights from reflection **as double-loop learning: Generalising from experiences**. Expressed by patterns or roots of a problem (e.g., "The best way I found to deal with this is …")	3
10	**Drawing conclusions and implications from reflection** by suggesting to apply new practice or reporting on changes *done or planned* (e.g., "Will definitely try and do … in the future")	3
Q1	**Questions for *information*** on the experience (e.g., "what do you mean by …" or "what happened afterwards")	2b
Q2	**Questions triggering discussions**, asking for an *interpretation* of a situation, for opinions or proposals (e.g., "what do people think about …")	2b

Coding Level 2: Articulations Used to Refer to Others

Referring to each other and relating to experiences shows interest in other content, which is important for the creation of results from reflection (Daudelin 1996; de Groot et al. 2013; Fleck and Fitzpatrick 2010). Exchanging experience enables participants to learn from each other. Therefore, contributions to a thread in which **experiences are linked to others** (code 4) are crucial (de Groot et al. 2013; van Woerkom and Croon 2008). Similarly, one may **link knowledge, data, values and other sources** (which do not stem from or explicitly refer to experiences) to experiences (code 5; Boud 1985). While these ways of referring to experience are similar (Daudelin 1996), linking experiences to each other constitutes reflection processes while linking experiences to existing knowledge often refers to existing solutions (Zhu 1996). We can therefore assume that **linking experiences to each other has a stronger effect on reflection results than linking experiences to knowledge**. Two comments on the same report from one of our cases show the differences between these ways to refer to each other:

A: *I have been in the same situation. I usually just tell my manager with an apology and reason and then ask if she wants to re-arrange it.* [code 4]

B: *I would [...] suggest staying late and working harder.* [code 5]

Referring to each other includes **challenging** or **supporting interpretations of actions** (Fleck and Fitzpatrick 2010; Raelin 2002; Tigelaar et al. 2008) as covered by codes 6a and 6b (see an example for 6b in the section below): We thus assume that the **occurrence of codes 6a and 6b positively influence the occurrence of results**. Questions play a special role in reflection, as they trigger engagement. Along with Zhu (1996) we differentiate questions for additional information (code Q1) from questions to provoke discussion (code Q2, see the first example above). The former is supposed to increase activity in reflection, while the latter should improve the quality of outcomes (Daudelin 1996; Zhu 1996). We thus assume that **questions have a positive impact on the occurrence of results**.

Coding Level 3: Articulations Used to Describe Results from Reflection

Learning from reflection means thinking towards solutions. This step was described above as a differentiator to similar concepts. Learning may start with **solution proposals** (Daudelin 1996; code 8). We differentiate **advice** (code 7) from solution proposals, understanding it as proposals given without explanation or relation to experiences, and therefore as **support that does not stem explicitly or directly from reflection**. Solutions proposals based on experiences are often more valuable (Hatton and Smith 1995), and therefore we assume that **solution proposals have more impact on results from reflection than advice**.

Results from reflection also include **insights** (learning) and **change**. Reflection participants may either gain a better **understanding of (single) experiences** (code 9a), which is related to single-loop learning (Argyris and Schön 1978), or they may draw **more general conclusions** on the reasons behind problems (code 9b), which is related (Greenwood 1998) to double-loop learning (Argyris and Schön 1978). **Deriving change** (code 10) is the final and constructive step of reflection (Daudelin 1996; Moon 1999). Given their direct relation to reflection in the analysis we use the **occurrence of any code 8, 9 or 10 as an indicator for results from the reflection process**. The example below shows a statement from one of our cases with learning (code 9b) and change (code 10) mentioned.

I do agree [code 6b] *that the less you want to communicate, the harder you'll likely find it to maintain high standards.* [code 9b] *Will definitely try and be resilient if/when this happens.* [code 10]

Analyzing Collaborative Reflection in Practice

We applied the coding scheme described above to four cases (see Table 3) in which workers used the "TalkReflect App", which was designed to support collaborative reflection, in different settings. The app supports reflection activities such as the documentation of experiences, sharing these experiences and collaboratively reflecting on them. It includes features proposed by related work:

- **Creating experience reports**: Users can document experiences and personal reflections. Figure 1 (left) shows an experience report (no. 1) with a personal reflection (2). Reporting on experiences may trigger reflection (Scott 2010).
- **Sharing experience reports**: Private to users initially, experience reports can be shared. Once they are shared, other users can find and mark them as favorites [Figs. 1(4, 5)]. Sharing experiences with others can be regarded as asking for feedback or opinions (cf. van Woerkom and Croon 2008).
- **Commenting on experience reports**: Users can comment on shared experience reports (Fig. 1 left, 3) to describe similar experiences, suggestions or other reflective content.

Table 3 Studies conducted with the TalkReflect App

Case	Interns	Service	Care	Hospital
Users	18	12	9	9
Days	51	80	50	42
Reports[a]	24	45	15	25
Comments	47	65	25	39
Time	Sep–Oct 2013	Aug–Oct 2013	Aug–Sep 2013	July–Aug 2013

[a]Total amount of reports and comments, later analysis is based on a selection of threads (see results section)

Fig. 1 The TalkReflect App with an experience report (*left*) and shared reports (*right*)

Besides the core features the app includes additional features such as feedback (e.g. via a 'like' button for helpful comments) and it allows for creating custom groups for sharing reports with certain co-workers (e.g., omitting superiors).

In all cases daily interaction with others (patients, residents, relatives, clients, citizens or colleagues) was found to be demanding by the participants and their superiors. The app was used to improve this. The study was conducted in the second half of 2013. Table 3 provides an overview of the cases, which shows that group sizes and usage periods varied. In all cases the app was moderately used (concerning the number of reports and comments created), which shows that there was a demand for collaborative reflection support in all cases.

Two of the cases took place in a public administration unit of a large city in the UK. The first case included interns working in different departments of the organization (referred to as the **interns** case in this paper). The organization wanted them to learn how to interact with colleagues and members of the public professionally, and to take away learnings for future work. The second case involved two departments providing similar services to the public (referred to as the **service** case). These departments were to be merged, which involved processes and physical workplaces. The aim here was to reflect on practices with the respective other department to support the merging process.

The third case was conducted in a British dementia care home (referred to as the **care** case). Staff used the app to improve their skills in conversations with residents and relatives. These skills are crucial for the wellbeing of residents as well as the reputation of the care home. Case four was done with physicians of a German hospital (referred to as the **hospital** case). The physicians and their superiors felt they needed to improve their abilities to conduct conversations with relatives. This puts physicians in an emotionally demanding situation, and the physicians felt they were not prepared well for this in medical school.

We chose these different cases to include diversity in the study, thus avoiding effects specific for certain domains or workplaces. Variations included the education of the participants, as physicians and interns held university degrees, while care staff is usually recruited from lower educational levels, and different hierarchies among participants, ranging from strict hierarchies in the hospital to no hierarchy among the interns. In addition, there were differences in the involvement of superiors: In the hospital and service cases a superior was very active and in the care and interns cases no superior was involved in using the app.

Methodology and Course of the Studies

All studies were done in a similar fashion. In the beginning the TalkReflect App was introduced to the participants by walking them through examples of reflection with the app and by letting them try/test it. It was then discussed how the app could be used in daily work, and how long the usage period would last. After that the studies were run without further intervention. By the end of the usage period the researchers collected feedback from the participants in group interviews, in which they were asked about their perception of using the app.

Results: Analyzing Reflection in the TalkReflect App

Two coders independently applied the scheme to the content created in the TalkReflect App. Before coding, we removed experience reports from the dataset that were not shared with others or not commented on by others than the original author in order to analyze collaborative reflection only. After coding we removed all threads without reflective content (e.g. no explicit relations to experiences). For example, we removed a thread in which participants discussed dinner dates. This created a set of 65 threads (see Table 4). Coding was done in a rigid way to ensure that only reflective contributions were coded. For example, even if a comment sounded like it related to experiences (e.g., "this should be done another way") it was only coded as linking experiences to each other (code 4 in Table 2) if an explicit reference (e.g., a key phrase like "in my experience") was present.

After coding, the coders compared their results, discussed differences to ensure they had used the coding scheme in a similar fashion, and adapted their coding if necessary. This procedure resulted in a total of 689 codes (291 and 298 codes) with an average for Krippendorff's Alpha of 0.91. To even increase the quality of the final dataset we only included the intersection of codes from both coders.

What Happened Inside the App? Results of Coding

The distribution of codes from the four studies is shown in Table 4. To show the differences in the proportions of codes applied to threads from the different cases, high and low values for each code are highlighted in the table. In addition, to analyze whether the proportions of codes differ significantly between cases we conducted $\chi 2$-tests and (where the prerequisites for a $\chi 2$-test were not met) Exact Fisher Tests. In addition Table 4 includes combined variables of codes 8, 9 and 10 to show differences between the cases.

Table 4 shows that the interns and service cases have higher values for levels 2 and 3 of the coding scheme (codes 4–10, Q1/2) than the care and hospital cases. While the difference is moderate for some codes, for example the value of the combined variable of codes 8, 9 and 10 (summarizing all results from reflection) is about twice as high in the interns and service cases than in the other two. The care case however shows a much higher amount of codes 2b (emotions of others) and 3 (initial interpretation of experiences) compared to the other cases.

What the App Was Used for: Differences Between the Groups

The differences of code proportions (Table 4) suggest that the participants used the TalkReflect App for different purposes and to a different extent.

In the **care** case the app was mainly used to document and share experiences, while figures for most codes on levels 2 and 3 are low. Emotions and initial interpretations

Table 4 Percentage of codes applied to threads from the cases (left) and groups (right), including combined codes for (8), 9 and 10

Code	Level	Interns	Service	Care	Hosp.	G1: Int. & Serv.	G2: Care & Hosp.
Threads		17	20	10	18	37	28
1	1	100%	95%	100%	100%	97%	100%
2a	1	35%	25%	20%	17%	30%	18%
2b^{EF}	1	6%	10%	80%	39%	8%^{CHI}	54%^{CHI}
3	1	29%	30%	70%	28%	30%	43%
4^{CHI}	2a	65%	20%	40%	22%	41%	29%
5	2a	41%	20%	0%	17%	30%	11%
6a	2a	0%	0%	0%	6%	0%	4%
6b	2a	29%	40%	20%	33%	35%	29%
7	3	59%	70%	20%	67%	65%	50%
8	3	41%	45%	10%	17%	43%^{CHI}	14%^{CHI}
9a	3	12%	10%	20%	0%	11%	7%
9b	3	35%	10%	0%	11%	22%	7%
10	3	12%	15%	10%	6%	14%	7%
8 9 10^{CHI}	3	71%	55%	30%	28%	62%^{CHI}	29%^{CHI}
9 10	3	47%	30%	30%	11%	38%	18%
Q1^{EF}	2b	41%	20%	10%	0%	30%^{CHI}	4%^{CHI}
Q2^{CHI}	2b	59%	65%	10%	6%	62%^{CHI}	7%^{CHI}

Black cells highlight high values, cells in light grey low values. Differences of the proportions of codes marked by *CHI* are significant ($p < 0.05$) with a $\chi 2$-test and differences marked by *EF* are significant ($p < 0.05$) with an exact fisher test

may have occurred often because dementia care is an emotionally demanding job, in which it is very hard to understand the behavior of people being cared for. A typical example of a report reads "*BB 21* [anonymous code for the resident] *said he is unhappy living here, he wants to leave and live on his own*". While in some threads experiences were related to others (40 %) the app was thus mainly used to **document and share** experiences and related emotions, but rarely for reflection on shared experiences.

The **hospital** case shows low values for follow-up activities such as referring to experiences and results of the reflection process. There is an exception for advice. An example for this can be found in one participant stating "*If you get blamed you can also offer a conversation with a senior physician to the relatives*" after another user had described a difficult experience with relatives of a patient. Most of advice given (8 of 12 occurrences of code 7) stems from the same user and therefore we conclude that results documented in the app mainly stem from this user giving advice (rather than from reflection of these cases). This conclusion is backed up by feedback from participants (see below).

The **interns** and **service** cases show higher values for codes 4–10 and Q1/2. This indicates higher activity on levels 2 and 3 in our reflection model, and especially higher interest in shared experiences and comments (indicated by asking questions). There are differences among the cases: the interns case shows more occurrences of codes 4 and 5 (relating experiences or knowledge to shared experience) as well as more results on the level of double-loop learning (code 9b). Despite these differences we can conclude in these cases the app was used on all three levels of our reflection model in both cases, and that these cases created significantly more results from reflection than the other two cases ($\chi 2 = 8.117$, $p < 0.05$ for codes 8, 9, 10; similar for codes 2a and Q1/2, see Table 4).

The differences among the cases led us to the creation of two groups: Group 1 (G1 in Table 4) consists of the interns and service cases, which used the app on all levels of the model in Table 1, and G2 contains the care and hospital cases, who mostly used the app on level 1 and (partly) level 2. Table 4 shows that the coding values between the groups differ considerably for levels 2b and 3 ($\chi 2 = 7.2$, $p < 0.01$ for codes 8, 9, 10; $\chi 2 = 20.4$, $p \leq 0.01$ for Q2). In our analysis we use the differentiation between the groups to identify which types of contributions supported reflection in the app: Focusing our analysis to G1 means focusing on those threads from the cases in which the app was used on all levels of reflection.

How App Usage Was Influenced: Context Factors and Explanations

The differences in the distribution of codes allow us to identify cases in which the app was used for all levels of reflection and thus to analyze the impact of certain articulations as described above, but do not explain why the interns and service cases differed from the care and hospital cases. Feedback given by participants in the interviews, which is described and discussed in Prilla (2014) as well as Prilla and Renner (2014) helps to explain these differences. From the feedback we can identify different constraints on using the app in the different cases: In the interns and care cases staff used the app in a self-directed way, while in the service and hospital cases we were told that one participant (a manager and a senior physician) facilitated the discussion. In the service case the manager was very active, providing topics, commenting on statements and asking questions. This caused high activity in the app. In the hospital case physicians told us that the senior physician provided advice (code 7) for many reports after a short period of time, which prevented some physicians to create further comments (as advice from a senior is not questioned in this hospital). Opportunities for face-to-face communication also differed: Care home and hospital staff worked on the same floor, the interns worked in different departments and in the service departments were located in different buildings. Some physicians told us that they had often already known experiences reported in the tool, and care staff mentioned that it was easier to discuss face-to-face than in the tool. **This difference may be the main reason for the differences in usage between G1 and G2**, as the value added by the app was lower for G2 than for the interns and service cases.

What Leads to Reflection Results: An Exploratory Analysis

The coding scheme shown in Table 2 was created with the underlying assumption that all types of articulations represented in the scheme are of (equal) importance to reflection. As can be seen from Table 4 the codes are not evenly distributed and there are differences between the cases, which suggests that in our cases different types of articulations had different impact.

In an exploratory analysis we investigated the impact of these articulations. For this we used correlation analysis to find possible dependencies between codes, and $\chi 2$-tests to determine differences in the proportions of codes. While we investigated relations between all codes we had a particular look at G1 and the interns and service cases to focus on impact on levels 2b and 3 of our model.

We found several moderate correlations between codes 2a (mentioning own emotions), 4 (linking own experiences to shared experience report) and 5 (linking knowledge to shared experience reports) to the combined variable of codes 8, 9 and 10 as well as some strong correlations between code 4 and code 9_10 (Table 5). These correlations can be found for all threads, for threads of G1 and for threads of the service case. This suggests that codes 2a, 4 and 5 may have had an effect on results from the reflection process. Cross tables and corresponding $\chi 2$-tests show similar results: If we separate the threads by the combined variables of codes 8, 9 and 10 we can find significant differences in the proportions of codes 2a, 4 and 5 (see Table 6), again with strongest effects for code 4. This supports the potential effect of the articulations depicted by the codes on results from the reflection process. There are only a few other correlations among codes and no

Table 5 Selected correlations between codes

All threads			G1			Service		
Codes	R	p	Codes	R	p	Codes	R	p
2a/4	0.324	<0.01	2a/4	0.426	<0.01	2a/4	0.577	<0.01
2a/9_10	0.339	<0.01	2a/10	0.435	<0.01	4/9a	0.667	<0.01
4/9_10	0.515	<0.01	4/9a	0.422	<0.01	4/9_10	**0.764**	<0.01
5/9_10	0.322	<0.01	4/9_10	**0.718**	<0.01			

Bold figures depict strong correlations

Table 6 Cross tabs for combined variables of codes 8, 9, 10 as categories

All threads				G1			
Category	Code	$\chi 2$	p	Category	Code	$\chi 2$	p
8_9_10	2a	3.8	<0.05				
8_9_10	4	6.8	<0.01	8_9_10	4	10.4	<0.01
8_9_10	5	6.8	<0.01	8_9_10	5	5.5	<0.05
9_10	2a	7.5	<0.01	9_10	2a	4.4	<0.05
9_10	4	17.2	<0.01	9_10	4	19.1	<0.01
9_10	5	6.7	<0.05	9_10	5	4.4	<0.05

Table 7 Regression analysis for threads from G1, using the combined variables of codes (8), 9, 10 as dependent variables

Dependent variable: 8_9_10				Dependent variable: 9_10			
Model	R^2	F	Sig.	Model	R^2	F	Sig.
2a	0.069	2.6	<0.05	2a	0.12	4.8	<0.05
2a, 4	0.283	6.7	<0.01	2a, 4	0.517	18.2	<0.01
2a, 4, 5	0.296	4.6	<0.01	2a, 4, 5	0.52	11.9	<0.01
2a, 4, 5, Q2	0.324	3.8	<0.01	2a, 4, 5, Q2	0.55	9.8	<0.01

other significant differences in the proportion of codes than shown in Table 6. Therefore we focused further analysis on codes 2a, 4 and 5, as they are likely to have impact on results of reflection.

We used linear regression to determine the impact of codes 2a, 4 and 5 on the combined variable of codes (8), 9 and 10, that is, to which extent a certain code can explain the variance of these variables. An analysis of all threads revealed only minor explanation of variance. Looking at G1 and G2 separately we reached considerable results for G1. The regression models are shown in Table 7.

Table 7 shows that code 4 (linking own experiences to shared experiences) has the strongest influence in the model, explaining 21 % of the variance of the variable 8_9_10 and 40 % of the variance of the variable 9_10. By removing code 2a, which is moderately correlated to code 4 within threads of G1($r = 0.426$, $p \leq 0.01$), from the model the impact of code 4 even rises ($R^2 = 0.282$, $F = 13.7$, Sig. ≤ 0.01 for codes 8, 9, 10; $R^2 = 0.515$, $F = 37.2$, Sig. ≤ 0.01 for codes 9, 10). This shows that the occurrence of code 4 has had an effect on the occurrence of results such as (proposals), learning and change in the threads of G1.

The other codes for articulations with potential impact on the results of the reflection process in cases G1 have moderate to literally no explanatory value. Code 2a (own emotions) explains 7 % of the variance in variable 8_9_10 and 12 % of the variance in variable 9_10, which suggests that emotions can have a slight impact on the occurrence of results. As code 2a is correlated to code 4, it is also likely that it had an influence on the occurrence of code 4 rather than on results from the reflection process.

Code 5 does not add much to the regression model and therefore has no considerable impact on the occurrence of results from reflection. This emphasizes the difference between collaborative reflection and other conversations on past experiences by showing that the decisive difference between them actually created a difference in the impact on results in G1.

The analysis also shows that other types of articulations such as emotions of others (code 2b), initial interpretations (code 3) and supporting or challenging assumptions (codes 6a/b) did not have an impact on results from reflection. There is also no considerable impact of solution proposals (code 8) to results. This does not mean that these types of articulations do not support reflection and learning from it at all: there may be influences, which just did not become obvious in our studies. Furthermore, some codes like 2b (for G1) and 6a were rarely used and may therefore not have shown impact in our data.

Also the role of questions remains unclear from this analysis. Despite being seemingly obvious from the (significant) difference in the proportions of codes Q1 and Q2 between the groups shown in Table 4, there is no significant correlation for them, and the regression model shows negligible explanatory value of Q2 (and Q1, which is not shown in the table).

Discussion: Implications for the Design of Collaborative Reflection Support

The results of our analysis provide insights for tool support of collaborative reflection, which we summarize in two themes. First, they help us to differentiate between levels of support for different kinds of groups and constraints. Second, they provide insights on how to guide collaborative reflection processes in terms of facilitating communication.

Tailoring Support for Groups: Levels and Scale of Support

The participants in the interns and service cases used the app for all levels of our model, and the participants of the care and hospital cases mostly stuck to level 1. Together with the feedback given by the participants described above, this led us to the creation of suggestions for the design of support for different groups. We suggest three levels of support:

- **Support level 1**: The care and hospital cases can be differentiated from the other cases in that the participants formed a co-located group in which members interacted frequently as part of their jobs. In such groups face-to-face interaction is the preferred means of communication. Therefore, support for collaborative reflection in these groups can focus on enabling people to **write down, share and sustain experiences**, leaving reflective communication to face-to-face situations. Tools may also remind users of existing experience reports, show them relevant experiences to foster face-to-face reflection or remind them to write down and share results from reflection.
- **Support level 2**: In the hospital case most activities following sharing experiences were focused on giving advice. This suggests that even in co-located situations reflection tools provide meaningful support by **sharing experiences, getting feedback on them and sustaining the feedback**. A tool may route experience reports to experienced users in order to have them comment on the experience. The terminating effect of advice in the hospital case (see above) suggests that there is a need to guide users of such tools away from giving advice (7) to providing solution proposals (8).

- **Support level 3**: The service and interns cases were conducted in a (partly) remote setting that made frequent face-to-face communication difficult. The TalkReflect App allowed the participants to share and discuss their experiences, thus adding extra value by providing an additional communication channel. In such contexts tool support **offers means for experience exchange and discussion as part of collaborative reflection and may thereby lead to documentation and sustainment of results from reflection**. This, however, either needs intrinsically motivated participants (interns case) or support by facilitation (the manager in the service case) to succeed.

The proposed support levels can provide a framework for further work. In particular, they may help to create appropriate collaborative reflection tool designs by analyzing group characteristics such as co-location, communication preferences and the need to get and sustain feedback **upfront**. In our further work the application and evaluation of these levels in additional cases of collaborative reflection will play a major role.

In addition, the levels point to design issues of scope and scale for collaborative reflection support. Support for levels 1 and 2 is appropriate for small, co-located groups, but it might not always be the best support option overall. For example, physicians in the hospital case may have benefitted from exchanging experiences in talking to relatives with colleagues outside their ward (e.g., from a different hospital). This upscaling of support adds value to tools like the TalkReflect app and makes support level 3 applicable to co-located groups like in the hospital case. Therefore, besides asking how a particular group can be supported in collaborative reflection we should ask for the most appropriate scale in order to provide adequate support for collaborative reflection.

Guiding Collaborative Reflection: Fostering Helpful Articulations

Our analysis reveals that articulations such as emotions, linking experiences to each other, linking knowledge to experiences and asking questions co-occur with results documented from reflection processes. It also shows that in our cases the only considerable impact on results among these articulations can be shown for linking experiences to each other. This **supports** our assumption that linking experiences has a larger impact on reflection results than linking knowledge, but **speaks against** assumptions made for emotions, questions and other articulations.

Concerning the **positive impact of linking experiences to each other**, we can conclude that reflection support tools should facilitate this actively. This may be done by making users aware of relevant content (i.e. content similar to theirs) or by prompting users to share similar experiences through questions (e.g., "Have you been in a similar situation? What did you do?"). **Linking knowledge to experiences did not have an impact** on results but is similar to linking experiences in its intention. Tools may thus provide a frame for users by prompting them to link their statements to experiences rather than linking them to knowledge or not mentioning a link to experiences. Concerning the support levels described above, this may also be key in turning a situation in which mostly advice (code 7) is given to one in which solution proposals (code 8) are provided.

For (own) **emotions and questions** we did not find considerable impact on reflection results. However, this does not mean that they are not supportive in collaborative reflection. Especially given the differences in using questions triggering discussions (code Q2) between G1 and G2 we may rather take the occurrence of emotions and questions in threads of collaborative reflection as a sign of engagement and moderation that keeps threads going and triggers people to contribute. Further work will have to look closer at these types of effects.

It is surprising that **solution proposals did not have an impact** on learning (codes 9a and 9b) and change (code 10). There is a significant difference between the distribution of these codes on G1 and G2 (see Table 4). Therefore, solution proposals might be used as a differentiator between types of reflection groups as discussed above. It may simply be that we did not see an effect on learning and change because proposals were not suitable or not applied for other reasons.

Conclusion and Outlook

This paper deals with an approach of analyzing the impact of tools supporting collaborative reflection. It is based on content analysis and complemented by feedback from users of the tool. By applying this approach to four cases of using the TalkReflect App we investigated whether and how the app was used and what led to results created in the app. We found that there were different ways in using the app, which relate closely to purposes and constraints of collaborative reflection in the respective groups. From this we derive suggestions for levels and scale of support. In addition, we found that certain types of articulations in the app facilitate the creation of results in the app, and we have created design suggestions to foster these articulations.

The results of our analysis suggest that our approach is an appropriate way to go forward in research on collaborative reflection. The size of our study and the number of threads analyzed are not sufficient to explore the full value added by the coding scheme, problems of its application and adaptations needed. Therefore, we are preparing additional studies, and we invite others to do so as well.

Our work contributes to the state of the art in research on collaborative reflection in two ways. First, it provides a **novel scheme for the analysis of collaborative reflection content** and an **initial study** of applying it. Second, it shows **how tools may be designed to enable groups to reflect together on different levels and scopes of support**. We are, however, aware of the fact that our results are mainly based on the content created in the tool, and that reflection also (or mainly as in some of our cases) happens in face-to-face interaction. Therefore our results do not allow more general insights on collaborative reflection. We rather suggest that it should be combined with other approaches focused on social interaction. It can then complement qualitative data from ethnography, interviews or experience sampling, and help to explain usage data such as frequency of tool usage in order to create more general insights on collaborative reflection inside and outside tools.

References

Argyris, C., & Schön, D. A. (1978): *Organizational learning: A theory of action perspective*. UK: Addison-Wesley.

Baker, D. F. (2010). Enhancing group decision making: An exercise to reduce shared information bias. *Journal of Management Education, 34*(2), 249–279.

Bannon, L., & Schmidt, K. (1992). Taking CSCW seriously: Supporting articulation work. *Computer Supported Cooperative Work, 1*(1), 7–40.

Baumer, E. P., Khovanskaya, V., Matthews, M., Reynolds, L., Sosik, V. S., & Gay, G. K. (2014): Reviewing reflection: On the use of reflection in interactive system design. In *Proceedings of DIS 2014*.

Bjørn, P., & Boulus, N. (2011). Dissenting in reflective conversations: Critical components of doing action research. *Action Research, 9*(3), 282–302. doi:10.1177/1476750310396949.

Boud, D. (1985). *Reflection: Turning experience into learning*. London: Kogan Page.

Boud, D., Cressey, P., & Docherty, P. (2006). Productive reflection at work: Learning for changing organizations. New York: Routledge.

Crowston, K., & Kammerer, E. E. (1998). Coordination and collective mind in software requirements development. *IBM Systems Journal, 37*(2), 227–245.

Daudelin, M. W. (1996). Learning from experience through reflection. *Organizational Dynamics, 24*(3), 36–48.

Davis, E. A. (2000). Scaffolding students' knowledge integration: Prompts for reflection in KIE. *International Journal of Science Education, 22*(8), 819–837.

De Groot, E., Endedijk, M. D., Jaarsma, A. D. C., Simons, P. R.-J., & van Beukelen, P. (2013). Critically reflective dialogues in learning communities of professionals. *Studies in Continuing Education*, 1–23. doi:10.1080/0158037X.2013.779240

Dennis, A. R., George, J. F., Jessup, L. M., Nunamaker, J. F, Jr, & Vogel, D. R. (1988). Information technology to support electronic meetings. *MIS Quarterly, 12*(4), 591–624.

Ellsworth, P. C., & Scherer, K. R. (2003). Appraisal processes in emotion. In *Handbook of affective sciences* (Vol. 572, pp. V595).

Fleck, R., & Fitzpatrick, G. (2010). Reflecting on reflection: framing a design landscape. In *Proceedings of the 22nd Conference of the Computer-Human Interaction Special Interest Group of Australia on Computer-Human Interaction, OZCHI'10* (pp. 216–223). Brisbane, Australia: ACM. doi:10.1145/1952222.1952269.

Greenwood, J. (1998). The role of reflection in single and double loop learning. *Journal of Advanced Nursing, 27*(5), 1048–1053.

Hatton, N., & Smith, D. (1995). Reflection in teacher education: Towards definition and implementation. *Teaching and Teacher Education, 11*(1), 33–49. doi:10.1016/0742-051X(94)00012-U.

Hoyrup, S. (2004). Reflection as a core process in organisational learning. *Journal of Workplace Learning, 16*(8), 442–454.

Introne, J. E., & Drescher, M. (2013). Analyzing the flow of knowledge in computer mediated teams. In *Proceedings of the 2013 Conference on Computer Supported Cooperative Work* (pp. 341–356). ACM.

Isaacs, E., Konrad, A., Walendowski, A., Lennig, T., Hollis, V., & Whittaker, S. (2013). Echoes from the past: how technology mediated reflection improves well-being. In *Proceedings of the SIGCHI Conference on Human Factors in Computing Systems, CHI'13* (pp. 1071–1080). Paris, France: ACM. doi:10.1145/2470654.2466137

Kolb, D. A. (1984). *Experiential learning: Experience as the source of learning and development*. Englewood Cliffs, NJ: Prentice-Hall.

Lockhorst, D., Admiraal, W., Pilot, A., & Veen, W. (2003). *Analysis of electronic communication using 5 different perspectives*.

Marcu, G., Dey, A. K., & Kiesler, S. (2014). Designing for collaborative reflection. In *Proceedings of PervasiveHealth'14*.

Moon, J. A. (1999). *Reflection in learning and professional development: Theory and practice*. New York: Routledge.

Newman, D. R., Webb, B., & Cochrane, C. (1995). A content analysis method to measure critical thinking in face-to-face and computer supported group learning. *Interpersonal Computing and Technology, 3*(2), 56–77.

Porges, Z., Yang, X., Desai, A., Ho, C., Pallegedara, R., Razzaque, R. et al. (2014). Achieve: Evaluating the impact of progress logging and social feedback on goal achievement. In *Proceedings of the Companion Publication of the 17th ACM Conference on Computer Supported Cooperative Work and Social Computing, CSCW Companion'14* (pp. 221–224). Baltimore, Maryland, USA: ACM. doi:10.1145/2556420.2556498

Power, D. J., & Sharda, R. (2009). Decision support systems. In *Springer handbook of automation* (pp. 1539–1548). Berlin: :Springer.

Prilla, M. (2014). User and group behavior in computer support for collaborative reflection in practice: An explorative data analysis'. In C. Rossitto, L. Ciolfi, D. Martin, & B. Conein (Eds.), *COOP 2014—Proceedings of the 11th International Conference on the Design of Cooperative Systems*. Berlin: Springer.

Prilla, M., Pammer, V., & Krogstie, B. (2013). Fostering collaborative redesign of work practice: Challenges for tools supporting reflection at work. In *Proceedings of the European Conference on Computer Supported Cooperative Work (ECSCW 2013)*.

Prilla, M., & Renner, B. (2014). Supporting collaborative reflection at work: A comparative case analysis. In *Proceedings of ACM Conference on Group Work (GROUP 2014)*. ACM.

Prinz, W., & Zaman, B. (2005). Proactive support for the organization of shared workspaces using activity patterns and content analysis. In *Proceedings of the 2005 International ACM SIGGROUP Conference on Supporting Group Work* (pp. 246–255). ACM.

Raelin, J. A. (2002). I don't have time to think! versus the art of reflective practice. *Reflections, 4*(1), 66–79.

Reynolds, M. (1999). Critical reflection and management education: rehabilitating less hierarchical approaches. *Journal of Management Education, 23*(5), 537–553.

Roschelle, J., & Teasley, S. (1995). The construction of shared knowledge in collaborative problem solving. In *Computer Supported Collaborative Learning* (pp. 69–97). Heidelberg: Springer.

Schön, D. A. (1983). *The reflective practitioner*. New York: Basic Books.

Scott, S. G. (2010). Enhancing reflection skills through learning portfolios: An empirical test. *Journal of Management Education, 34*(3), 430–457.

Suchman, L. A. (1987). *Plans and situated actions: The problem of human-machine communication*. Cambridge: Cambridge University Press.

Tigelaar, D., Dolmans, D., Meijer, P., de Grave, W., & van der Vleuten, C. (2008). Teachers' interactions and their collaborative reflection processes during peer meetings. *Advances in Health Sciences Education, 13*(3), 289–308.

Van Woerkom, M., & Croon, M. (2008). Operationalising critically reflective work behaviour. *Personnel Review, 37*(3), 317–331.

Vince, R. (2002). Organizing reflection. *Management Learning, 33*(1), 63–78.

Weick, K. E. (1995). Sensemaking in organizations (Vol. 3). Thousand Oaks, CA: Sage Publications, Inc.

Wever, B. D., Schellens, T., Valcke, M., & Keer, H. V. (2006). Content analysis schemes to analyze transcripts of online asynchronous discussion groups: A review. *Computers and Education, 46*(1), 6–28. doi:10.1016/j.compedu.2005.04.005.

Zhu, E. (1996). Meaning negotiation, knowledge construction, and mentoring in a distance learning course. In *Proceedings of Selected Research and Development Presentations at the 1996 National Coventions of the Association for Education Communications and Technology.*

Keeping Distributed Care Together: Medical Summaries Reconsidered

Troels Mønsted

Abstract Summaries in the medical record have traditionally offered health professionals good cognitive support by guiding reading of the medical record and supporting communication and collaboration in clinical teams. However, because of increased distribution of chronic care and fragmentation of the medical record, summaries are becoming increasingly incomplete and have lost some of their ability to mediate collaboration in clinical teams and support situated sensemaking. Based on findings from a project aimed at studying and designing IT to support collaboration among health professionals in distributed, chronic care, this article present a detail study of current use of summaries and discusses how a new type of summary can be designed to offer better support for distributed, chronic care. Overall I argue that we must maintain an appropriate balance between structure and flexibility, while reconsidering the readership, the authorship, and the maintenance of summaries.

Introduction

Modern medical work at hospitals offers a great deal of interdisciplinary collaboration; most types of care involve several individuals that usually represent different professional groups, including physicians, nurses, secretaries, laboratory technicians, etc. Traditionally, collaboration at hospitals has mainly taken place within the boundaries of a single organization, either collocated or inter-departmental; care has been organized so that a patient was admitted, then treated by a clinical team, and then either discharged or referred to another care provider. As a result, information systems have typically been anchored locally, as exemplified by the widespread paper-based medical records, and primarily served to support work and collaboration within the confines of a single organization.

T. Mønsted (✉)
University of Copenhagen, Copenhagen, Denmark
e-mail: monsted@di.ku.dk

© Springer International Publishing Switzerland 2015
N. Boulus-Rødje et al. (eds.), *ECSCW 2015: Proceedings of the 14th European Conference on Computer Supported Cooperative Work, 19–23 September 2015, Oslo, Norway*, DOI 10.1007/978-3-319-20499-4_8

143

In recent years, there has been a strong trend towards distributing care across multiple care providers through closer integration of primary and secondary care and through distribution of dedicated responsibilities among highly specialized teams working at different hospitals. This is partly motivated by increased professional specialization in healthcare. Furthermore, the healthcare system feels the pressure of an ageing population where more citizens suffer from (several) chronic conditions. This has made it necessary to consider how chronic care can be reorganized to meet both the requirements of quality and efficiency of care.

Distributed chronic care critically exposes the challenges in modern healthcare, as inter-organizational collaboration is currently not well supported by information systems; rather, the information infrastructure in Danish healthcare appears as a silo-based and fragmented cluster of records and IT systems (Bansler et al. 2013). Partly sparked by the chronic care model (Wagner et al. 1996), increased attention is paid to the re-organization of chronic care and how development of a new and better information infrastructure can contribute to increased continuity and quality of care. The chronic care model suggests that greater emphasis is placed on making patients active contributors to own care, for instance by learning self-management skills (by monitoring important symptoms, talking to physicians, and using resources in society), and by creating better collaboration and coordination among health professionals (Wagner et al. 1996; Roland 2013). As argued by Winthereik and Vikkelsø (2005), health information systems have great potential as change agents in our attempts to achieve a greater integration between the multiple health providers involved in care of chronic disease, and thus design and development of improved information infrastructures are key challenges to the continuous development of healthcare. In particular, development and redesign of medical records are challenging as this infrastructure has ramifications to practically all types of work at hospitals; medical records fulfill administrative and legal purposes, they serve as a means to support clinical research, quality assessment, to communicate observations, to justify decision and to coordinate activities (Rosenbloom et al. 2010).

For health professionals, medical records are probably the single most important information device; they are used to write and read patient information (Berg 1996), and to position their activities in relation to a past illness trajectory and an anticipated future (Mattingly 1998). The institution of the medical records is, however, for several reasons, under severe pressure: First, more patients suffer from chronic conditions. As a consequence, illness trajectories become longer and produce more information. Second, increased use of e.g. illness-specific databases, specialism-centric systems and stand-alone devices means that the medical record as a single, centralized artifact has seized to exist. Today, records can rather be understood as a distributed system or ecology of artifacts (Fitzpatrick 2004; Bardram and Bossen 2005) that, in the words of (Berg and Bowker 1997: 515) encompass "(...) *all written, typed, or electronically stored traces of any aspect of patient treatment that has official status within the hospital system* (...)". To achieve overview of a patient case, health professionals therefore currently gather information and assemble narratives from many different artifacts and systems

(Bossen and Jensen 2014). Third, due to increased specialization of clinical work and a trend towards centralizing clinical competences, courses of treatment are increasingly distributed as patients are treated by specialists at different units. This is often referred to as Integrated Care (Kodner and Spreeuwenberg 2002). As a result of these trends, the medical record has become obese and fragmented (Bansler et al. 2013) and for health professionals, it is now a rare privilege to have access to a complete set of patient data, let alone that this is presented in a digestible format.

In recent years, the issue of how clinical data can be rendered reusable in medical records, among other reasons, to counter the possible danger of developing information silos in healthcare has received great attention. In this regard, Rosenbloom et al. (2010) argue that the tension between structure and flexibility must be taken into account. While a high degree of structure and standardization is typically favored by those who reuse data, flexibility and narrative expressivity are often valued by busy writers of clinical notes (Rosenbloom et al. 2010). Yet, there is a tendency towards more structuring of new generations of medical records, as seen by numerous implementations of medical records that, as a consequence, are found typically to offer better support for secondary work (audit, administration, research, reimbursement), rather than primary medical work (diagnostic work, patient consultations, operations, examinations, etc.) (Greenhalgh et al. 2009), for instance by increasing time taken to retrieve information (Car et al. 2008) and by not offering sufficient cognitive support (Stead and Lin 2009).

This tension between structure and flexibility of clinical information systems, I argue, is deeply rooted in a more fundamental tension between different logics of medical work and on different ideas on how medical records serve clinical practice.

Different Logics of the Medical Record

The medical record is often portrayed as a repository of information that serves to provide health professionals with the best possible overview of patient information, to support them in making good clinical decisions. This logic suggests a strong foundation in the biomedical tradition where medical reasoning is portrayed as the practical application of scientific knowledge. Exemplified by the evidence-based regimen (Sackett et al. 1996) this implies "(...) *the conscientious, explicit, and judicious use of current best evidence in making decisions about the care of individual patients. The practice of evidence based medicine means integrating individual clinical expertise with the best available external clinical evidence from systematic research*" (Sackett et al. 1996).

From this stance, medical work is about the application of clinical guidelines that mandates therapy to achieve a precisely defined target (Singer et al. 2002). The main virtue of the record is to support medical work providing an accurate account of patients and illnesses (Berg 1997), and the core of the medical record is structured data that can be reused for many different purposes. This logic is more often than not strongly influencing health IT development. For instance, Greenhalgh et al. (2009) found six assumptions that characterize development of medical records in the UK (in this case specifically electronic medical records). These describe how records are predominantly seen as a container for patient information that can seamlessly be integrated in clinical work, and improve effectiveness and efficiency of clinical work. Hereby, new generations of medical records are expected to drive changes in staff and patient interactions and replace most, if not all, previous systems, and this centralized information infrastructure will gain value, the more distributed and widespread it becomes (Greenhalgh et al. 2009).

Second, other portraits of the medical record dispute the idea that data can be extracted, transferred and reused while retaining its meaning. Greenhalgh et al. (2009) conclude that "(…) *clinical data must be interpreted in context and "framed" before they become meaningful.*" (Greenhalgh et al. 2009: 763). De-contextualized clinical information therefore needs to be re-contextualized (Reddy et al. 2001) and 'universal codes' need to be localized (Winthereik 2003).

Following this logic, medical reasoning cannot be characterized purely as the application of science or technical skills, but "(…) *the ability to work out how general rules—scientific principles, clinical guidelines—apply to the particular patient*" (Montgomery 2006: 5), and perspectives on *sensemaking* (Weick 1995) are increasingly portrayed in literature (see e.g. Jensen and Aanestad 2006; Albolino et al. 2007; Battles et al. 2006; Jordan et al. 2009). Clinical guidelines do therefore not *mandate* care but are an important resource for situated medical reasoning where information is put together with conditional certainty (Hunter 1996; Montgomery 2006). This position goes hand in hand with a logic of medical records that to a lesser extent emphasizes its ability to distribute structured data but rather foreground the interpretative and narrative content, as "(…) *interpretive reasoning required to understand signs and symptoms and to reach a diagnosis is represented in all its situated and circumstantial uncertainty in narrative.*" (Montgomery 2006: 46). Other studies suggest that clinical notes containing naturalistic prose are more accurate, reliable, and understandable for clinicians reviewing medical records (Rosenbloom et al. 2010: 2). Such an interpretative stance on medical reasoning therefore emphasizes the narrative content of the medical record.

The two different logics described here produce significantly different ideas of how the medical record serves medical work. In the first logic, the medical record is typically seen as a *representation* of the patient's condition and past illness trajectory. This perspective stems from the idea that a record can appear as a passive copy that repeats an event or stores this for future reference (Berg 1996: 500). The second logic is typically associated with the point of view that the record is a "*force in itself, mediating the relations that act and work through it*" so that "*social interaction cannot be said to constitute the meaning of the medical record since the record is part and parcel of that interaction; 'social interaction is transformed through it.*" (Berg 1996: 501). Berg and Bowker (1997) furthermore argue that the record is far from a 'post hoc *depiction of times passed and spaces explored*' and that it, rather than representing clinical facts and events, feeds into the very constitution of these.

When clinical collaboration at hospitals mostly took place within the confines of a single organization and when the information system was still a relatively organized collection of documents, the medical record served well as a tool that supported health professionals in making sense of a patient case and coordinated collaboration within clinical teams. With the increasing fragmentation of the information infrastructure in healthcare, the medical record as we know it is, however, losing its position as a central force that keeps together the many strands of chronic care. This is particularly apparent in cases of distributed care where the record is becoming increasingly insufficient as a tool to make sense of a patient's illness trajectory. Based on findings from a project aimed at designing IT support for distributed, chronic care, this article discusses how summaries in the medical record, if an appropriate balance between structure and flexibility is found, can support collaboration and sensemaking in distributed, chronic care.

Methodology

The research presented in this paper has been conducted as part of the Co-constructing IT and Healthcare (CITH) where the research group has investigated requirements for design of IT to support distributed care of patients with chronic heart arrhythmia that requires implantation of an ICD device (Implantable Cardioverter Defibrillator). ICD care involves the effort of health professionals from at least two hospitals (a specialized ICD center at a university hospital and a cardiology department at a local hospital). The overall goal of the project has been to contribute to a safe and secure life of the patients through improved communication and collaboration between all involved parties. The project has furthermore advanced the conceptual and practical understanding of how to model, develop and implement socio-technical IT solutions for communication and collaboration within heterogeneous and distributed networks of health professionals.

The project here presented has been specifically aimed at designing digital service that supports collaboration between two groups of physicians contributing to ICD care: physicians specialized within electro-physiology from the ICD center at the university hospital and physicians specialized within cardiology from a local hospital. The study had a duration of 1½ years and was conducted as a combined fieldwork and design inquiry, drawing intensively on workplace studies and the inventory of the Participatory Design toolbox. The paper is, therefore, partially based on ethnographic data and on insights that emerged through design activities.

As part of the fieldwork, we conducted semi-structured interviews with numerous health professionals from four major hospitals in the capital region of Denmark. We also conducted approximately four weeks of observations, covering referral practices, admission, physical examination, implantation, and various types of follow-ups of ICD patients. Finally, we made in-depth studies of the main information systems in use, including medical records at two hospitals and adjacent IT systems.

The collaborative design process included five workshops with participation of five physicians from two major hospitals. Using various design techniques, including inspiration card workshops (Halskov and Dalsgaard 2006), paper mock-ups (Ehn and Kyng 1991), and generative prototyping (Cramer-Petersen 2013), an iteratively developed prototype was used to elicit requirements from the users, and incrementally design and test various properties, including the role, functionality, and interface design (Houde and Hill 1997). In between the workshops, the researchers conducted follow-up studies, and exposed the prototype to real use through field tests to challenge and develop its practical feasibility.

Software Prototype

During the project, the research team designed, developed, and tested the fully functional software prototype coSummary. This design focuses on situations where healthcare professionals need to gain an overview of a particular illness trajectory within a short period of time, e.g. when admitting a patient, at patient consultations and at rounds. The design was informed by insights from fieldwork the outcome of five co-design workshops.

coSummary is divided into an input and output screen. The input screen consists of 46 input fields (primarily multiple choice fields), sorted into five main categories. All input fields are accompanied by a comment field where the user can add additional descriptive notes. When a healthcare professional submits a finished input form, the system automatically generates the "summary" that is presented on the output screen. The output screen presents a highly condensed summary that is divided into three groups: (1) Positively confirmed information. This is the main part of the summary and shows information on the patient, e.g. core information on the heart condition, ICD device, etc. (2) Blank fields. This group contains input fields that have so far not been filled out. This may indicate factors that it may be relevant for the reader to investigate. (3) Negatively confirmed information: This group contains information that is confirmed as irrelevant. A healthcare professional may e.g. have specified that a patient does not suffer from diabetes.

While coSummary in itself represents a very detailed suggestion for a new type of summary that may support collaboration in distributed care, the prototype also served to explore the tension between structure and flexibility in new generations of medical summaries. The contribution in this paper focuses on the fundamental considerations of the role, issue, and potential for medical summaries and a sensemaking tool in distributed, chronic care (Fig. 1).

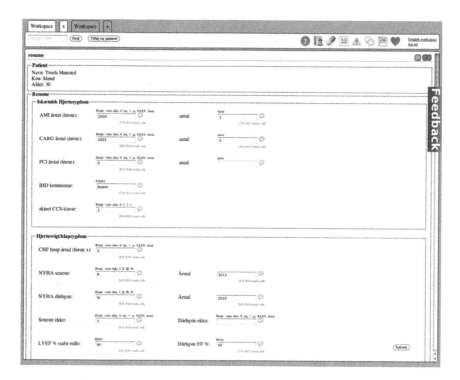

Fig. 1 coSummary input screen

A Case of Distributed Chronic Care

ICD care, while it in contrast to many other types of chronic care requires a great deal of technical expertise from patients and health professionals (Bjørn and Markussen 2013), exemplifies how chronic care can be distributed across multiple organizationally distributed care providers where the patients' are also important contributors through monitoring technology. An Implantable Cardioverter Defibrillator (ICD) is an advanced device that can automatically detect and restore normal heart rhythm in case of atrial fibrillation or heart failure. This treatment is offered to patients with chronic heart arrhythmia that cannot be treated with medicine alone. The responsibility for ICD care is overall divided between an ICD center[1] and a local hospital. Before implementation of an ICD device, a patient is most often initially diagnosed at a local hospital, either because of sustained heart arrhythmia or because the patient is admitted with acute heart failure. If physicians at the local hospital find indications that the patient meets the criteria for ICD care, the patient is referred to one of the ICD centers. Here, the patient will undergo examinations that may lead to implantation of the device (Fig. 2).

---

[1]In Denmark there are a total of five ICD centers.

Fig. 2 Physician reading the medical record

After implantation, the patient will attend two types of follow-ups. One takes place at the ICD center and is referred to as the *device follow-up*. Here, health professionals monitor and assess technical aspects of the device (remaining battery level, therapies given, programming of thresholds, etc.). This takes place either at a consultation or through remote monitoring. The other follow-up is referred to as the *medical follow-up*. These take place as a consultation at the patient's local hospital. Here, a cardiologist assesses the patient's current condition and the progress of the treatment, and the aim is to adjust until a pre-defined target is reached.

A medical follow-up represents a typical situation where a medical record is in use in clinical practice, and therefore very well describes the constraints the health professionals' experience when reading the medical record. First of all, 15 min are allocated for a medical follow-up and the cardiologist is therefore rather busy completing all the necessary duties, including preparation (by reading the medical record), conducting physical examinations (e.g. blood pressure or ECG diagrams), interviewing the patient, deciding on adjustments of the treatment, and documenting his activities by dictating progress. Second, in order to perform medical reasoning well, and thereby work out how general clinical guidelines apply on the specific patient case, the physician has to position his activities in relation to a past illness trajectory and an anticipated future. Here, the physicians are, however, very challenged in keeping together information from a medical record that spreads across a range of information systems, including a paper folder, a local database (Hjerterplus), dedicated databases, e.g. Labka (laboratory tests) and www.icddata.dk (basic information about a patient's device and results from device monitoring).

Summaries in the Medical Record

> We have a nineteen hundred pages record here. I can't remember that I've seen him
> before. Okay. There is a note from December where we have summarized a bit. December
> 2008, more than a year ago. There is also a very good summary if we go back to March
> 2008. (cardiologist, local hospital)

While IT systems are increasingly entering the scene at hospitals, the main
body of the medical record[2] at the hospitals in this study was a paper folder. This
paper folder consists of a vinyl cover that holds the following documents in three
pockets at the front: Cave (medical allergies), latest dispatch letter, information
about referring institution, patient's ID, signed consent, and nursing notes. Inside,
the content is sorted in the following categories: progress notes, cardiographic
tests, paraclinical tests, ECG and holter, and dispatch letter. In total, these documents often comprise several hundred pages.

Progress notes form, so to speak, an integrative core of the medical record
(Bansler et al. 2013). Physicians use progress notes to, in a very concise format,
document the past medical history, current condition, clinical findings, assessments and treatment plan of a patient. Progress notes are written following each
encounter with a patient. They may therefore have many different authors and
may contain information about several conditions and testify different courses of
treatment. In spite of the multitude of authors, progress notes follow a relatively
consistent set of genre rules. For instance, the composition follows a consistent
pattern whereby clinical data is documented and communicated. However, progress notes are also consistently used to express uncertainty and ambiguity, and
therefore often contain an element of doubt.

Progress notes fulfill a central role for the delivery of daily clinical practice,
also at medical follow-ups, and they support medical reasoning by making other
health professionals' view on the patient's condition and the past illness trajectory visible to the reader. However, the strength of the progress notes, their high
granularity of detail, is arguably also their weakness. As the amount of information recorded in the medical record rapidly grows, it also becomes increasingly
difficult to read. The medical record has swollen to proportions that makes it hard
to digest and in some cases, the medical record contains several hundred progress
notes. In those situations, physicians will most often look for a more comprehensive type of progress note that is referred to as the 'summary'.

Summaries share many of the genre characteristics of progress notes (see
example in Fig. 3); the language is very concise, the composition follows a relatively consistent pattern, the substance varies, and the summaries express clinical
judgment, including elements of insecurity and doubt. Summaries do, however,
stand out from ordinary progress notes in some important ways. First, they generally present an account of the patients' illness history in *less detail* but with

---

[2]The description of the medical record and progress notes presented here is based on Bansler
et al. (2013). The analysis of the summaries has not previously been published.

Admission 08.02.07 CWARD
64-year-old male admitted for ablation. Participates in the ARISTOCRAT
project.

Allergy
Does not tolerate Propofol, caused convulsions previously. Does not tolerate
patches.

Previous
1992; stroke without residual deficit.
2000; Acute MI,
2001; CABG,

2002; PCI w stent.
Then several coronary angiograms
DC conversion x2, latest in June 2006.

Risk
Smoking through many years and in large scale, but no consumption since '00.
Increased BP, now well controlled.
Increased cholesterol, now well controlled.
No DM.
Highly predisposed for ischemic heart disease on father's side.

Present
Ischemic heart disease since 2000. Previously CABG and PCI in 2002. Coronary
angiogram several times.
Atrial fibrillation with DC-conversion 2 times, latest in August 2004. Holter
monitoring in January 2007 showed one occurrence of 3.8 seconds of non-
sustained VT and atrial fibrillation.
Occasional chest discomfort and sometimes also angina at rest and during
activity. Not certain if Nitroglycerin works on these pains. Is in NYHA cl.
2.

Other organ systems
CNS: No residual deficit after stroke in 1992.
CP: See above.
GI: No complaints.
UG: No complaints.
Extr.: Tendency to swollen legs, but not currently on diuretic treatment.

Fig. 3 Example of a summary

emphasis on the *overview*. While ordinary progress notes are used to document
observations and decisions from a single patient encounter in rich detail, e.g. a
physical examination or a medical follow-up, and therefore represent a narrow,
clinical gaze, summaries are used to provide overview of the broader trends in
an illness trajectory. Guided by genre rules they do this in a relatively structured
way, while they are still flexible enough to allow the author to express nuances.
Summaries typically contain information about the patient's chief complaints,
diagnosis, significant events in the past clinical history and present condition,
although in and by reading the summary, a trained health professional will be able
to construct a narrative of the broad aspects of the patient's illness trajectory and
identify the conditions that the patient is diagnosed with or under suspicion for.
Second, summaries are most often *authored infrequently*. While ordinary progress notes are entered in the medical record following all patient encounters,
summaries are authored much more infrequently, not only because it is a relatively time-consuming task, but also because summaries are mainly authored to
document certain events. Summaries are most often authored as *admission notes*

Medicine
```
tabl. Selo-Zok 50 mg x 4 (currently paused)
tabl. Imdur 60 mg x 2
tabl. Inspra 25 mg x 1
tabl. Aspirin75 mg x 1
tabl. Apurin 300 mg x 1
tabl. Furix 40 mg x 4
tabl. Kaleoric 750 mg x 4
tabl. Marevan after schedule (currently paused)
tabl. Odrik 2 mg x 1
tabl. Akarin 20 mg x 1
tabl. Zarator 40 mg x 2
tabl. Centyl Mite 1 mg x 1
```
(08.02.07)   cont....
```
tabl. Rilamir 0.25 mg x 1
Nitrospray p.n.
tabl. Felden 20 mg. p.n.
tabl. Kodein 25 mg, max 2 x 4 daily.
tabl. Pinex 1 g max. x 4
tabl. Ketogan p.n.
```

Objective
```
Awake and relevant with good colors. No signs of cyanosis, jaundice or
anemia.
BMI Above average.in good general condition.
St.c.: Irregular heart rate = p.p. No audible murmurs.
St.p.: Ves. resp. all over. No audible rales.
Extr.: Slim and free moving. Good peripheral pulse.
```

Fig. 3 (continued)

when a patient is either admitted to the hospital or transferred between wards. On some occasions, for instance in cases of complex diagnosis that require a thorough review of the past clinical history of the patient, summaries can also be authored. As a result, no formal requirements or established work practices exist, which ensure that there are recent summaries available, and often the reader will experience that the most recent one dates months or even years back. Third, summaries are *situated* in the sense that the content, while very flexible in format, is framed by a certain situation, purpose, and genre. When a summary for instance is authored upon admission of a patient, this takes place in the light of clinical findings (a diagnosis or symptoms) and the summary follows the plot of a specialized health professional (a cardiologist, oncologist, diabetologist, etc.). Thus, summaries are far from neutral representations of a past illness trajectory; rather they represent the clinical gaze of a certain medical specialism at a certain hospital. As a result, summaries both contain information that is generic, but also information that is tied up to clinical and organizational codes, e.g. abbreviations of persons, units and symptoms. Fourth, summaries are an important source of *cognitive support* in medical work that supports sensemaking. Summaries are, like narratives, far from neutral representations of past events, but an account that includes, excludes, and provides interpretation (Feldman et al. 2004). To make sense of the specific, we, however, also need to have a sense of the whole (Bruner 1991). Summaries provide this whole to the reader in two ways: First, they provide the reader with a relatively comprehensive overview of the patient's condition, as seen from a specific clinical perspective. Second, they provide the reader with indications of what elements of the patient's condition that need to be investigated further. Thereby, summaries guide what parts of the remaining record that the physician needs to read.

Finally, summaries are *read frequently*. In contrast to the infrequent authorship, summaries are often in use at for instance medical follow-ups in ICD care. Here, physicians usually look for summaries as the first thing when preparing for a patient consultation. For the same reason, they utter frustration that the availability of such summaries is highly inconsistent. In spite of the benefit this may have on the quality of care, they are very time-consuming to produce, and health professionals often prioritize their time differently, e.g. so they can receive more patients at consultations or spend more time with the individual patient. Despite that summaries offer some cognitive support within the institutional and clinical framing from where they emerged, their role is challenged by the increased specialization and organizational distribution of chronic care.

Summaries in Distributed Chronic Care

Summaries have traditionally been widely used and fulfilled an important role in distributed ICD care. Summaries have provided health professionals with a relatively fulfilling overview of the patient's condition, past illness trajectory, previous examinations, and other conditions or comorbidities that it may be relevant to take into account. This has been achieved through a fine balance between structure and flexibility that allows them to, while remaining relatively structured and efficient to read for a trained professional, be quite expressive by documenting the patient's illness trajectory with a relatively high degree of nuance. More than being a mere representation of the patient's condition, the quality of the summaries is to be found in their ability to support health professionals in making sense of a patient's illness trajectory and providing them with clues of what to investigate further, and hereby guide reading of the medical record. This role as an important sensemaking device is, however, diminishing in distributed chronic care. This may partly be explained by the fragmentation of the information infrastructure that increases by the number of health providers involved in a course of treatment. The result is that summaries from one hospital, while accessible through an IT system (provided that the patient has given informed consent), are often not read by physicians from other hospitals. Furthermore, as substantial amounts of clinical data are stored locally at other hospitals, for instance in dedicated databases, the author of a summary rarely has full access to data on the particular patient. As a consequence, summaries often provide a less complete overview, in cases where care is distributed across multiple healthcare providers. Another more fundamental reason is that medical information does not always preserve the same meaning and connotations when it travels across organizational, professional, and personal boundaries. As argued by Reddy et al. (2001), sharing information in clinical setting is just as much a challenge of recontextualizing this information as it is to decontextualize it, and as shown by the following case, this also applies in ICD care.

Case: How Many Electrodes Are There Supposed to Be?

As part of the CITH, we experimented with the transferability of summaries between electro-physiologists from an ICD center and cardiologists from a local hospital, both groups involved in distributed ICD care. As part of designing a new summary, we produced and experimented with a highly specialized subtract of ICD data to see how cardiologists from the local hospital made sense of this. During a test, a cardiologist from a local hospital noticed that a patient only had two electrodes (broadly referred to as *leads*) implanted and not the third LV (left ventricular) electrode. This drew his attention as the summary also stated that the patient had a CRT device implanted, which normally requires three electrodes. The cardiologist therefore concluded that the patient in fact had a CRT-D device (an ICD device with pacemaking capabilities). He suggested that the implanting physician could have forgotten either to implant the LV electrode or to record this information. An electro-physiologist from the ICD center who was also present and who implants ICDs on a regular basis, explained that they sometimes fail to implant all electrodes[3] due to complications that occur during the routine, or they choose to implant a CRT device if they assess that the patient will need the LV electrode within reasonable time, as they will then be able to reuse the CRT device. The cardiologist argued that this kind of information should appear in the ICD database, as it is otherwise confusing to him. The electro-physiologist objected, as it really is not that straightforward; what they can tell from the available data is that the device is not programmed to use the third electrode, so the patient actually has an LV electrode implanted. Or maybe the patient did not wish to have the LV electrode implanted, as this would involve open-heart surgery. The electro-physiologist furthermore explained that when information in the ICD information is ambiguous, they normally contact the operating physician. Finally, the electro-physiologist recalled that a patient from an ongoing research project had experienced sustained false therapies, probably because of a defect electrode that caused the ICD to maldetect arrhythmia. In this case, the LV electrode was therefore deactivated, which could also be the case here. This, apparently very concise, information can therefore be interpreted in different ways:

- The implantation team forgot to implant the LV electrode
- The implantation team forgot to record information about the LV electrode
- The implantation team failed to implant the LV electrode due to complications
- The implantation team chose to implant a CRT device in advance, expecting that the patient would need this within reasonable time

---

[3]The device can partially function without the third electrode.

- The patient experienced a large number of inappropriate therapies, why the LV electrode had been deactivated.

As shown with this case, it can be a significant challenge for health professionals to make sense of even very specific clinical information. While this challenge of de- and re-contextualizing information is not an uncommon phenomenon in healthcare, it is expressed particularly clearly in distributed chronic care: As health professionals form new, distributed collaborative networks, information increasingly travels across traditional professional and organizational boundaries, changing the context and often the meaning and connotations of these categories. Hereby we run the risk that distributed care becomes poorly aligned, decreasing continuity of care. It is therefore of crucial importance to ensure that information included in summaries for distributed chronic care, is sufficiently meaningful for the readers.

Summaries Reconsidered

Summaries in the medical record have traditionally offered good support for medical sensemaking and collaboration in clinical teams, by enabling health professionals to provide and access an overview of the patients current condition and past illness trajectory in a relatively structured, yet flexible format. In distributed chronic care, the fragmentation of the medical record and the sheer amount information of produced have however cause the summaries to loose some of their value, mostly because they provide a less complete overview of patient information. Distribution of care furthermore complicates the use of existing types of summaries. This is partly because summaries from one hospital, while technically possible, is often not read by health professionals at other hospitals. Moreover, the meaning and connotations of clinical information is often very specialized or dependent on local standards or habits, and therefore does not always travel well across professional or organizational boundaries.

As a response to such challenges, the possibility for, either manually or automated by a computer system, aggregating data from medical records into overviews that are more easily accessed by health professionals has received great attention. As an example, the concept of *summary records* has been envisioned as an approach to assist health professionals getting an overview of patient data by providing health professional with subtracts of information from the medical record. Extending the idea of a dossier représentatif that Schneider and Wagner (1993) describe as an approach to support local practices by different, dedicated views that link to a core record, the hope is that summary records can contribute to a better, more efficient, and safer healthcare system by efficiently providing readers with a structured overview of e.g. medication, medical history, allergies, laboratory reports, referrals, and discharge letters (Greenhalgh et al. 2010). In an evaluation of an implementation of a shared electronic summary record in

England, Greenhalgh et al. (2010) found a general positive effect of summary records, not least with regard to prevention of medication errors. However, they also found that adoption was compromised by several issues, including a lack of trust in the quality of the content of the summary record and a lack of fit with existing organizational routines. Automated summary records represents a very practical approach to providing health professionals with an overview of patient data, that very well respond to the issue of time that is currently one of the causes for the irregular authoring of summaries. If such summaries are to amount to a collaborative tool that also support situated sensemaking in specialized types of distributed, chronic care, such as ICD care, I however argue that two other issues must be taken into account. First of all, the information needs of health professionals in chronic care are typically very specialized, why some elements of the patient's illness trajectory are of greater relevance for the reader than others. In the case of ICD care it is for instance important for the cardiologist to be able to access a range of key indicators for the patient's heart condition, while information on other conditions such as diabetes is of peripheral interest. Second, in order to function as a force that mediate the relations that act and work through it and thereby support health professionals in aligning their activities, and in order to support health professionals in reasoning about how the general guidelines of ICD care apply on the individual case in all of its circumstantial uncertainty, the summary should not merely be a structured representation of the patient's current and past condition, but also possess enough flexibility to allow health professionals in expressing assessments, ambiguity and doubt, as traditional summaries did.

In order to fulfill these demands, the CITH project experimented with new design principles for medical summaries in the coSummary prototype. Based on these experiences, I propose that the *readership, authorship*, and *maintenance* of summaries are reconsidered, in order to create a better fit with distributed, chronic care: First, as I have previously shown, traditional summaries are not authored with a specific *readership* in mind. Instead, they are produced as documentation of certain events, most commonly upon admission of the patient. As a result, traditional summaries typically contain a relatively broad set of information, potentially on several conditions. In contrast, coSummary was designed specifically to address the information needs that physicians have when assessing the physical condition of the patient and technical condition of the device following implantation. To address the need for accessing more nuanced considerations, all data fields in coSummary were supplemented by a free text option, in which the health professionals could add comments.

Second, with regard to *authorship*, medical summaries are traditionally written by a single health professional, typically the physician responsible for admission of the patient. This first of all frames the content of a summary, as this is shaped by the clinical gaze of this individual and is influenced by his training, experience, professional interests, genre rules in the organization and the information that is available in the medical record and the information systems at the particular hospital. Basing summaries on individual authorship, furthermore, makes it a relatively comprehensive duty, which may explain why summaries do not regularly appear in medical records. To ensure the quality and completeness of the information presented in a summary, the design of coSummary was based on a principle of *co-authorship* whereby in principle all health professionals dealing with a patient, add information to the summary, for instance following a patient consultation.

Third, to introduce co-authorship, would also require reconsideration of the *maintenance* of summaries. A central principle that underpins current progress notes, including summaries, is that they, once written, are filed in the medical record at the hospital. Here, they are kept in chronological order among other progress notes. As the summaries are never updated, they describe the condition of the patient at a certain point in time from the perspective of the author and as the summaries (for reasons earlier described) are authored infrequently, they are not always very relevant for the reader. To increase the probability that the information in a summary is relevant and up-to-date, the coSummary prototype was designed to make it possible to maintain existing summaries, by allowing health professionals to enter new information or update existing entries when they observed change in the patient's condition. This was facilitated by a web interface that allows the health professional to easily access the editing functionality, for instance after a consultation.

Altogether, the experiences from CITH with experimenting with and testing these design principles through the coSummary prototype suggest that while it will save the health professionals little or no time when authoring a summary, the practices of keeping up-to-date and reading the summary that emerged are promising. For the health professionals, coSummary provides a very meaningful overview of a patient's heart condition which, estimated by the participating cardiologists will safe them important time that they will otherwise spend on reading progress notes in the medical record.

While the results presented in this paper is the outcome of a project dealing with care of a single chronic condition, it is important to recognize that the challenges of introducing a new generation of specialized and collaboratively authored medical summaries is further exacerbated if we take into account the general increase in the number of patients treated for multimorbidity. Multimorbidity is defined as the presence of two or more long-term conditions (either physical or mental diagnoses) in a patient and in recent years the prevalence in Denmark has increased significantly (Moth et al. 2012). As a consequence, a large fraction of patients in chronic care suffers from more than one condition. For instance, chronic heart arrhythmia is often associated with other lifestyle-related conditions, including diabetes and COPD (a severe lung disorder typically caused by smoking). Each of these conditions follow different care regimens, but as clinical guidelines generally focus on single conditions rather than combinations of disease (Boyd and Kent 2013), multimorbidity requires health professionals to actively seek information on other diseases, assess possible cross-effects of different types of therapy, and potentially prioritize these therapies, in order to avoid unwanted consequences, such as polypharmacy (Flesch and Erdman 2006). Multimorbidity therefore critically extends the challenges of designing collaborative summaries, and should therefore be taken into account in future studies.

Conclusion

In this article, I have presented findings from a project aimed at designing improved support for distributed care of patients with chronic heart arrhythmia focusing on how distributed collaboration among health professionals can be improved through IT-support. Overall, the study has revealed that summaries fulfill an important role for collaboration in clinical teams as well as for situated sensemaking. Because of a relatively structured, yet flexible format that allow health professionals to summarize patient data and pass on information with a certain level of nuance, ambiguity, and doubt. However, because of increased distribution of care and pronounced fragmentation of the medical record, the summaries are becomingly increasingly incomplete, as authors rarely have access to a full set of patient data. By experimenting with design principle for a new generation of medical summaries through the software prototype coSummary, I propose that we, to satisfy the specialized information needs of health professionals involved in distributed chronic care, engage in developing regimen-centric summaries, designed to present specialized information in a relatively high degree of detail. This however also requires that we reconsider some of the principles that underpin current summaries. By focusing the readership of summaries on members of a care regimen, introducing co-authorship of summaries and enabling ongoing maintenance, we can support health professionals in forming stronger collaborative networks across organizational boundaries, and we provide them with improved support in keeping together complex cases of distributed, chronic care.

Acknowledgments   The research was supported by the Danish Council for Strategic Research as part of the CITH project (2008–13). I thank physicians and patients at the local hospital and ICD center for allowing us to observe and interview them, in particular physicians Helen Høgh Petersen, Jesper Hastrup Svendsen, Olav Wendelboe Nielsen, René Husted Worck, and Steen Abildstrøm. I also thank all other researchers affiliated to the CITH project who have contributed to this study: Pernille Bjørn, Finn Kensing, Kjeld Schmidt, Erling Havn, Tariq Andersen, and Jonas Moll. A special dedication goes to Professor Jørgen Bansler for his great contribution to the ideas presented in this article, through discussions and feedback on the manuscript.

References

Albolino, S., Cook, R., & O'Connor, M. (2007). Sensemaking, safety, and cooperative work in the intensive care unit. *Cognition, Technology and Work, 9*(3), 131–137.
Bansler, J., Havn, E., Mønsted, T., & Schmidt, K. (2013). Physicians progress notes—The integrative core of the medical record. In *European Conference on Computer-Supported Collaborative Work ECSCW'13*, September 21–25, 2013 (pp. 123–142).
Bardram, J. E., & Bossen, C. (2005). Mobility work: The spatial dimension of collaboration at a hospital. *Computer Supported Cooperative Work, 14*(2), 131–160.
Battles, J. B., Dixon, N. M., Borotkanics, R. J.,Rabin-Fastmen, Kaplan, H. (2006). Sensemaking of patient safety risks and hazards. *Health Research and Educational Trust, 41*(4), 1555–1575.
Berg, M. (1996). Practices of reading and writing: the constitutive role of the patient record in medical work. *Sociology of Health and Illness, 18*(4), 499–524.

Berg, M. (1997). *Rationalizing medical work: Decision-support techniques and medical practices*. Cambridge: MIT Press.

Berg, M., & Bowker, G. C. (1997). The multiple bodies of the medical record: Toward a sociology of an artifact. *The Sociological Quarterly, 38*(3), 513–537.

Bjørn, P., & Markussen, R. (2013). Cyborg heart: The affect apparatus of bodily production of ICD patients. *Science and Technology Studies, 2*, 14–28.

Bossen, C., & Jensen, L. G. (2014). How physicians 'Achieve Overview'—a case-based study in a hospital ward. In *Proceedings of CSCW'14* (pp. 257–268).

Boyd, C. M., & Kent, D. M. (2013). Evidence-based medicine and the hard problem of multimorbidity. *Journal of General Internal Medicine, 29*(4), 552–553.

Bruner, J. (1991). The narrative construction of reality. *Critical Inquiry, 18*(1), 1–21.

Car, J., Black, A., Anandan, C., Cresswell, K., Pagliari, C., McKinstry, B. et al. (2008). *The impact of health on the quality and safety of healthcare*. University of Edinburgh and Imperial College London.

Cramer-Petersen, C. (2013). Between generative prototyping and work of synthesis in design: Interplay and adding value in the early concept development. In *Proceedings of Co-Create 2013 Conference*.

Ehn, P., & Kyng, M. (1991). Cardboard computers: Mocking-it-up or Hands-on the future. In J. Greenbaum & M. Kyng (Eds.), *Design at work: Cooperative design of computer systems*. Hillsdale, NJ: Lawrence Erlbaum Associates.

Feldman, M. S., Sköldberg, K., Brown, R. N., & Horner, D. (2004). Making sense of stories: A rhetorical approach to narrative analysis. *Journal of Public Administration Research and Theory, 14*(2), 147–170.

Fitzpatrick, G. (2004). Integrated care and the working record. *Health Informatics Journal, 10*(4), 291–304.

Flesch, M., & Erdmann, E. (2006). The problem of polypharmacy in heart failure. *Current Cardiology Reports, 8*(3), 217–225.

Greenhalgh, T., Potts, H. W. W., Wong, G., Bark, P., & Swinglehurst, D. (2009). Tensions and paradoxes in electronic patient record research: A systematic literature review using the meta-narrative method. *Milbank Quarterly, 87*(4), 729–788.

Greenhalgh, T., Stramer, K., Bratan, T., Byrne, E., Russell, J., & Potts, H. W. W. (2010). Adoption and non-adoption of a shared electronic summary record in England: A mixed-method case study. *BMJ, 340*, c3111.

Halskov, K., & Dalsgård, P. (2006). Inspiration card workshops. In *Proceedings of the ACM Conference on Designing Interactive System DIS* (pp. 2–11).

Houde, S., & Hill, C. (1997). What do prototypes prototype? In M. Helander, T. Landauer & P. Prabhu (Eds.), *Handbook of human-computer interaction* (2nd ed.). Amsterdam: Elsevier Science B.V.

Hunter, K. (1996). "Don't think zebras": Uncertainty, interpretation, and the place of paradox in clinical education. *Theoretical Medicine and Bioethics, 17*(3), 225–241.

Jensen, T. B., & Aanestad, M. (2006). How healthcare professionals make sense of an electronic patient record, adoption. *Information Systems Management Information Systems Management, 24*(1), 29–42.

Jordan, M. E., Lanham, H. J., Crabtree, B. F., Nutting, P. A., Miller, W. L., Stange, K. C., & McDaniel, R. R, Jr. (2009). The role of conversation in health care interventions: enabling sensemaking and learning. *Implementation Science, 4*(15), 1–13.

Kodner, D. L., & Spreeuwenberg, C. (2002). Integrated care: meaning, logic, applications, and implications—a discussion paper. *International Journal of Integrated Care, 12*(2), 791–806.

Mattingly, C. (1998). *Healing dramas and clinical plots: The narrative structure of experience*. Cambridge: Cambridge University Press.

Montgomery, K. (2006). *How Doctors think. Clinical judgment and the practice of medicine*. Oxford: Oxford University Press.

Moth, G., Vestergaard, M., & Vedsted, P. (2012). Chronic care management in Danish general practice—a cross-sectional study of workload and multimorbidity, *BMC Fam .Pract, 13*, 52.

Reddy, M. C., Dourish, P., & Pratt, W. (2001). Coordinating heterogeneous work: Information and representation in medical care. In *Proceedings of European Conference on Computer-Supported Cooperative Work 2001* (pp. 239–258).

Roland, M. (2013). Better management of patients with multimorbidity. *BMJ, 346*, 2510.

Rosenbloom, S. T., Denny, J. C., Xu, H., Lorenzi, N., & Stead, W. W. (2010). Data from clinical notes: A perspective on the tension between structure and flexible documentation. *JAMIA, 18*, 181–186.

Sackett, D. L., Rosenberg, W. M. C., Muir, J. A., Haynes, B. R., & Richardson, W. S. (1996). Evidence based medicine: What it is and what it isn't. *BMJ, 312*, 71.

Schneider, K., & Wagner, I. (1993). Constructing the 'Dossier Représentatif'. *Computer Supported Cooperative Work (CSCW), 1*(4), 229–253.

Singer, G. M., Izhar, M., & Black, H. R. (2002). Goal-oriented hypertension management: Translating clinical trials to practice, *hypertension. Journal of the American Heart Association, 40*, 464–469.

Stead, W. W., & Lin, H. S. (2009). *Computational technology for effective healthcare*. Washington, D.C.: The National Academies Press.

Wagner, E. H., Austin, B. T., & Von Korff, M. (1996). Organizing care for patients with chronic illness. *The Milbank Quarterly, 74*(4), 511–544.

Weick, K. E. (1995). *Sensemaking in organizations*. New York: Sage Publications.

Winthereik, B. (2003). "We fill in our working understanding": On codes, classifications and the production of accurate data. *Methods of Information in Medicine, 4*, 489–496.

Winthereik, B. R., & Vikkelsø, S. (2005). ICT and integrated care: Some dilemmas of standardising inter-organisational communication. *Computer Supported Cooperative Work CSCW, 14*(1), 43–67.

Constructing Awareness Through Speech, Gesture, Gaze and Movement During a Time-Critical Medical Task

Zhan Zhang and Aleksandra Sarcevic

Abstract We conducted a video-based study to examine how medical teams construct and maintain awareness of what is going on in the environment during a time-critical, collaborative task—endotracheal intubation. Drawing on a theme that characterizes work practices in collaborative work settings—*reading a scene*—we examine both vocal and non-vocal actions (e.g., speech, body movement, gesture, gaze) of team members participating in this task to understand how these actions are used to display status of one's work or to acquire information about the work status of others. While each action modality was helpful in constructing awareness to some extent, it posed different challenges, requiring team members to combine both vocal and non-vocal actions to achieve awareness about each other's activities and their temporal order. We conclude by discussing different types of non-vocal actions, their purpose, and the need for computational support in this dynamic work setting.

Introduction

Despite its importance and influence on both social and technical research in CSCW, the concept of awareness remains difficult to grasp (Gross 2013). A number of workplace studies have served to define awareness in cooperative work, showing how actors align and integrate their distributed but interdependent activities by tacitly monitoring the work of others (e.g., Heath and Luff 1992; Hutchins 1995; Berndtsson and Normark 1999). Yet many questions about awareness in

Z. Zhang (✉) · A. Sarcevic
College of Computing and Informatics, Drexel University,
3141 Chestnut Street, Philadelphia, PA, USA
e-mail: zz87@drexel.edu

A. Sarcevic
e-mail: aleksarc@drexel.edu

© Springer International Publishing Switzerland 2015
N. Boulus-Rødje et al. (eds.), *ECSCW 2015: Proceedings of the 14th European Conference on Computer Supported Cooperative Work, 19–23 September 2015, Oslo, Norway*, DOI 10.1007/978-3-319-20499-4_9

cooperative work remain unanswered (Schmidt 2002), calling for further research (Gross 2013). Questions such as what actors monitor for and what they ignore, what features of work are displayed and what features remain hidden, what the actors are able to perceive about the actions of others, and which indicators play a key role in determining the current state of affairs, become increasingly important as we consider the design of meaningful computation environments to support awareness (Schmidt 2002).

Awareness is especially critical in medical work. Many CSCW studies have paid attention to this concept (e.g., Bossen 2002; Reddy et al. 2006; Svensson et al. 2007) and many systems have been developed to support it (e.g., Bardram et al. 2006). Yet, as found out by a recent review of CSCW research in healthcare, most studies focus on understanding how work is collaboratively carried out in everyday practice (Fitzpatrick and Ellingsen 2013). Few studies have examined how workers achieve or sustain awareness through moment-to-moment analysis of interactions among clinicians. Those that looked into embodiment in medical teamwork focused on smaller groups and isolated events (e.g., Hindmarsh and Pilnick 2007), or on the collaborative use of artifacts (Svensson et al. 2007).

Our goal is to design a computational environment to support awareness and work coordination during complex and high-risk medical activities such as emergency medical and trauma resuscitation. Although emergency medical teamwork has been studied extensively, little is known about how members of trauma or emergency medical teams achieve and sustain awareness during critical resuscitation moments. For the purposes of this research, we define awareness as an ongoing, dynamic process that is being shaped by emerging information and events, and is observable through coordinative actions in the environment.

In this paper, we describe a video-based study of 11 simulated trauma resuscitations conducted to understand how resuscitation team members coordinate work during a highly collaborative, life-critical medical task—endotracheal intubation, or insertion of a tube into the patient's trachea to secure an unobstructed airway. We examine how vocal and non-vocal actions (e.g., speech, body movement, gesture, gaze) constitute work practices that are then used to achieve and maintain awareness. To corroborate findings from video analysis, we draw from materials collected over five years of fieldwork, including observations, video review of resuscitations, and interviews with team members.

To interpret our findings, we draw on Suchman's (1997) work on centers of coordination and on one theme in particular that characterizes work practices in these workplaces—*reading a scene*. As Suchman described it, reading a scene involves assembling the knowledge about past, present and future events 'through juxtaposition and interpretation of verbal reports, visual images, and various forms of text in real time' (1997, pp. 49). Although rarely called a center of coordination, trauma resuscitation shares many characteristics of such a center: (a) strict division of labor, (b) collocated team members, (c) team-dependent task coordination, and (d) diverse sources of information. Where it differs from centers of coordination is in the lack of tools and technologies to facilitate work coordination. Resuscitation bay instruments, such as vital signs monitors and sensors, provide data about the patient's physiological status. This sensor-based data, however, provides limited contextual information about team activities. Awareness of who is around or what others are doing is achieved through verbal communication, with dedicated roles calling out and reporting different types of information. The means by which resuscitation teams coordinate and communicate are therefore radically affected. Exploration of these mechanisms through the lens of the *reading a scene* theme allows for new insights as well as for the re-examination of challenges in designing computational environments to support awareness in high-risk cooperative work.

We contribute to CSCW in three ways. First, we are adding knowledge to the growing body of CSCW research concerned with the interplay of embodied action and speech in co-present, ephemeral and time-critical settings. Second, by drawing on a Suchman's theme characterizing the centers of coordination, we show how different types of 'immaterial mechanisms' (Bossen 2002) are used in coordinating tasks and constructing two critical types of awareness in trauma resuscitation—activity and temporal awareness. Finally, we discuss implications for computational environments in supporting awareness in this work setting.

Related Work on Awareness and Embodied Action

The literature on awareness within CSCW is vast, spanning different foci and areas of research. Below we review key studies of awareness in centers of coordination and critical care settings, as well as those that focused on the interplay between speech, embodied action, and object manipulation as mechanisms for achieving awareness.

Awareness in Centers of Coordination and Critical Care Settings

Seminal studies of collaborative work in centers of coordination such as London Underground line control rooms (Heath and Luff 1992), air traffic control (Berndtsson and Normark 1999; Hughes et al. 1992), airport operations rooms (Goodwin and Goodwin 1996) and ship navigation (Hutchins 1995) have shown that collaborators tacitly monitor each other to maintain representations of their work, and to plan and organize their own conduct. Specifically, these studies examined the ability of actors to see and analyze events using a range of artifacts and systems, while aligning their activities in an unobtrusive and seamless fashion. Similarly, CSCW studies of awareness in critical care settings have found that clinicians use a variety of mechanisms, processes and artifacts to coordinate work and achieve awareness. For example, Reddy and colleagues (Reddy and Dourish 2002;

Reddy et al. 2006) showed the importance of temporal rhythms and patterns in orienting clinicians in an intensive care unit (ICU) toward future activities. Bardram et al. (2006) and Bardram and Hansen (2010) studied the processes of planning and scheduling activities in the operating suites with a focus on technology design to promote spatial, temporal and social awareness for improved coordination and communication in this environment.

This body of work has produced rich accounts of how activities are carried out and how awareness is achieved in high-stakes work settings through the collaborative use of coordination mechanisms, such as various artifacts and technologies (Schmidt and Simone 1996). Our paper extends this line of research, but focuses on the use of immaterial coordination mechanisms, like speech and embodied action. In doing so, we perform moment-to-moment, fine-grained analysis of both vocal and non-vocal actions to identify the mechanisms by which multidisciplinary medical teams construct and maintain awareness during a highly collaborative, time-critical medical task.

Awareness and Embodied Action

The team-driven nature of medical work has provided an opportunity for studying the use of different media and embodied resources for achieving awareness in a range of clinical environments. For example, Koschmann et al. (2011) found that surgeons establish common references to particular locations of the surgical field by coordinating their talk and gestures with their hands and instruments. Svensson et al. (2007) analyzed passing of instruments among clinical staff during surgery, and found that the arrangement, configuration and passing of an instrument relied upon the participants' abilities to see and prospectively anticipate actions of others. Mentis and Taylor (2013) observed the use of new intraoperative imaging technologies during neurosurgery, showing how medical images are constructed and embodied with the actions by which surgeons manipulate the body.

Examined together, these studies are concerned with the use of instruments, tools and artifacts as coordinative mechanisms. In addition, most of them involved an analysis of new technologies or digital interventions, which to some extent either transformed or changed the ways in which workers interacted with each other. There are, however, important works that focused on bodily conduct alone in complex interactional and organizational contexts, such as studies by Hindmarsh and Pilnick (2002, 2007) and Goodwin et al. (2005). In particular, Hindmarsh and Pilnick (2002) examined the patient's social and interactional impact on the organization of work and communication among members of the anesthetic team, identifying several key practices and skills associated with in situ teamwork. For example, they found that members of anesthetic teams conduct certain tasks in tandem and mutually monitor each other's work by seeing or overhearing conversations, which allows them to efficiently orient to the trajectories of colleagues' actions. In their follow-up study on embodiment and ephemeral teamwork in preoperative anesthesia, Hindmarsh and Pilnick (2007) used the endotracheal intubation task to examine the bodily conduct of medical personnel as a coordinative resource. Their observations showed how participants success-fully anticipate the future activities of colleagues based on their intimate under-standing of the trajectories of actions and by making sense of emerging conduct of colleagues. The authors highlighted the importance of placing the body at the heart of the analysis of work and organization, calling for future studies of social interaction and work practices to follow their suit.

Although we examine the collaborative practices of medical professionals using a similar context—the work of anesthesia and the endotracheal intubation task, our study differs from this previous work in two significant ways. First, prior studies examined intubation during preoperative anesthesia as an isolated event with only two roles participating in the task, the anesthesiologist and his or her assistant. In contrast, we examine how this task is performed in the larger context of trauma resuscitation and with more players, making the "scene" much larger and more complex than that of preoperative anesthesia. Second, the anesthesiologists and their assistants come from the same training background, with overlapping skills and knowledge, whereas the personnel involved in intubating a trauma patient comes from different disciplines and backgrounds, possessing a range of skills. The context of our study is therefore highly multidisciplinary and hierarchical, providing an opportunity for new insights about the interplay between embodied action and speech, as well as their use as resources for achieving and sustaining awareness.

Background: Trauma Resuscitation and Intubation Task

The setting for our study is the *resuscitation bay*, a complex but low-technology work setting in which medical team members engage in time-critical, high-stakes management of a critically injured patient. Although team members follow estab-lished protocols and guidelines, their performance efficiency primarily rests on their ability to coordinate actions with one another and with the dynamic changes of the patient's physiological systems. Typical trauma resuscitation involves 8 to 12 medical specialists from various disciplines, depending on the hospital size, the severity of injury, and the corresponding level of trauma activation (American College of Surgeons 2006). A high-level response to a severely injured patient includes an attending surgeon, an emergency medicine physician, surgical and emergency residents, emergency department nurses, a scribe nurse, a radiology technician, an anesthesiologist, a respiratory therapist, a critical care nurse, secu-rity officers, and a social worker. In contrast, the resuscitation team response to a less severely injured patient might initially include an emergency physician and nurses until the attending surgeon arrives. Patients in need of endotracheal intuba-tion are considered critical and usually require full trauma team activation. Trauma teams are formed ad hoc upon receiving patient arrival notification, with members called from different hospital units, which makes their prior acquaintance with each other less likely. Teams are also hierarchical, with clear division of labor and delineation of responsibilities. For instance, attending surgeons, surgical fellows or emergency medicine physicians assume the leadership role (*team leader*). Anesthesiologists and respiratory therapists control airway, cervical spine, and ventilation. Surgical residents perform hands-on patient examination (*physician doer*). Emergency department nurses draw and administer medications and fluids, establish intravenous (IV) access, and assist with other hands-on tasks (*medication nurse*, *nurse left* and *nurse right*). The *scribe* nurse is responsible for creating and maintaining the full record of the trauma activation. Each role is strategically positioned around the patient bed to ensure timely and efficient completion of the resuscitation process: respiratory therapist and anesthesiologist are at the head of the bed, physician surveyor is at the right side, bedside nurses stand on both sides, scribe is at the foot of the bed, and team leader stand in the back.

Of all resuscitation tasks and activities, endotracheal intubation—a time-critical, multi-step procedure, with each step comprising several sub-steps—is probably among the most challenging and demanding tasks in terms of team coordination. It starts with the leader and anesthesiologist making a decision to intubate the patient. Depending on the patient's age and medical history, they then agree upon a set of medications to render the patient unconscious and paralyzed. Because medications are usually pushed via intravenous (IV) access, the leader must also ensure that an IV is placed before medications are drawn. The leader will therefore monitor the work of the nurse right, whose task is to place an IV. In the meantime, the anesthesiologist prepares the intubation equipment (laryngoscope handle and blades, stylet, and tubes), while the respiratory therapist performs pre-oxygenation. Administration of intubation medications follows next. Because the use of anesthetic, sedative and paralytic drugs is potentially dangerous given the effects they produce, their preparation and administration are carefully executed and monitored through six steps: they are ordered by the anesthesiologist or team leader, the medication nurse prepares them, gives them to the bedside nurse (nurse left), who then checks them for correctness, administers them, and acknowledges they have been given. The administration of medications and the start of intubation must be tightly coordinated because of the limited duration of drug effects. Right before starting, the anesthesiologist will position the patient, tilting his or her head, lifting chin and thrusting jaw, to ensure smooth insertion of the tube. As the anesthesiologist starts with intubation, the respiratory therapist stops pre-oxygenation and removes the oxygen mask. The anesthesiologist then places laryngoscope in oropharynx, while another team member (usually a nurse or physician doer) applies cricoid pressure. The tube is then inserted and laryngoscope is removed from the patient's mouth. The respiratory therapist immediately connects the tube to oxygen and starts patient ventilation. The anesthesiologist confirms tube placement by reporting its position at the lip. Determining the presence of CO_2 in exhaled air using a small device called CO_2 indicator and auscultating the patient's chest for breath sounds signal the end of endotracheal intubation. In summary, the intubation procedure involves the work of seven medical specialists, whose actions and movements require fine-grained, moment-to-moment coordination. Because mutual awareness of each other's actions is critical for timely and effective completion of the patient's intubation, we felt this procedure provided an ideal case for studying how both vocal and non-vocal actions constitute work practices that are then used to achieve and maintain awareness during a time-critical medical task.

Methods

The core of our data are video records of 11 high-fidelity simulated trauma resuscitations originally performed in a pediatric Level 1 trauma center in the U.S. mid-Atlantic region. A total of nine unique trauma teams performed two clinical scenarios. The first scenario (Scenario A) involved a 5-year-old female injured in a high-speed car accident. Teams were required to respond with interventions including intubation and fluid administration to stabilize blood pressure. The second scenario (Scenario B) involved a 3-year-old male hit by a car. Although teams performing this scenario were expected to carry out only chest decompression and fluid administration to stabilize blood pressure, they also proceeded with patient intubation. Four teams performed Scenario A only, two teams performed both Scenario A and Scenario B, and three teams performed Scenario B only. Because both scenarios involved critically-ill patients, they required full trauma team activations, with eight core team members comprising each team: a team leader (attending surgeon or emergency medicine physician), a physician doer (surgical resident), an airway physician (anesthesiologist or critical care fellow), a respiratory therapist, two bedside nurses, a medication nurse, and a scribe nurse. Participants were recruited from a pool of physicians and nurses who normally serve in these roles and participate in trauma resuscitations in the hospital. Simulations were performed in the actual resuscitation bay using high-fidelity patient mannequins and the usual medical equipment and materials available. Two video cameras captured each simulation—one provided an overhead view and the other provided a side view of both the team and the room.

Patient simulators have been used to teach and evaluate team performance in a range of medical events. Prior research on simulators has shown that participants frequently 'suspend their disbelief' and perform in a manner similar to actual clinical scenarios while fully realizing they are working on the patient simulator (Nackman et al. 2003). Even so, relying solely on simulations poses several limitations. To validate our analysis of simulation videos, we draw from a large corpus of data collected over five years of fieldwork at the same research site. These data include notes from in situ observation and video review of tens of live resuscitations, transcripts of interviews and focus groups with clinicians serving in different trauma team roles, and video review sessions with trauma team members commenting on teamwork while watching a resuscitation video.

Video Review of Simulations and Data Analysis

Our primary data analysis involved systematic review of video recordings and transcripts of 11 simulations. We focused on a few minutes of action in each video (i.e., endotracheal intubation fragment), performing moment-to-moment analysis of speech, gesture, gaze and body movement of all team members participating in the task. We considered the fragment starting when a team member (usually team leader) ordered patient intubation or verbally confirmed the need to intubate the patient. The ending point was when the anesthesiologist or bedside nurse reported CO_2 monitor reading (for assessing the adequacy of ventilation), and the physician doer reported the status of breath sounds. On average, video fragments were 3.8 min long, ranging from 2 to 6 min.

While reviewing the videos, we paid specific attention to instances in which vocal and non-vocal actions were used to achieve an overview of the situation, understand the current status of team members' tasks, display the status of tasks occurring either subsequently or in parallel, and perceive the overall progress of the intubation task. In doing so, we were interested in how the interactions among team members were collaboratively produced with respect to trajectories of actions, team members' verbal and non-verbal communication, and the manipulation of various artifacts. Detailed transcripts of both speech and action served to clarify the character of actions and to explore the relationship between vocal and non-vocal actions. As we progressed with the review, we began to identify common patterns of action and common practices of coordination, as well as how different mechanisms (speech, bodily conduct, gaze) contributed to constructing awareness and accomplishing this time-critical task.

To better illustrate the observed patterns of action and coordination practices, we provide brief excerpts from transcripts that include descriptions of actions (e.g., 'turns gaze toward nurse') and accompanying utterances. Where possible, we also show gestures and body movement through video images, and highlight them by circling the action of interest. Following the human subjects protection rules mandated by the ethics committee approving this study, we anonymized our data and completely blurred the faces appearing in the video images.

Findings

We present findings in three parts. We start with examples of verbal communication as the most common mechanism for achieving and sustaining awareness about the current state of affairs. We then describe how gesture and body movement contributed to work coordination and awareness. By describing these three mechanisms one at a time, we show the strengths and weaknesses of each, highlighting their successes and failures in securing awareness. We conclude with examples of work in which all three mechanisms interacted with each other, allowing for smooth and timely coordination and awareness.

Achieving Awareness Through Speech

Successful management of patients during trauma resuscitation is largely reliant on the flow of clear, concise and accurate information among medical team members. To coordinate tasks and make decisions, the leader relies on other people in their designated roles to acquire, retain, validate and report the needed information. When assigning tasks, the leaders often direct orders to the team as a whole rather than to an individual. For instance, a request for the latest set of vital signs is typically given as *"Can we get the vitals"* versus *"Pat, can you give me the vitals."* Orders and inquires can also be directed to specific individuals when there is a need for specific information or task, such as intubating the patient or establishing IV access. Similarly, when reporting task-related information, a team member can direct his or her report to the entire team (e.g., when administering fluids), or to a specific role (e.g., when working on a task with another team member). In the excerpt below, we show a typical information exchange between the leader, anesthesiologist (Anst), medication nurse (MedN), and left and right bedside nurses (NurseL, NurseR) as they start preparing for patient intubation (Fig. 1).

As seen in this example from Team 2, Scenario A, the leader started by asking the anesthesiologist to prepare for intubation. The anesthesiologist acknowledged and the leader then turned to the medication nurse and ordered intubation medications. Soon after, the team's focus turned to the status of IV access and nurse right's work. As soon as the medication nurse approached the bed with syringes ready in her hand, the nurse left, whose task is to administer medications, inquired about the status of IV access. Although potentially visible by just glancing at the patient body, the status of an IV is usually confirmed verbally for a simple reason: the line can be established but it may not work properly, so the nurse right, who either established it or checked it upon the patient arrival (in case IV access was established en route to the hospital), confirms it is set. Here, we saw how both the leader and nurse left inquired about the status of IV access, even though they could see the nurse right working on it. We also saw the nurse right responding to inquiries and, after successfully completing her task, announcing that she was "in". Once the IV was established, the team proceeded with administering fluids and medications, and finally with patient intubation. Although we only showed an excerpt here, this was an example of a heavily verbalized intubation case. Because the leader needed specific information and tasks to be completed, his orders and inquires were directed to specific roles. We also noticed the use of personal pronouns playing an important role in achieving team awareness. Expressions such as *"What do we have for access?"* or *"We are working on it here"*, as opposed to *"Can I have etomidate and succinylcholine please"* or *"I am working on it"*, served as implicit expressions of responsibility for various actions, thereby making other team members aware of who is in charge of a task.

Unlike body movement or gesture that can be easily missed if one is not looking in a particular direction, speech and vocal sounds can reach all actors by being overheard regardless of their targeted direction. Heath and Luff (1992) described

00:04:37	Leader	[Turns gaze toward Anesthesia] Prepare to intubate, (name), if you would please.
	Anst	[Gaze goes to Leader, head nod]
00:04:40	Leader	[Orients toward Med Nurse at the workbench on the right, facing away the team] Can I have etomidate and succinylcholine please?
00:04:43	MedN	[Facing away the team, nod]
00:04:44	Anst	I have a 5-O tube ready.
00:04:45	Leader	Okay.
00:04:47	Leader	[Gaze goes to patient] Be careful of the cervical spine obviously.
00:04:48	MedN	[Approaches bedside, medication syringes in hand]
00:04:51	NurseL	[Gaze to Nurse R] Um, do we have access?
00:04:53	NurseR	[Looks down, works on IV access] Not yet.
00:05:14	Leader	[Gaze toward Nurse L] And what do we have for access, (name)? Have we been working (…)?
00:05:16	NurseR	I am working on it!
00:05:18	NurseL	[Gaze toward Leader] We're working on it right here, do we want an I/O?
00:05:19	Leader	[Gaze toward Nurse R] Can you get it, (name)? Yeah, let's get something a little bit bigger.
00:05:23	NurseR	Okay.
00:05:24	Leader	Keep me posted on that, okay? If you haven't gotten it within about a minute or two, let's go to I/O access.
00:05:24	NurseR	Alright, I am in!
00:05:30	Leader	[Gaze toward Nurse Right] You're in?
00:05:32	NurseR	[Gaze toward Leader] Yeah, I'm in!
00:05:32	Leader	Okay.

Fig. 1 Excerpt from Team 2, Scenario A

how overhearing conversations contributed to peripheral monitoring of the actions in the Line Control Rooms on London Underground. Similarly, we noticed how overhearing exchanges between the anesthesiologists and leaders triggered other team members' actions. Most often, we observed the medication nurse overhearing the leader and anesthesiologist's discussion about the intubation plans. As shown in the excerpt below from Team 3, Scenario B, the medication nurse would immediately start preparing medications using the information she overheard, rather than wait for the leader's direct order (Fig. 2).

Often times, however, speech alone is not sufficient enough for team members to acquire information or achieve awareness about the work status of others.

00:08:26	Anst	[Turns gaze toward Leader] Getting drugs? Are we getting any drugs?
00:08:28	MedN	[Gaze toward Anesthesia]
00:08:29	Leader	Yes, what do you think?
00:08:29	MedN	[Turns toward workbench, facing away, starts opening cabinets with syringes]
00:08:30	Anst	I think, uh, we'll get some etomidate and succs to intubate.
00:08:50	MedN	[Turns around facing the team, holds medication syringes in her hand]

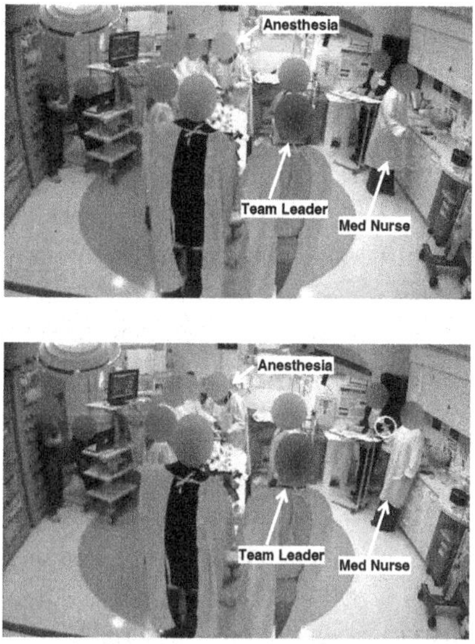

Fig. 2 Excerpt from Team 3, Scenario B

Although important, words are often misheard or lost in the shuffle, especially in the noisy and crowded environment of the resuscitation bay. Another problem is human error; team members often forget to report out loud the status of their activities as they become engrossed in their tasks, or they only provide partial reports (Sarcevic et al. 2012). The challenges in using speech as a sole mechanism for achieving awareness highlight the need for using other channels to convey status of one's activity, including gesture and body movement.

Efficient Uses of Gesture and Movement in the Absence of Speech

In the resuscitation bay, with the patient positioned in the center of the room, trauma team members perform a dynamic set of activities surrounding the patient, such as examining the patient, moving around the patient, assembling and arranging medical tools and equipment, or checking the patient's vital signs by looking at the vital signs monitor. Working side-by-side makes it easier for team members to monitor each other's activities and assess the relevance of those activities to their own work. At the same time, they carry out various embodied actions, indirectly displaying their ability to recognize the trajectory of other team members' actions and to anticipate their next move. This ability to make sense of the current conduct and anticipate future activities helps ensure smooth coordination, even when verbal communication is absent.

00:06:09	NurseR	[At the bedside, standing next to Physician Doer, fetches the IO drill for inserting intraosseous line]	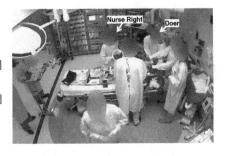
00:06:09	Doer	[Holds the patient's neck, controls for cervical spine]	
00:06:10	Anst	[Turns gaze toward Nurse Right]	
00:06:10	Doer	[Turns gaze toward Nurse Right]	
00:06:56	NurseR	[Orients her body toward Physician Doer, arm with the IO drill extended toward Physician Doer].	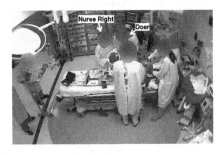
00:07:00	Anst	[Takes over cervical spine control]	
00:07:02	Doer	[Takes the IO drill from Nurse Right and starts inserting the line]	

Fig. 3 Excerpt from Team 5, Scenario B

Because responsibilities are clearly specified for each role, team members pay particular attention to activities that are highly relevant to their tasks. Often times, however, some roles would assist with tasks that have limited relevance to their own work, as illustrated below in the example from Team 5, Scenario B (Fig. 3).

We enter this sequence as the team prepares to establish interosseous (IO) line to administer fluids and medications. The physician doer has just volunteered to immobilize the patient's cervical spine, while the anesthesiologist prepares intubation equipment and respiratory therapist ventilates the patient. Establishing IO access is the nurse right's responsibility, so we see her taking the IO drill instrument out of the box (action circled in the first video image). It took the nurse about 40 seconds to configure the IO drill. In theory, both nurse right and physician doer can perform this task. In this case, however, the physician doer has easier access, because he is closer to the patient's right leg. Recognizing the situation, the nurse right performs a series of subtle movements, displaying the readiness of the IO drill and implicitly asking physician doer to insert the IO: holding the IO drill in one hand and waiting for a few seconds, orienting her body toward physician doer, extending her arm toward physician doer, and then pulling back (action circled in the second video image). The anesthesiologist also recognizes the nurse's intention, so she takes over cervical spine control. A second later, the physician doer takes the instrument and starts inserting the IO.

This excerpt illustrates how the anesthesiologist, nurse right and physician doer coordinated their activities without talking to each other. They were able to recognize each other's gestures and body movement, making sense of actions around them and anticipating each other's needs. As others have found in similar contexts, this timely and smooth coordination between actors rests on their ability to understand the character and trajectory of actions performed by others to which they can contribute (Hindmarsh and Pilnick 2007).

Speech, Gesture and Movement Combined for Complete Awareness

In Fig. 1 from Team 2, Scenario A, medication nurse approached the bed with pre-pared syringes, but did not verbally announce this information to the team. Rather, it was nurse left who noticed her presence, 'reading' her gesture as a signal that medications were ready for administration. Although gesture and body movement serve as important mechanisms by which team members can display their status, the crowded nature of the resuscitation room often makes these channels difficult to see. In the cases we reviewed, we noticed how team members crowd around the patient, leaving little room for movement, especially when treating pediatric patients. Because activities happen in parallel (e.g., one nurse may be taking manual blood pressure while another is drawing blood from the same arm), team members push their ways in order to complete tasks.

Combining speech with gesture or body movement provides for a more efficient mechanism for displaying activity status. Preparing medications is a good example, given the many steps in the process and the importance of keeping the team aware of the completion of each step. The following excerpt is again from Team 2, Scenario A, continuing a minute after the first excerpt stopped (Fig. 4).

Here, we could see how speech, body movement and gesture together constituted the work and allowed for smooth and timely coordination of activities. At the beginning of the excerpt, we found the medication nurse standing at the bed-side, verbally announcing medication types and dosages. As we described before, such verbal reports serve to make the entire team aware of one's task status, or in this case, of the readiness of intubation medications. The leader, however, asked for a pause before administering medications to first assess the patient's neurological status using Glasgow Coma Scale (GCS). As the leader reported the score, the anesthesiologist turned her gaze toward the leader. Because GCS assessment is a critical step before patient intubation, the anesthesiologist paid particular attention to this information, illustrating again how team members remain sensitive to the specific information or tasks that are closely related to their roles and responsibilities. In addition, the anesthesiologist nodded two times, displaying her agreement with the leader's assessment—that is, the GCS score was critically low and intubation was necessary. Soon after, the leader checked in with nurse right about the status of fluid administration. The nurse right responded using both an utterance and deictic gesture, pointing toward the medication nurse who was assisting

00:06:18	MedN	[Stands next to Nurse Left, holds syringes, orients toward her and hands over syringes] That's 8 mg of etomidate and 50 mg of succynocholine.

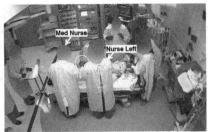

00:06:22	Leader	Let's just hold those for a second. Let's get a formal GCS [neuro] count. Eyes no response, verbal no response, motor no response. So Glasgow is 3, so go ahead.
00:06:32	Anst	[Gaze toward Leader, nod]
00:06:34	Leader	[This] certainly confirms our decision to intubate.
00:06:36	Anst	[Gaze toward Team Leader, another nod]
...		
00:07:06	Leader	[Gaze toward Nurse Right] Are our fluids going in?
00:07:08	NurseR	[Points toward Med Nurse, who is now helping with fluid administration] Nobody started fluids yet, she's getting them.

00:07:10	Leader	[Gaze toward Medication Nurse]
00:07:12	NurseL	[Waves hand with medications, orients toward Team Leader, gaze toward Team Leader] And I have an RSI ready.

Fig. 4 Excerpt from Team 2 Scenario A continued

with fluids (gesture circled in the second video image). In turn, the nurse's gesture directed the leader's attention to the specific team member (medication nurse), making him aware of who was taking care of the task. At the end of this sequence, the nurse left oriented her body and head toward the leader and waved the hand in which she held medications, displaying their readiness (gesture circled in the third video image). The nurse left augmented her gesture by verbally reporting that medications were ready.

Even with speech and gesture combined, team members can often miss the clues because they are either busy with their own tasks or the person reporting on their status isn't doing enough of "displaying" to be noticed by others. Consider for example an excerpt from Team 8, Scenario A, when the anesthesiologist was busy preparing intubation equipment and missed other activities around the bed (Fig. 5).

In this excerpt, we saw the nurse left reporting the status of medications two times, first announcing they were ready, and then announcing medication names as she was administering them. Even so, the anesthesiologist was busy with monitoring vital signs and preparing equipment, so she missed these verbal cues. To

00:05:30	Anst	[Looks at the vitals monitor, turns to Doer] Can you take over the bagging?
00:05:32	Doer	[Gaze toward Anesthesia] Sure.
00:05:33	Anst	[Hands the bag to Doer, turns around toward intubation cart, facing away the bed, starts preparing intubation equipment].
00:05:40	NurseL	[Starts administering medications] Etomidate in. Succs in.

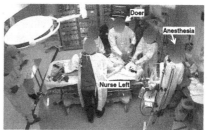

| 00:05:40 | Anst | [Turns back toward patient, intubation equipment ready in her hand] |
| 00:05:52 | | [Anesthesia puts the laryngoscope on the bed, Doer hands the bag over to Respiratory, Doer starts holding the patient's head, Respiratory starts bagging the patient] |

| 00:06:01 | Anst | [Gaze toward Nurse Left] (Name), meds are in? |
| 00:06:03 | NurseL | [Gaze toward Anesthesia] Yes, meds are in. |

Fig. 5 Excerpt from Team 8, Scenario A

obtain the needed information, she had to ask nurse left directly if medications were administered. There were cases, however, when the lack of information or when missing a report created bigger commotion among team members. In one live event, for example, we observed the anesthesiologist inquiring about the status of intubation medications six times. Upon closer inspection, we uncovered that team members in charge of preparing and administering medications did not communicate with the anesthesiologist about their work status, leaving the anesthesiologist unsure where they were along the six steps in the medication preparation process.

Comments about closed-loop communication were frequently heard as we interviewed various team members, further confirming how neither of the mechanisms for displaying and monitoring work status can be sufficient alone. In combination, however, these different mechanisms constitute meaningful work practices that help facilitate smooth and timely coordination, as each mechanism helps making up for the shortfalls of the others.

Discussion and Conclusion

In this paper, we conducted a video-based study to examine how medical teams construct and maintain awareness of what is going on in the resuscitation environment during a high-critical, collaborative task—endotracheal intubation. We examined both vocal and non-vocal actions (e.g., speech, body movement, gesture, gaze) of team members working on this task to characterize different types of mechanisms by which they either display the status of their work or monitor the environment to acquire information about the work status of others. To interpret our findings, we drew on the 'reading a scene' theme that Suchman (1997) adopted and then used to characterize work practices in collaborative work settings such as centers of coordination.

Our findings showed how the co-present resuscitation team members leveraged different types of 'immaterial mechanisms' (Bossen 2002) to construct and sustain awareness in a time-critical environment. According to Bossen (2002), immaterial coordination mechanisms include routines, procedures and habits like division of labor, peripheral awareness and even knowledge about a worker's background or experience. Similarly, we observed that team hierarchy and standardized protocols played an important coordinative role in completing complex resuscitation tasks. Here, however, we extended the term immaterial mechanism to also include vocal and non-vocal actions by which trauma team members coordinate their work. As we saw through the excerpts, they took advantage of working side-by-side to not only visually check the status of ongoing activities but to also overhear conversations, which in turn triggered their own actions. The work around and on the patient was dynamically configured through the use of speech, gesture, gaze, and body orientation. While speech was used to obtain or report specific information, gestures and body orientation were used for different purposes. For example, extending one's arm while holding an object expressed an intent of passing that object; nodding was primarily used for simple answers like 'yes' or 'no'; pointing was used to direct one's attention, while hand waving was used to draw attention. Similarly, orienting one's body or head was also used to draw attention. What became clear from our analysis, however, was that each mechanism alone was helpful in constructing awareness to some extent, posing several challenges along the way. For instance, because the resuscitation room could easily become chaotic and noisy, verbal communication was often subject to failure, leading to misunderstanding or information loss. Or, when gestures were unsuccessful in communicating the information, it was because they were missed and rarely because they were misunderstood. To overcome these challenges, team members took advantage of their ability to 'read the scene' and combine speech with gesture or body movement for a more efficient way to achieve awareness about each other's activities and their temporal order.

Prior work has found that maintaining mutual awareness within a team of clinicians is central to the coordination of work in hospitals (Heath et al. 2002). Our data showed that by explicitly requesting information, overhearing conversations, or seeing actions of others, the resuscitation team members were able to obtain information about the status of ongoing activities of each other (i.e., *activity awareness*). Often times, however, while working on their own tasks, team members missed both verbal and non-verbal clues in the environment. As shown above, we observed several cases with the anesthesiologists lacking awareness about the status of medications, which in turn triggered additional (multiple) requests for information.

Temporal awareness is especially critical when working on time-critical tasks such as intubation. Common approaches to keeping track of temporal order of most medical activities include schedules or knowing the temporal rhythms and patterns of work practices (Reddy et al. 2006). In contrast, keeping track of time during intubation relies on intimate monitoring of and being sensitive to another team member's activity in order to project the trajectory of actions and time one's contribution to the task. As our findings showed, the anesthesiologist must know the exact moment of administering medications so that intubation can be performed within the limited timeframe of drug effects duration. Or, as the anesthesiologist is inserting the tube, the respiratory therapist must closely monitor each move that the anesthesiologist makes to be able to attach the ventilation bag to the tracheal tube in a timely manner. One possible explanation for such a relatively smooth coordination between the anesthesiologist and respiratory therapist with almost no conversation at all could be their intimate knowledge and understanding of each other's work, which in turn precludes the need for intense articulation work (Bossen 2002). In contrast, coordinating the timing of administering medications with intubation requires more effort on behalf of all team members.

The question then is how best to approach the design of computational environments to address the challenges in achieving and sustaining awareness of activities and their temporal order during highly intense and time-critical medical work. On one hand, the activities performed by various team members and the manner in which they were performed showed how the organization of the intubation task unfolded naturally. Clinicians undertook their work by either 'reading' the actions of others and responding to them, or making them visible to others on the team. Most of the time, this visibility of embodied actions allowed for smooth coordination and timely completion of activities such as passing instruments, inserting the tube, or ventilating the patient. It is our belief then that such natural task organization can hardly benefit from any technological intervention, for it would only get in the way. On the other hand, we observed critical moments and commotion among team members when the needed information was not reported, or when it was missed or lost in the shuffle. It is here that we argue for technology support in constructing and maintaining awareness of ephemeral and historic information such as task parameters, timing and types of interventions, and patient data. The challenge is that such information is internalized in memories of those who performed tasks and is available only if reported voluntarily or requested. A possible solution is to externalize this information by augmenting the use of speech, given its key role in making this ephemeral and historic information available to the team. The whiteboard-like, digital wall display has proven useful in supporting awareness of medical teams (Bardram et al. 2006). A quick glance at the wall display to obtain information about different task parameters in real time (e.g., timing, types and dosages of administered medications) may speed up the process and preclude the need for redundant inquires by the anesthesiologist, leader and other roles. The challenge, however, is in accurate and timely capture of such information from the environment. While verbal reports could be potentially captured using speech recognition, this approach can be problematic when we take into account the noise or parallel speech, though vocabulary is rather limited so algorithms could be trained. Manual data entry has been tried, but was found challenging due to the rapid pace of events (Fitzgerald 2009).

Our findings showed that medical resuscitation teams heavily rely on speech and bodily conduct to communicate the information and keep each other aware of activities during time-critical tasks. Similar behaviors have also been observed in other work domains. There are ongoing efforts in automatic capture and recognition of human activities during collaborative work in order to support teamwork and decision making. Our future work will explore how important it is to capture these actions and the extent to which this can be achieved.

Acknowledgments This work is supported by the National Science Foundation under Grant No. #1253285. We would like to thank our research team members for their support, as well as to the medical staff at the research site for their participation. Thanks also to the anonymous reviewers for their constructive suggestions and recommendations.

References

American College of Surgeons. (2006). *Resources for optimal care of the injured patient.* Chicago, IL: American College of Surgeons.

Bardram, J. E. & Hansen, T. R. (2010). Why the plan doesn't hold—a study of situated planning, articulation and coordination work in a surgical ward. In *Proceedings of the 2010 ACM Conference on Computer-Supported Cooperative Work (CSCW 2010)* (pp. 331–340). Savannah, Georgia, USA.

Bardram, J. E., Hansen, T. R., & Soegaard, M. (2006). AwareMedia: A shared interactive display supporting social, temporal, and spatial awareness in surgery. In *Proceedings of the 2006 ACM Conference on Computer-Supported Cooperative Work (CSCW 2006)* (pp. 109–118). Banff, Alberta, Canada.

Berndtsson, J. & Normark, M. (1999). The coordinative functions of flight strips: Air traffic control work revisited. In *Proceedings of the 1999 ACM Conference on Supporting Groupwork (GROUP 1999)* (pp. 101–110). Phoenix, Arizona, USA.

Bossen, C. (2002). The parameters of common information spaces: The heterogeneity of cooperative work at a hospital ward. In *Proceedings of the 2002 ACM Conference on Computer Supported Cooperative Work (CSCW 2002)* (pp. 176–185). New Orleans, Louisiana, USA.

Fitzgerald, M. (2009). Trauma reception and resuscitation project'. *Injury, 40*(1), S15.

Fitzpatrick, G., & Ellingsen, G. (2013). A review of 25 years of CSCW research in healthcare: Contributions, challenges and future agendas. *Computer Supported Cooperative Work (CSCW): An International Journal, 22*(4–6), 609–665.

Goodwin, C., & Goodwin, M. H. (1996). Seeing as a situated activity: Formulating planes. In Y. Engestrom & D. Middleton (Eds.), *Cognition and communication at work* (pp. 61–95). Cambridge: Cambridge University Press.

Goodwin, D., Pope, C., Mort, M., & Smith, A. (2005). Access, boundaries and their effects: Legitimate participation in anaesthesia. *Sociology of Health and Illness, 27*(6), 855–871.

Gross, T. (2013). Supporting effortless coordination: 25 years of awareness research. *Computer Supported Cooperative Work (CSCW): An International Journal, 22*(4–6), 425–474.

Heath, C., & Luff, P. (1992). Collaboration and control: Crisis management and multimedia technology in London underground line control rooms. *Computer Supported Cooperative Work (CSCW): An International Journal, 11*(1–2), 69–95.

Heath, C., Svensson, M. S., Hindmarsh, J., Luff, P. & Vom Lehn, D. (2002). Configuring awareness. *Computer Supported Cooperative Work (CSCW): An International Journal, 11*(3–4), pp. 317–347.

Hindmarsh, J., & Pilnick, A. (2002). The tacit order of teamwork: Collaboration and embodied conduct in anesthesia. *The Sociological Quarterly, 43*(2), 139–164.

Hindmarsh, J., & Pilnick, A. (2007). Knowing bodies at work: Embodiment and ephemeral teamwork in anaesthesia. *Organization Studies, 28*(9), 1395–1416.

Hughes, J. A., Randall, D. & Shapiro, D. (1992). Faltering from ethnography to design. In *Proceedings of the 1992 ACM Conference on Computer-Supported Cooperative Work (CSCW 1992)* (pp. 115–122). Toronto, Ontario, Canada.

Hutchins, E. (1995). *Cognition in the wild.* Cambridge, MA: The MIT Press.

Koschmann, T., LeBaron, C., Goodwin, C., & Feltovich, P. (2011). Can you see the cystic artery yet? A simple matter of trust. *Journal of Pragmatics, 43*(2), 521–541.

Mentis, H. M. & Taylor, A. S. (2013). Imaging the body: Embodied vision in minimally invasive surgery. In *Proceedings of the 2013 ACM Conference on Human Factors in Computing Systems (CHI 2013)* (pp. 1479–1488). Paris, France.

Nackman, G. B., Bermann, M., & Hammond, J. S. (2003). Effective use of human simulators in surgical education. *Journal of Surgical Research, 115*(2), 214–218.

Reddy, M. C. & Dourish, P. (2002). A finger on the pulse: Temporal rhythms and information seeking in medical work. In *Proceedings of the 2002 ACM Conference on Computer-Supported Cooperative Work (CSCW 2002)* (pp. 344–353). New Orleans, Louisiana, USA.

Reddy, M. C., Dourish, P., & Pratt, W. (2006). Temporality in medical work: Time also matters. *Computer Supported Cooperative Work (CSCW): An International Journal, 15*(1), 29–53.

Sarcevic, A., Marsic, I., & Burd, R. S. (2012). Teamwork errors in trauma resuscitation. *ACM Transactions on Computer-Human Interaction (TOCHI), 19*(2), July 2012, article 13.

Schmidt, K. (2002). The problem with awareness. *Computer Supported Cooperative Work (CSCW): An International Journal, 11*(3–4), 285–298.

Schmidt, K., & Simone, C. (1996). Coordination mechanisms: Towards a conceptual foundation of CSCW systems design. *Computer Supported Cooperative Work (CSCW): An International Journal, 5*(2–3), 155–200.

Suchman, L. (1997). Centers of coordination: A case and some themes. In L. B. Resnick, R. Saljo, C. Pontecorvo, & B. Burge (Eds.), *Discourse, tools, and reasoning: Essays on situated cognition* (pp. 41–62). Berlin: Springer-Verlag.

Svensson, M. S., Heath, C., & Luff, P. (2007). Instrumental action: the timely exchange of implements during surgical operations. In *Proceedings of the 10th European Conference on Computer-Supported Cooperative Work (ECSCW 2007)* (pp. 41–60). Limerick, Ireland.

Online Social Networks and Police in India—Understanding the Perceptions, Behavior, Challenges

Niharika Sachdeva and Ponnurangam Kumaraguru

Abstract Safety is a concern for most urban communities; police departments bear the majority of responsibility to maintain law and order and prevent crime. Police agencies across the globe are increasingly using Online Social Network (OSN) (such as Facebook and Twitter) to acquire intelligence and connect with citizens. Developing nations like India are however, still exploring OSN for policing. We interviewed 20 IPS officers and 21 citizens to understand perceptions, and explored challenges experienced while using OSN for policing. Interview analysis, highlights how citizens and police think about information shared on OSN, handling offensive comments, and acknowledgment overload, as they pursue social and safety goals. We found that success of OSN for policing demands effective communication between the stakeholders (citizens and police). Our study shows that OSN offers community-policing opportunities, enabling police to identify crime with the help of citizens. It can reduce the communication gap and improve coordination between police and citizens. We also discuss design opportunities for tools to support social interactions between stakeholders.

Introduction

Police departments across the globe are increasingly using Online Social Networks (OSNs) to connect with citizens and share law and order[1] related information. For instance, in 2011 riots, UK Police used Twitter to provide localized

---

[1]In this paper, we use 'law and order' synonymous with social issues like theft, crime, traffic.

N. Sachdeva (✉) · P. Kumaraguru
Cybersecurity Education and Research Center (CERC), IIIT-Delhi, New Delhi, India
e-mail: niharikas@iiitd.ac.in

P. Kumaraguru
e-mail: pk@iiitd.ac.in

© Springer International Publishing Switzerland 2015
N. Boulus-Rødje et al. (eds.), *ECSCW 2015: Proceedings of the 14th European Conference on Computer Supported Cooperative Work, 19–23 September 2015, Oslo, Norway*, DOI 10.1007/978-3-319-20499-4_10

information, dispel rumors, reassure citizens and to find looters. After the riots, looking at the impact of OSN (Twitter) on policing, the UK government emphasized the need for each police force to develop an OSN communications plan (Home Affairs Committee 2011). Thousands of citizens in developed countries post content and follow police departments such as Boston police and UK police. Citizens provide useful content to police, e.g., situational information, participate in online beat programs[2] needs in different geographical area. and identify—victims, accused, missing people, lost or stolen vehicles (GMP police).

OSNs have demonstrated massive potential to reform policing; however, it introduces various challenges (Davis et al. 2014). Firm legal restrictions on public disclosures and police impression as "coercive arm of the state," make it difficult to communicate with citizens (Denef et al. 2013). Further, past events show that the police misunderstood the citizens' expectation resulting in reputation loss of the department (Los Angeles News 2014). OSN attributes like openness, volume, and velocity at which information spreads also introduce unique challenges for the police. For example, during Vancouver riots (2010), police had no procedure in place to collect citizens' tweets with possible suspect clues (mentioning @VancouverPD) (The COPS Office and the Police Executive Research Forum 2013).

Research shows benefits, effectiveness, and challenges of using OSN by police in developed world (Cobb et al. 2014; Palen and Vieweg 2008; Semaan and Mark 2012). However, need for OSN mediated communication, collaboration, and connectedness between citizens and police in developing nations is largely unexplored. With the increased penetration of OSN in developing countries like India, police are exploring the effectiveness of OSN as a communication channel to maintain law and order (Nayak 2014). Unlike the developed world, police organizations in India lack adequate police personnel. According to the United Nation guideline, 270–280 police personnel are recommended per 100,000 citizens (Express News Service 2013). The policing department in India has only 130 personnel per 100,000 citizens and there is only one IPS (Indian Police Services) officer for every 359,953 citizens Ministry of Home Affairs (2010). In contrast, the US has 233 police officers per 100,000 people (Wu et al. 2012). This lack adequate police personnel results in many under-policed areas in India. Police have felt the need to obtain community collaboration to accomplish its increasingly vast duties and is exploring use of technology like OSN to reach community (Express News Service 2013). However, police personnel have limited exposure to technology (The Economics Times 2014). These limitations (inadequate number of police personnel and technology exposure) make it difficult to adopt findings of OSN use by police in developed world to facilitate policing needs in developing countries like India.

To address these gaps, we study (largely unexplored) needs, challenges, and preparedness of police and citizens for using OSN in a developing nation like India. In this work, we adopt multi-stakeholder approach to examine the OSN use for community policing in India. Our approach includes interviews of 21 citizens and 20 IPS officers who lead and command various police and intelligence organizations in India. Our

---

[2]In Police Beat programs, individual police officer is held responsible for community's policing.

work provides an insight about how OSN can help Indian police to build a community and communicate with citizens to achieve community-policing goals. This knowledge can help improve policing services and facilitate community-policing efforts.

Research Objective

In this work we analyze, *whether OSN based technology can be adopted to support communication and collaboration for making safer society in developing countries like India.* To analyze our research objective, we study the following supporting aspects: Why police and citizens can use OSN for improving policing and preventing crime? Which are the different kinds of OSN platforms police is exploring to use? What is the target audience that the police want to reach through OSN? We also analyze the challenges police and citizens think they might face while using OSN for communication and collaboration. The work particularly aims to analyze the role of OSN in supporting collaboration between police and citizens to fight crime, recover from ongoing threats, and maintain law and order.

Our Contributions

Our research builds upon prior knowledge of OSN use by citizens, first responders, and organizations for effective collaboration (Cobb et al. 2014; Shklovski et al. 2008; Stoll et al. 2012; Voida et al. 2012). This research is essential to devise appropriate communication strategies, collaboration methods, and laws and regulations. Our findings are:

- Citizen participation on OSN increases the human resource available with police to identify offenders.
- OSN can help to reduce communication gap and improve coordination between police and citizens.
- Four challenges that can hinder use of OSN for community policing. These include—maintaining meaningful communication, information verification overload, immediate acknowledgement of information shared, and lack of technical expertise and policies to handle information generated on OSN.
- Identify how technological innovation and CSCW research can help support better community policing on OSN.

Related Work

Many studies show how OSN has played an effective role during events involving law and order issues like the Boston bombings, Sichuan earthquake (2008), Haiti earthquake (2009), Oklahoma grassfires (2009), and Chile earthquake (2010).

Gupta and Kumaraguru (2012), Gupta et al. (2013), Mendoza et al. (2010), Qu et al. (2009), Starbird and Palen (2011), Vieweg et al. (2010). These studies demonstrate that OSN provides critical real time information and reduces the misinformation during crisis events. Research shows that citizens use OSN for public coordination during a crisis situations; researchers have categorized public response and shown different communities which developed during crises on OSN (Gupta et al. 2012; Hughes et al. 2008). Research also show that police organizations need effective communication strategy to provide timely information to citizens (Chermak and Weiss 2005; Denef et al. 2013; Heverin and Zach 2010). These studies provide insights on different strategies and activities that police perform on OSN. Recent studies show that OSN is a plausible resource for police forces to reach citizens (Denef et al. 2011). Police in developed nations have realized the effectiveness of OSN in various activities such as investigation, crime identification, intelligence development, and community policing (Denef et al. 2011; IACP 2013; Lexis Nexis Risk Solutions 2012). Few studies explore technology for community interaction and collaboration to prevent crime (Heverin and Zach 2010; Lewis and Lewis 2012).

Benefits of OSN are also accompanied by various challenges like interactivity and pace of information diffusion (Denef et al. 2011). Police departments in developed countries have made reasonable efforts and progress to adopt OSN. Developing nations like India are also influenced by OSN and police (in these regions) are still evolving skills to use OSN for policing (Plane 2013). Few studies in India show that OSN was used to spread misinformation and public agitation during crisis events such as Mumbai terror attacks (2011), Muzzafarnagar riots and Assam disturbance (2012) (Gupta and Kumaraguru 2011; Kumaraguru 2013). These studies report that in these events, panic was spread through fake images, messages, and videos on OSN.

Surveys have shown that OSN introduced challenges for police officers such as fake/impostor accounts which target law enforcement agencies, security and privacy concerns, civil liabilities and resource constraints like time and technical skill of the staff (IACP 2013; Lexis Nexis Risk Solutions 2012). Another challenge was easy accessibility of OSN to malicious people who can modify or spread rumors, making sharing information a complex task (Denef et al. 2013). These studies provide little insight about—rationale and expectations of police behind these actions and acceptance of these actions by citizens.

To best of our knowledge, it is the first study that examines police and citizens' behavior and expectation regarding OSN use for community policing in India. HCI and CSCW research can improve the communication and collaboration between the two stakeholders (police and citizens) for better policing. For this, insight into the technological interactions between these stakeholders is required. Our research expands on the existing literature of OSN for law and order situation and provides a focused study addressing these specified research gaps. We believe that the insights from our study will provide opportunities to develop better communication strategy for police and citizens.

Background

To understand OSN role in collaboration and communication to fight crime, we discuss interaction strategies of police and community policing approach.

Community Policing Approach

Community policing aims to achieve following: (a) offering decentralized decision-making that empowers field officers to identify crime, (b) prioritizing the problem with the help of local citizens, and (c) introducing transparency in the policing. To achieve these objectives two prime components are recognized— community partnership paradigm and problem-solving approach (Community Policing Consortium 1994). We discuss each of these components below.

Community partnership involves maintaining orderliness and safe neighborhoods with the help of citizens. For this partnership, Indian police introduced provisions such as neighborhood watch committee; join beat constables to perform night beats, and arrange social and cultural get-togethers to understand neighborhoods. These activities of community partnership help develop trust between the police and the community. Police need to develop community trust before involving citizens in decisions-making process. With increased trust, police are able to get valuable information available with the citizens about their neighborhoods. Therefore, community partnership involves developing relationships that increase "bond of trust" by maintaining community contact and frequent communication with citizens (Community Policing Consortium 1994).

Problem solving approach involves four aspects: Information exchange, problem identification, problem solving, and Trust. It involves identifying common concerns for citizens and the police. The prioritization happens with help of citizens, e.g., a police team might think that burglary is the biggest problem in their locality, however, community might consider women assault and harassment as a bigger concern. Once the problems are prioritized, police work at providing solutions to the issues raised by citizens. Problem-solving approach considers those solutions as best that can satisfy community members to improve safety, reduce anxiety, and strengthen the ties between police and citizens (Community Policing Consortium 1994).

The provisions so far adopted for community policing are mostly non-technology based. Realizing the potential of OSN and to involve citizens in policing activities, Indian police have made its presence on various OSNs such as Twitter and Facebook. Table 1 describes Twitter followers and Facebook likes of the popular Indian police pages. In this work, we use the knowledge of community policing components and analyze role of OSN to facilitate policing. We also identify the design challenges that need to be addressed to increase OSN role in community partnership and problem solving. We found that for almost all the police departments, number of followers on Twitter is less in comparison to Facebook likes. Given that

Table 1 Twitter followers and Facebook (FB) likes on police pages

Police departments	Likes	Followers	Post	Joined
Bangalore city[b]	105,463	12,100	Yes	2011
Bangalore traffic[b]	249,968	8045	Yes	2012
Chennai[a]	50,979	1108	Yes	2013
Delhi traffic[a]	202,858	2,59,000	Yes	2011
UP police PR[a]	8304	4585	Yes	2013

[a]Shows both FB and Twitter profiles were not verified
[b]Shows Twitter page was verified
"Post" shows if others were allowed to post on FB
"Joined" shows year in which the page came in existence

the number of likes is more on Facebook than followers on Twitter (for most of the departments), wherever appropriate, we provide examples from Facebook.

Methodology

In this research, we conducted a multi-stakeholder study consisting of 41 semi structured, in-depth interviews. We recruited all police officers through word-of-mouth and mailing lists dedicated for IPS officers; IPS is one among the three All India Service (Ministry of Home Affairs 2010). We completed 20 individual interviews with IPS officers, each of about an hour. In our study, 95 % participants were male and 5 % were female; 20.00 % were in the age group 25–34 years, 10.00 % were 35–44 years, 55 % were 45–55 years and 15 % were 55–65+ years. They provided services in different states and three officers served special branches. They were of the rank ADG (Additional Director General), DGP (Director General of Police), and above. Interview questions comprised of topics such as the need for police to use OSN, how OSN has been helpful so far to police, understand OSN usage policies followed by departments, and challenges in adoption of OSN. Among eight officers who used OSN for official purposes, only two officers had used OSN for more than two years. Rests were planning to use OSN for official purposes.

Next, we interviewed 21 citizens to understand their perspective on the presence of police on OSN. Citizen participants' demography was diverse (e.g. age group, education, and occupation). Interview questionnaire for citizens comprised of different topics such as, ways in which citizens will like police to help through OSN, and preferred OSN for communication with police. Most citizen participants reported using OSN like Facebook for the last three to five years, whereas police officers reported recent use (almost an year) for policing activities. Ten citizens were aware of Facebook police pages; among these, six had heard or visited police pages on OSN and three mentioned that they had visited these pages to communicate with police. Citizens in the interviews consisted of 57.14 % male and 42.86 % female; 23.81 % were between the ages of 18–24 years, 42.86 %

were 25–34 years, 14.29 % were 35–44 years, 9.52 % were 45–54 years, and 9.52 % were 55–65+ years. Participants were from a broad range of educational background: teaching/research (25.53 %), fashion designing (11.76 %), MBA (5.88 %), computer/IT (29.41 %), and other fields (29.42 %).

These interviews (both citizens and police) were conducted by one of the authors and she met the interviewee one on one. Few interviews were conducted through telephone. We chose to conduct interviews in English as it is the common business language used in the country. All interviews were recorded and transcribed for analysis. We used randomly generated numbers to identify the subjects in our notes so as to maintain subjects' privacy. Participants were shown consent information, after they agreed to participate in our study. Recruitment approach followed in this work has also been used in other CSCW studies (Semaan and Mark 2012).

Qualitative Analysis: We applied limited grounded theory analysis on interview responses. An analyst iteratively assigned codes: open codes, axial codes and dimensional codes. Grounded theory method allows coding by a single analyst because of the intense labor involved in the coding process (Charmaz 2006). Initially, 25 codes were developed, which were condensed to four categories— why OSN, preferred OSN, target audience, and limitation of OSN for policing. Over successive iterations of coding, 3 categories—why OSN, preferred OSN and limitation of OSN categories became independent dimensions with their own subcategories. Participants gave mixed and nuanced responses for target audience; therefore we combined tentative subcategories as one category.

During the process, we developed various memos based on the incidences and cases shared by the participants and relationships observed between the categories. We used conceptual memos to note the meaning of codes and record when events happened, and respective consequences. Authors are aware that the core aspect of grounded theory method is an emerging theory from comparisons of codes and successive iterations. However, in this paper authors do not report a full theory analysis and use these categories in combination with quantitative results to understand the policing scenario on OSN. This limited use of grounded theory for interpreting data is an established research approach (Charmaz 2006; Muller et al. 2014; Muller and Kogan 2012).

Results

In this section, we report participants' perception, evaluate the current status of OSN for policing and the associated challenges.

Why Are OSN Needed?

Three themes emerge from our analysis of the interviews: (1) OSN can support policing by increasing citizen participation to identify crime, (2) OSN can reduce the communication gap, and (3) OSN can improve co-ordination between the police and citizens. We now discuss these themes and support these inferences through evidences from content analysis of Facebook pages. We refer interviewed IPS officers as P1...P20, and citizens as C1...C21. To analyze the situation on actual position on OSN, we provide anecdotal evidences from Facebook pages, which substantiate the perceptions of IPS officers and citizens on use of OSN.

Increase Citizen Participation to Identify Crime

Officers express that OSN can help increase the personnel (citizen volunteers) available for police to identify offenders. According to officers, using OSN, citizens can easily report defaulters and lawbreakers. P7 says, "OSN can be used to create a community of people who will be using it (OSN) [to identify crime]." Another officer states that before the introduction of OSN, only traffic police on roads were responsible for catching traffic violators, but now anybody can use OSN pages to post pictures of traffic violators. P17 says, "Delhi Traffic Police page involves public [citizens] in finding traffic violators, on the basis of which challans [fine] are issued. So our limited resources are increased, and we can catch many more people by seeking help of public [than before]." Officers believe that using OSN, citizens can provide real time content to inform about crime. For example, P9 states, "Young people are using OSN on the mobile devices. They can upload real time content [from the crime location]."

Consistent with police officers, citizens also agree that OSN pages can help report issues related to traffic and crime. These issues include traffic congestion, accidents, beggars, corruption, and other issues with public transport. Most citizens remark that they will like to use OSN pages to report traffic issues like unruly behavior of taxi or autorickshaw drivers. For example, C1 says, "I use public transport like autorickshaw; they [auto drivers] either overcharge or harass passengers by refusing to go. I will like to report these cases." According to citizens, OSN can also provide opportunities to engage with police to report crime such as theft, neighborhood issues, and crime against women. C13 states, "if I see a girl in a vulnerable situation I might give this information [on the Facebook page of police], and they [Police] can take instant action." C12 says that she can instantly geo-tag the crime location in the Facebook post to help officers receive quick information about exact location of the crime.

Facebook content analysis shows that citizens use these pages to report activities such as the use of tinted dark glasses in cars, crimes against women, and neighborhood issues like drunk men on streets. For example, A citizen complains about drunk men and posts a video as an evidence, "I am posting a video as well of people drinking openly at XXX wines, sec 1X-1Z road. I had posted pics from the same location on 13th Aug as well" (see Fig. 1). These observations show that citizen participation on OSN can increase the personnel available for identifying crime and law offenders.

Fig. 1 Citizen posted an image on Facebook to report illegal use of streets for alcohol consumption

Reduce the Communication Gap

We find that OSN can reduce the communication gap between police and citizens in three ways: (1) OSN can help understand the public opinion about various law and order issues, (2) OSN can help get feedback from citizens, and (3) OSN allows citizens to overcome social pressures to approach the police.

Understand citizen opinion: Officers mention that OSN can provide effective understanding of public sentiments and opinion. P3 states, "Whenever we think of OSN, we think it in terms of what are the aspirations of the public [citizens], what they want from us, what are their grievances and how we can address them." Officers report OSN to be better than existing media (such as television) to gauge public opinions. P3 states, "OSN is more representative; police delivery [of services] can be more up to mark. On TV we are not sure of how many people are interviewed, they show only 2–3 people. This number cannot be used to show mass opinion." According to officers, understanding the opinion of citizens is important for early crime detection, crime prevention, and for reducing communication gap between police and citizens. Similar to police officers, few citizens also agree that police can know about public opinion using OSN. C6 states, "Your status speaks everything. They [Police] can know what is going in mind of citizens and take action accordingly."

Feedback from citizens: Officers believe that OSN based feedback (both positive an negative) from citizens can bridge the gap between police and public. We asked officers, what will be their reaction to the message such as Scenario A, I will like to thank the police to improve law and order. P9 says, "make it reach as many people as possible and post it. Helps to show a positive image of your organization. Good feeling among the community and for people." P12 says, "further propagate such message; these tweets are hardly to be seen. Definitely they will boost up the moral." Officers considered it important to reply to feedback posts to keep the connection with citizens and show that citizens' views are respected. P8 says, "convey thanks for posting; it should be taken cognizance of. The other person should feel that somebody is taking note of his thoughts." Officers said that they will also appreciate negative feedback and take appropriate actions. We showed officers a post, Scenario B, in which a citizen had complained about unavailability of police on a highway where a girl was being beaten. P1 says, "we will check if actually it is happening and take action; subsequently will post about the action." Officers believed that OSN can help explain the reasons for such lapse so that people can understand the situation better. Adding, further officers mentioned that in the absence of OSN, police depend upon exiting media such as television and newspaper to explain their decisions. On these media, the police views are presented as understood by the journalists. However, with OSN police officers can directly communicate with citizens and express their views (without influence of journalists). P4 says, I would like to use OSN to give official version of any information. Because they [citizens] always hear the story from what media [television or newspaper] has to say which always might not be correct. [Using OSN] They [citizens] can hear what we have to say directly from us. Police version is the correct version and people should start trusting it [police version] instead of media [television or newspaper].

We showed the above-discussed scenarios—A and B to citizens. Few citizens said that they will like to spread/reply to positive messages. C1 says, "There are certain situations when police really give their best. [I will share this post to] Encourage police and let others know that police is doing something." More citizens mention that they will share or like a post in Scenario B than Scenario A, so that police are more informed about the issue. Citizens believe that like or share utility might let police understand the gravity of the situation. A citizen mentions that if many people complain about the same issue police might take some action.

In Facebook posts, we find that citizens appreciate police for the good work and share what troubles them. For example, a citizen complains about an undisciplined drunk police constable (see Fig. 2). Such posts can help police understand citizens' concern, which play a significant role in reducing communication gap. Understanding the citizen's need for anonymity, police say in a post that citizens need not reveal their identity if they want to help solve violent crimes. Thus, content analysis of Facebook pages shows that OSN can reduce the communication gap between citizens and police by encouraging frequent exchange of information and feedback.

Provides anonymity: The third method which helps reduce the communication gap is OSN's ability to facilitate anonymous communication between police and citizens. Many citizens mention that they will prefer an anonymous platform to communicate with police. C7 says that he will like to make an anonymous

Fig. 2 Post showing police acknowledging citizens' concern regarding undisciplined police constable. This post received 102 likes

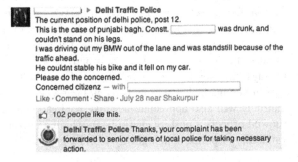

complaint on OSN against local Member of Legislative Assembly (MLA, politician), and illegal activities of a local shopkeeper, which otherwise is not possible as these influential people can harm him. Citizens report that they are fearful and concerned about their security, therefore, use fake-profiles to share information with police. For example, C16 states, "I created a fake profile to post pictures of traffic offenders, so that law offenders are punished, but they do not get to know that I complain about them." Some officers also acknowledge that citizens may not feel comfortable revealing their identity on Facebook, and may use pseudonyms similar to undercover informers. These observations show that OSN helps overcome social fears and pressures while communicating with police.

Improve Coordination

In this section, we show that OSN can improve coordination between police and citizens by keeping citizens informed and delivering targeted messages.

Keep citizens informed: Officers mention that the police can use OSN to keep citizens informed about various arrangements. For example, P15 states, "OSN help in disseminating information and forewarn [citizens] about areas that might see a conflict." Further, P2 states, "OSN can help inform citizens about jewellery snatching cases, time it can happen, and precautions to be taken." Officers show interest in posting wide variety of advisories (an official announcement or warning) through OSN such as crime alerts, safety tips for women, children and senior citizens, places to avoid during major events and natural calamities like cyclone or floods. An officer states, "A cricket match and a popular festival happened on the same day; we were expecting a large gathering for both the events. These crowds were required to cross each other's route to reach their destinations. To avoid traffic, we issued instructions through public post on OSN; this proved helpful to manage the crowds and avoid traffic on roads." Citizens also view OSN as a means to obtain timely alerts from police. C7 says, "Suppose there is a threat in Delhi, and they [Police] give me alerts on it [OSN] then I would have liked to follow it [police Facebook page]." Such alerts can keep citizens informed and improve coordination.

Targeted communication: Officers acknowledge the need to communicate appropriate advisories to appropriate audiences for improving coordination with them. These advisories are communication-intensive, highly social, cultural, and influence social networks in the real world. Officers in different regions have different needs and priorities for issuing these advisories. For instance, P1 states that OSN can be used to spread awareness regarding social evil practices of witch-hunting in northeast India. 3 Officers from Haryana (a state in North India) mention that they will like to create awareness about women, children and senior citizen safety as one agenda. Few citizens also mention that they will like or share an advisory only when it is relevant to their network. This suggests that OSN can help in spreading targeted messages to improve coordination.

Fig. 3 Image posted by
Delhi Traffic Police on
Facebook informing citizens
about traffic diversion
for Independence day
celebrations

Consistent with the interview analysis, we find that the police use Facebook pages to keep citizens informed about policing arrangements. A police post informs citizens which roads will be closed for general traffic from 5.00 AM to 9.00 AM (see Fig. 3). Another post informs citizens about criminals and states "Nataraja@Mallu, a notorious rowdy involved in assault, extortion, kidnapping & attempt to murder booked under Goonda Act today." To target specific audiences, we find that Delhi police maintains a dedicated page for North Eastern Indian citizens who were recently victimized in the city.

Which OSN Police Prefer to Reach the Citizens?

We asked officers, which OSN do you use for your day-to-day activity to maintain law and order? We find that police organizations are using or planning to use a variety of OSN platforms. Among these, Facebook and WhatsApp are the most preferred networks. Some platforms are used to communicate with citizens (Facebook and Twitter) and some are used only within the organization (WhatsApp and YouTube). Sixteen officers prefer Facebook over other OSN for activities involving citizen participation; among these sixteen, 6 officers use only Facebook. P4 said: "Facebook is more interesting. Personal viewpoint can be expressed and it is more interactive. People [citizens] prefer to give their inputs through Facebook." Some officers advocate the need of dedicated Facebook pages for policing tasks. P19 says, "Depending upon the need of the department they can have it [a Facebook page] for specific purposes like woman's extortion cell, child abuse cell, and extortion cell." Few officers mention using Twitter; these officers believe that Twitter requires less time as it is used by few people. P15 says, "Actually it is the matter of how much time you can devote. Facebook gets too big and involves many more people [whereas on] Twitter you make a small comment and it is done."

For personal and within organization use, officers use mobile-based applications like WhatsApp and BlackBerry Messenger. Many officers feel that WhatsApp is better than Facebook to get instant information about the current situation on the ground. P13 says: "During a gathering or law and order situation, the usual question is how many people [are there]. Then they [officers in control rooms] start guessing, if officers on duty have a phone they can click the picture and upload it, so that in the control room, we have an idea." Officers further add that WhatsApp showed when the person was last seen online and therefore cannot deny receiving the message. P12 mentions, "Nobody can deny that he or she have received a message." While comparing Facebook with WhatsApp, P18 says, "With WhatsApp, we can send an audio file as well. We can transfer photos, images instantly with WhatsApp. I feel Facebook is terrible in this case. Suppose you want to upload an image to Facebook, it will take a lot of time." Officers feel that policing requires instant response, as time plays a crucial role and can make or break things.

Who Is the Target Audience?

We asked officers, who are the target audience you want to reach through OSN. We find that there was no clear understanding of target audience on OSN among the officers. P6 says, "every citizen is our target audience, but audience is limited to account holders [on OSN]." Similarly P4 remarks, "persons who are using it [OSN], affluent classes, students younger generation who can afford to use the Internet." Few officers who feel that younger population and students are common audience on OSN believe that OSN can help reach and connect with youth better. P3 says, "Youth is sometimes available only on OSN; what they have to say is sometimes not available on traditional media/sources of information. They have very strong ideas which are otherwise missed out."

Few officers say that currently OSN was restricted to urban areas and did not have good reach in rural areas. P9 says, "Urban sector, yes we can find some information. Rural areas, it is not of priority [to reach through OSN]." We find similar views among few officers regarding the use of mobile phone applications like WhatsApp; P13 believes that there are few WhatsApp users in India. The limited reach restricts efforts to use OSN for policing by some agencies in urban areas only; but in the past, we find that OSN effect percolated to rural areas in crises situations like riots in Muzzafarnagar and Assam Hindustan Times (2013); Press Trust of India (2013). This shows that officers have limited understanding of OSN reach and audience it impacts. Officers do not mention any distinction in the population on different platforms and believe that OSN can be used to connect with anybody.

OSN Challenges and Overheads

We now discuss the following four challenges that can hinder community-policing efforts using OSN: maintain meaningful communication, verification overhead, acknowledgment overhead, and lack of technical capabilities.

Maintain Meaningful Communication

Participants acknowledge the need for maintaining information exchange through OSN that is meaningful to improve policing decisions and arrangements (here after referred as meaningful information). We identify two factors that can inhibit this meaningful information exchange on OSN: (1) unclear and generic information from police and (2) violent and abusive content from citizens.

Citizens remark that advisories during riots help take appropriate decisions but think that some police posts are too ambiguous and may not help take appropriate decisions. For instance, citizens find that police advisory released on Facebook asking citizens not to trust any rumors posted on OSN during Muzzafarnagar riots (See Fig. 4) was too generic to be enforced. For example, C4 states, "This information is useless. If my friend is tweeting or sharing (Fig. 4) how will I know that it is not fake. The post says not trust any tweet, why should I trust this post." However, most police officers feel that it is useful to share such information.

Officers fear that on OSN, citizens may use inappropriate expressions and informal language to communicate their thoughts. P10 states, "Expectation of people how police should use OSN is not based on the clear understanding of law enforcement agencies. They think that the way they use informal style language on Facebook accounts, law enforcement will also do the same. That is not possible." An officer mentions that Twitter profile and Facebook wall have the potential to create havoc. Officers also express inability to remove or control the spread of abusive content from the official pages. They believe that removing inappropriate comments may give the impression that the police are censoring the page and may obstruct community-policing initiatives. Similar to interview analysis, online posts on Facebook pages show that citizens post abusive content. For example, in reply

UP Police PR shared Pro TO Dgp UP's status.
September 8

कृपया FACEBOOK, TWITTER, YOU TUBE, WHATSAPP पर
प्रचारित किसी भी प्रकार की अफवाह, वीडियो क्लीपिंग पर विश्वास न करें।
उपद्रवियों पर सख्ती से काबू पाया जा रहा है।

Fig. 4 Advisory shown to participants posted by UP police on Facebook "Please, do not trust any rumor, video clipping shown on Facebook, Twitter, YouTube, WhatsApp. Nuisance creators are being controlled sternly." Post received 26 likes

to a police post informing citizens about arrest of a criminal, a citizen posts comments like "Shoot all bloody rapists," "bastard," and "That bastard private parts should be cut so it sets an example for others too."

Verification Overhead

Officers believe that information obtained from OSN is a starting point, and it is essential to verify the information. P17 states, "Any information is just information as long as it is there. After that it has to be verified, correlated with other information, for this piece of information to go to the category of intelligence." Officers also mention about various techniques they may use to verify the information available on OSN. One approach is to look at the number of responses (multiple posts) posted related to an issue. P3 states, "More are the number of responses that we check, more we are close to the truth." Another approach that officers mention for virtual verification is to check the source of the information. Citizens also agree that information obtained from OSN is not completely trustworthy and requires verification. However, most citizens say that if information comes from police pages, it will be trustworthy and will need no verification. Citizens (similar to police) rely upon the source of the information to judge its reliability. C12 states, "I do not trust the information, I verify the source of it." Analysis of behavioral data shows that police may ask citizens for additional information for verification. For example, one of the police pages posted, "Thanks, Kindly re-post the pictures with clearly visible R/C [Vehicle Registration] No., time and place also so that proper action can be taken against the police personnel." In some cases, police request citizens to contact an officer who can verify the details and take action. For example, "Dear [name], Please visit at [XXX] Police Station and lodge a complaint with the details, and they will take necessary action in this regard. Thank you;" shows police need to verify information shared on OSN.

Acknowledgement Overload

OSN users often expect a quick response when they post a complaint or a request on OSN (Kelly 2014). We analyze citizens' view on how long police can take to respond to a citizen's request. Citizens' expectation varied from few minutes to a week. C5 states, "if police has to use OSN, then there should be a team who should be checking it every second." For some citizens, type of complaint and volume of complaints received on OSN influence frequency of acknowledgement. C14 states, "That depends upon the issue, traffic problems can be answered in 1 or 2 days. Children/people who need immediate help like accident cases should get an immediate response." Very few citizens state that the police should send an immediate acknowledgement that they have received the complaint. According to police officers, responses cannot be provided immediately. Few officers say that they can respond once in a day and for some officers it depends on the need. This expectation difference between police and citizens can inhibit the active use of OSN for policing. Analysis of Facebook pages shows that the police do acknowledge citizens' post, for example in a post police states, "Dear [name], Your post has been conveyed to High Ground Police Station (080-229XX587/XX83), They will assist you in this regard. Thank You."

Lack of Technical Teams and Policies

Officers think that lack of manpower who are capable of handling OSN pages of police inhibits social media adoption for community policing. They also mention about the need for guidelines and policies, which can lead to uniformity and clarity in decisions while using OSN.

Most officers believe that police departments require trained people who can help leverage the benefits of OSN. P9 states, "Team of better people as of now, it is a resource constraint for us who can help us use it better." Officers think that the OSN team should be acquainted with police decisions and be very specific about content they post on OSN. P3, while discussing characteristics of the person handling OSN page states, "Person, who can be very specific about what he speaks; for now, he will share very limited type of information."

Officers mention the need for policies that can help understand the pros and cons of using OSN. For example, P4 states, "It [OSN for policing] is still in an experimental phase but to leverage its benefits, policy has to be built, keeping in mind—OSN usage, pros, and cons. Like Facebook's servers are outside India, so how information [confidential] can be saved [stored] on them." Officers mention a need for guidelines on content to be posted. They believe guidelines on content are important to generate information that can keep citizen communities interested during lean periods (time when there is no crisis to deal with). Few officers think that policy can help define boundaries and extent to which OSN should be used by police. P5 states, "Centralized guidelines should be there on how to use Facebook, Twitter and YouTube otherwise everybody will start using it in his or her ways. Thus, the current absence of OSN policies and guidelines limit the use of OSN for policing.

Discussion

In this work, we explore how OSN can facilitate community policing in India. Consistent with the previous research in the developed world, we find that OSN can help involve citizens in policing through various ways: increasing citizen participation in neighborhood watch, reducing communication gap and improving coordination between "grassroots" members of community and police department (Heverin and Zach 2010). Researchers in the CSCW field are uniquely positioned to develop tools necessary to support police-citizen relationship on OSN. Current

CSCW research investigates OSN use by first responders and citizens primarily during crisis situations, which are event-driven and have specific goals to be achieved in a short term (Denef et al. 2013). It is unclear how this knowledge can be used for day-to-day communication in policing activities that are diverse and are not time bound. We find that effective policing through OSN requires identifying the needs, planning activities, creating useful content to be shared, and constantly communicating with citizens. We now discuss OSN role to facilitate frequent contact and ease information exchange as required in different components of community policing in day-to-day policing.

OSN Role in Community Partnership Paradigm: Lack of communication is frequently cited as a major problem resulting in lack of trust in services offered by police (Lewis and Salem 1981). Our study shows that OSN provides opportunities for police to keep citizens informed about policing arrangements and decisions. However, officers in our study think that they need to understand the content and characteristics of interaction that can happen on OSN during "lean periods" (when no major event is happening of law and order interest). This can help keep the community involved and get persistent visibility to police. We think that persistent presence on OSN can also help police to get quick visibility during high impact events like blasts where communication need has been felt the most.

Our study shows that police believe OSN can help reach the desired set of population and can provide opportunity to have a constructive dialogue and exchange feedback among police and citizens. However, police say that constant communication needs to be constantly guided through specialized 24×7 OSN teams, policies, and guidelines. We find that though OSN facilitates quick information exchange between police and residents, designing appropriate nudges that educate about the legal and social implications of abusive content can reduce the misuse of OSN. This can help improve effective communication between the two stakeholders. Defamatory content can be a major block for successful adoption on OSN by police. Most citizens during interviews mention that abusive content should not be used on OSN while expressing disagreement on police actions. We find that, in recent events, defamatory content posted against a politician on Facebook and WhatsApp led to violent protests in Mumbai, India. Police filed a complaint against the accused, but lacked concrete means to educate citizens about implications (legal and social) of such content.

Citizens often fear police and feel that revealing facts about crime may expose them to criminals; these apprehensions hinder police—community association (Community Policing Consortium 1994). Prior work in developed world suggests that citizens may not trust community-policing technology that does not keep their submission anonymous (Lewis and Lewis 2012). Similarly, in our study, we found that citizens prefer to use OSN as it provides anonymity that can help citizens reach police without social pressures and fear; thus, OSN facilitates community contact and partnership. OSN provides a platform where citizens can hold police accountable for taking action against crime but not expose themselves to criminals or other social pressures. However, anonymous posts involve legitimacy issues that make it difficult for police to take actions. We believe that technological solutions require amalgamation of security and CSCW domain such that the proposed technology can provide anonymity to citizens, but also keep minimal checks to authenticate information if needed.

OSN for facilitating problem solving: We find that both citizens and police believe that using OSN, citizens can inform the police about vulnerable streets in the city, report geo-tagged posts that can give instant information about the location of the crime to the police. Citizens can also post images and videos of unsafe neighborhoods. This information exchange can facilitate two important aspects of community policing: (a) the problem-identification and (b) prioritization based on citizen's input. Problem-solving approach suggests that best solutions are those that satisfy the community. Police after examining OSN generated content can identify priorities of different communities and use this information to make appropriate judgment to satisfy the safety needs of citizens. This can help make community feel safer and can generate trust in police. Police Officers in our study mention that OSN can help explain reasons for lapse in policing arrangements directly to citizens without involving journalists (as needed in other mediums like television and newspapers). This can help citizens understand the situation at hand and also encourage information exchange to address the lapse.

We find that for success of OSN, police will need to acknowledge the information exchanged through OSN; our work shows this can be an overhead for the police. Therefore, the police departments need a technology that can imbibe an effective acknowledgment system on OSN platforms. We find that citizens' preference for response time on the post varied depending upon the case. An analysis of communication patterns can reveal expectation of citizens regarding response time to complain. This knowledge can be used to design a semi–automated acknowledgement system. Social tools can also help classify the content posted by citizens on OSN in various categories, and police departments can set flags to send an acknowledgement based on the category. This can help reduce the overhead and enable frequent OSN use.

We also find that legitimacy of information exchanged through OSN can impede the information exchange during problem-solving process. Setting up OSN profiles and pages, can get a large number of posts for police to address. Legitimacy of this information is also a concern for police and they feel it is challenging to verify all the information posted on OSN. However, police feel that multiple responses on the topic can be a good indicator that the information is legitimate and verified. Tools and applications can be built to ease this verification and validation. These tools can provide cross-platform verification and get responses from different OSN, resulting in increased pace at which police obtains responses from different platforms on the issue. Alerts can be generated to inform police about the verification being done on the content; this can expedite the police decision.

As we conclude this paper, we believe that this work outlines the requirements (as extracted from our interviews) for a socio-technical solution that can facilitate two important component of community policing—community partnership and problem-solving process. This study creates an understanding about policing requirements from OSN. This study also provides designers and researchers with insights for designing technology that empowers and encourages police—citizen communities to address social issues. Community policing so far has been addressed using non-technology tools but community oriented platforms like OSN can act as a facilitator and catalyst to policing.

Limitations

This study provides insights on perceptions, behavior and challenges for OSN use in community policing, however, there are some limitations to this work. We only study users from urban and suburban areas where OSN influence is high. It will be interesting to study a broader space. Other communities for e.g. OSN users in rural areas may prefer different technologies like voice based solutions for community policing. The number of male policemen in our study is dominant, however male and female ratio in our study, is representative ratio of the genders in IPS (Joshi 2012). Another potential limitation is of the interview methods that analyze perceptions of the participants and cannot measure the behavior of subjects. We present preliminary evidences of actual behavior using Facebook content but think that behavior can be understood through further analysis in future studies.

Acknowledgments We would like to thank all participants for sharing their views with us. We would also like to thank TCS for funding the project through Ph.D. fellowship. Our special thanks to Mr. Nandkumar Sarvade who helped us connect with IPS officers. We would like to thank CERC and Precog members for supporting us throughout the project; special thanks to Aditi Gupta and Siddhartha Asthana.

References

Charmaz, K. (2006). Constructing grounded theory: A practical guide through qualitative analysis. Thousand Oaks, CA, USA: Sage.

Chermak, S. & Weiss, A. (2005). Maintaining legitimacy using external communication strategies: An analysis of police-media relations. *Journal of Criminal Justice*.

Cobb, C., McCarthy, T., Perkins, A., Bharadwaj, A., Comis, J., Do, B., & et al. (2014). *Designing for the Deluge: Understanding and supporting the disturbed*. Collaborative Work of Crisis Volunteers. CSCW.

Community Policing Consortium. (1994). *Understanding community policing. A framework for action*. Technical report, Bureau of Justice Assistance.

Davis, E. F., Alves, A. A. & Sklansky, D. A. (2014). *Social media and police leadership: Lessons from Boston*. Technical report, NIJ and Harvard's Kennedy School of Government.

Denef, S., Bayerl, P. S. & Kaptein, N. (2013). Social media and the police—Tweeting practices of British police forces during the August 2011 riots. In *Proceedings of CHI 2013* (pp. 3471–3480).

Denef, S., Kaptein, N., Bayerl, P. S. (2011). ICT Trends in European Policing.

Express News Service. (2013). Is community policing need of the hour? http://www.newindianexpress.com/states/karnataka/article1430481.ece

Gupta, A., Joshi, A. & Kumaraguru, P. (2012). Identifying and characterizing user communities on twitter during crisis events. *Workshop on UMSocial*, Co-located with CIKM.

Gupta, A., & Kumaraguru, P. (2011). *Twitter explodes with activity in Mumbai blasts! A lifeline or an unmonitored daemon in the lurking?*. Technical report, IIIT-Delhi.

Gupta, A., Kumaraguru, P. (2012). Misinformation on Twitter during crisis events. In *Encyclopedia of social network analysis and mining (ESNAM)*. Springer publications.

Gupta, A., Lamba, H. & Kumaraguru, P. (2013). $1.00 per RT #BostonMarathon #PrayForBoston: Analyzing fake content on twitter. eCrime Research Summit.

Heverin, T. & Zach, L. (2010). Twitter for city police department information sharing. In *Proceedings of ASIST 2010*.

GMP police, 'GMP on social media'. http://www.gmp.police.uk/content/section.html?readform& s=BF065D29498499728025796100424FED

Hindustan Times. (2013). Video that sparked communal violence in Muzaffarnagar reaches other districts. http://www.hindustantimes.com/India-news/lucknow/Video-that-sparked-Muzaffarnagar-clashes-makes-its-way-to-other-districts/Article1-1120683.aspx

Home Affairs Committee. (2011). Home Affairs Committee concludes police failed to appreci-ate magnitude of riot task. http://www.parliament.uk/business/committees/committees-a-z/ commons-select/home-affairs-committee/news/plsd-report-publication/

Hughes, A., Palen, L., Sutton, J., Liu, S. & Vieweg, S. (2008). "Site-seeing" in disaster: An examination of on-line social convergence. ISCRAM.

IACP. (2013). 2013 IACP Social Media Survey. http://www.iacpsocialmedia.org/Portals/1/ documents/2013SurveyResults.pdf

Joshi, S. (2012). Only 442 women police stations across India: Police research data. http://www. thehindu.com/todays-paper/tp-national/tp-newdelhi/only-442-women-police-stations-across-india-police-research-data/article4236877.ece

Kelly, G. (2014). Social media marketing requires prompt response times.http://www.businesstex ter.com/social-media-marketing-requires-prompt-response-times/

Kumaraguru, P. (2013). *Riots in Muzaffarnagar (Uttar Pradesh), India*. September, 2013. Technical report, IIIT-Delhi.

Lewis, S. & Lewis, D. A. (2012). Examining technology that supports community policing. In *Proceedings of CHI 2012* (pp. 1371–1380). ACM.

Lewis, D. A., & Salem, G. (1981). Community crime prevention: An analysis of a developing strategy. *Crime and Delinquency, 27*(3), 405–421.

Lexis Nexis Risk Solutions. (2012). Survey of Law enforcement personnel and their use of social media in investigations. www.lexisnexis.com/investigations

Los Angeles News. (2014). NYPD Twitter campaign backlash spreads to LAPD. http://abclocal. go.com/kabc/story?section=news/local/los angeles&id=9514478

Mendoza, M., Poblete, B. & Castillo, C. (2010). Twitter under crisis: Can we trust what we RT?. In *1st Workshop on social media analytics SOMA*.

Ministry of Home Affairs. (2010). Indian Police Service (IPS). http://mha1.nic.in/ips/ips home.htm

Muller, M., Geyer, W., Soule, T. & Wafer, J. (2014). Geographical and organizational common-alities in enterprise crowdfunding. In *Proceedings of CSCW 2014* (pp. 778–789).

Muller, M. J. & Kogan, S. (2012). Grounded theory method in HCI and CSCW. In J. Jacko (Ed.), *Human computer interaction handbook*. CRC Press.

Nayak, V. (2014). 92 Million Facebook users makes India The Second Largest Country [STUDY]. http://www.dazeinfo.com/2014/01/07/facebook-inc-fb-india-demographic-users-2014

Palen, L. & Vieweg, S. (2008). The emergence of online widescale interaction: Assiatance, Alliance and Retreat. CSCW.

Plane, B. (2013). [Infographic] How police departments use twitter. http://connectedcops. net/2013/04/23/infographic-how-police-departments-use-twitter/

Press Trust of India (2013). Social media if misused becomes a threat to social security: Shinde. http://tech.firstpost.com/news-analysis/social-media-if-misused-becomes-a-threat-to-social-security-shinde-215320.html

Qu, Y., Wu, P. & Wang, X. (2009). Online community response to major disaster: A case study of Tianya forum in the 2008 China Earthquake. In *Proceedings of 42nd Hawaii International Conference on System Sciences*.

Semaan, B. & G. Mark (2012). 'Facebooking' towards crisis recovery and beyond: Disruption as an opportunity. In *Proceedings of CSCW 2012* (pp. 27–36).

Shklovski, I., Palen, L. & Sutton, J. (2008). Finding community through information and communication technology in disaster response. CSCW.

Starbird, K. & Palen, L. (2011). "Voluntweeters": Self-organizing by digital volunteers in times of crisis. In *Proceedings of CHI 2011* (pp. 1071–1080).

Stoll, J., Foot, K. & Edwards, W. K. (2012). Between us and them: Building connectedness within civic networks. In *Proceedings of CSCW 2012* (pp. 237–240).

The COPS Office and the Police Executive Research Forum. (2013). *Social media and tactical considerations for law enforcement*. Technical report.

The Economics Times. (2014). NCRB to connect police stations and crime data across country in 6 months'.

Vieweg, S., Hughes, A., Starbird, K. & Palen, L. (2010). Micro-blogging during two natural hazards events: What twitter may contribute to situational awareness. In *Proceedings of CHI 2010*.

Voida, A., Harmon, E. & Al-Ani, B. (2012). Bridging between organisation and the public: Volunteer coordinators. Uneasy relationship with social computing. In *Proceedings of CHI 2012*.

Wu, Y., Lambert, E. G., Smith, B. W., Pasupuleti, S., Jaishankar, K. & Bhimarasetty, J. V. (2012). An exploratory comparison of policing views between Indian and U.S. College Students. *International Criminal Justice Review*.

The Work of Infrastructuring: A Study of a National eHealth Project

Miria Grisot and Polyxeni Vassilakopoulou

Abstract In this paper we examine a national initiative to further develop the Norwegian healthcare information infrastructure. Specifically, we analyse the work of a project team engaged in the design and development of new web-based capabilities for communication between citizens and primary healthcare practitioners. We foreground the work of infrastructuring which entails conceptualising new technological capabilities not as standalone objects, but as elements in larger arrangements that are sociotechnical in nature. Our findings show how the work within the project was shaped by concerns for embeddedness and durability that led to certain design decisions. Furthermore, we find that these decisions had significant repercussions on the development process and created a complex situation where the cooperation of an evolving constellation of multiple actors was required. Our research contributes an initial understanding of how an infrastructural project is different to projects aimed to the development of specific software artefacts.

Introduction

Recently, Monteiro, Pollock, Hanseth and Williams argued that the CSCW field needs to take account of the ways in which computer support at work has changed over the last 20 years and called for a shift of focus from artefacts to infrastructures (Monteiro et al. 2013). Practically, they asked for studies that go beyond self-contained informatics' applications destined for specific work settings and situations of use (artefacts) and for more research on unbounded, interconnected

M. Grisot · P. Vassilakopoulou (✉)
Department of Informatics, University of Oslo, Oslo, Norway
e-mail: xvasil@ifi.uio.no

P. Vassilakopoulou
e-mail: miriag@ifi.uio.no

© Springer International Publishing Switzerland 2015
N. Boulus-Rødje et al. (eds.), *ECSCW 2015: Proceedings of the 14th European Conference on Computer Supported Cooperative Work, 19–23 September 2015, Oslo, Norway*, DOI 10.1007/978-3-319-20499-4_11

infrastructures that span localities and temporal scales. They justified their call by referring to the wider turn towards systems' openness and interconnectivity which is fuelled by technological trends (e.g. virtualization, new flexible modes for linking applications via web-services, social computing). With this paper we respond to this call by studying the work entailed in the design and development of a national healthcare information infrastructure.

We have studied the eDialogue project which is an on-going Norwegian Government effort to extend the national eHealth platform (called HealthNorway). HealthNorway currently gives access to personal health data sets, and to quality assured health information. The aim of the eDialogue project is to introduce new, additional web-based services for one-to-one communication between citizens and primary healthcare practitioners. The project is not only about organising work to implement additions to what is already in place. More importantly, it is about coordinating multiple actors in order to ensure that the new capabilities offered will be interweaved with existing arrangements and will be able to support evolving needs. Working for the introduction of novel technologies within healthcare is especially challenging because novelty has to link to historically built conventions of practice and to technologically congested landscapes that are the outcome of intensive digitalization efforts undertaken during the last decades. We refer to this work as the work of infrastructuring.

Infrastructures are "pervasive enabling resources in network form" necessary to human activities (Bowker et al. 2010, p. 98). From the perspective of system builders infrastructuring is work that is cross-disciplinary, political, aiming at integrating differences while keeping a holistic view (Hughes 1979). The work of infrastructuring is frequently overlooked, and is loaded with significant ethical and political concerns (Star and Bowker 2002). Infrastructuring entails dealing with inherited strengths and limitations of the existing sociotechnical installed base (Hanseth et al. 1996; Star 1999). Moreover, it entails a development effort that is multi-relational: socio-material, socio-historical and processual (Karasti and Syrjänen 2004). In infrastructure development work, different participants engage in complex collaborative processes for concerted action (Karasti and Baker 2004; Karasti et al. 2010). We continue these lines of research by investigating the work of infrastructuring in a case of relatively simple electronic services development that proved to require complex and demanding coordination.

In this paper we foreground the work of the team engaged in infrastructuring. Specifically, we explore two concerns that are especially relevant in the early stages of design and development (before use) when key decisions have to be taken: embeddedness and durability. Embeddedness refers to how "infrastructure is sunk into, inside of, other structures, social arrangements, and technologies" (Bowker and Star 1999, p. 35). From a system builder's perspective it is a concern related to how to set up infrastructures that are likely to blend in existing technologies and practices. As infrastructures are never built "de novo", but they always develop amidst a stream of technical antecedents, social conventions and professional rules (Ciborra and Hanseth 1998), a concern for embeddedness relates to decisions about how to intertwine novelty with existing technologies and conventions of practice. Nowadays, new infrastructural developments cannot link to conventions of practice without attaining embeddedness to multiple heterogeneous technologies that are already in use and have become integral parts of everyday activities. It is a situation where infrastructures come out of multiple different technologies controlled by distributed actors. Several studies have explored the evolution of relationships among people, organisations and technologies during infrastructuring work and have pointed to issues related to the creation of synergies, the alignment of interests and goals, the motivation of participation and cooperation sustainment (Bietz et al. 2010; Pennington 2011; Procter et al. 2011; Spencer et al. 2011).

The concern for durability refers to the need to form strategies for future infrastructure evolution. Ribes and Finholt have introduced the concept of the "long now" to help us understand the forward looking concerns of infrastructural development, concerns that relate to the fact that today's planning will effect tomorrow's sustainability and evolvability of infrastructures (Ribes and Finholt 2009). Similarly, Karasti, Baker and Millerand identified a temporal orientation (infrastructure time) that goes beyond project time (Karasti et al. 2010). Steinhardt and Jackson labelled this aspect of infrastructure development "anticipation work" (Steinhardt and Jackson 2015). Catering for a wide range of potential users and uses currently and in the future is challenging (Pollock and Williams 2010); the need for durability cannot be addressed by developing today all capabilities needed for imaginary scenarios of possible organisational contexts and practices that will exist in the future, instead, approaches that allow openness and adaptability are needed (Avital and Te'eni 2009).

The aim of our study is to explore and understand the particularities of working to design and develop technologies in projects with an infrastructural orientation, i.e. projects that are not oriented towards delivering self-contained applications (artefacts). Specifically, we focus on the decisions taken in the eDialogue project with attention to concerns of embeddedness and durability, and to the work implications of those decisions. Our research contributes a more fine grained understanding of what a shift from artefacts to infrastructures entails and insights on the intricacies of the work of infrastructuring.

The remaining of the paper is structured as follows. First, we describe the method we used to collect and analyse our empirical data, and then we provide an overview of the empirical setting. Subsequently, we present our analysis. Finally, we conclude by discussing our research findings and possible directions for further research.

Method

The impetus for our study comes from our involvement in an ongoing research project on the interplay between new information technologies (IT) and existing modes of organizing within Norwegian healthcare. Within this project we study new patient-oriented, web-based technologies. We take a process approach where we examine how "things change over time" (Pettigrew 1997). As one of the research activities in this project, we have conducted a case study on the eDialogue project with a focus on the activities of the project team members. In particular, our study has focused on examining how the project team members deployed their activities and cooperated in order to extend the information infrastructure that is already in place by creating new links and adding new technical capabilities.

The study had a first phase in the period January-June 2013 with a focus on the overall visions. In this phase we assembled and analysed a range of academic, government and industry studies, and programmatic and strategic government documents on the deployment of technologies in the Norwegian healthcare sector. A second phase of data collection took place from August 2013 to December 2014 with intensive fieldwork. In this second phase we have focused more closely on the eDialogue project. We have attended weekly project meetings, workshops, and other thematic meetings. In addition, we have conducted a total of 28 open-ended semi-structured interviews with various members of the project team, including the project managers. Interviews lasted approximately 1 h each and have been recorded and fully transcribed. Finally, we reviewed preparatory meeting documents, presentation slides, reports, and project deliverables as we have been granted access to a shared directory with project documents. In summary, the research reported is based on data collected using a combination of fieldwork and documents' analysis (Table 1).

We have approached our study by engaging in infrastructural inversion (Bowker 1994), and focusing on the activities that result to the functioning of the infrastructure (the design and development work of the project team), rather than those supported by the infrastructure (e.g. healthcare practitioner—patient communication practices). Infrastructural inversion in our case is witnessed when the effort to design and develop the new eDialogue services makes visible to the

Table 1 Data sources

Source	Description
Interviews	28 semi-structured interviews with project team members. All interviews were fully recorded and transcribed verbatim
Observations during weekly meetings, workshops and thematic meetings	49 weekly meetings (status meetings with the presence of the whole team, standard duration of 60 min each). Detailed notes taken 1 design workshop (full day) 5 thematic meetings (approximately 60 min each)
Document analysis	Phase 1: Norwegian Healthcare Strategic Planning Documents; Policy, Regulation and Standards Documents; Phase 2: Project documents (reviewed preparatory meeting documents, presentation slides, reports, and project deliverables)

project participants the existing (or non-existing) infrastructural components. Thus, we followed closely the project work and the trajectories of project participants. During interviews we asked participant to identify key decisions taken as the project evolved. The material from the interviews helped us to map key concerns in the project work which we have then enriched with information from the project documentation. We have then focused on those design decisions related to our specific interest to understand how concerns for embeddedness (Bowker and Star 1999) and durability (Ribes and Finholt 2009) shaped the work of the design team. We have then organised the analysis in two steps. First we described how key decisions were reached and how concerns emerge from discussion of alternatives and rationales provided by the participants. Second we have analysed implications of the key decisions for project work making an effort to foreground the work to make these decisions work.

Case Background

The empirical material for this paper is sourced from the study of the eDialogue project which is an on-going Norwegian Government initiative to enable digital communication between citizens and General Practitioners (GPs). The eDialogue project builds upon and extends the capabilities put in place through an initiative with a wider scope: HealthNorway. HealthNorway is a national web-based platform which was launched in 2011 with the aim to provide a basis for the development of new electronic health services and a single point of access to existing services. Through HealthNorway citizens can access data related to their own health from various sources (national summary records, e-prescription records, vaccination records) and browse quality assured health information (on prevention and treatments, patient's rights, and quality indicators for healthcare facilities).

The efforts for eDialogue officially started in 2012 with a preparatory study. The whole endeavour was initiated, ran and funded by the governmental agency which is bestowed with the authority to implement national health policies and to ensure secure and simple information flows in the health and care sector (from now on referred as the Agency). The Agency had already developed and launched the HealthNorway platform and had an interest in extending it. In its initial form the platform supported only one-way information access (citizens accessing their own health data and general health related information) and the aim with eDialogue was to extend it in order to support interactive services (exchange of information between citizens and healthcare providers both asynchronous and synchronous). The outcome of the preparatory study for eDialogue was the specification of four new types of electronic services that would have to be supported: booking of appointments, renewal of prescriptions, electronic contact for administrative purposes and e-consultation. The study was concluded in September 2012, then, a pre-project ran to evaluate the feasibility, relevance and expected benefits of the new services. The final report of the pre-project was published early in 2013

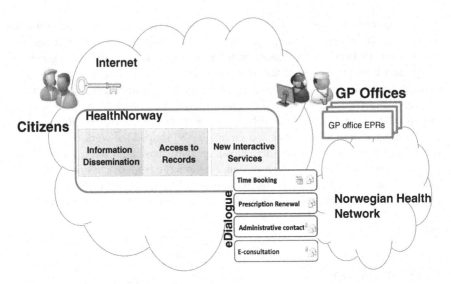

Fig. 1 The positioning of eDialogue in relation to HealthNorway

and confirmed the desirability of all four services. Subsequently, a fully-fledged eDialogue project started in spring 2013. The new services are now (January 2014) in testing phase and a pilot will run during 2015 in a number of GP offices.

As already explained, eDialogue is not meant to be a standalone suite of electronic services but rather, it is conceptualised as an extension of the existing HealthNorway platform. Furthermore, it has to relate to other technologies in place such as the various Electronic Patient Record Systems (EPRs) that GP offices use and the secure, closed network that connects healthcare units throughout Norway. Currently, 98 % of GP offices, 97 % of municipalities, all hospitals and all pharmacies are connected to this network (Norsk Helsenett 2014). This network is vital for all electronic exchanges of information with healthcare providers and is developed and managed by a government enterprise (Norwegian Health Network—NHN). Figure 1 provides a graphical overview of how eDialogue's expands HealthNorway.

Case Analysis

In the paragraphs that follow we present our analysis of the eDialogue case. The analysis is structured in two parts: first, we identify key decisions related to embeddedness and durability concerns, and then, we analyse the implications of these decisions for project work.

Decisions Related to Concerns for Embeddedness and Durability

Embeddedness concerns shape decisions on how to reach citizens and GP offices.

During the early stages of the project conceptualisation there was a need to decide how eDialogue would reach citizens and GP offices. For the citizens' side a major concern was to ensure a seamless user experience. This could not be achieved by simply providing a single gateway to different types of disparate services via HealthNorway. The design of the user interfaces for eDialogue services would have to ensure that new visual elements and additional screens follow the same styles adopted for the rest of the site to ensure a consistent users' experience, furthermore, synthetic overviews of information would have to be provided. A team member said: "*we want this information from your GP to be linked to information from other instances, from hospitals so that you can see everything together*". Another informant said that "*the argument was that the users would expect to have everything in one place to build their own timeline of data*". Hence, the project participants were concerned with how the new services would become embedded into the already established service offering of HealthNorway. Following the same logic, it was decided to re-use authentication mechanisms which were already employed by HealthNorway for identifying citizens. This way, citizens would access after a single log-in the whole spectrum of HealthNorway electronic offering (both old and new services).

For the interface with the healthcare practitioners' side the project team aimed to ensure embeddedness within the pre-existing work arrangements. For instance, they wanted to avoid the introduction of a new system that would require extra work e.g. additional authentication procedure, and additional work to learn how to use it. Alternatives were discussed and it was decided to make use of the existing EPRs in GP offices and extend them with a module that would provide access to the new interactive services. Norwegian GPs already use EPR systems for documenting and accessing patient health information, and are familiar with how to use the systems. The decision to reach out for the GP offices via the existing EPRs implied that the private software companies that developed the EPRs would have to be enrolled to the project in order to adjust their products. By enrolling the EPR vendors to the eDialogue project, the project team became dependant to the collaboration with the vendors for the development of the GP's interface. Vendors were assigned the task of reconfiguring the existing EPRs by applying their understanding about GP office practices and by working with users' panels that they have established while developing and improving their EPR systems.

Durability Concerns Shape Decisions on Message Routing

The decision to link the healthcare practitioners' side with the citizens via the existing EPR systems created the need to think about the linkage itself. Since

GPs' EPRs were already linked to the secure network (Norwegian Health Network—NHN), they could be easily physically linked to HealthNorway. But for the actual information exchange to happen there would be a need to put in place a mechanism to route the messages exchanged between GPs and citizens. It was soon realised that routing is a "cross cutting need"; other actors in the sector would also need some kind of mechanism for routing messages. An informant said: "*a solution that is just for us would not help the sector at all because if one doctor wants to communicate with the hospital or two doctors with each other, or the public health institute with a doctor, this solution would not help*". Thus the decision about the type of routing mechanism was shaped not only by concerns within the project but also by a concern for the sector. This meant that the routing mechanism would potentially constitute a core lasting component of the sector infrastructure upon which various services could be built. It needed to be a solution that could support the routing of various types of messages exchanged between heterogeneous actors. This forward looking concern was translated to a discussion on how to create a solution that would be durable.

The concerns about ensuring durability related to various aspects of how to make the solution relevant in the long term. First, they decided to adopt a messaging standard that would work with different type of messages. This decision was also related to the requirement of the Agency for Public Management and eGovernment (Difi) for ensuring re-use. One of the architectural principles defined by the Difi stipulates that: "*any solution that is established must be developed in a manner that enables it to be reused in other contexts and within other frameworks*" (DIFI 2009). Finally, it was decided to have the routing mechanism developed and owned by NHN (the network provider). As NHN is another governmental entity (fully owned by the Ministry of Health and Care Services) the full assignment of the development and maintenance of the routing mechanism to this third party was politically unproblematic. As NHN already provides the network to the sector, it has the technical capabilities and institutional resources available to support all potential new users in the future. Furthermore, the involvement of NHN would ensure greater visibility and create better opportunities for further reuse. By creating favourable conditions for wide adoption of the new routing mechanism within the sector its potential for being sustained in the long term was strengthened.

Durability Concerns Shape Decisions About Data Storage

Another key decision was the one about storing and making available for retrieval messages exchanged between citizens and GPs. From the healthcare practitioners' side the messages would be sent from the EPR systems and consequently, they could be stored there and considered part of the patient record. However, storing them only at the EPRs would not be a good solution for ensuring accessibility for the citizens. For instance, GPs would likely switch off their computers after working hours or might have temporary network connection problems potentially disrupting access. Although eDialogue was initially envisioned as a thin mediating layer between citizens and healthcare practitioners, it was soon realised that an archive would be needed. The archive would serve the need for making messages continuously available and also, would provide a number of opportunities for further development in the future, ensuring that the eDialogue services will be expandable ensuring durability.

The project team considered the possibility to develop the archive in-house. However, this option was discarded based on concerns over future oriented requirements for scalability. In the future the archive would probably need to also include messages from the hospitals with attachments of heavy files from picture archiving and communication systems (PACS) and extracts from records. An informant explains the potential for future developments around the archive as follows: *"So that a hospital doesn't print out and sends to a patient, but the patient can access his or her information in only one place, and whether it is information generated or synchronised, you will find it in one place, and you decide if you want to print it out or if you want to download"*. In this case the forward looking concern for durability meant to select a solution that would be able to expand and scale in the long term. Another aspect of durability was related to maintainability in the long term, this would be better ensured by the adoption of an already mature, standard solution. An informant explains: *"a standard solution is giving us quite a few things, it is stable, it is well proven so we know it works, it has been handling huge databases for other customers around the world, so we know is capable of taking this amount of data, it is of course secure, it has very good support for security within the solution, and all the kind of basic services you need like putting in documents, deleting, changing who can access a document, logging everything that is happening, all these are kind of standard"*.

The requirements for the archive were initially assessed against standard storage solutions already in use for e-government services and an ongoing national initiative to put in place a national secure digital mailbox. By looking at the specifications of these storage solutions it was identified that not all of them would provide good encryption support. Although storage encryption is not currently a regulatory requirement it made sense to adopt encryption for a national archive of sensitive health related data to ensure preparedness for stricter regulations that could be introduced in the future. Furthermore, it became evident that it would be good to manage the storage solution within the project and not to rely on a shared generic public sector resource because the team recognized a great potential for future developments of eDialogue services based on the archive. In this case the concern for durability related to the long term management and control of the new component, as the archive could prove to be the cornerstone of all upcoming citizen oriented electronic health services. An informant clarified: *"maybe, we do not know, maybe the archive will have an important role (...) potentially we talk of*

Table 2 Key eDialogue project tasks

Concerns	Key tasks	Description of eDialogue project activities (external actors marked by underlining)
Embeddedness	1. Develop citizens' interface by extending HealthNorway	Elicit user requirements, develop a concept, implement the graphic interface, develop functionality and link to the other components
	2. Develop healthcare practitioners' interfaces by extending EPRs	Develop specifications for <u>EPR vendors</u>. Work with vendors to refine specifications. Negotiate collaboration terms. Check deliveries, integrate components and collaborate with vendors to fix problems
Durability	3. Develop message routing mechanisms	Develop specifications for <u>NHN</u>. Prepare terms' agreement. Check deliveries, integrate components and collaborate with NHN for fixing problems
	4. Put in place an archiving solution and link it to other components	Develop specifications and call for tenders. Evaluate proposals. Prepare contract for <u>solution provider</u>. Check deliveries, integrate components and collaborate with archive solution provider for fixing problems

terabytes and petabytes, so it is big, if this is widely used it will probably be in a few years the biggest database in Norway". Differently to the routing mechanism which was conceptualised as a generic solution for all types of actors within healthcare, the archive was viewed as a component dedicated to citizens' storage needs now and in the future.

Key Project Tasks Resulting from Decisions Taken

The decisions described in the previous paragraphs, were taken during the early stages of the project. Based on these decisions, the overall project plan was developed and key project tasks were defined (summarised in Table 2). Tasks one and two are about reaching citizens and GPs. The related decisions show the project team's concerns for embeddedness. Tasks three and four are about satisfying the needs for message routing and storage. The related decisions show the project team's concerns for durability as new reusable components with significant growth potential are favoured. The table also describes the involvement of key external actors in each of the tasks.

The Implications of Decisions for Project Work

The project was conceptualised from the start as an infrastructuring effort with a focus on embedding the novel services in the existing landscape and developing new components that would be durable and reusable. The decisions that were taken made the project activities complex and created the need to manage multiple interdependencies among a number of actors. A project participant commented: *"there is a lot of complexity to handle, it seems simple but it is not. Of course it is complex there are multiple providers, 5 platforms and 4 different languages involved."* This complexity required the team to work on different levels in relation to the sector, to the existing platform, to various EPR vendors and to other technology providers. In the next subsections we analyse the project work by elaborating on: the work to achieve sector-wide agreement, the work with specifications before reaching maturity, the work with multiple different paces, the work with nested interfaces and the work of assembling parts.

Working to Achieve Wide Agreement

The development of the routing mechanism and the procurement of the archive solution made the work of the project team less about the eDialogue services and more about the design of patient-oriented services in general in the context of HealthNorway. Thus, work had to be expanded to include complex "anchoring" work both internally to the Agency and externally. For instance, the development of the routing mechanism as a new component that would be durable and reusable for the health sector created the necessity to expose the architectural blueprints to sectorial fora and ensure agreement before actually proceeding to implementation. Furthermore, the decision to purchase the archive initiated a process for building consensus internally in the Agency. Consensus to the decisions taken was critical as one of the project participant explained: *"ForumY is very important when solutions like this are developed and planned, so our risk was that they would say no, and we would have to start from scratch again. But they found it to be a good work foundation."* Consequently, much of the work of the project team was directed towards engaging other interest groups, explaining, obtaining consensus and stimulating interest.

Working with Specifications Before Reaching Maturity

The project team had to work and coordinate with several external actors were technically involved in the project and had to develop specific components: (a) the EPR vendors which are companies of different sizes and with different interests, then, (b) the vendor of the archive solution and (c) the Agency that would develop and maintain the message routing mechanism. Thus ordering work within the project was far from trivial. To ensure synchronisation of deliveries the specifications for external actors had to be developed very early in the process and much before the internal development team would start work. A project participant said: *"the vendors wanted the implementation guide before they would sign the agreement and I fully understand this of course. But the problem on our side, was that the functional side was actually just beginning to be worked out at the time (...) we had to take a lot of decisions that maybe would not be the same today, now that the functional side has done a lot of work, maybe something would have now been different."* Additionally, at the early stages of the project not all the legal preparations that would delineate the design space were completed. Working within healthcare where a number of strict privacy laws and regulations apply dictated a close collaboration with lawyers in order to clarify things and also to try and change the rules in place when needed. One of the lawyers working with the project said about project members: *"sometimes they forget they need to be within the legal framework because you cannot just do whatever you want and make it work technically, it has to be within the legal frame which is not easy for the technologists to see, or they do not want to see because they are creative and they want to make good solutions."* Changing the laws and regulations would require very lengthy processes. One of the lawyers working with the project said: *"it can take years. That's why we wanted to ask just for a policy or agreement thing. Because we know that it can take years for new regulation."* Thus, project participants had the difficult task of preparing full specifications for the external actors involved in technical development without having available a fully developed legal framework.

Working with Multiple Different Paces

The different types of external actors' involvement had their own paces and this entailed different work requirements and agreements. For the archive, a public procurement process had to be followed, with an open call, a prequalification process, a formal evaluation and ranking of proposals and contracting. For the EPR vendors the situation was different as there are only three specific companies that provide EPRs to the Norwegian GP offices and all of them had to be engaged to ensure full national coverage. This means that vendors had to be persuaded to participate and a negotiations' period was needed. A project participant said: *"one of the things that were difficult was that the three vendors are very different, they have very different organization, they have very different culture of how they communicate and work (...) It took time to understand how to cooperate with them, even if the agreements are equal, we can cooperate differently in practice."* Finally, working with the network provider (that was also given the responsibility for message routing mechanisms) had its own particularities as this is another governmental agency. A project participant said: *"when it comes to NHN we have agreements, or when we come to a point we have agreements. But we have a sort of cooperation and dialogue before we have the agreement, before the really start to work with something, so you can say we work with NHN like they are a kind of friend, until a certain point, then we have to make an agreement about what they are going to do for us, price, at what time and so on.*" Thus the project team had to learn to negotiate and cooperate according to different modalities with the various partners in the process, and on top they had to learn to articulate work across multiple negotiation and cooperation lines.

Working with Nested Interfaces

Developing the user interface for the citizens as part of the overall HealthNorway platform proved also to be tricky. This work had three facets. First, it dealt with envisioning the positioning for the eDialogue within HealthNorway. A project participant said: "*so we cannot just make eDialogue an island in this portal, we have to know now how important eDialogue is, is this what most people want when they come in here? Is it other stuff? (...) What does the user see when logging on? Is it your next appointment or your newest article or what is it?*" Thus, in order to develop the specific interface to citizens, the project participants had to work out the overall user experience within HealthNorway and to relate the interface concept to the "big picture". Second, this work entailed involving users in design by organizing panels of representatives with informational roles. A project member informed us: "*we are going to establish a new user panel with eight users, we had one last year but now we are going to have a new one, (...) including sick people, healthy people, someone with a foreign background (...) and we also have a GP panel (..) but they are also giving important information about the patient, so when I say ok so 'what does the patient want?' and they say "they are very much into book and choose", then maybe the calendar should be the focal point.*" Finally, the work of the project team dealt also with developing an understanding of the current practices of patient-GP communication as these would shape future patterns of use by the citizens. The project members did not only rely on the information gathered from GPs participating in the panel established by the project, but also, organised visits and observation sessions in GP offices.

Working to Assemble the Parts

Finally, the project team engaged in the work of assembling the parts. Putting everything together and testing the whole development from end to end proved to be challenging. For instance, not all parts were completed at the same moment but full testing would only be performed when all the links in the chain were available. In addition, fixing errors was challenging as it was not always obvious where the causes were to be found and alterations in one of the parts would sometimes require adjustments to the rest of them. Obviously, canonical agile development where all testing has to be completed within each sprint was not fully applicable and a lot of testing had to be performed at the end of the process. At the beginning of 2015 testing and fixing was almost completed and final preparations for piloting were underway. Modifications and adjustments decided after piloting will again require complex coordination among the various actors.

Discussion and Conclusion

The case analysis presented in the previous section has focused on how concerns related to the embeddedness and durability of the infrastructure shaped eDialogue's design and development. A concern for achieving embeddedness led to the decision to provide novel technological capabilities by extending existing technologies in use: the EPR systems and the HealthNorway presentation layer. By introducing the new information exchange functionality to GP offices via the existing EPR systems the project team is aiming to link to the existing technologies in place and the conventions of practice. By extending existing interfaces used by citizens the project team aims to create a coherent and homogeneous space for all electronic interactions of the general public with the healthcare system. Furthermore, a concern for durability (anticipating future evolution) has shaped decisions related to the message routing mechanisms and the archiving solution. The aim there was to ensure that new developments will be extendable and reusable in the future. Overall, these specific concerns led to decisions that defined the character of the project and created the need for close cooperation with multiple actors (the Agency, the EPR systems' providers, NHN, a software house that provided an archive solution).

Our empirical material relates to the early stages of infrastructural design and development (before use) and our analysis is focused on those early stages. We suggest that an understanding of the early work required for systematic infrastructural development is essential in order to grapple with the particularities entailed in putting infrastructures in place. Such an understanding can support a shift of focus from artefacts to infrastructures (Monteiro et al. 2013) and provide insights to those engaged in introducing further computer support within today's already digitised work settings where there is little scope for introducing new closed systems and tools. The early stages of infrastructure development entail visionary work performed under uncertainty by multiple actors, in different institutional settings, that have to coordinate their activities and technically interweave their outputs. As we have shown with our case study, the problem that we now have to address is how to introduce new technological capabilities that afford connections to what is already in place, mobilizing and recombining pre-existing resources, blending resiliently in the already densely populated landscapes.

Our primary goal in this paper was to understand the work of the project team engaged in the eDialogue project. For this project the development of specific functionality was only a small fraction of the total effort required: most of the work entailed conceptualising the different components in the infrastructure, negotiating with stakeholders in the sector, agreeing on long term mutual relationships, and coordinating internal work with the work of external actors that were gradually enrolled to the project. Additionally, quite differently to what would have happened in an application development project, the key challenges were less about modularising the work required for a well-defined delivery and more about developing a sensitivity to the constraints and singularities of all the actors enrolled and the emerging interdependencies. We have shown that the work for eDialogue entailed further developing what was already in place (for instance by using the EPRs in the GPs offices), mobilising and recombining pre-existing resources (for instance the health network and the institution that supports it), and how to add new versatile, reusable components (for instance by introducing the archive). We conceptualise this form of design and development work as infrastructuring.

Other researchers have engaged in a discussion on the work of infrastructuring (Aanestad et al. 2014; Pipek and Wulf 2009). Overall these studies denote an urge to develop an approach that emphasises a processual view in order to capture infrastructures 'in the making' but also to capture users' engagement with the technologies and the ensuing modifications when technologies are introduced in various local setting. For instance, Pipek and Wulf make a clear distinction between compromises made during design–before-use and those made during design–in-use and explicitly use the notion of infrastructuring to denote "all activities that contribute to a successful establishment of usages" (Pipek and Wulf 2009). The focus of our paper is explicitly on work before new technologies are introduced to use.

Within its explicit scope of researching design and development before use our study offers important insights on what the shift from artefacts to infrastructures entails. *First*, we show the repercussions of infrastructural concerns in the design and development process. We find that decisions driven by concerns related to the embeddedness and durability of the infrastructure created the need for distributed collective work. However, the constellation of the collaborating actors is not pre-defined but evolves dynamically, making cooperation, work synchronization and work assemblage very challenging. *Second*, by recounting the implications of these decisions for the subsequent unfolding of work we associate the configuration of software processes to the specifics of the technology under development (unbounded, interconnected, spanning localities and temporal scales). Although CSCW research has addressed recent changes in software process such as agile development and global development (Avram et al. 2009; Bjorn et al. 2014; Cohn et al 2009; Dittrich et al. 2009), these changes have been discussed as important contemporary trends and have not been explicitly linked to the specifics of technologies developed. From our case analysis it becomes evident that tailored software processes are needed when aiming for technologies that will have infrastructural qualities. However, it is difficult to be more specific about software process requirements by drawing from one singular case. Our exploratory research has been designed to generate an initial understanding of how a project conceptualised to be of infrastructuring nature is different to a project aiming for the development of a specific artefact. Further research including cross case analyses could provide a basis for methodological reflections on plausible types of collaborative software processes for extending infrastructures.

References

Aanestad, M., Jolliffe, B., Mukherjee, A., & Sahay, S. (2014). Infrastructuring work: Building a state-wide hospital information infrastructure in India. *Information Systems Research, 25*(4), 834–845.

Avital, M., & Te'eni, D. (2009). From generative fit to generative capacity: Exploring an emerging dimension of information systems design and task performance. *Information Systems Journal, 19*(4), 345–367.

Avram, G., Bannon, L., Bowers, J. M., Sheehan, A., & Sullivan, D. (2009). Bridging, patching and keeping the work flowing: Defect resolution in distributed software development. *Computer Supported Cooperative Work (CSCW), 18*(5–6), 477–507.

Bietz, M., Baumer, E., & Lee, C. (2010). Synergizing in cyberinfrastructure development. *Computer Supported Cooperative Work (CSCW), 19*(3–4), 245–281.

Bjorn, P., Bardram, J., Avram, G., Bannon, L., Boden, A., Redmiles, D., de Souza, C., & Wulf, V. (2014). Global software development in a CSCW perspective. In *Proceedings of the Companion Publication of the 17th ACM Conference on Computer Supported Cooperative Work and Social Computing.*

Bowker, G. (1994). *Science on the run: Information management and industrial geophysics at Schlumberger, 1920–1940.* Cambridge: MIT press.

Bowker, G., Baker, K. S., Millerand, F., & Ribes, D. (2010). Toward information infrastructure studies: ways of knowing in a networked environment. In J. Hunsinger, L. Klastrup & M. Allen (Eds.), *International handbook of internet research* (pp. 97–117). Berlin: Springer.

Bowker, G., & Star, S. L. (1999). *Sorting things out: Classification and its consequences.* Cambridge: MIT Press.

Ciborra, C., & Hanseth, O. (1998). From tool to Gestell: Agendas for managing the information infrastructure. *Information Technology and People, 11*(4), 305–327.

Cohn, M. L., Sim, S. E., & Lee, C. (2009). What counts as software process? Negotiating the boundary of software work through artifacts and conversation. *Computer Supported Cooperative Work (CSCW), 18*(5–6), 401–443.

DIFI. (2009). *Overarching ICT architecture principles for the public sector.*

Dittrich, Y., Randall, D., & Singer, J. (2009). Software engineering as cooperative work. *Computer Supported Cooperative Work (CSCW), 18*(5–6), 393–399.

Hanseth, O., Monteiro, E., & Hatling, M. (1996). Developing information infrastructure: The tension between standardization and flexibility. *Science, Technology and Human Values, 21*(4), 407–426.

Hughes, T. P. (1979). The electrification of America: The system builders. *Technology and Culture* 124–161.

Karasti, H., & Baker, K. S. (2004). Infrastructuring for the long-term: Ecological information management. In *Proceedings of the 37th Annual Hawaii International Conference on System Sciences,* 2004.

Karasti, H., Baker, K. S., & Millerand, F. (2010). Infrastructure time: long-term matters in collaborative development. *Computer Supported Cooperative Work (CSCW), 19*(3–4), 377–415.

Monteiro, E., Pollock, N., Hanseth, O., & Williams, R. (2013). From artefacts to infrastructures. *Computer Supported Cooperative Work (CSCW), 22*(4–6), 575–607.

Norsk Helsenett. (2014). About us. URL https://www.nhn.no/english/Pages/about.aspx.

Pennington, D. (2011). Bridging the disciplinary divide: Co-creating research ideas in escience teams. *Computer Supported Cooperative Work (CSCW), 20*(3), 165–196.

Pettigrew, A. (1997). What is processual analysis? *Scandinavian Journal of Management, 13*(4), 337–348.

Pipek, V., & Wulf, V. (2009). Infrastructuring: Towards an integrated perspective on the design and use of information technology. *Journal of the Association for Information Systems, 10*(5), 447–473.

Pollock, N., & Williams, R. (2010). e-Infrastructures: How do we know and understand them? Strategic ethnography and the biography of artefacts. *Computer Supported Cooperative Work (CSCW), 19*, 521–556.

Procter, R., Rouncefield, M., Poschen, M., Lin, Y., & Voss, A. (2011). Agile project management: A case study of a virtual research environment development project. *Computer Supported Cooperative Work (CSCW), 20*(3), 197–225.

Ribes, D., & Finholt, T. A. (2009). The long now of technology infrastructure: Articulating tensions in development. *Journal of the Association for Information Systems, 10*(5), 375–398.

Spencer, D., Zimmerman, A. S., & Abramson, D. (2011). Special theme: Project management in e-science: challenges and opportunities. *Computer Supported Cooperative Work (CSCW), 20*(3), 155–163.

Star, S. L. (1999). The ethnography of infrastructure. *American Behavioral Scientist, 43*(3), 377–391.

Star, S. L., & Bowker, G. (2002). How to infrastructure. In L. Lievrouw & S. Livingstone (Eds.), *Handbook of new media: Social shaping and social consequences* (pp. 151–162). London: Sage.

Steinhardt, S., & Jackson, S. (2015). Anticipation work: Cultivating vision in collective practice. In *CSCW'15*, Vancouver, BC, Canada.

How Do User Groups Cope with Delay in Real-Time Collaborative Note Taking

Claudia-Lavinia Ignat, Gérald Oster, Olivia Fox, Valerie L. Shalin and François Charoy

Abstract A property of general interest of real-time collaborative editors is delay. Delays exist between the execution of one user's modification and the visibility of this modification to the other users. Such delays are in part fundamental to the network, as well as arising from the consistency maintenance algorithms and underlying architecture of collaborative editors. Existing quantitative research on collaborative document editing does not examine either concern for delay or the efficacy of compensatory strategies. We studied an artificial note taking task in French where we introduced simulated delay. We found out a general effect of delay on performance related to the ability to manage redundancy and errors across the document. We interpret this finding as a compromised ability to maintain awareness of team member activity, and a reversion to independent work. Measures of common ground in accompanying chat indicate that groups with less experienced team members attempt to compensate for the effect of delay. In contrast, more experienced groups do not adjust their communication in response to delay, and their performance remains sensitive to the delay manipulation.

Introduction

Computer science work, including Ellis et al. (1991), Sun et al. (1998) and Ignat and Norrie (2008), provides the technical capability to distribute document editing among multiple users. Synchronous or real time collaborative editing allows

C.-L. Ignat (✉) · G. Oster · F. Charoy
Inria, 54600 Villers-lès-Nancy, France
e-mail: claudia.ignat@inria.fr

C.-L. Ignat · G. Oster · F. Charoy
LORIA, Université de Lorraine, CNRS, 54506 Vandoeuvre-lès-Nancy, France

O. Fox · V.L. Shalin
Department of Psychology, Wright State University, Dayton, OH, USA

© Springer International Publishing Switzerland 2015
N. Boulus-Rødje et al. (eds.), *ECSCW 2015: Proceedings of the 14th European Conference on Computer Supported Cooperative Work, 19–23 September 2015, Oslo, Norway*, DOI 10.1007/978-3-319-20499-4_12

a group of people to modify a shared document at the same time. One user's changes appear to other users almost immediately with very small time intervals of inconsistent document status. Real-time collaborative editing has gained in popularity due to the wide availability of free services such as Google Drive. Existing real-time collaborative editing tools are currently used in scenarios involving only a small number of people (e.g. up to 10) contributing to a shared document such as a research paper or project proposal or meeting notes. However, scenarios involving large number of users are currently emerging, such as group note taking during lectures or conferences. Existing tools are not currently designed to support this change completely in terms of the number of users, ultimately limiting the number of users that can simultaneously edit a document.

The requirements for group performance in the case of a large number of users are not established. One system property of general interest is delay. Delays exist between the execution of one user's modification and the visibility of this modification to the other users. This delay has many causes: network delay due to physical communication technology be it copper wire, optical fiber or radio transmission; time complexity of various algorithms for ensuring consistency, where most of them depend on the number of users and number of operations that users performed; the type of architecture such as thin or thick client. Understanding the requirements associated with delay informs the broader research community in the domain of collaborative editing, which continues to develop merging algorithms under the uniform assumption of high responsiveness requirements for real-time collaboration. Potentially, modest delay is well-tolerated and can suspend further optimisation research. Worse, high responsiveness could interfere with user productivity under certain circumstances.

Not all groupware applications appear sensitive to delay. For example, Dourish and Bly (1992) claim: *"We can tolerate a certain amount of delay; image updates may only occur every ten minutes, and so the user will not expect up-to-the-second information."* Others argue that usability limitations of otherwise effective groupware may yield to adaptations in work practice (Olson and Olson 2000). Some designers even suggest the benefit of delay warnings, so that users can adjust their strategies if they are aware of system conditions (Vaghi et al. 1999; Gutwin et al. 2004). Some work has examined the effect of network delay on multi-player real-time games on the order of 1 s delay (Gutwin 2001). But, no study has been done in collaborative editing where much longer delays result from other factors than network delay. Such factors include consistency maintenance algorithms that may scale with the number of users and operations (Ahmed-Nacer et al. 2011).

In this paper we aim to evaluate the performance consequences of delay in real-time collaborative document editing. Setting up an experiment with numerous users that edit concurrently a shared document would not be possible with current tools. Existing tools restrict the number of users editing a document and most of them are not open-source in order to allow code instrumentation for an analysis of user behavior. We instead mapped the real-world setting to a laboratory task that permits the systematic manipulation of delay. First, we used a simulation with GoogleDocs to estimate the range of delays, taking into account the number of users and their typing speed. Then we examined the effect of simulated delay within this range on a note taking task performed by a small group of users. As GoogleDocs code is not open source, we used another well-known editor, EtherpadLite, that we instrumented for introducing artificial delays. In particular, we analysed the effect of delay on the error rate and redundancy during the collaborative process. We also examined compensatory strategies for dealing with delay such as coordination.

We structure the paper as follows. We start by presenting our research questions and related work. We then describe our collaborative note taking task and design of artificial delays that we introduced in our experiment. We then present the experimental procedure we followed and the dependent measures. We next present results of our experimental design followed by a discussion. Concluding remarks are presented in the last section.

Research Questions and Related Quantitative Research

None of the field studies on collaborative writing tools such as the one presented by Tammaro et al. (1997) or usability studies such as the one presented by Noël and Robert (2004) provides quantitative behavioral evidence to define limits for collaborative editing technology. While delay certainly affects the performance of the individual, our interest lies in the consequence to real-time collaborative editing and the compensatory strategies at the team level that users adopt to overcome the negative effect of delay. Olson and Olson (2000) claim that coupling between sub-tasks influences tolerance for delay. Collaborative note-taking has the potential to maximize sub-task coupling between users, and provides an ideal task for identifying the range of delay tolerance. In the remainder of this section, we consider the existing research and its implications for our study along three dimensions: The likely range of effective delay, informative outcome measures, and informative collaborative measures.

To examine the effect of delay experimentally we require a range of delay values to study. Studies of the effect of delay in gaming environments such as the ones presented by Gutwin et al. (2004) and Vaghi et al. (1999) examine tasks with time constants (or turns) on the order of 700 ms. Results suggest performance decrements with delays as small as 200 ms (Gutwin et al. 2004). However, 200 ms delays are much smaller than delays in collaborative editing that are in the order of magnitude of several seconds. As shown by Karat et al. (1999), the average typing frequency is around 2 characters/s. We therefore expect that the task-time constant of collaborative editing is proportional to the time to type a word, or 2.5 s for an average of 5 characters per word. We should not expect delay effects in such tasks below this level of delay. However, the absence of a clear precedence for our paradigm suggested the need for a supplementary simulation study to determine a likely effective range of delay.

For studying the effect of delay in real-time collaborative editing we also require an outcome metric that quantifies group performance in terms of the quality of the document and a process metric for quantifying the compensatory communication in response to limitations of the collaboration technology. In what follows we review quantitative research related to these two metrics and we define our research questions.

Need for an Outcome Metric Olson et al. (1993) exemplifies the need for an outcome metric to evaluate the quality of the work produced with groupware. While Erkens et al. (2005) developed an outcome metric for prose quality, it was not sensitive to the experimental manipulations, permitting conclusions only about post hoc covariates and process. Some researchers such as Birnholtz et al. (2013) focus only on process measures, with unclear implications for outcome.

Candidate metrics for text quality appear in research that investigates writing skill apart from the technology. The skill models resulting from this research identify the facets of composition at multiple levels of analysis, including goals, processes and cognitive demand (Hayes 2012). Two points from Hayes (2012) concern us here. First, he notes the cognitive demand of transcription, including spelling and writing. Second, he relies on quantified topics to score written essays. In fact topics and topic transitions define different levels of writing proficiency.

Latent semantic analysis (LSA) by Landauer and Dumais (1997) provides methods for comparing the content of two documents. LSA uses a reference lexicon to describe the frequency of lexical terms in a document. Similar to factor analysis, an approximation of the full frequency matrix merges similar terms and represents the document in question, which among other applications, permits comparison against other documents. One of the limitations of LSA is that it does not account for grammar or word order. However, emphasis on lexical items in Landauer and Dumais (1997) converges with emphasis on topic in Hayes (2012) rather than detailed propositional analysis.

Our research questions concerning the outcome metrics related to document quality follow:

RQ1 How does delay influence the quality of the final document in terms of the number of grammar errors?

RQ2 How does delay influence the quality of the final document in terms of the amount of redundancy?

RQ3 How does delay influence the quality of the final document in terms of the number of keywords from the transcript?

These research questions assume an independence of quality metrics. This is not necessarily the case. For example, a redundant text with increased length might very well be responsible for an increase in grammatical errors, as participants become unable to monitor and correct each other.

Compensatory Communication Communication provides a backup for local uncertainties in the coordination of coupled tasks (Tremblay et al. 2012). Participants might discuss alternatives to articulating the task, or manage their own communication. Collaborative editing often includes a chat capability, allowing direct type-written communication between team members. Whether or not chat is task-related, chat establishes links between team members and tells the group something about what the writer is doing, even if only to indicate that the writer is not doing task-related work. An analysis of chat language can inform us about the collaborative process.

Other work has examined chat content during collaborative editing. For example, Birnholtz et al. (2013) used a categorization scheme driven by an interest in group sentiment. While some of our dimensions are similar, we chose individual lexical measures that are inspired by psycholinguistics, and avoid the challenge of quantifying units of analysis (such as phrases or sentences), multiple categorizations of the same phrase and inter-rater reliability. Our approach has precedence. For example, Gibson (2010) examined the prevalence of first words in the examination of turn taking behavior in face-to-face interaction. Both Birnholtz et al. (2013) and Gibson (2010) base their analyses on Schiffrin (1987), who also relies on single word measures.

Similar to Birnholtz et al. (2013), we examined accord language (both agreement and objection terminology) as an attempt to manage both the dialogue between participants as well as the task itself. In spoken language, accord participates in dialogue management by providing feedback to the present speaker, and controlling turn-taking (Clark and Krych 2004). Accord language also facilitates the management of the task, including transitions within and between sub-tasks (Bangerter and Clark 2003).

Classic work on the English language suggests that orderly discourse attaches new information to understood (given) information (Chafe 1976). Drijkoningen and Kampers-Manhe (2012), Dimroth et al. (2010) confirm that French, the language used in our empirical work, respects the given-new convention. Clark and Haviland (1977) demonstrated that language produced in this way facilitates comprehension, by allowing recipients to attach new information to previously activated old information. Thus, we say *"Pierre ate a banana"* to introduce the idea that Pierre ate an unspecified banana and *"Pierre ate the banana"* to describe what happened to a previously identified, specific banana. In the first case the referent is indefinite, and in the second case the referent is definite. As the previous example illustrates, one device for marking given and new information is the determiner. The definite determiner *"the"* appears with an established, specific referent, while an indefinite determiner *"a"* appears to introduce a new referent. Participants may be introducing new information in an orderly fashion, or they are aware of what others are doing and know. In either case, respect for the given-new convention suggests the presence of shared context and common ground.

Our research question regarding the effect of delay on compensatory communication follows:

RQ4 How does delay influence the use of accord language and definite determiners as an indication of common ground in the chat?

Delay and compensatory communication may interact with a third variable, collaborative experience. Experienced users may make assumptions regarding tool functionality. Delay could catch them by surprise. Inexperienced users may be more unsure about how the process works. Therefore our final research question follows:

RQ5 How do delay, experience, and compensatory collaboration effort interact to affect task performance?

Experimental Editing Task

We selected a collaborative note taking task where delay is likely problematic. A group of four participants had 15 min to: (i) listen to a 12 min audio taped interview (ii) take notes for assigned topics (iii) consolidate the notes to reduce redundancy (iv) eliminate grammatical and spelling errors.

The task has at least several methodological advantages. First, the source interview provides a content-based performance standard. A performance standard is more challenging for more open-ended collaborative editing tasks. Second, the distribution of task assignments promoted interactivity and dependency. Third, the note taking task loads on transcription, with known cognitive demand. This task should therefore bound the tolerance for delay in collaborative editing.

In order to test the effect of delay we introduced artificial delays between a user's modification and its appearance to other users. In order to determine potentially effective values of delay we performed some measurements using simulations with GoogleDocs. We used Selenium WebDriver Java 2.44.02 to simulate users that type simultaneously on the same shared document with different typing speeds. One user simulated a reader that only reads the document. Another user simulated a writer that writes special strings that the reader will read. Other users were simulated as dummy writers that write some non-meaningful text. The role of dummy writers was to simulate concurrent access to the document. Writers can insert or delete text. We measured the delay as the difference of time between the writer inserts a particular string and the time when the reader reads this string. To eliminate clock synchronisation issues, both writer and reader were executed on a same computer. We analysed how the delay depends on the number of users and the typing speed of the users. We varied the number of users from 1 to 50 (the maximum number of users that can simultaneously edit a document in GoogleDocs) and the frequency speed from 1 to 10 characters/s.

Karat et al. (1999) mentions that the average rate for transcription is 33 words per minute (wpm), and 19 words per minute for composition. The same study reports that, when the group was divided into "fast", "moderate" and "slow" groups, the average speeds were 40, 35, and 23 wpm respectively. As the common conversion factor between words per minute and characters per minute is 5, we chose to report here on an average frequency of typing of 2 characters/s. Figure 1 shows the results we obtained for repeated measures of the delay in terms of the number of users that concurrently modify the document with a typing speed of 2 characters/s. For this typing speed, when the number of clients exceeded 38 we

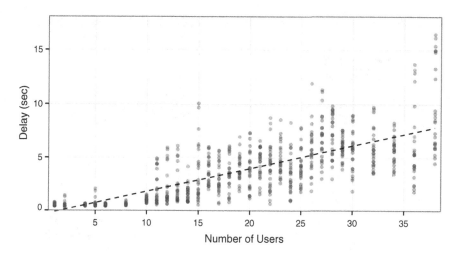

Fig. 1 Delay measurements in GoogleDocs according to the number of clients for a typing speed of 2 characters/s

faced substantial client disconnections and the collaborative editing process was stopped. We therefore reported for the results obtained for number of clients varying from 1 to 38.

Even a small number of users incurs delay between 1 and 2 s. Moreover, 4 s delays are a common result for more than 11 users. Based on this analysis we introduced artificial delays of 0, 4, 6, 8 and 10 s into the experimental design.

Methods

Participants

Eighty students affiliated with a French university participated in this experiment, in mixed gender groups of 4. Due to a change in instructions (see below) we dropped three groups of initial participants. The analysis below includes the remaining sixty eight participants.

The participants ranged in age from 21 to 27. All participants used French in their daily activities. An electronic announcement solicited participation. One of the researchers organized interested participants into sets of 4 and scheduled the session. All participants received a 10 Euro gift certificate for their participation.

Apparatus

The experiment was conducted using four GNU/Linux desktop computers in a classroom setting. Participants were separated by partitions and could not directly

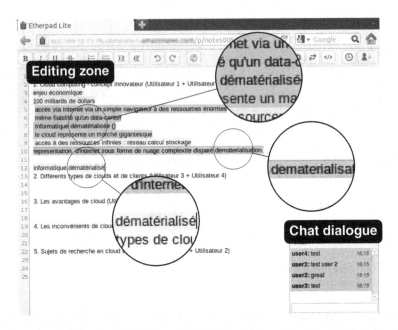

Fig. 2 Etherpad editor—each modification is highlighted with a color corresponding to the user who performed it

observe other team members while they worked, although typing activity was audible. The server running the Etherpad application was hosted on an Amazon Elastic Compute Cloud (EC2) instance located in the US East (Northern Virginia) Region. Each desktop ran the Mozilla Firefox web browser executing the Etherpad web client application. Etherpad hosted the task stimuli and a Chat dialogue facility (see Fig. 2). User operations appeared color-coded in both the text and chat. Etherpad relies on a client-server architecture where each client/user edits a copy of the shared document. When a user performed a modification it was immediately displayed on the local copy of the document and then sent to the server. The server merged the change received from the user with other user changes and then transmitted the updates to the other users. When a user edited a sequence of characters, the first change on the character was immediately sent to the server, while the other changes were sent at once only upon reception of an acknowledgement from the server. With each change sent to the server, it created a new version of the document. Gstreamer software enabled the video recording of user activity. We also instrumented Etherpad to register all user keyboard inputs on the client side and to introduce delays on the server-side. The editor window displayed 50 lines of text. Users editing above the field of view of a collaborator could cause the lines within the collaborators' view to "jump" inexplicably. Such a property is consistent with the inability to view an entire document as it undergoes modification from multiple team members.

Task and Stimuli

Participants listened to a 12 min, 1862 word interview on cloud computing,[1] divisible into five main sections.

Procedure

The entire procedure was approved by a US University institutional review board. Participants began the session with informed consent for three different experimental tasks and a survey conducted in the same sequence:

- A proofreading task, in which participants corrected a short text, containing several grammatical and spelling errors
- A sorting task, in which participants located the release dates of an alphabetized list of movies, and sorted them accordingly and
- A note taking task, in which participants listened to a 12 min interview on the topic of cloud computing, and provided an integrated set of notes on the interview
- All participants completed a follow-up questionnaire at the completion of the three task series.

The second task was analysed by Ignat et al. (2014). The task that we present in this paper is the third task, on note taking. Scripted instructions (translated here into English) for this task follow: *"Researchers will provide you and your team with an audio lecture. Your task is to take notes on this lecture using the editing tool and assemble a unified report for your team. After the end of the audio you will have three additional minutes. Please work as accurately as you can while still being efficient. You are free to coordinate your efforts with your team mates as you like at the beginning and throughout the task, using the chat interface at the right side of the screen."* The task took 15 min. In the first 12 min participants listened to the audio tape and took notes on the shared document by using the Etherpad editor. After the end of the audio, participants were allowed 3 additional minutes to revise their notes and generate a reconciled summary of their notes by continuing to use the collaborative editor.

Initial review of data from the first three groups showed that participants took their own notes separately for the whole interview. That is, the shared document was not structured according to the main parts of the audio interview. This resulted in redundancy across the entire audio content, which was replicated four times. Furthermore, the quality of the summary suffered. As each participant wrote only the most important information, significant detail was missing.

---

[1]The 12 min interview is available online at the following url: https://interstices. info/jcms/i_60795/calculer-dans-les-nuages.

We decided to drop the first three groups of participants and change the instructions. We divided the shared document into five sections corresponding to the five main parts of the audio interview. For each section of the document two participants were assigned the role of taking notes of the main content of the corresponding audio part. The other two participants were assigned the role of revising the notes taken by the first two participants. The roles were inverted for each section of the document. This is consistent with real world collaborative note taking tasks during meetings where the discussion subtopics are usually known before the meeting. We added the following phrases to the above presented instructions for the task: *"In order to help you coordinate on this task we divided the document into five sections corresponding to the five main parts of the audio lecture. For each section we assigned two among you to take the main role on taking notes. These two participants are identified by their identity (User1, User2, User3 or User4) right after the title of each section. Each participant knows his/her identity from the previous tasks. The other two participants not mentioned after the section title have the role of revising the notes taken for that section. Your roles turn for each section."*

Design

The note taking task was conducted with teams of 4 participants for each level of the continuous independent variable Delay, tested at 0, 4, 6, 8 and 10 s in addition to the 100 ms delay inherent in the EC2. Three teams experienced 0 s condition (i.e. no delay was introduced), three teams experienced 4 s delay condition, four teams experienced 6 s delay condition, three teams experienced 8 s delay condition and four teams experienced 10 s delay condition. While participants viewed their own document changes in real-time, they viewed other participants' changes according to delay condition. Chat was implemented in real time for all conditions. Delay conditions were tested in random order, and all groups experienced a single level of delay across the three-task session.

Dependent Measures

Number of words is computed by the number of words in the text base. For each group in the experiment we examined recorded versions of the shared document at every minute. For each document version we computed its total number of words by using a script written in Python.

Keywords is one measure of document content and quality. Keywords is computed as the number of main keywords present in the final version of the document provided by each group of users. We identified 121 keywords or short phrases distributed over the document sections. Keywords included nouns, (e.g., *"services"*, "*clients*"), verbs, (e.g., "*payer*", "*consommer*") and adjectives, e.g., ("*cohérence*"). Crucially, we included misspellings as corresponding to the presence of keywords. For each section in the final document we automatically identified the number of keywords corresponding for that section as present or missing. We examined the number of keywords divided by the number of words as well as an arcsin transformation of this ratio measure. These give consistent results and we report only the transformed metric here.

Redundancy is a second measure of document content and quality. Redundancy is computed as the sum of redundancies of each section in the document. Redundancy of a section was measured by analysing the recorded videos of the collaborative editing session. Redundancy of a section represents the maximum number of occurrences in that section of any topic present in the audio. The topic contained one or more keywords belonging to that section. This measurement was performed on the document version that corresponded to the end of that section in the audio. Redundancy of a section can be equal to 0, 1, 2, 3 or 4, as a topic can be replicated maximum 4 times corresponding to the maximum number of participants. The redundancy sum at 12 min corresponds to the end of the audio, prior to the 3 min proof-reading opportunity. A binary redundancy metric captured the redundancy that remained at the end of the proofreading period, that is, whether the redundancy was caught and repaired. For example, we can notice in Fig. 2 that redundancy of Sect. 1 of the document is 3 as three users marked down the idea of "*dematerialised computer science*": two users wrote "*informatique dématérialisé*", while the third one wrote "*démateralisation*" as shown by the three zoomed zones depicted in the figure. We therefore find a triple repetition of the base of the keyword "*dematerialisation*".

Error Rate serves as a third measure of document quality. Error rate is computed using *Reverso* tool.[2] Reverso checks misspellings and grammar of a text in any language. For each group we generated the versions of the shared document at every minute during the experiment and we computed the number of errors for every such version by using reverso. The number of errors was computed automatically using a script written in Python. We examined the number of errors divided by the number of words as well as an arcsin transformation of this ratio measure. These give consistent results and we report only the transformed metric here.

We also examined covariates obtained from the chat behavior and survey responses.

Chat Behavior included the number of words, accord language, and definite determiners. For accord language we tallied all versions of "*oui*" ("*ouai*", "*ouis*", "*ouaip*"), negation ("*ne*", "*not*", "*naan*"), "*OK*" ("*ok*", "*k*", "*d'accord*") and objection ("*sinon*", "*objection*", "*contre*"). We did not tally the words paired with "*ne*" such as "*pas*", "*rien*" etc., to avoid double counting. We did not tally "*si*", which is a version of "*yes*" used in response to negation, because it also means "*if*". For definite determiners we tallied "*le*", "*la*", "*les*", "*au*" and "*aux*", but adjusted the count of "*la*" to exclude the case of "*de la*".

---

[2]Reverso tool is available on-line at http://www.reverso.net/.

Survey responses examined here include: (a) Which exercise did you find most difficult? Why? (b) Did anything annoy you about the text editor? If, yes, why? (c) What was the impact of the collaborative editing tool for note taking task? (Using a 10 point Likert scale) Explain. (d) Have you previously used collaborative tools? We split the groups by the consistency of experience. In the high experience groups, all members had previous collaborative editing experience. In the low experience groups, one or more members lacked collaborative editing experience.

Results

We used regression modeling to describe the quantitative consequences of delay condition to performance measures. We show the consequences of delay to document content and errors, and suggest the role of document redundancy as a mediator of these relationships. Subsequent analysis of redundancy shows that the more experienced groups manage redundancy less purposefully and are hence subject to the effect of delay. Low experienced groups attempt to manage redundancy as revealed by chat metrics for common ground.

Performance Measures

We examined both document content and errors as performance measures. For the purposes of contrast, we also examine subjective ratings.

Document Content The text base is larger for the high delay groups at 15 min, $F(1, 15) = 5.198$, $p = 0.0377$, $\beta = 0.5073$, adjusted $R^2 = 0.2078$. We characterized document quality as the ratio of keywords to number of words in the text base (or version of the shared document) at 15 min. Proportion of keywords is negatively related to delay condition, $F(1, 15) = 7.8610$, $p = 0.0134$, $\beta = -0.5864$, adjusted $R^2 = 0.3001$. Quality content decreases with delay condition. Finally, document redundancy at 12 min is a function of delay condition, $F(1, 15) = 14.66$, $p = 0.0016$, $\beta = 0.7030$, adjusted $R^2 = 0.4605$. Figure 3 illustrates the relationship between delay condition and proportion of keywords and word count. In summary, delay increases the text base, decreases the proportion of keywords and increases the redundancy.

Error Proportions at 15 min Error rate is a function of condition, $F(1, 15) = 15.94$, $p = 0.0012$, $\beta = 0.7178$, adjusted $R^2 = 0.4829$. The error proportion metric is negatively correlated with the proportion of keywords, $F(1, 15) = 26.98$, $p = 0.0001$, $\beta = -0.8017$, adjusted $R^2 = 0.6188$.

Redundancy and error rate are correlated, $F(1, 15) = 27.17$, $p = 0.0001$, $\beta = -0.8027$, adjusted $R^2 = 0.6206$. Figure 4 illustrates this relationship between

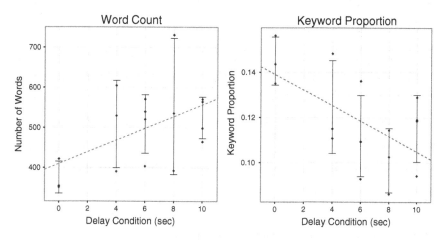

Fig. 3 Number of words (*left*) and proportion of keywords (*right*) as a function of delay condition

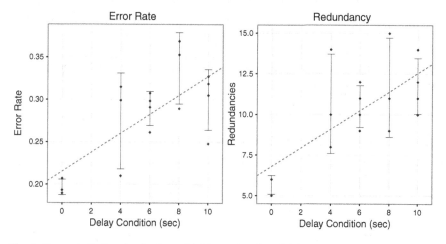

Fig. 4 Error rate (*left*) and redundancy (*right*) as a function of delay condition

delay condition and error rate and redundancy. Thus, error rates, like document content measures, appear sensitive to delay condition.

Subjective Difficulty Ratings Editor difficulty ratings are not related to delay condition $F(1, 15) = 3.487$, $p = 0.0815$. Editor difficulty ratings do not correlate with any of the performance measures: Error rate, $F(1, 15) = 1.87$, $p = 0.1916$, Redundancy at 12 min, $F(1, 15) = 0.1343$, $p = 0.7191$, Proportion of keywords $F(1, 15) = 0.377$, $p = 0.5484$ and Word count $F(1, 15) = 0.0067$, $p = 0.9359$.

Mediation Analyses

A model of grammatical error rate with both delay and redundancy suppresses the relationship between delay condition and error rate. A corresponding graphic for this mediation analysis and beta weights appear in Fig. 5.

	R	Adj. R^2	β
Analysis 1: error rate = delay condition	0.6949	0.4829	
Delay condition			0.7178**
Analysis 2: redundancy = delay condition	0.6786	0.4605	
Delay condition			0.7030**
Analysis 3: error rate = redundancy	0.7878	0.6206	
Redundancy			0.8027***
Analysis 4: error rate = delay condition + redundancy	0.8042	0.6467	
Delay condition			0.3035
Redundancy			0.5893*

$* p \leq 0.05, ** p \leq 0.01, *** p \leq 0.001$

A similar mediation analysis suggests a similar, albeit non significant mediation of redundancy, disrupting the relationship between delay condition and proportion of keywords.

These suggest that managing redundancy is the process that contributes to the observed effects of delay on outcome.

Redundancy Management Analyses

We examined covariates recovered from both the questionnaire and chat behavior to better understand the factors that influence the management of redundancy. We

Fig. 5 Redundancy at 12 min mediates the relationship between delay condition and grammatical error rate at 15 min

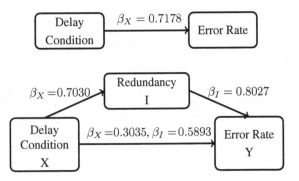

divide the exposition into two sections: Redundancy awareness as indicated in the questionnaire and common ground as indicated in the chat.

Redundancy Awareness Some groups did complain about the difficulty in managing redundancy. Redundancy Awareness appears in two places in the post hoc questionnaire. Those who found the note taking task most difficult sometimes referred to redundancy. Participants also sometimes explained their ratings for the editor in terms of the ability to manage redundant text. Examples illustrating these explanations are provided in English: "*We are lacking time to organise, therefore we write the same things, taking notes on the same thing at the same time is generally complex when we do not know in advance what will be said*" (a group in condition 8) and "*Difficult to divide the tasks, we obtain a lot of redundant text (multiple participants write almost the same thing)*" (a group in condition 4).

In all groups except two, at least one group member complained about the management of redundancy. However, this awareness metric was unrelated to the measurement of redundancy at twelve minutes, $F(1, 15) = 0.1182$, $p = 0.7358$, or the resolution of redundancy $F(1, 15) = 0.1572$, $p = 0.6973$.

Experience A model of redundancy with delay, experience and delay × experience suggested an interaction between the effect of delay and experience, $t(13) = 2.287$, $p = 0.0396$. To pursue this interaction, we split the data by experience level. Groups in which all participants were experienced with collaborative editing show a persisting effect of delay $F(1, 6) = 18.1$, $p = 0.0054$, $\beta = 0.8666$, adjusted $R^2 = 0.7096$. Groups in which some of the participants were less experienced do not show the same sensitivity to delay $F(1, 7) = 1.815$, $p = 0.2199$, adjusted $R^2 = 0.09244$. Figure 6 illustrates the relation between redundancy

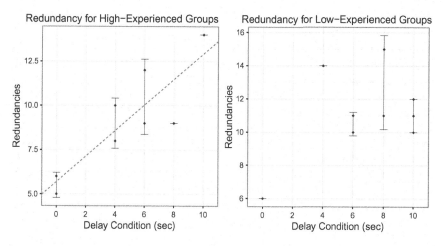

Fig. 6 Delay condition predicts redundancy for high collaborative experience (*left*) groups, but not for low experience groups (*right*)

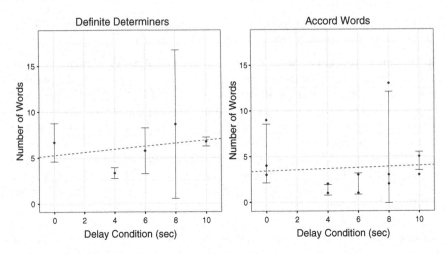

Fig. 7 Definite determiners (*left*) and agreement (*right*) by delay condition

and delay condition for groups with high and respectively low collaborative experience.

Chat Behavior The metrics for definite determiners and agreement are highly correlated $F(1, 15) = 10.09$, $p = 0.0063$, adjusted $R^2 = 0.3622$ (see Fig. 7). In the spirit of factor analysis, we added the two metrics to create an aggregated measure, Common Ground. A model of redundancy with delay and common ground reveals significant effects for both delay condition, $t(14) = 4.587$, $\beta = 0.7514$, $p = 0.0004$ and common ground $t(14) = -2.274$, $\beta = -0.3725$, $p = 0.0392$. Common ground opposes the effect of delay condition on redundancy. A model of redundancy with delay and total chat word count is not significant for total chat word count, $t(14) = -1.549$, $p = 0.1436$, confirming that the common ground findings are not an artifact of word count.

Finally, we examined the effect of common ground and delay condition for both the high and low experience groups. In general, the average amount of common ground behavior does not differ between the high and low experience groups ($M = 10.25$ words, $SE = 2.93$; $M = 9.78$ words, $SE = 1.20$). However, for the high experience groups, a model of redundancy with delay and common ground reveals that delay condition is significant $t(5) = 5.307$, $p = 0.0032$ but common ground is not $t(5) = -1.811$, $p = 0.1300$. In contrast for the low experience group, delay misses significance $t(6) = 2.336$, $p = 0.0582$ but common ground is significant $t(6) = -5.142$, $p = 0.0021$. The negative value suggests that common ground comprises an effort to decrease redundancy. Thus, the general effect of common ground suggested by the overall analysis is localized to the low experience groups. High experience groups do not use common ground in the same way.

Discussion

We examined the effect of delay on collaborative note-taking task, using levels of realistic delay consistent with an independent simulation. The collaborative note-taking task creates dependency and interactivity in collaborative editing, and permits the measurement of task outcome with reference to transcribed audio tape. Here we return to our original questions regarding the relationship between delay and collaboration effort before turning to implications for design.

Delay

We demonstrated a general hinderance of delay on four performance measures, such that delay increases grammatical errors and redundancy and decreases the proportion of key words relative to the text base. We also showed that text redundancy mediates the relationship between delay condition and grammatical errors. Given the increase in word count that we also observed, the effect of delay is to increase redundancy and create a larger, more erroneous and less manageable text base to be corrected after the audio tape is completed. A similar, albeit non-significant relationship between redundancy, delay condition and proportion of key words is consistent with the role of redundancy as a mediator between delay and performance.

We suggest that delay interferes with the ability to monitor team members' activities and adjust ones behavior accordingly. In effect, delay forces independent, redundant work.

Delay, Collaboration Effort and Experience

A complete account of the delay effect must also consider the effect of collaboration effort and experience. In general common ground opposes the effect of delay on redundancy. However experience interacted with delay, such that redundancy increased with delay for the high experience groups, but not the low experience groups. While both groups appeared to exercise the same amount of collaboration effort overall, the low experience groups adjusted their collaboration effort to manage the redundancy, while the high experience groups did not. Thus, the high experience groups appear to be caught off-guard when the editor did not operate as expected, and they did not attempt compensatory collaboration effort by means of communication through chat. This is the case although the task in question was third in a three-task series, and thus participants had previous opportunity to discover the delay and adjust accordingly.

Implications for Design

As our primary purpose was to demonstrate the effect of delay in collaborative editing, and motivate continuing work on the optimization of collaborative editing algorithms, we chose delay values that were highly likely to disrupt performance. This work is the first to study effect of delay in collaborative note taking. Results of both the simulation and experimental studies suggest refinement of the limits of delay in the range of 0–4 s in order to analyse the limit of user tolerance to delay. Testing small levels of delay will establish the shape of the delay-performance function. This function needs not be linear, and knowledge of a critical point will help further constrain design.

The study we performed shows that reducing delay influences the efficiency of the group and the quality of note taking. This finding is important because the choice of the underlying architecture of the collaborative editor has an impact on the delay or feedthrough time, which measures the time from a user performing an action to other users seeing the result (Graham et al. 2006). An architecture with a thick client, where computations are executed on the client side rather than on the server side is more suitable for minimizing feedthrough time. Popular collaborative editing systems such as GoogleDrive, relying on the Jupiter algorithm for synchronizing changes, do not rely on a thick client architecture. As a result, transformations among operations necessary for synchronizing changes are performed not only on the client side but also on the server side. Executing transformations on the server side introduces additional delay. Choosing synchronisation algorithms where computation is done only on the client side such as SOCT2 by Suleiman et al. (1998) or LogootSplit by André et al. (2013) reduces the delay. Among these families of algorithms, CRDTs support a better scalability in terms of number of users and feature better time complexities for integration of remote operations (Ahmed-Nacer et al. 2011).

Conclusions

In this study we evaluated the performance consequences of simulated network delay in real-time collaborative note taking. We designed an artificial note taking task where groups of four participants must take notes on an audio lecture and revise their notes in a limited period of time. Results of our study show that the general effect of delay on this task is to encourage independent work. We showed that delay increases grammatical errors and redundancy, resulting in a decreased quality of the task content. Measures of accompanying chat indicate that less experienced groups attempt to compensate for the effect of delay. In contrast, more experienced groups do not adjust their communication in response to delay, and their performance remains sensitive to the delay manipulation.

To our knowledge this study is the first to evaluate the effect of delay on performance of collaborative note taking and efficacy of compensatory strategies on this task. This initial study is fundamental for the refinement of the limits of tolerable delay in real-time collaborative editing. Establishing the shape of the delay performance function places fundamental constraints on the choice of collaborative editing architecture and underlying synchronisation mechanisms.

Acknowledgments The authors are grateful for financial support of the USCoast Inria associate team, the Inria internships programme and the research program ANR-10-SEGI-010 and for sabbatical support from the Department of Psychology, Wright State University. The authors thank Vinh Quang Dang for his help on simulations with GoogleDocs.

References

Ahmed-Nacer, M., Ignat, C.-L., Oster, G., Roh, H.-G., & Urso, P. (2011). Evaluating CRDTs for real-time document editing. In: *Proceedings of the Eleventh ACM Symposium on Document Engineering—DocEng 2011* (pp. 103–112). Mountain View, CA, USA: ACM Press.

André, L., Martin, S., Oster, G., & Ignat. C.-L. (2013). Supporting adaptable granularity of changes for massive-scale collaborative editing. In: *International Conference on Collaborative Computing: Networking, Applications and Worksharing—CollaborateCom 2013* (pp. 50–59). Austin, TX, USA: IEEE Computer Society.

Bangerter, A., & Clark, H. H. (2003). Navigating joint projects with dialogue. *Cognitive Science, 27*(2), 195–225.

Birnholtz, J. P., Steinhardt, S. B., & Pavese, A. (2013). Write here, write now!: An experimental study of group maintenance in collaborative writing. In: *ACM SIGCHI Conference on Human Factors in Computing Systems—CHI 2013* (pp. 961–970). Paris, France: ACM.

Chafe, W. (1976). Givenness, contrastiveness, definiteness, subjects, topics and points of view. In: *Subject and Topic* (pp. 25–55). USA: Academic Press.

Clark, H. H., & Haviland, S. E. (1977). Comprehension and the given-new contract. In: *Discourse Production and Comprehension* (pp. 1–40). New York: Ablex Publishing.

Clark, H. H., & Krych, M. A. (2004). Speaking while monitoring addresses for understanding. *Journal of Memory and Language, 50*, 62–81.

Dimroth, C., Andorno, C., Benazzo, S., & Verhagen, J. (2010). Given claims about new topics: How romance and germanic speakers link changed and maintained information in narrative discourse. *Journal of Pragmatics, 42*(12), 3328–3344.

Dourish, P., & Bly, S. (1992). Portholes: Supporting awareness in a distributed work group. In: *Proceedings of the SIGCHI Conference on Human Factors in Computing Systems—CHI 1992* (pp. 541–547). Monterey, CA, USA: ACM.

Drijkoningen, F., & Kampers-Manhe, B. (2012). Word order in French and the influence of topic and focus. *Linguistics, 50*(1), 65–104.

Ellis, C. A., Gibbs, S. J., & Rein, G. (1991). Groupware: Some issues and experiences. *Communications of ACM, 34*(1), 39–58.

Erkens, G., Jaspers, J., Prangsma, M., & Kanselaar, G. (2005). Coordination processes in computer supported collaborative writing. *Computers in Human Behavior, 21*(3), 463–486.

Gibson, D. R. (2010). Marking the turn: Obligation, engagement, and alienation in group discussions. *Social Psychology Quarterly, 73*(2), 132–151.

Graham, T. N., Phillips, W. G., & Wolfe, C. (2006). Quality analysis of distribution architectures for synchronous groupware. In: *International Conference on Collaborative Computing: Networking, Applications and Worksharing—CollaborateCom2006*. Atlanta, GA, USA: IEEE Computer Society.

Gutwin, C. (2001). The effects of network delays on group work in real-time groupware. In: *Proceedings of the Seventh Conference on European Conference on Computer Supported Cooperative Work—ECSCW 2001* (pp. 299–318). Bonn, Germany: Kluwer Academic Publishers.

Gutwin, C., Benford, S., Dyck, J., Fraser, M., Vaghi, I., & Greenhalgh, C. (2004). Revealing delay in collaborative environments. In: *Proceedings of the SIGCHI Conference on Human Factors in Computing Systems—CHI 2004* (pp. 503–510). Vienna, Austria: ACM.

Hayes, J. R. (2012). Modeling and remodeling writing. *Written Communication, 29*(3), 369–388.

Ignat, C.-L., & Norrie, M. C. (2008). Multi-level editing of hierarchical documents. *Journal of Computer Supported Cooperative Work, 17*(5–6), 423–468.

Ignat, C.-L., Oster, G., Newman, M., Shalin, V., & Charoy, F. (2014). Studying the effect of delay on group performance in collaborative editing. In: *Proceedings of International Conference on Cooperative Design, Visualization and Engineering—CDVE 2014* (pp. 191–198). Mallorca, Spain: Springer International Publishing.

Karat, C.-M., Halverson, C., Horn, D., & Karat, J. (1999). Patterns of entry and correction in large vocabulary continuous speech recognition systems. In: *Proceedings of the SIGCHI Conference on Human Factors in Computing Systems—CHI 1999* (pp. 568–575). Pittsburgh, PA, USA: ACM.

Landauer, T. K., & Dumais, S. T. (1997). A solution to plato's problem: The latent semantic analysis theory of acquisition, induction, and representation of knowledge. *Psychological Review, 104*(2), 211–240.

Noël, S., & Robert, J.-M. (2004). Empirical study on collaborative writing: What do co-authors do, use, and like? *Computer Supported Cooperative Work, 13*(1), 63–89.

Olson, G. M., & Olson, J. S. (2000). Distance matters. *Human-Computer Interaction, 15*(2), 139–178.

Olson, J. S., Olson, G. M., Storrøsten, M., & Carter, M. (1993). Groupwork close up: A comparison of the group design process with and without a simple group editor. *ACM Transactions on Information Systems, 11*(4), 321–348.

Schiffrin, D. (1987). *Discourse markers*. Cambridge: Cambridge University Press.

Suleiman, M., Cart, M., & Ferrié. J. (1998). Concurrent operations in a distributed and mobile collaborative environment. In: *Proceedings of the International Conference on Data Engineering—ICDE 1998* (pp. 36–45). Orlando, FL, USA: IEEE Computer Society.

Sun, C., Jia, X., Zhang, Y., Yang, Y., & Chen, D. (1998). Achieving convergence, causality preservation, and intention preservation in real-time cooperative editing systems. *ACM Transactions on Computer-Human Interaction, 5*(1), 63–108.

Tammaro, S. G., Mosier, J. N., Goodwin, N. C., & Spitz, G. (1997). Collaborative writing is hard to support: A field study of collaborative writing. *Computer-Supported Cooperative Work, 6*(1), 19–51.

Tremblay, S., Vachon, F., Lafond, D., & Kramer, C. (2012). Dealing with task interruptions in complex dynamic environments: Are two heads better than one? *Human Factors, 54*(1), 70–83.

Vaghi, I., Greenhalgh, C., & Benford, S. (1999). Coping with inconsistency due to network delays in collaborative virtual environments. In: *Proceedings of the ACM symposium on Virtual reality software and technology—VRST 1999* (pp. 42–49). London, United Kingdom: ACM.

Configuring Attention in the Multiscreen Living Room

John Rooksby, Timothy E. Smith, Alistair Morrison, Mattias Rost
and Matthew Chalmers

Abstract We have conducted a video study of households in Scotland with cohabiting students and young professionals. In this paper we unpack five examples of how mobile devices are used by people watching television. In the examples we explore how screens are used together (a) in a physical ecology, (b) in an embodied way, (c) in an orderly way, and (d) with respect to others. We point out that mobile devices are routinely used to access media that is unconnected and unrelated to media on television, for example for sending and receiving messages, browsing social media, and browsing websites. We suggest that mobile devices are not used to directly enhance television programmes, but to enhance leisure time. We suggest that it is important, when considering mobile devices as second screens, not just to treat these as a design topic, but to pay attention to how they are interactionally integrated into the living room.

Introduction

Screen-based devices are often used in front of the television. Reports by Google (2012), Nielsen (2014) and others have addressed the scale of this phenomenon. Jokela et al. (2015), Google (2012) and others have presented generalised patterns of how televisions and other devices are used together. Cruickshank et al. (2007), Cesar (2008) and others have identified opportunities for integrating mobile devices with the televisions. However, such studies can obscure the very thing they seek to draw attention to: the mundane everyday phenomenon of using a second screen. In this paper we will explore the *local particulars* of using second screens.

J. Rooksby (✉) · A. Morrison · M. Rost · M. Chalmers
University of Glasgow, Glasgow, UK
e-mail: john.rooksby@glasgow.ac.uk

T.E. Smith
University of Edinburgh, Edinburgh, UK

© Springer International Publishing Switzerland 2015
N. Boulus-Rødje et al. (eds.), *ECSCW 2015: Proceedings of the 14th European Conference on Computer Supported Cooperative Work, 19–23 September 2015, Oslo, Norway*, DOI 10.1007/978-3-319-20499-4_13

We will look beyond generalised descriptions of how much time is spent doing this or that, or what combinations of media are most common. Instead, we will examine in detail the real world, real time ways in which mobile devices are used when watching television.

This paper presents five examples from a video study of four households in Scotland. The examples show cohabiting students and young professionals watching television. Our analysis will draw upon the idea of "multi-screening". Rather than treat this as a matter of direct or technical integration between televisions and mobile devices, we will examine the integration of second screens into the living room in terms of its practical accomplishment on a mundane everyday basis. We see the integration of second screens into the living room as an *interactional* issue. This paper does not produce design requirements or opportunities, but seeks to characterise and make sense of a domestic setting into which mobile technology and new media are entering.

Television and Second Screens

According to a study commissioned by Google (2012), we are living in "*the new multi-screen world*". They found that people in the USA spend 4.4 h of their leisure time in front of screens each day, and that two or more screen-based devices are routinely used in sequence or in parallel. They found that 77 % of the times people watch television, they also use a second screen. Clearly, using a device in front of a television is common, but these numbers tell us little about how and why this happens.

Home Media

The term "second screen" is commonly invoked with respect to the use of mobile devices or other smaller screens in conjunction with a primary display. These primary displays are typically larger screens, often a television. Hess et al. (2011) characterise the relationship between televisions and second screens in terms of "cross media", and "parallel media". Cross media is the use of a second screen to directly interact with or display information from the primary screen. Parallel media is the use of a second screen in a way that has no technical integration with the primary display, and which may or may not be related to what is on screen.

The academic literature on second screens focuses predominantly on cross media. Cruickshank et al. (2007) developed an application for displaying programme information on a mobile device. Cesar et al. (2008) describe the design of second screen technology in order to control, enrich, share and transfer television content. Ley et al. (2013), and Ogonowski et al. (2013) examine how cross media systems are used through equipping and running living laboratories.

Some work does focus on parallel media, particularly the use of social media during television shows. For example Basapur (2012) describes the use of a *"socially generated information feed"*, and Schirra et al. (2014) discuss how people use Twitter while watching a soap opera. Other work has looked at the use of mobile search while watching television. Some other work on show-relevant app use, for example mobile search, or reading television guides also exists.

Little attention has been paid to what Jokela et al. (2015) term "unrelated parallel media". One reason may be that cross media is more readily a design topic: it is reasonable to build and trial a cross media system but less so a parallel media system. Another reason is methodological. There is very little observational work on watching television. It is overwhelmingly studied in a laboratory setting (e.g. Geerts et al. 2008; McGill et al. 2014b), or indirectly through logs (e.g. Schirra et al. 2014), surveys (Courtois and D'Heer 2012; McGill et al. 2014a), probes (Bernhaupt et al. 2008) and interviews. These methods have strengths, but they each miss the mundane, everyday, *invisible* (Tolmie et al. 2002) uses of technology. Some video studies of naturally occurring television watching do exist, for example Juhlin and Önnevall (2013) have presented a study of how people gesture when watching sports games in a public bar. They argue that it is important to complement laboratory work with ethnographic fieldwork in ordinary environments. Juhlin and Önnevall chose to study bars because of the relative ease of access to these settings, using these as a proxy for the home.

The Home

Watching television is a common domestic pastime, and a valued social activity for many households (Bernhaupt et al. 2008). Of course, the television is not the be all and end all of life in the living room. Watching television can include actively concentrating on what is on-screen, or what Brown and Barkhuus (2006) refer to as passive viewing: times when the television is on, but other activities take precedence. Geerts et al. (2008) point out that people engage with the television and interact with co-present others differently depending on the genre of show. For example people talk more during news, sports and quiz shows than those that require more concentration. Eichner (2014) has pointed out that many popular shows have a predictable format to which viewers can orient to and engage with.

Crabtree et al. (2003, 2012), O'Brien et al. (1999), Tolmie (2013) and Tolmie et al. (2002, 2008) draw our attention to the social and physical organisation of home life. They point out that to study work in CSCW need not be to study a job-of-work, but can encompass practices of home and family life. Shove (2003, 2003) pays attention to materiality in the home. Barnham and Harrison (2013) treat collocated couples as a design topic, and Neustaedter et al. (2012) refer to family life as a continuous "work in progress". Laurier and Wiggins (2011) have used video to study family meal times. Little attention, particularly video ethnography has paid attention to television viewing, but it is within this CSCW and Sociological literature on domestic life *in practice* that this paper sits.

A Video Study of Watching Television

In this paper we use examples taken from a video study of people watching television in their own homes. We recruited four households in Scotland for the study. Two households were cohabiting heterosexual couples, one household had two cohabiting heterosexual couples, and a fourth had two female friends. The participants were young professionals or students in their 20s and early 30s. We recruited and selected the households using criteria including (a) every member of the household was an adult, (b) every member of the household allowed us to log their mobile phone and consented to being videoed, (c) the household ordinarily watched television in a shared living room. Criterion (a) reflected ethical issues in logging mobile devices, whereas (b) and (c) reflected more pragmatic concerns.

We began the study by installing software on each householders' mobile iOS and Android devices to log the name and time of the apps they used. Additionally we requested that each household videoed themselves when watching television. We visited each household and installed two video cameras, one facing towards the television and one away towards where people were likely to sit. We told the households to turn these cameras on and off as they wished, asking for at least three evenings/periods of video data. We generated over 18 h of footage in the study. We watched through this footage, taking summary notes and identifying analytical themes. We then went back and transcribed several sequences in depth, and organized data sessions to discuss and analyse these. Where the sequences contained conversation, we transcribed this in Jefferson format. However, many of the sequences involved watching in silence or with little talk. Therefore we also created visual transcripts using a graphic transcription format (see Laurier 2014 and Stokoe 2012).

Examples

We will discuss five examples. A graphic transcript is presented for each example (Figs. 1, 2, 3, 4 and 5). Each transcript represents a sequence of video data. The transcripts are selective, in that particular frames from the two video cameras have been selected. Figures 4 and 5, which both represent relatively long sequences (75 and 210 s respectively) have been simplified for the paper.

Example 1 (Fig. 1): Household one watch Downton Abbey
F11 and M11 (household one) are a cohabiting couple. Figure 1 shows them sitting on their sofa watching Downton Abbey (a period drama) using an on-demand

Fig. 1 Household one watch Downton Abbey

Fig. 2 Household two watch The Thick of It

Fig. 3 Household three share chocolate while watching Four Lions

service. F11 uses a controller to fast forward through mid-show advertisements. They had been holding hands to this point but break hands to pick up the controller. The couple care about Downton Abbey, they have put their digital devices to the side and pay attention.

Example 2 (Fig. 2): Household 2 watch The Thick of It

F21 and F22 (household two) are housemates. Figure 2 shows them watching The Thick of It (a comedy). They have accessed this show using an on-demand service via a games console. They selected this programme following a short discussion of what they should watch while eating dinner. At the start of Fig. 2, they can be seen to be eating their meal. F21 finishes her meal and pushes her table forward. She gets up, looking across to F22's plate. F22 is not eating but has not finished her meal. F22 has received an SMS message, and is typing a reply. F21 leaves the room and comes back without her plate. F22 continues eating.

Example 3 (Fig. 3): Household 3 watch Four Lions

M31 and F31 (household three) are a cohabiting couple. In Fig. 3 they are watching the comedy film Four Lions. The couple are watching the film shortly after midnight, and are drinking and snacking as they watch. M31 is paying more attention to the film than F31. F31 appears to be following along, but is also using the Facebook app on her phone. M31 takes a bar of chocolate from a plastic bag and begins to open it. F31 looks across to the chocolate and then raises her eyes to M31. M31 notices this and turns to F31. As they make eye contact, F31's expression changes slightly, her eyes widen and she tilts her head forward a little.

M31 asks *"chocolate?"* F31 moves her gaze back to Facebook and nods and smiles. M31 then gives her a piece of chocolate. F31 browses Facebook while eating the chocolate.

Fig. 4 Household four watch Strictly Come Dancing

Example 4 (Fig. 4): Household 4 watch Strictly Come Dancing

Two couples, F41 and M41, and F42 and M42, live together in household four. In Fig. 4, F41 and M41 sit together on one sofa, and F42 on another (M42 has gone out to play football). They are watching Strictly Come Dancing, a game

Fig. 5 Household four watch Educating Yorkshire

show in which celebrities compete in a dancing competition. The example begins at a tense point where the names of the dancers facing possible elimination in a *"dance off"* are about to be revealed. The females groan together at the announcement *"Julien and Janette"*. At this point F41's phone sounds a notification. Earlier she had left her phone on a surface behind her, and now it is out of reach. She and M41 turn around to look at it, then look at each other. F41 smiles at M41, at first with a closed mouth, and then with raised eyebrows and her teeth showing. M41 gets up to retrieve the phone, something that F42 teases him for, calling him *"a loser"*. M41 hands F41 her phone. She opens Snapchat (a picture messaging app), looks at a picture, then tilts it to M41 who is already looking over her shoulder, and finally she shows it to F42. Then, M41 and F42 both start looking at their own mobile phones; F42 opens Instagram and M41 Facebook. On the television, one of the hosts of Strictly Come Dancing asks Julien how he feels about the lack of votes. F41 comments *"It's a shame, why do you think no one votes for him?"* to which F42 replies *"cos he's guff"* (slang, equivalent to *"he stinks"*).

Example 5 (Fig. 5): Household 4 watch Educating Yorkshire
In household four again, M42 and F42 are seated together, and F41 is sitting separately on another seat (M41 is at work). They are watching but paying little attention to the reality television show Educating Yorkshire. The show concerns life in an English school, with the focus during the example being on how to deal with children smoking. M42 is browsing the real estate app Rightmove. F41 is using her laptop to browse the website of a nightclub called Electric Circus. She announces that the band Pigeon Detectives are coming, and then asks F42 what they sang (evidently remembering the band's name, but not the music). F42 sings some of one of their hit songs, leaning across to M42 as she does so and raising her voice, as if to provoke him. F41 and F42 then realise *"that's on camera"* and laugh. F42 then offers to play a song on her phone. Despite F41 laughing *"Nooo"*, F42 opens the music app Spotify. While fetching the music she comments about what is happening on TV (a school boy is revealed to be a heavy smoker) *"eleven to twenty a day, God!"* F41 interjects that she is going away with her boyfriend on Friday. When the advertisements begin, F42 begins playing a Pigeon Detectives song. M42 begins changing channels, settling on another reality television show The Hotel of Mum and Dad. M42 then shouts at F42, saying they do not have to hear the music and that it is loud enough for the whole building to hear. F42 asks M42 why he is *"such a grumps"*.

Configuring Attention

Following Crabtree et al. (2013), we do not attempt to quantify or generalise across occurrences, but will unpack the examples we have presented. Our purpose is to explore the householder's methods: the mundane work of watching television.

The Ecology of Attention

In the five examples we can see that the households have each positioned a sofa or sofas facing the television. In Example 1 (Fig. 1) it can clearly be seen that F11 and M11 have set up their living room in such a way that they can spend time reclining and/or eating and drinking together while facing the screen. They have a footstool that doubles up sometimes as a table, and behind them they have a shelf where they place drinks. Objects are placed in and moved between various areas while they view. A glass of water can be seen behind the couple. M11 has his laptop open but to his side on the sofa. He also has placed his bag and some documents with his computer, providing a workspace. He is able to move back and forth between his work on one side and his partner on the other. Both F11 and M11 have mobile phones, which they keep with them and use during the evenings, typically to send and receive messages. F11 has placed hers on the arm of the chair. M11 has his beside him on the sofa, using his computer to charge it. Both of their devices kept on the opposite side to their partner. F11 and M11 have three remote controls in use. Two of these are placed on the arm of the sofa next to F11. The one she is using had been placed on the sofa away from the other two. It may not be ideal to have three controllers, but F11 and M11 seem to keep these organized, knowing which one they need and where this is.

In Example 2 (Fig. 2) the sofa is set opposite the television. The two women each have a table on which to place things. They use this for their meal and a drink, and F22 has also laid out various cosmetic products. This household has at least four remote controls, two of which are placed on F22's table. The controller for the Games Console, which is used to select what to watch, is placed on the sofa between them. Unlike the couples in our study, these two sit well away from each other throughout. Between them sit two dolls. F21 and F22 place their phones on their own table, keeping it screen up and beside their plate as if ready and waiting for a notification. In the first image in the figure, F22's phone has lit just as she receives a message. Neither housemate seems particularly interested in the show, far less so than household one were in Downtown Abbey (and far less so than they are in Dr Who on a subsequent evening). F22 looks down at her phone to write an SMS, ignoring the screen as well as her housemate. F21's silent check of F22's plate is one example of how visual rather than verbal coordination is at play in front of the television. The look orients to the possibility of F21 doing something for F22, but this possibility is not played out at that moment.

The sofa is, to borrow from Crabtree et al. (2003), a *centre of activity*. It is not just for sitting, but somewhere for watching, eating, drinking, using social media, working, holding hands, painting nails, and so on. These activities draw on and produce an *ecological habitat* in which various things are situated to facilitate various activities. The living rooms are set up for television watching, with comfortable seating set opposite the television screen. In addition, coffee tables and shelves are used to facilitate activities while watching. The mobile objects used by the participants, including mobile phones and laptops, but also plates of food, glasses of drink, remote controls, documents, cosmetics, and more, easily and unproblematically enter this configured space. These objects are not thrown in randomly but moved around in systematic, routine ways. There are places for food and drink, there are places to put phones and laptops, and so on. Remote controls, of which the households have several, were often placed in a particular configuration with some piled together, and others kept more readily to hand. Mobile phones were often kept to hand (not always, as Example 4 shows). Sometimes these were placed in the pocket, but often they were kept screen-up by the person's side.

Embodied Attention

Watching television is also an *embodied activity*. Reclining and being comfortable is clearly an important part of watching, to the point where getting up can make someone a *"loser"* (Example 4). The householders would often recline to watch television unless they were eating. We note the householders often adopted particular postures to facilitate watching television and using a device simultaneously. This involved moving the phone to slightly below eye level, making it possible to move between screens with just a shift of the eyes. When someone held their device lower and looked down (e.g. Fig. 2) this seemed to be to focus specifically on the device. These postures can serve what Brown et al. (2013) refer to as a "double duty". They are useful for the person, but also serve as a signal or cue to those around you as to what you are doing. Given that so much television watching goes on in silence, these cues are important.

We also note that couples can and do routinely cuddle or make physical contact with each other while both watching television and using a device. Sitting next to someone using a mobile device also affords looking and showing. In Example 4, M41 could see the Snapchat image sent to his partner, probably without F41 even needing to tilt her phone. The videos remind us that it is a particular affordance of the mobile phone (as opposed to the plated meal and, to some extent, the book and newspaper) that it can be used when embracing or in close contact with another.

As Heath et al. (2002) have pointed out of workplaces, attention is not just a matter of cognition or mental state but is demonstrably physical, embodied and gone about by the people involved in a methodical manner.

Sequentially Ordered Attention

Example 3 (Fig. 3) shows a couple watching a film. As with the previous examples, the living room is set up to facilitate various activities (including watching, eating and using mobile devices), and various objects (chocolate, drinks and a blanket) are made available for use while they watch. Even though F31 seems to be focusing on Facebook, she is not unaware of her surroundings. She has been laughing from time to time with the film, and she notices when her partner unwraps a chocolate bar. F31's posture is notable, she has adopted a position with her mobile device at chest height that enables her to move her attention back and forth between the screen just by moving her eyes. In the example, F31 solicits an offer of chocolate. She does this by turning to M31, looking at the chocolate in his hand, looking at his face, and smiling. When he asks "*chocolate?*" she shifts her gaze back to her mobile device (she is viewing Facebook), while nodding her head. F31 has not said anything, but her movements are communicative or *accountable*. Her shift of attention away from the screens and to her partner functions as a request because it plays to a common sense or routine sequence of action: a snack will be offered for sharing. As such, Example 3 portrays not just a sequence of activity, but activity that orients to and invokes a normative sequential order. Eating together does not just happen because chocolate exists, but is made to happen through coordinated, embodied, meaningful interaction.

Example 4 (Fig. 4) also features a female persuading her partner to do something by looking at him. When she receives a Snapchat message she persuades him to retrieve her phone, which she left earlier on a surface behind her. In this example, all parties orient to the sequence Schegloff (1969) terms the "summons-answer pair": when the phone sounds, pick it up. Notifications can be ignored if necessary (Tolmie et al. 2008), but the message arrives as music plays on Strictly Come Dancing, just after the announcement "*Julien and Jenette*". We suggest that the housemates are orienting here to the format of Strictly Come Dancing. Although F41 and F41 are following the show closely, it is not all consuming of their attention. As Eichner (2014) points out, many shows have a highly structured and predictable format that can be mastered by viewers and serve as a resource for how they watch. The householders know when to engage with Strictly Come Dancing, when to concentrate, when to groan (it is not a coincidence F41 and F41 groan together), when to give assessments and so on. Whereas in Example 2, F21 and F22 dip in and out of the Thick of It without paying much attention, F41 and F42 methodically attend to Strictly Come Dancing. They seem to know when to focus, when they can look away and so on.

After F41 has seen the Snapchat image and showed it to the others in the room, M41 and F42 also start engaging with their devices. It as if F41's Snapchat message leads to viewing social media being taken up as a group activity. But as they do this divergent activity, the females comment on the television show. When the presenter of Strictly Come Dancing invites a contestant to assess his performance, F41 offers her own assessment ("*it's a shame*") and invites F42 to give one too ("*why do you think…*"). Pomerantz (1984, p. 57) points out that assessments are produced as products of participation: they are claims of knowledge about what the speaker is assessing. F41's assessment and call to F42 for another, works to assert their on-going shared attention to the show. F41 is not just saying 'hey look at this', but is making a knowledge claim and calling for a further knowledge claim, with the effect that both women not only attend to the show but call upon and invoke a shared history of attention to this show. Even though F42's assessment "*he's guff*" is disaffiliative to F41's "*it's a shame*", the effect is to affirm on-going, convergent attention.

Tolmie et al. (2008) and Fischer et al. (2013) characterise notifications as interruptions. The notification in this example is out of the flow of on-screen events, but it is matter-of-course for the household. There is nothing disruptive, or unwelcome about it, the only problem is that someone has to stand up to get the phone. Tolmie et al., in their discussion of notifications, call on us to "*tackle the issue through a detailed exploration of how interruption handling is accountably managed and organized or ordered, including morally ordered, by cohorts*". By paying attention to how (a) the housemates organize getting the device and opening the image, and (b) the housemates organize ongoing shared attention to the television following the viewing of the image, we can see that they are engaging in behavior that orients to normative order. Their behavior is not controlled by this order, they are not made to answer the phone, are not made to give assessments, but they do this in and as orderly, coordinated viewing.

To call the notification in the example an interruption does seem something of a mischaracterization, in that the term implies that watching television is the important activity. Messages, social media and so on seem very much welcome parts of these householders' evenings. They are part and parcel of their leisure time in the living room. Certainly attention is accountably managed and organized in the course of watching together, but this must be done whether or not alerts are sounding or mobile devices are in use. In looking at mundane household life, we are led to look at what Brown et al. (2013) and others refer to as "*multi-activity*". The literature on multi-activity covers many settings, but is commonly concerned with family life. For example studies of family meal times (Mondada 2009; Laurier and Wiggins 2011) and family car journeys (Goodwin and Goodwin 2012) have to deal with how people handle multiple on-going activities. Similarly, to watch the television, multiple other events and activities (not just "interruptions") are oriented to and kept in check.

Coordinated Attention

The examples are each of people watching television together with others. It is not the case that watching together involves being quiet so that others can listen. We have seen that watching together is collaboratively achieved (e.g. the assessments of Strictly Come Dancing in Example 4). We have also seen that watching together can also involve doing things like eating together (Examples 2 and 3). Concerning Example 4, we argued that a notification sound is not necessarily interrupting the entertainment but is part of it. Note how when F41 opens the image, she allows M41 to have a look and then shows it to F42. The image arrives to her personal device, but is shared in the group. The reason for sharing is not that it is from someone they all know, but that it is a picture of a dog. As Fischer et al. (2013) describe, when a notification arrives to a group setting, the receiver of the message is accountable to the group. F41 did not necessarily have to share the picture, but would have had to explain it somehow.

In Example 5 (Fig. 5), F42 sits with her partner M42, and across from her friend F41. As with the other examples, this example highlights aspects of watching television together with others. However, in this example there is an argument about appropriate behaviour. F41 and F42 are having a jovial conversation about a local nightclub and start discussing a band they remember from their shared past. Meanwhile M42 is engaged with the property app Rightmove on his mobile phone. F41 and F42 have been following the television, while they talk, commenting on it at times. M42 does not communicate with F41 and F42 or comment on the show, but note that he has adopted a posture where he can move his eyes between the television and his phone. This is not the same posture as F31 in Example 3, but the effect is the same. M42 does not move or look at F42 when she is singing. Our impression here is not that the mobile phone has cut M42 off from his housemates, but that he is actively using it to cut them off. F42 for her part seems to be trying to provoke attention for M42; when she sings she leans in towards him, looks at him and raises her voice. Trouble does seem to be brewing at this point, and perhaps this is partly why F41 says "*nooo*" when asked if she wants to hear it, and introduces a new topic "*we're away Friday*" moments later. Whether or not F41 sees a confrontation brewing, she sees F42's comment "*do you want to hear…*" and her picking up the phone as indicative of an intention to play music.

It is interesting that F42 waits to the advertisements to play the music, as if it is acceptable for her to sing but not to play music during the programme itself. M42 also seems to orient to this, shouting not at her singing but at her playing music from her phone. Switching channels away from the advertisements and to another show may well have to do with underscoring the unacceptability of the music or to avoid the repost *but the advertisements are on*. While in the previous examples we have shown mobile devices being interwoven with watching, here the device is used in an unacceptable way. Devices are not unproblematic in the living room, but rather that they are (to the main extent) kept unproblematic. When it comes to having to regulate the use of someone's device, it is through a burst of anger. There is no subtle warning, as if F42 should know where the limit to acceptable behaviour is.

A difficulty for us as observers with explaining Example 5 is that the confrontation seems embedded in F42 and M42's relationship. It appears that F42 goes out to provoke him. All but one of our examples feature *couples* watching television. The fact that they are couples is relevant to how they watch. In Example 1, M11 and F11 hold hands and watch as a couple. In Examples 3 and 4, a female gives her partner not just a look, but a smile. In Example 4, M41 does not readily get up to retrieve the phone, but is called upon through F41's looking and smiling at him 'as a boyfriend' to do this favour. The look is intimate, F42's expressions are similar to those described in Kendon's (1990) account of a woman moving into a kiss. F42 orients to M41 and F41's relationship when she teases M41 for getting up, calling him a "loser". She orients to M41 as being subservient, to him doing her work. As Tolmie (2013) points out, intimacy is witnessable and actionable within mundane action. Tolmie argues that intimacy is a quality of action, rather than an action itself (e.g. not all kisses are intimate, and not all intimate kisses are intimate in the same way). Regarding Examples 3 and 4, were they sitting next to a stranger in the cinema or on the bus, they would probably not make requests in the same way, if at all. If such a look was given to a stranger, it would likely be interpreted as a request to be quiet, or met with a "what?" rather than taken as a request to be given something. Our point is, intimacy is recognisable not just from an action but in actions done in particular ways in particular contexts. This does not mean two people sitting together are in a relationship, but means they may have to do work to avoid this assumption. Perhaps this explains the dolls that sit between F21 and F22 in Fig. 2. With respect to Example 4, F41 could conceivably have sat next to F42's boyfriend and used puppy eyes to persuade him to pick up her phone, but F42 would probably be upset by this and do something other than tease.

The examples, in various ways, evoke an intimacy of domestic life. This is apparent in the gross sense that the living room is a domestic, private place, but is also apparent in the particulars of watching television. Intimate looks can be given which achieve particular ends. Boyfriends and girlfriends can sit together. Images can get shared first with a partner through virtue of the partner being closest. Television shows can be enjoyed together with a partner and together with a friend in somewhat different ways, and friends have a right to tease couples about their conduct. Whereas Examples 3 and 4 showed examples of couples sharing and doing things for each other, Example 5 is confrontational. However, it is still an intimate scene. The couple are sitting in close contact (a sort of embrace this time), eye contact is made, and cute and teasing language is used "*why such a grumps?*" What is at issue here is that technology does not feature in the living room as something that brings or breaks intimacy, but rather mobile devices are things that enter an intimate environment and are used with respect to intimacy. Mobile devices do not have fixed roles in this intimate behaviour. A mobile device is present in Example 4, but as something that is looked away from and then turned back to. Whereas in the previous Example 3 the mobile phone was the object central to a couple's interaction, in this case a bar of chocolate takes that centrality. Intimacy can be played out with relation to a variety of objects, of which the physical mobile phone is just one.

Validity of the Study

We have collected video of people using their own devices in their own homes, at times of their own choosing. We cannot claim our study has captured what would have happened in the households had our cameras not been there. The householders clearly designed some of their activities for the study. For example, in household two, a consideration in the decision to watch The Thick of It was that it was a program during which they didn't mind using their phones. After a while, this household seemed to stop trying to meet our imagined expectations, watching shows they genuinely enjoyed such as Dr Who and putting their devices aside. Other households were similar, for example household one seemed awkward until relaxing into Downton Abbey, during which they put aside their devices. Generally, the cameras seemed to be forgotten as the study progressed, in the sense that the participants stopped designing their actions for the study. Example 5 is a case in point. F41 and F42 remember the camera having sung out loud, which brings embarrassed laughter. But the presence of the camera rapidly becomes irrelevant; the laughter stops and the conversation moves on smoothly (to an argument—something that was unlikely to be "an act" for us). This is typical in video studies, that whether or not people know the camera is there, they end up carrying on (Rooksby 2013; Laurier and Philo 2006).

Our study has not uniformly captured ordinary life. This suggests it is problematic to do things such as count how often or for how long screens are used together (although possibly no less problematic than diary and other methods for this). Our choice has been to select and unpack individual examples. In doing so, it has been necessary to pay close attention to and reason about how the participants are orienting to the study itself. We have not selected examples that are devoid of an orientation to the study (as Example 5 clearly shows), but rather we have taken demand characteristics as another observable phenomena that is *done* by the participants as the watch television.

Implications of the Study

It is not our intention to draw out direct implications or ideas for designing home media. Rather we will speak to how the home is and can be seen and understood when designing and evaluating new technology.

- *Multi-screening as practice*: When displays are discussed in the computing and design literature, it is often with disembodied terms such as "screen" (e.g. multi-screening, second screens) or "media" (e.g. cross media, parallel media). The effect is to separate them from the physical and social environment in which they are used. The integration of mobile devices with the television is not, and need not be, in terms of there being a technical connection between devices, or there being a logical relationship between the media viewed on different devices. In the examples we do not see people using their mobile phones to control the television, or to discuss shows via social media. We see people actively interweaving unrelated media together. This interweaving is physical, embodied, orderly and coordinated.

- *Multi-screening as embedded in leisure time*: Mobile devices were not used in front of the television to enhance a television show. Rather, they seem to be in use to bring further things into leisure time, to create more possibilities for entertainment, pleasure and companionship. The idea that messages are "interruptions" or that devices are used to do "sequential" and "parallel" tasks seem mischaracterisations of leisure time. As Harper (2010, 2011) points out, when you examine examples of messaging and technology use, there is little evidence that people are as overloaded with floods of information. On the contrary, people seem to be actively bringing more things into their lives. We should not view the mobile device as being brought into television viewing, but the use of mobile devices, the watching of television, and so on as things being brought into leisure.

- *Multi-screening as constituent in social and intimate life*: It is apparent from our examples that mobile devices have found a place in domestic life. There are claims currently that mobile phones are overused (Lee et al. 2014) and distracting and disruptive to relationships Turkle (2011). However, our examples do not chime with this. We see people using devices while together, even when they embrace. These mobile devices do not seem to be fully demanding of attention (unless that is, the user is purposefully ignoring their partner—Example 5). Using Facebook did not seem to stop F31 noticing her partner was eating chocolate. These glances are fleeting, but the embraces we can see are much longer. Perhaps the relative youth of the study participants is of issue here, or perhaps mobile devices are simply becoming less troublesome. As Ling (2009) and O'Hara et al. (2014) suggest, over time people make a place for new technologies in their lives.

Conclusion

In sum, the examples show that paying attention to screens in the living room is not just an issue of cognition, but of the physical, embodied, and orderly management of media in the home. We suggest the design problem is not how to create integrated systems to meet cognitive ability, but to support the practical ways in which people bring media together in the living room. This is not to criticise cross media, but to say all media needs to find its place in the home.

Acknowledgments This work was funded by EPSRC award EP/J007617/1 A Population Approach to Ubicomp System Design. We thank the anonymous reviews, Eric Laurier at the University of Edinburgh, and our colleagues in the 'Populations' research programme.

References

Barnham, S., & Harrison, S. (2013). Designing for collocated couples. In C. Neustaedter, S. Harrison, & A. Sellen (Eds.), *Connecting families. The impact of new communication technologies on domestic life* (pp. 15–36). Berlin: Springer.

Basapur, S. et al. (2012). FANFEEDS: Evaluation of socially generated information feed on second screen as a TV show companion. In *Proceedings of EuroITV 2012*, pp. 87–96.

Bernhaupt, R. et al. (2008). Trends in the living room and beyond: Results from ethnographic studies using creative and playful probing. *Computers in Entertainment (CIE), 6*(1), 5.

Brown, B., & Barkhuus, L. (2006). The television will be revolutionised: Effects of PVRs and filesharing on television watching. In *Proceedings of ACM CHI '06*, pp. 663–666.

Brown, B., McGregor, M., & Laurier, E. (2013). iPhone in Vivo: Video analysis of mobile device use. In *Proceedings of ACM CHI '13*, pp. 1031–1040.

Cesar, P., Bulterman, D., & Jansen, A. J. (2008). Usages of the secondary screen in an interactive television environment: Control, enrich, share, and transfer television content. EuroITV 2008.

Courtois, C., & D'heer, E. (2012). Second screen applications and tablet users: Constellation, awareness, experience, and interest. EuroITV '12.

Crabtree, A., Rouncefield, M., & Tolmie, P. (2012). *Doing design ethnography*. Berlin: Springer.

Crabtree, A., Tolmie, P. & Rouncefield M (2013). How many bloody examples do you want? Fieldwork and generalization. In *Proceedings of ECSCW '13*, pp. 1–20.

Crabtree, A., Rodden, T., Hemmings, T., & Benford, S. (2003). Finding a place for Ubicomp in the home. In *Proceedings of Ubicomp '03*, pp. 208–226.

Cruickshank, L., Tsekleves, E., Whitham, R., Hill, A., & Kondo, K. (2007). Making Interactive TV easier to use: Interface design for a second screen approach. *The Design Journal, 10*(3), 41–53.

Eichner, S. (2014). *Agency and media reception. Experiencing video games, film and television*. Berlin: Springer.

Fischer, J. E., Reeves, S., Moran, S., Greenhalgh, C., Benford, S., & Rennick-Egglestone, S. (2013). Understanding mobile notification management in collocated groups. In *Proceedings of ECSCW '13*.

Geerts, D., Cesar, P., & Bulterman, D. (2008). The implications of program genres for the design of social television systems. ACM uxTV '08.

Goodwin, M. H., & Goodwin, C. (2012). Car talk: Integrating texts, bodies, and changing landscapes. *Semiotica 191*(1/4), 257–286.

Google. (2012). The new multiscreen world: Understanding cross-platform consumer behaviour. Think With Google Newsletter, August 2012.

Harper, R. (Ed.). (2011). *The connected home: The future of domestic life*. London: Springer.

Harper, R. (2010). *Texture: Human expression in the age of communication overload*. Cambridge: MIT.

Heath, C., Sanchez Svensson, M., Hindmarsh, J., Luff, P., & Vom, Lehn D. (2002). Configuring awareness. *Computer Supported Cooperative Work, 11*(3–4), 2002.

Hess, J., et al. (2011). Jumping between devices and services: Towards an integrated concept for social TV. In *Proceedings of EuroITV '11*, pp. 11–20.

Jokela, T., Ojala, J., & Olsson, T. (2015). A diary study on combining multiple information devices in everyday activities and tasks. In *Proceedings of CHI '15*.

Juhlin, O., & Önnevall, E. (2013). On the relation of ordinary gestures to TV screens. General lessons for the design of collaborative interactive techniques. In *Proceedings of CHI '13*, pp. 919–930.

Kendon, A. (1990). *Conducting interaction. Patterns of behaviour in focused encounters*. Cambridge: Cambridge University Press.

Laurier, E. (2014). The graphic transcript: Poaching comic book grammar for inscribing the visual, spatial and temporal aspects of action. *Geography Compass, 8*(4), 235–248.

Laurier, E., & Philo, C. (2006). Natural problems of naturalistic video data. In H. Knoblauch, J. Raab, H.-G. Soeffner, & B. Schnettler (Eds.), *Video-analysis methodology and methods, qualitative audiovisual data analysis in sociology* (pp. 183–192). Oxford: Peter Lang.

Laurier, E., & Wiggins, S. (2011). Finishing the family meal: The interactional organisation of satiety. *Appetite, 56*(1), 53–64.

Lee, U., Lee, J., Ko, M., Lee, C., Kim, Y., Yang, S., Yatani, K., Gweon, G., Chung, K. M., & Song, J. (2014). Hooked on smartphones: An exploratory study of smartphone overuse among college students. In *Proceedings of CHI 2014*.

Ley, B. et al. (2013). Impacts of new technologies on media usage and social behaviour in domestic environments. *Behaviour and Information Technology, 33*(8), 815–828.

Ling, R., & Donner, J. (2009). *Mobile communication*. Polity.

Mondada, L. (2009). *The methodical organization of talking and eating: Assessments in dinner conversations. Food and Quality Preference, 20*(8), 558–571.

McGill, M., Williamson, J., & Brewster, S. (2014a). How to lose friends and alienate people: Sharing control of a single use TV system. In *Proceedings of TVX '14*, pp. 147–154.

McGill, M., Williamson, J., Brewster, S. (2014b). Mirror, mirror, on the wall: Collaborative screen-mirroring for small groups. In *Proceedings of TVX '14*, pp. 87–94.

Neustaedter, C., Harrison, S., & Sellen, A. (2012). Connecting families: An Introduction. In C. Neustaedter, S. Harrison, & A. Sellen (Eds.), *Connecting families. The impact of new communication technologies on domestic life* (pp. 1–14). Berlin: Springer.

Nielsen. (2014). Cross platform report, Q1 2014. http://www.nielsen.com/. Accessed February 2015.

O'Brien, J., Rodden, T., Rouncefield, M., & Hughes, J. (1999). At home with technology. An ethnographic study of a set-top box trial. *Transactions on Human Computer Interaction (TOCHI), 6*(3), 282–308.

Ogonowski, C., et al. (2013). Designing for the living room: Long-term user involvement in a living lab. In *Proceedings of CHI '13*, pp. 1539–1548.

O'Hara, K., Massimi, M., Harper, R., Rubens, S., & Morris, J. (2014). Everyday dwelling with WhatsApp. In *Proceedings of CSCW '14*, pp. 1131–1143.

Pomerantz, A. (1984). Agreeing and disagreeing with assessments: Some features of preferred/dispreferred turn shapes. In J. M. Atkinson & J. Heritage (Eds.), *Structures of social action* (pp. 57–101). Cambridge: Cambridge University Press.

Rooksby, J. (2013). Does professional work need to be studied in a natural setting? A secondary analysis of a laboratory study of software developers. In Petre, M. & van der Hoek, (Eds.). *Software designers in action. A human centric look at design work.* Chapman Hall: CRC Press.

Schegloff, E. (1969). Sequence in conversational openings. *American Anthropology, 70*, 1075–1095.

Schirra, S., Huan, S., Bentley, F. (2014). Together alone: Motivations for live-tweeting a television series. In *Proceedings of CHI '14*.

Shove, E. (2003). *Comfort cleanliness and convenience: The social organisation of normality.* Oxford: Berg.

Shove, E. (2007). *The design of everyday life.* Oxford: Berg.

Stokoe, E. (2012). Moving forward with membership categorization analysis: Methods for systematic analysis. *Discourse Studies, 14*(3), 277–303.

Tolmie, P., Crabtree, A., Rodden, T., & Benford, S. (2008). Are you watching this or what? Interruption and the juggling of cohorts. In *Proceedings of ACM CSCW '08*.

Tolmie, P. (2013). *Everyday intimacy.* Saarbrücken: Lambert Academic Publishing.

Tolmie, P., Pycock, J., Diggins, T., MacLean, A., & Karsenty, A. (2002). Unremarkable computing. In *Proceedings of CHI '02*, pp. 399–406.

Turkle, S. (2011). *Alone together. Why we expect more from technology and less from each other.* Basic Books, 2011.

Measures and Tools for Supporting ICT Appropriation by Elderly and Non Tech-Savvy Persons in a Long-Term Perspective

Claudia Müller, Dominik Hornung, Theodor Hamm and Volker Wulf

Abstract Appropriation work of new media by the elderly who do not possess experiences in information and communication technologies (ICT) and related support of their acquisition of media competencies are in focus of this paper. A study based on ethnography and action research aiming at examining elderly and not tech-savvy persons' first steps in their appropriation of tablet PCs and internet applications is being provided. On the basis of socio-constructivist learning approaches we outline specific obstacles and constraints in the set-up of an appropriate learning environment for elderly ICT novices.

Introduction

Research work in the field of Ambient Assisted Living (AAL) to enable ageing at home is in most cases directed towards physical and cognitive problems associated with ageing and accordingly, ICT support is being developed to improve home care arrangements between different stakeholders, such as the patients and the care networks. Only few projects explicitly deal with the social side of elderly persons' wellbeing in a community perspective (e.g. Aarhus et al. 2009; Mynatt et al. 1999) which builds the ground of this paper. We report on action-research based

C. Müller (✉) · D. Hornung · T. Hamm · V. Wulf
University of Siegen, Siegen, Germany
e-mail: claudia.mueller@uni-siegen.de

D. Hornung
e-mail: dominik.hornung@uni-siegen.de

T. Hamm
e-mail: theo.hamm@yahoo.de

V. Wulf
e-mail: volker.wulf@uni-siegen.de

© Springer International Publishing Switzerland 2015
N. Boulus-Rødje et al. (eds.), *ECSCW 2015: Proceedings of the 14th European Conference on Computer Supported Cooperative Work, 19–23 September 2015, Oslo, Norway*, DOI 10.1007/978-3-319-20499-4_14

activities aiming at building a basis for collaborative learning between researchers and non tech-savvy tenants of a local neighborhood.

The activities reported on here are a part of a large-scale and long-term participatory design project directed to the development of a neighborhood portal for tenants of a local housing complex in a German city. The neighborhood portal is one attempt in a set of socio-technical measures to support social interaction, awareness and informal help in the neighborhood. The focus of this paper is the work the 'design team' consisting of researchers and elderly tenants had to do to build up a common realm of imagination towards the roles modern technologies could play in the elderlies' every-day lives in the future. Subsequently, appropriation and learning strategies are important themes which, however, have not been much discussed so far for the 'ageing at home' context.

Due to the demographic changes of our societies and the focus on ICT support in every-day contexts to leverage social problems in the elderly such as the increase of social isolation and decreasing societal inclusion, research on media learning and appropriation of new ICTs by the elderly is a topic which becomes increasingly important. However, appropriation of new media by elderly people non-affine to ICT and their acquisition of media competencies are objectives which have not been examined a lot.

We report results of an ethnography- and action research-based study focused on elderly and non tech-savvy persons' first steps in the appropriation of tablet PC and internet applications which may contribute to their quality of life in the sense of getting new channels to communicate and to stay socially connected and informed. Since two years we regularly meet a group of elderly people in bi-weekly workshops and support as well as observe their appropriation processes of the new media.

To make sure the elderly tenants may as well benefit from the online portal and will be able to contribute to this digitally-based channel of ICT, the workshop series has been introduced as a learning forum to help elderly to get access to the new media.

Methodologically and conceptually speaking, we ground our work in socio-constructivist learning approaches (Andresen et al. 2000; Baker et al. 1999; Stahl et al. 2006; Wegerif 2006), which focus on informal and social learning, such as Communities of Practice (CoP) (Lave and Wenger 1991).

Wegerif (2006, p. 1) postulates for younger learners in the networked society that it becomes more and more important "*to teach flexible thinking and learning skills, particularly to create skills of learning to learn*". We see this equally important for elderly people trying to approach the new media. However do we see certain obstacles and constraints in contrast to younger users of the Internet and devices in the media uptake and learning processes in the elderly who so far did not have contact with digital media. For this specific group of learners we identify several themes and obstacles, which are in stark contrast to concepts, tools and methods aiming at knowledge and competence building of younger learners in school or professional settings. In this paper we would like to shed light on the following objectives which seem to need special discussion for the elderly:

Firstly, how to tackle the challenge to get elderly people motivated to start a learning way of new media and secondly how to set-up a socio-constructivist learning environment, which in the case of the elderly must be deeply grounded in their everyday life interests, needs and wishes. From here then, we wish to discuss the balance which needs to be found between learning offers of general and specific, practice-based knowledge. Finally, the question of how to build-up a sustainable framework for the elderlies' appropriation and learning support is of utmost importance against the background of the learning capabilities and interests of the very target group.

Related Research

Human-centered technology research and learning theory both have been motivated by and grounded on cognitivist assumptions and theories (Bannon and Bødker 1991; Stahl 2011) for several decades.

Vygotsky's and Leontiev's influence via the inclusion of Activity Theory into these fields of research shifted the focus from individual's mental processes towards group interactions (Bannon and Bødker 1991; Engeström 1987; Kuutti 1995), communication (Wegerif 2006) and the role of artifacts as mediators of informal learning as well as bearers of highly contextualized knowledge (Baker et al. 1999; Bannon and Bødker 1991; Stahl et al. 2014; Suchman 1987). The shift from analyzing internal mental processes towards social interactions involved developing new methods in order to adequately describe and frame the observed phenomena.

Lave and Wenger (1991) coined the term of Legitimate Peripheral Participation (LPP), which is based i.e. on Vygotsky's (1978) zone of proximal development, in an effort to describe the highly social process of gradually integrating novices into an established community by taking part in their ongoing practices, routines and habits, thus being able to adopt and refine skills, informally learn basic principles and develop an identity inside the community.

As a framework for establishing LPP as a praxeological concept Lave and Wenger (1991) introduced the concept of Communities of Practice (CoP) with its three keystones (a) joined enterprise (an overarching community goal); (b) mutual engagement (connecting all members to a consistent social entity) and (c) shared repertoire (development of common language, values, and resources). CoP are well cited in human-centered ICT research (Draxler et al. 2012; Rohde et al. 2007; Stahl 2011) as well as in learning research (Hung and Chen 2005; Rohde et al. 2005).

Under the term of technology appropriation researchers describe suitable measures for the support of successfully adapting certain artifacts to a certain practice, a crucial process regarding the acceptance and future use of technology (Overdijk and Diggelen 2007; Draxler et al. 2012; Stevens et al. 2010).

The abovementioned influences are discussed under the theoretical frame of (social) constructivist learning, which partially supersedes the earlier concepts of cognitivist, instruction-oriented learning and teaching. As a result informal and situated learning in the form of problem-based (Wood 2003) and technologically enhanced (Jahnke et al. 2014; Twidale et al. 2005) learning settings, as well as a growing interest in practice-based approaches (Kuutti and Bannon 2014; Wulf et al. 2011) fuel future research opportunities in human-centered and collaborative ICT research fields such as CSCL, CSCW and HCI.

As Beringer et al. (2011), Ekeland et al. (2010) and Müller et al. (2012) describe an anchoring in real practice, i.e. in actually occurring problems and existent habits, is a crucial aspect not only in working with elderly people and ICT but also in elderly education. The researchers claim that former assumptions should be superseded where seniors themselves are seen as problems due to their alleged bodily and mental restraints and argue for a wider implementation of qualitative methods, like action research (Lewin 1946, Hayes 2011) and participatory design workshops (Bødker 1996), in order to gain a deeper understanding of seniors' everyday lives.

These measures in combination with technologically enhanced, collaborative learning settings on the one hand provide much deeper insights in seniors' everyday lives for research and development, on the other hand empower the seniors by offering learning possibilities and enhance their lives by supporting the appropriation and use of technology. Current literature provides very few examples of successfully implemented long-term projects with ICT and seniors (Mynatt et al. 1999; Naumanen and Tukiainen 2009).

Another challenge for the development of training and educational measures for home based systems is skill development regarding digital literacy (Kommers 2010), a problem, which often applies not only for non-professional home contexts (elderly patients and elderly spouses as informal carers) but also in care professions, which are often additionally gendered (women are more often lacking ICT competences and familiarity due to socialization processes).

A further important aspect is the inclusion of social media to enable social and organizational embedding of learning tools to support negotiation processes between people and motivate contacts and communication rather than this can be done by only documents and learning artefacts (Richter and Koch 2008). In many practical situations these potentials can only be gained by securing privacy and intimacy (Löser and Herrmann 2011), thus a combination of open and closed learning arrangements must be aimed at. First research agendas of the integration of social media in e-learning have been developed by Greenhow (2009) who focused on in situ-learning and everyday-embedding or Kafai and Peppler (2011) who researched into the linking of smaller learning groups and bigger groups of interest.

Setting and Methods

Our work with seniors is based in a participatory design project of the development of a web-based neighbourhood platform together with a housing company and a group of voluntary, interested tenants in a German city quarter. All of these tenants are between 60 and 86 years of age and without initial knowledge in the area of new media and ICT. The platform offers several possibilities including a digital bulletin board, a platform for local professional services to present themselves as well as a communication network for the tenants to ask for or offer help, organize social events and exchange goods.

Before being able to invite the elderly tenants to become partners in a participatory design project who did not use new media and—for many of them—were initially not very interested in the media topic, we firstly were challenged to get them interested and motivated and to enable them to evaluate if the new media practices would be fitting to their every-day practices. This is to say that before a participatory design process could be started, we had to open up a shared space of thinking and of possibilities of futures practices, for both sides, the elderly tenants as well as for the researchers who needed to learn about their interests, needs and daily practices. This process was being accomplished for about 9 months.

First of all this appropriation and learning approach involved introducing the 10 participants to mobile devices, mobile applications and certain web-based technologies in order to develop a sense for the technology. We provided them with tablet computers accompanied by an introduction to the very basic handling of these devices as well as providing opportunities to discuss and solve specific problems that they faced when using the tablets at home. These measures were complemented by informal chats about topics of interest for the elderly people in order to get to know their daily live routines, hopes, fears and wishes.

The participants gradually explored certain features like photography, photo sharing via email, instant messaging, video conferencing and usual web browsing, always supported by our expertise and grounded in their daily lives (we will elaborate further on this below in the empirical section). We observed the ongoing appropriation process of the seniors with the tablet computers and mobile applications in biweekly workshops in a community room of the housing company situated next to the housing complex. In total we conducted about 50 regular and three larger-scaled workshops up to now. After the first 9 months of work with the tablets, we were able to take up discussions dedicated towards the development of the neighborhood portal. From that time on until today (altogether two years now) the workshop topics alternated between technology appropriation/learning and portal development, following an established structure of one hour of "troubleshooting" and informal chatting with coffee and cake followed by the actual workshop for another two hours.

The overall methodology combines elements from qualitative data analysis (Flick et al. 2004) and action research (Lewin 1946; Hayes 2011). From the beginning, project reflection, activities for learning support and idea generation for the portal design were framed by means of theoretical sampling regarding data collection, documentation, open coding, analysis, reflection and further planning. The documentation mainly consisted of interview transcripts, field notes and photos, as well as artifacts like screenshots made by the participants and email or instant messenger conversations. The larger-scaled workshops were additionally documented by partially transcribed audio and video recordings.

Empirical Findings

Getting Access and Fostering Motivation

The first contact to elderly tenants was established at an assembly of the tenants organized by the housing company. We were able to casually chat with some attendees in order to get in contact with potentially interested people. After the first tenant assembly, we joined a regular activity called "coffee and cake with the caretaker", which had been established by the local caretaker as an offer to elderly tenants to come together and chat. We deliberately took this chance to get in closer contact to the mostly (up to 15) elderly participants regularly visiting this event, after some first experiences with a high skepticism and reluctance towards the technology issue. In the course of these meetings, we brought some mobile devices and demonstrated and discussed different usage possibilities, based on the ongoing informal talks about the seniors' everyday lives.

When some elderly tenants signaled interest in getting deeper into tablet usage, we started to organize an own bi-weekly workshop in the community room, commencing the "tradition" of starting the sessions with coffee and cake (see Fig. 1). At that point of the project, we also were able to hand out mobile devices to about 15 interested elderly people. The workshops were essentially aimed at spanning up a bridge between actual practices of the peoples' conduct of every-day life and the ability to imagine possible futures of meaningful ICT support, i.e. to span up a

Fig. 1 Coffee, cake and cooperative technology exploration

shared thinking space of future possibilities (in a similar vein as, e.g. described by Brandt et al. (2010).

Two essential features are the basis of the workshops: First, the handing over of off-the-shelf technology and support in individual and group-based appropriation, which is strongly linked to the persons' every-day life issues. Second, based on subsequent diffusion of technology usage meaningful to the individuals, an engagement in concrete participatory design sessions can be started. The final goal is then to bring the former participants to a status where they possess a certain level of skills to operate the technology in for them meaningful ways, and perhaps more importantly, to get over their skepticism, anxieties and negative self-images in respect to new media and instead foster their pleasure to see themselves as capable and important contributors to the design project.

We chose off-the-shelf tablets and smartphones so that the participants could benefit from a huge app repository and many sources of support. Additionally, they could get used to touch-sensitive interaction which is important for the use of the outdoor displays which show the neighborhood portal in front of the tenements. A third reason for the selection of off-the-shelf technology versus custom software is to foster sustainable usage after the end of the project. As many persons in the social networks of the elderly participants (such as children, grandchildren or neighbors) are meanwhile used to mobile devices, they are being seen as one possible way to get help in case of trouble with the device.

Co-constructing "Anchor Points"

In order to elicit "anchor points" to bridge their actual every-day practices with the new media, we ground our work in subsequent dialogs about their everyday life contexts and how ICT might contribute to their quality of life. In the beginning, we started with a demonstration of simple photo and video functionalities on the tablets because some of the elderly had brought pictures to the workshops in order to show us their families or places they liked, such as their former favorite holiday destination or their former hometowns.

We took this notion and started the presentation of the tablets with introducing the photography features, i.e. how to take pictures and videos, how to safe and find them on the device. As this practice was being perceived as both, very easy and joyful, taking pictures and making videos became a major issue for the next couple of weeks (see Fig. 2). Next, some participants wished for the possibility to exchange their pictures, because, as one said: "It is a pity. I am never on the pictures I take myself. And Hilde has all the nice pictures of me."

This was an excellent starting point for introducing the concept and use of email, including the creation of an email account for everyone. The participants learnt that email is an excellent way of contacting grandchildren, children and friends and when the feature of attaching a file was explained and understood by the participants the possible use of email developed to become manifold. However,

Fig. 2 Participants taking photos with their tablets

it also became evident that constant repetition and usage of the medium was necessary and a key to understanding and memorizing the functionalities. Nowadays, for most, writing and receiving emails is not a novelty anymore but has become a part of their live and a contribution to their quality of live.

Stepwise Introduction of Online Features and Mobile Apps

Other starting points for the increasing use of online features included sports or cultural events such as Formula One races or the Eurovision Song Contest. Especially for the male participants the soccer scores are of interest and the ability to have in-depth reports on teams, coaches and games are highly appreciated and are a clear motivation to use the tablet in their home environment. Another popular app was a companion app from a TV station, which was introduced by a participant, providing in-depth information on shows and the TV program. The lady had played around with her daughter on the tablet and the daughter then had installed that app for her. After the lady demonstrated her new app to the other participants some of them were interested in having that app themselves. Interestingly, the app was even downloaded by a participant who did not even watch the station, but who wanted to be able to participate in the chat on that topic.

By this, new themes emerged for the neighbors who were not that familiar to each other and they started conversations that were not possible before.

Downloading apps was found to be rather easy and very handy, hence the other participants quickly started downloading a variety of apps by themselves. Most participants are well versed in downloading apps now while always avoiding charged ones, still being afraid of additional charges, which they might not have been aware of. Often, they wait for the next workshop to ask us to be sure the app is cost-free. This means, that sometimes they do not take up these new veins for some 14 days until they again have the chance to ask us and make sure they will not be charged.

Taking the clues from the group to create adequate learning points has been crucial in maintaining a keen interest in the new possibilities and motivation for further learning experiences. A further need was created when one of the participants discovered an app to create collages of photos. She had seen the possibilities when she was visiting her son. This idea was picked up by the group, so we ran a workshop dedicated to this particular app. As the app is only available in English we translated the buttons and features for the group and additionally prepared a short handbook providing screen shots of every interaction step with the collage app, which could be taken home by the participants to practice further after the workshop.

In one of the workshops we heard that one of the participants has a daughter-in-law living on the Philippines. She told us that she was sad that they could not talk a lot together on the phone, as she was not yet fluent in German and still learning. We introduced Skype to her so she could try it out at home. In the next workshop she reported that they had talked and also used the chat feature, which enriched their communication enormously. This was such a practical example to the group that now all of them have installed and use Skype to communicate with family members who are not living in the vicinity. The possibility not only to communicate verbally but also to see the other person hit off incredible well with the group and has extended their imagination to the possibilities to ICT.

As we always start the workshops with coffee and cake, baked by one of the female participants in turn, and one of the researchers is vegan, so he cannot participate in the common meal, the ladies regretted this. In the next workshop two ladies proudly presented a vegan cake and told us that they first informed themselves about what it means to live vegan on Wikipedia, and then browsed for vegan cake recipes on YouTube. Here we could observe how quickly their abilities to conduct online research and gather information on new topics have improved when a clear motivation was at hand.

Another anecdote where a participant had seen a huge benefit in using the tablet was when she started to send daily photos of her holiday to the group and maintained a communication throughout the stay. Besides increased options for information, communication and staying connected, also direct improvements of problems in every-day live were being observed, e.g. when another one ordered spare parts for her wheeled walker online.

The possibility to see their neighborhood area from a birds-eye perspective via "Google Maps" is another example how important it is to take the individual interest of participants as starting points for learning. After they discovered this feature they all first showed the group which ways they usually take and extended the concept to show each other were they grew up. When a new researcher was introduced to the group one of the ladies took him on a virtual tour through her home village and showed him where she had lived, went to school and were the beach was for swimming.

Self-actualization and biography and reminiscence work thus is another feature much loved and needed by the elderly people which is enormously being supported by means of new media and internet. Yet, these new abilities also permanently create new problems: "*How do I access the wifi in a Hotel?*" or "*Why do I not have access to the internet at every point on an island?*" For these kinds of problems we provide individual help in the first part of the workshops, the "trouble shooting" session.

Changes in Attitudes Towards the New Media by Ongoing Practice

Besides observing that the elderly successively integrated the new technology in their individual every-day life context and by this, how their disinterest, anxieties and barriers towards the new media subsequently decreased, we also were able to observe a change in their overall attitude. In the beginning of our work we often were confronted with utterances such as:

> It is nice that you want to teach us to use these new technologies, but as we are old it might be of more worth for you to work with the young who really need these skills in school or on their job!" or "I do not know if this is good for me, what will other people think when I as such an old person am running around with a tablet PC. I think it is a bit embarrassing.

This confirms research results on attitudes towards ICT by elderly people and hence a high degree of self-marginalization of the elderly when reflecting their active integration and contribution in participatory design projects (Müller et al. 2012). However, by the subsequent processes of sense-making of ICT usages in their every-day life circumstances, also a process of change of identity as an ICT user occurred. In contrast to the peoples' shyness and reluctance in the uptake of the tablet usage, today we see them being proud of having mastered their first steps of appropriation of the technology:

> I was at my grand-daughters 20th birthday and her friends looked at me and probably thought:' what does this old lady do with that tablet?' When I took all these pictures they saw they were really nice and asked me if I would send them. That was fun for me!

In the last months we have seen a definite change in the way our group utilizes new technology and how much self-esteem the individuals draw from these new abilities. New subjects and themes are sometimes researched in online searches by the individuals themselves. Some participants are very good at baking cakes and have expanded their knowledge by referring to internet pages. Another is taking

Fig. 3 Self-made christmas decoration and cake

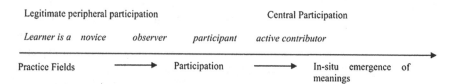

Fig. 4 Scaffolding continuum, Hung and Chen (2005), p. 229

tips and hints from the internet for handcrafting her own Christmas decoration. This is her own interest which she now can pursue by herself and thereby adding a new dimension to her life (Figs. 3 and 4). For those participants, the 'decorators' and 'bakers', the workshops have the additional purpose to serve as an audience which is always pleased to receive the nice table decorations. Likewise the self-made cakes are getting a lot of praise which the single-living participants do not get so often.

We see that the mastery of conducting internet researches is then linked to other more 'traditional' skills which both in a sum are highly acknowledged in the group.

Self-help Measures: Face-to-Face, Manuals and Tools

Reflecting about measures for self-help when tablet usage problems occur, is an important task since the project resources only allow us to meet the group bi-weekly and as well as in regard to the end of the project in six months from now. With the increase of the usage in their home environments the usage problems increase alike, resulting in a lot of questions and problems that have to be discussed in the workshops (e.g. notifications about updates in the apps). Sometimes, the participants experience the problems as such gravely that they stop using the tablet until the next time they see us. Thus, we developed some methods and introduced tools to bridge the time span between our bi-weekly face-to-face meetings.

As the participants may keep their tablets after project end and utter the wish to go on in their usage and learning process, we need to think about an appropriate long-term support. This, as a keystone for the project success, involves establishing routines whereby the individuals are able to solve any upcoming problems either themselves or are able to ask other persons or resources for help. Therefore, aids were introduced to the group since the beginning of the project in form of individual as well as group level support.

Language Issues

Initially the group had to learn a whole set of new vocabulary and a plethora of new concepts. As the group is composed of native German speakers the difficulties can be easily seen as many terms are English—even in the German help sections of manuals. Hence the first step was to create a list of translations and explanations in paper format. However, it sometimes is hard to find the right balance between going on with a (rather established) English term or a German translation. In some cases, people memorize English terms very easily, and then do not feel that the translation is necessary. An example is the handling of the term "screenshot": when we explained the concept of screenshots and used a German term, this resulted in the group going quiet, looking at us and saying *"You mean screenshot. Why don't you say this?"* This shows that we have to handle a balance between common ICT terms and specific adapted terms for people lacking the knowledge. When the participants understand the terms against the background of their practice and integrate them in a sense-making process, then the general terms are being accepted—and even wished for. This demonstrates the successful learning curve from their point of view and it fills them with pride that they are capable to participate in this "technical speech" environment. In addition, we offered a diverse portfolio of aids to our group apart from simply translating if necessary. The key to understanding the use of the tablet, apps and portal are discussions with the group and individuals where we try to explain the frameworks and concepts needed to understand modern IT based technology. Without a very basic understanding of these only one-time solutions can be offered.

Handbook

Therefore we have written a handbook explaining the basic functions of the tablet with sufficient screenshots from the original tablet. The intention of the handbook is to provide the individuals with a short manual explaining basic functions to use at home. In order to help individuals with specific problems in handling apps or the tablet we have created stencils of the tablet where we can draw and include annotations during the workshops. Here, we use a pattern we often observe: the people often use notes and write down the solutions given by us to be able to read them and repeat the related tablet interactions later on at home. When we see that a specific way of problem solving is of interest for others, too, we approach that in one of the following workshops, so they can help each other when they need to repeat the way of problem solving (e.g. in the handling of a specific app) later on.

Individual Help Strategies

As the group has progressed in using different media of communication such as email, *SKYPE* and *TELEGRAM* (similar to *WHATSAPP*), we were able to introduce these channels for asking us or the group for help. Based on this, we exercised making a screenshot and sending it. This supported the demonstration of a usage problem and its explanation. Before the participants were capable to use the described channels and tools for asking for help we had offered a support hotline for some hours per week where they could call in case of questions or problems. This hotline was used very rarely because describing problems on the telephone seemed to be rather impractical and beyond their capabilities.

One typical source of tablet usage problems was the change of the user interface after a software update. To date most members of the group wait for the researchers to explain the changes or to help them to get the "old" interface back. It often happens that they feel that it was their fault that the interface changed by inadvertently changing the settings of an app. As the people only then are interested in learning new issues when they are of direct relevance to their every-day life, they are not much interested to dig deeper into the ICT framework and to learn about why e.g. updates in general are important and they do not see a point in the change of interfaces which for them seem good when they are being understood by them.

As we had chosen the way to set-up our work on off-the-shelf hard- and software, we always have to deal with the need to leverage the newly learned skills and the changes brought by the software providers. This problem can be exemplified by a problem which occurred with GMX mail. One of the participants had problems accessing her email account via the internet but was able to access via the GMX app. The website reported general log-in problems but also GMX had run an update. After checking the status of the updates and updating the browser the problem remained. Only after de-installing and re-installing the app, the problem was solved. We spent two days chatting and calling each other to solve the problem. In the end her neighbor suggested the solution.

This provides an example of individual help strategies which they now can use to solve problems by themselves. They have learned sufficient terms, concepts and vocabulary so that they can ask for help and search out different sources for help in order to solve their problems. In fact they are self-assured enough now to ask people outside of our group for help and to devise their own help strategies.

An additional source of help is a SAMSUNG app which involves calling a cost-free hotline and downloading an app which enables the hotline to enter the tablet directly. Naturally, they will only deal with problems related to the tablet and pre-installed apps. But using this system requires first of all trust and an adequate usage of terms. The problem was that after an update the screen-shot function had been changed. Therefore we decided to use the help-line instead of searching for button ourselves. We sat down with one of our more experienced users and downloaded the app and then called the help-line. Here the main problem was one of trust and the fear of incurring unwanted costs. Only after we insured her twice that it actually was cost free, she was willing to make an assisted call. After SAMSUNG had shown and explained the solution she was pleased with the result and now would be willing to call without assistance.

Discussion

The set-up of an environment for elderly people in order to learn to manage a mobile technology, such as a tablet computer, encompasses a lot of aspects which already have been reported in work on informal learning environments based on socio-cultural theories of learning, such as e.g. in (Lave and Wenger 1991; Stahl et al. 2006; Wood 2003). However, for the target group of elderly and not tech-savvy people there are certain aspects which we think need further consideration, such as finding ways to raise interest and motivation to get in touch with new media, social learning issues and appropriation support. In the following, we make use of the concepts of Legitimate Peripheral Participation (LPP) and Communities of Practice (CoP) (Lave and Wenger 1991) and the scaffolding metaphor (Hung and Chen 2005) to analyze potentials and barriers to building up a social learning environment for elderly ICT novices.

Experience-Based and Open-Ended Formulation of a Joint Enterprise

A joint enterprise is a major basis for learning partners to be able to exchange knowledge or, in the case of vocational training, to gradually grow into a professional group by legitimate peripheral participation (Lave and Wenger 1991). By means of the pre-defined project goal of co-developing a neighborhood portal, we had not been able to get elderly tenants interested in cooperating with us because we were lacking a common realm of thinking in regard to their possible future

ICT support. That's why the initial pre-defined joint enterprise had to be extended: in order to be able to talk about design decisions in a participatory design sense, another joint project in setting up interest and motivation for technology usage and to learn first steps had to be set up. Here, the joint sub-project enabled the researchers to learn about the tenants' everyday practices, their thoughts, wishes and needs, and this was then a basis for suggesting ICT support which was valued as meaningful by the participants in form of an ongoing dialog. Thus, in the first couple of months, the researchers had to carefully bring in usage options based on the "anchor points" they derived from ongoing dialogs with the workshop participants on their every-day life.

Dealing with the Problem of a Missing Common Repertoire

An important facet of a shared repertoire in a CoP is the shared language and the terms being used in the field of learning. This is lacking here to certain extents and we have to accept that the two parties—elderly tenants and researchers—will never come to the end of sharing a common repertoire, which will contribute to an autonomous usage of the tablets by the workshop participants. This is a special problem of people not being able to speak and understand English—and based on this the IT terms—which is quite common in the elderly generation in many countries and is one of the major barriers to ICT adoption. There are attempts in designing special elderly-related tools, which provide only limited access to Internet applications, which then may be controlled for their usability and choice of terms being used. We—in contrast—have chosen to work with off-the-shelf software and hardware in regard to a coming project end and the related chances to substitute our help by other media users being capable to help from their family and friend networks. This choice certainly has its special costs and constraints as long as software and hardware providers do not pay special attention to the elderly customers' appropriation needs.

Another important aspect here is the reflection of the question of what 'should the elderly learners learn to be capable to manage their tablets autonomously?' We perceived here certain limits: as we have seen that learning in the elderly must be closely linked to sense-making processes embedded in every-day practice anchor points, we will not be able to provide them with a 'curriculum' covering all possible usage options (and troubleshooting strategies) so that they may act autonomously in the future. There will always be a difference in the knowledge, and the 'common repertoire' we strive for, is strongly constructed by the researchers. However, we are still developing a common repertoire, which may be limited, but nevertheless useful for the individual learning paths of the participants as well as for the set-up of a collaborative thinking space of future possibilities for the overall design approach.

Mutual Engagement to Identify "Anchor Points" and to Raise Pride in the Own Practice

The notion of mutual engagement is a concept that points at the highly relevant need to step into an ongoing dialog with the elderly. Only when "anchor points" from their every-day life may be connected by the researchers to technical features and applications, a process of sense-making can start and motivation and interest in learning will being taken up by the elderly. Mutual engagement also depicts processes of development of pride in mastering the new media, which was formerly far away from their every-day life. After constant interaction with the media, the development of a new facet of their construction of identity as a technology user could be observed.

The learning support we provided is most notably appropriation support (Stevens et al. 2010). Only by appropriating an object (such as a software tool) a sense-making process can be initiated. In the case of the non tech-savvy elderly with a high barrier towards ICT based on their reluctance, their self-image and non-available knowledge and usage experiences, the provision of links to their every-day life circumstance were pivotal to open up a common space of possibilities.

This process was based on both, social learning processes among each other in their group, but also triggered by the research team, who subsequently proposed new applications in the dialog with the people. Learning processes thus were positioned on experience-based learning, i.e. the "*appropriation of something that is to them personally significant or meaningful (sometimes spoken of in terms of the learning being 'true to the lived experience of learners')*" (Andresen et al. 2000, p. 2). The lived experiences of the elderly are different environments than in other learning arrangements, such as at schools or in professional settings, and are linked to different learning targets and objectives in dealing with new media. The media landscape on the other hand is rapidly changing. This means we have to balance learning capabilities and interests on the one hand and the rapid media changes on the other. We introduced ways for a general handling of the tablets, but were not able to dig deeper into concepts and frameworks, which then would have been too overwhelming for the elderly we worked with, as the relation to their actual practices would have been missing.

The Metaphor of Scaffolding as a Lens to Learning Support for Elderly and not Tech-Savvy Persons

The 'scaffolding' metaphor used in pedagogics seems to be a workable lens to highlight potentials and barriers in the set-up of measures to secure sustainability of learning in the elderly. Some scholars see Vygotsky's concept 'zone of proximal development' as a basis for the scaffolding metaphor, which denotes a process of learning by which *"individuals progress in their skills and experience and gradually require less structure and guidance"* (Rieber 2000).

Hung and Chen (2005) introduce the "scaffolding continuum" (Fig. 4), which describes an evolution of a learner from the role as a novice, via an observer and participant to an active contributor in the end, similar to the concept of LPP (Lave and Wenger 1991). Equally is the idea that the need for support in handling the learning objectives subsequently decreases as the learner gradually becomes an expert, which is being denoted as 'fading'.

The idea, that a learner in the beginning of his/her learning endeavor is being provided with tools, materials and personal advice by a tutor which in the course of the learning route may subsequently being reduced is only partly realizable for the target group and the learning objectives at hand. As demonstrated, it will be hardly possible to install such a learning environment to support the full process of the elderly learners from being a novice to becoming an autonomous operator of the tablet PCs. In different degrees of intensity all of them will be in need of support and help when certain problems with their devices occur after the researchers' withdrawal at the end of the project.

In the case of the elderly and against the background of their lacking capabilities and interests in the acquisition of conceptual knowledge in order to be able to transfer their knowledge from one application to another, the focus must therefore be strongly set onto setting up practice-based scaffolds as measures and tools for (self-) help. Instead of aiming at rolling-out a course on the overall features and concepts of tablet PCs and internet usage on the tablets, it seems more sensible to follow the two paths: (1) Setting up appropriation support linked to real and lived experiences to the elderly learners and, (2) Preparing measures, tools and social networks for (self-) help.

Conclusion

We have presented an action-research based project in the context of the development of a local neighborhood portal aiming at supporting social interactions among the elderly tenants. We described specific measures to open up a common thinking space between the elderly and us researchers and a step-wise approach to enable sense-making activities in the non tech-savvy people towards the usage of tablet PCs in the context of their every-day lives. We used the Communities of Practice concept (Lave and Wenger 1991) for the discussion of our empirical findings to make visible some specificities when aiming at supporting ICT learning by non tech-savvy elderly in an experience- and community-based approach.

Acknowledgments We warmly thank all the participants and project partners for their attendance and endurance in this project. The project is funded by the German Federal Ministry of Family Affairs, Senior Citizens, Women and Youth.

References

Aarhus, R., Aaløkke Ballegaard, S., Grönvall, E., & Bo Larsen, S. (2009). Ageing in communal place: Ethnographic studies of social interaction in senior housing communities. In *Workshop at ECSCW 2009 on Enhancing interaction spaces by social media for the elderly*, Vienna, Austria, September 7, 2009.

Andresen, L., Boud, D., & Cohen, R. (2000). Experience-based learning. In G. Foley (Ed.), *Understanding adult education and training* (2nd ed., pp. 225–239). Sidney: Allen & Unwin.

Baker, M., Hansen, T., Joiner, R., & Traum, D. (1999). The role of grounding in collaborative learning tasks. In P. Dillenbourg (Ed.), *Collaborative learning: Cognitive and computational approaches* (pp. 31–63). Oxford: Elsevier Science/Pergamon.

Bannon, L., & Bødker, S. (1991). Beyond the interface: Encountering artifacts in use. In Carroll, J. M. (Ed.), *Designing interaction: Psychology at the human-computer interface* (pp. 227–253). Cambridge: Cambridge University Press.

Beringer, R., Sixsmith, A., Campo, M., Brown, J., & McCloskey, R. (2011). The "acceptance" of ambient assisted living: Developing an alternate methodology to this limited research lens. In Abdulrazak, B., Giroux, S., Bouchard, B., Pigot, H., & Mokhtari, M. (Eds.), *Toward useful services for elderly and people with disabilities* (pp. 161–167). Berlin, Heidelberg: Springer.

Bødker, S. (1996). Creating conditions for participation: Conflicts and resources in systems development. *Human-Computer Interaction, 11*, 215–236.

Brandt, E., Binder, T., Malmborg, L., & Sokoler, T. (2010). Communities of everyday practice and situated elderliness as an approach to co-design for senior interaction. In *Proceedings of OZCHI '10*, pp. 400–403.

Draxler, S., Stevens, G., Stein, M., Boden, A., & Randall, D. (2012). Supporting the social context of technology appropriation: On a synthesis of sharing tools and tool knowledge. In *Proceedings of CHI '12*, pp. 2835–2844.

Ekeland, A. G., Bowes, A., & Flottorp, S. (2010). Effectiveness of telemedicine: A systematic review of reviews. *International Journal of Medical Informatics, 79*(11), 736–771.

Engeström, Y. (1987). *Learning by expanding*. Helsinki: Orienta-Konsultit.

Flick, U., von Kardorff, E., & Steinke, I. (2004). *A companion to qualitative research*. London: Sage.

Greenhow, C. (2009). Social networking and education: Emerging research within CSCL. In O'Malley, C., Suthers, D., Reimann, P., & Dimitracopoulou, A., (Eds.), In *Proceedings of the 9th International Conference on Computer Supported Collaborative Learning—Volume 1 (CSCL'09)* (Vol. 1, pp. 454–458). International Society of the Learning Sciences.

Hayes, G. R. (2011). The relationship of action research to human computer interaction. *ACM TOCHI, 18*(3), 18.

Hung, D., & Chen, V. (2005). Preserving authenticity in CoLs and CoPs: Proposing an agenda for CSCL. In *CSCL '05*, pp. 227–231.

Jahnke, I., Svendsen, N., Johansen, S., & Zander, P. (2014). The dream about the magic silver bullet–the complexity of designing for tablet-mediated learning. In *GROUP '14*, 2014.

Kafai, Y., & Peppler, K. (2011). Beyond small groups: New opportunities for research in computer-supported collective learning. In *Proceedings of the 2011 computer-supported collaborative learning (CSCL) conference*, pp. 17–24.

Kommers, P. (2010). Education and lifelong learning. In Study on the social impact of ICT' (EU-SMART PROJECT: CCP Nr.55A—SMART Nr.2007/0068, http://ec.europa.eu/information_society/eeurope/i2010/docs/eda/social_impact_of_ict.pdf.

Kuutti, K. (1995). Activity theory as a potential framework for human-computer interaction research. In B. A. Nardi (Ed.), *Context and consciousness: Activity theory and human-computer interaction* (pp. 17–44). Cambridge: The MIT Press.

Kuutti, K., & Bannon, L. J. (2014). The turn to practice in HCI : Towards a research agenda. In *Proceedings of CHI '14*, pp. 3543–3552.

Lave, J., & Wenger, E. (1991). *Situated learning: Legitimate peripheral participation.* Cambridge: Cambridge University Press.

Lewin, K. (1946). Action research and minority problems. *Journal of Social Issues, 2*(4), 34–46.

Löser, K.-U., & Herrmann, T. (2011). Privacy, trust and the practice of learning management systems. In *Proceedings of the 2011 Computer-Supported Collaborative Learning (CSCL) Conference*, pp. 811–817.

Müller, C., Neufeldt, C., Randall, D., & Wulf, V. (2012). ICT-development in residential care settings: Sensitizing design to the life circumstances of the residents of a care home. In *Proceedings of CHI '12*, pp. 2639–2648.

Mynatt, E., Adler, A., Ito, M., Linde, C., & O'Day, V. (1999). The network communities of SeniorNet. In *Proceedings of ECSCW '99*, pp. 12–16.

Naumanen, M., & Tukiainen, M. (2009). Guided participation in ICT-education for seniors: Motivation and social support. In *39th IEEE Frontiers in Education Conference*, pp. 1–7.

Overdijk, M., & Diggelen, W. (2007). Appropriation of a graphical shared workspace: The learner-tool connection. In *CSCL '07*, pp. 570–572.

Richter, A., & Koch, M. (2008). Functions of social networking services. In: *Proceedings of the 8th international conference on the design of cooperative systems.* Institut d'Etudes Politiques d'Aix-en-Provence, Carry-le-rouet, France, pp. 87–98.

Rieber, L. (2000). The studio experience: Educational reform in instructional technology. http://it.coe.uga.edu/studio/ (04/30/2015).

Rohde, M., Klamma, R., Jarke, M., & Wulf, V. (2007). Reality is our laboratory: Communities of practice in applied computer science. *Behaviour & Information Technology, 26*(1), 81–94.

Rohde, M., Klamma, R., & Wulf, V. (2005). Establishing communities of practice among students and start-up companies. In *CSCL '05*, pp. 514–519.

Stahl, G. (2011). Theories of cognition in CSCW. In *ECSCW '11*.

Stahl, G., Koschmann, T., & Suthers, D. (2006). Computer-supported collaborative learning: An historical perspective. In R. K. Sawyer (Ed.), *Cambridge handbook of the learning sciences* (pp. 409–426). Cambridge: Cambridge University Press.

Stahl, G., Ludvigsen, S., Law, N., & Cress, U. (2014). CSCL artifacts. *International Journal of Computer-Supported Collaborative Learning, 9*(3), 237–245.

Stevens, G., Pipek, V., & Wulf, V. (2010). Appropriation infrastructure: Mediating appropriation and production work. *Journal of Organizational and End User Computing, 22*(2), 58–81.

Suchman, L. (1987). *Plans and situated actions: The problem of human-machine communication.* Cambridge: Cambridge University Press.

Twidale, M., Wang, X., & Hinn, D. (2005). CSC*: Computer supported collaborative work, learning, and play. In *CSCL '05*, pp. 687–696.

Vygotsky, L. (1978). Mind in society: Development of higher psychological processes. Massachusetts: Harvard University Press.

Wegerif, R. (2006). A dialogic understanding of the relationship between CSCL and teaching thinking skills. *International Journal of Computer-Supported Collaborative Learning, 1*, 143–157.

Wood, D. (2003). Problem based learning. *BMJ, 326*(February), 328–330.

Wulf, V., Rohde, M., Pipek, V., & Stevens, G. (2011). Engaging with practices: Design case studies as a research framework in CSCW. In *Proceedings of CSCW '11*, pp. 505–512.

Part II
Exploratory Papers

CSCW and the Internet of Things

Toni Robertson and Ina Wagner

Abstract The Internet of Things (IoT) promises a massive increase in interconnectivity between objects and spaces requiring some sense of cooperation and interaction between them. We suggest the explicit conceptualization of the cooperation between objects and spaces as cooperative work and explore some of the visions, analogies and exemplary illustrations of the IoT using key CSCW concepts: coordination mechanisms, differences across contexts, common information spaces, and awareness. The paper begins a reflection on how CSCW concepts and approaches can inform an understanding of the IoT from a social and practice perspective raising crucial questions for the design of these technologies in the future. An issue of paramount importance will be negotiating the boundaries between (networks of) objects and people, making them transparent, understandable and adaptable.

Introduction

There is a rapidly growing body of research efforts focused on a corpus of emerging technologies grouped under the term Internet of Things (IoT). The term itself is defined in a number of ways. Atzori et al. (2010), in their influential survey of the visions, enabling technologies, applications and open issues of the IoT, suggested that its many and various definitions testify to the strong interest in it and 'the vivacity of debates on it' (p. 2788). They defined the basic idea of this 'novel paradigm' as:

T. Robertson (✉)
Engineering and Information Technology, University of Technology Sydney, Sydney, Australia
e-mail: toni.robertson@uts.edu.au

I. Wagner
Department of Informatics, University of Oslo, Oslo, Norway
e-mail: ina.wagner@tuwien.ac.at

© Springer International Publishing Switzerland 2015
N. Boulus-Rødje et al. (eds.), *ECSCW 2015: Proceedings of the 14th European Conference on Computer Supported Cooperative Work, 19–23 September 2015, Oslo, Norway*, DOI 10.1007/978-3-319-20499-4_15

the pervasive presence around us of a variety of things or objects—such as Radio Frequency Identification (RFID) tags, sensors, actuators, mobile phones etc.—which, through unique addressing schemes, are able *to interact with each other and cooperate with their neighbours* to reach common goals (*Ibid.,* our emphasis).

Other definitions of the IoT include 'a plethora of heterogeneous objects interacting with the physical environment' (IoT-A 2010) or a more formal, glossary definition: 'the global network connecting any smart object' (*Ibid.*). Such technology-driven definitions of emerging or still unthought-of technologies are both common and familiar to us because they enable a focus on a new domain of technical endeavour with its range of technological hurdles still to be solved. In the case of the IoT the emphasis is on the massive increase in interconnectivity between objects (in particular) but also between different spaces and indeed anything else that might be connected via the Internet to something else. This increased interconnectivity has led to a recognition of the need for contributions from different fields of research, including those such as CSCW that have developed resources to enable understandings of the sociotechnical aspects and implications of technology design and use (e.g. Atzori et al. 2010). It has also motivated predictions that the IoT will play a pivotal role in helping to address many of today's societal challenges as well as more extreme predictions of far-reaching economic and social transformation of society.

Schmidt (2011, p. 384) recently remarked: 'Epoch-changing transformations of human society are indeed proclaimed at a frequency that seems to match the business cycle perfectly'. And claims from the IoT literature that '*all* the objects in the world' (our emphasis) can and will be connected (e.g. Raiwani 2013; Bassi and Horn 2008) obviously do not withstand much scrutiny. But enormous numbers of objects are already connected to the Internet and many, many more will be so very soon. Examples of the IoT resonate strongly with Weiser's (1991) vision for ubiquitous computing, of interactive and communications technologies that not only disappear into the fabric of everyday life but are indistinguishable from it. The distinctions between ubiquitous technologies and IoT technologies are contested and can vary between different perspectives with the former even being retrospectively redefined to make room for the 'new' vision of the IoT (e.g. Raiwani 2013). But considered as one instantiation of Weiser's vision, the IoT promises to significantly extend, enrich, and even shift the relationship between people and the world around them gradually resulting in a genuine paradigm shift.

Within CSCW the underlying assumption/commitment has been that cooperative technologies and applications enable, mediate and support cooperation between people (e.g. Rodden et al. 1992) particularly, though not necessarily exclusively, by appropriately connected artefacts and/or good design practices reducing and constraining the amount of articulation work necessary in cooperative work (e.g. Schmidt and Bannon 1992). Combinations of, and interconnectivity between, people, technologies, various artefacts and spaces to enable cooperative work and other cooperative activities have defined the field and its various foci within the wider context of ongoing technology development. In the recent Jubilee Issue of the CSCW Journal, Schmidt and Bannon (2013) described the process of CSCW development:

> New technologies with collaborative potentials are emerging [...] and researchers engaged in their development or application may join the CSCW movement as they realise that their problems are related to problems already studied within CSCW or that they might benefit from building on what has been learned in CSCW, while researchers already engaged in CSCW research may explore the potentials of these new technologies (p. 347).

With the development of new technologies come new potentials for collaboration that in turn have provided opportunities to critique, re-evaluate and extend the fundamentals of the field (e.g. Schmidt and Bannon 2013; Bjørn et al. 2014).

The IoT brings many more objects and spaces into the mix, relying on some kind of cooperation between those objects and spaces to accomplish particular activities within the wider network (Atzori et al. 2010). These activities may or may not be directly linked to cooperative activities between people. Here our particular interest has been piqued by the notion of large numbers of objects 'able to interact with each other and *cooperate* with their neighbours to reach common goals' (Atzori et al. 2010, our emphasis). We wonder what it might mean when the metaphor of cooperation is applied to objects and space and if it might be a fruitful exercise to take this cooperation between objects seriously, as a kind of cooperative work that can be thought about from a perspective informed by the concerns and insights of CSCW. We have already learned from Actor Network Theory the value of taking seriously the non-human actors in sociotechnical networks, so the notion of objects and other non-human actors cooperating with each other to reach common goals is neither particularly novel nor farfetched. Indeed within the IoT literature we already find initiatives to converge the IoT and Social Networks into a Social Internet of Things (SIoT) as a way to provide structure for network navigability, establish 'trustworthiness' and new models of relationships between objects and spaces to address IoT related issues (Atzori et al. 2012). We emphasise that we are not seeking to attribute any sense of intent to objects as we might for cooperation between people or indeed to inadvertently humanise objects and spaces in any way. Our aim in this paper is to explore the explicit conceptualization of cooperation between objects and spaces as cooperative work as a way to uncover how some of the central themes and issues in CSCW might inform both the critique and design of IoT technologies.

The Cooperative Work of Interconnected Objects and Spaces

Those of us working within CSCW and related fields know that future technologies, no matter how great and heroic the technical challenges overcome in their making, will be just as situated within everyday material and social contexts as those that already exist or have been used in the past. Objects will still act within the resources of their situations just as we will still act within the resources of ours (Suchman 1987). But these everyday material and social contexts and our capacities to act in them will be changed by new technologies in all kinds of ways. So considering visions and examples connected with the IoT from a CSCW perspective poses some challenges. Within CSCW arguments are usually based on rich material from observational studies of work. Within the IoT literature arguments are generally based on, or at least illustrated by, various visions, analogies and use cases to help envisage what these future technologies might be like and how they might be used. However, positioning visions of the IoT within a framework of cooperative work enables using some of the important concepts from CSCW to orient our thinking about these new technologies.

To ground our further discussion, we start with one recent example of a potential IoT application in the field of logistics management that is derived from the work of Atzori and his colleagues (Atzori et al. 2010, 2014)

> Advanced cars, trains, buses as well as bicycles along with roads and/or rails are becoming more instrumented with sensors, actuators, and processing power. Roads themselves and transported goods are also equipped with tags and sensors that send important information to traffic control sites and transportation vehicles to better route the traffic, help in the management of depots ... and monitor the status of the transported goods (p. 2793).

The potential context for this example assumes: almost every link of the supply chain can be monitored by real time information processing technologies based on Radio Frequency Identification (RFID) and Near Field Communication (NFC); real time access to the Enterprise Resource Planning (ERP) program enables potential customers to be kept informed about the availability of products and where they currently are; route optimization to save time and fuel; information about the type and status of goods plus delivery times; and the monitoring of perishable goods to avoid uncertainty in quality for purchasing and distribution decisions (*Ibid.*).

This potential IoT application is further developed in a later paper (Atzori et al. 2014) that explores how the relationship structures of social technologies, such as friends, groups, liking, sharing and following etc., might suggest ways of organising the connections/relationships between objects:

> Chests of perishable goods know the quality and quantity of their contents (set by the producer) are able to continuously monitor the status of the environment, and know their current position. They make this information available to the rest of the network according to specific rules defined by the owner (the carrier) (p. 103).

This information is then shared with appropriate devices associated with the owner (dynamically via some kind of defined 'social' relationship within the network), such as a management system that deals with transport scheduling. The position of the chests is shared with other objects with common 'working locations' with the chests, such as warehouses, trucks and delivery destinations, to plan the storage and transport of goods. Information about the quantity of the foods, origins, quality (predefined and set by the owner), and location is shared with appropriate marketing venues that can share information about when a chest is sold with the chest itself and, the original management system and whoever and whatever might need it (again dynamically according to the 'social' relationships between the various actors in the network) (*Ibid.*).

This is a relatively straightforward example of a possible application of the IoT in a complex work context. How can we explore examples like this from a CSCW perspective? Our discussion in the reminder of this section draws on the fundamental CSCW concepts of coordination mechanisms, differences across local contexts, awareness and information spaces.

Coordination Mechanisms

CSCW research has developed a, by now, quite elaborate understanding of (work) practices. The concept of work has been elegantly described by Schmidt (2011, p. 375) as a polymorphous concept comprising activities that are considered 'necessary or useful in a practical way'. Work practices in modern societies often involve multiple, often geographically distributed, cooperating practitioners, representing different perspectives. The practices these practitioners engage in are characterised by a certain regularity in the sense that they follow particular agreed upon criteria of correct conduct. Moreover, many modern workplaces have to cope with multiple interdependencies, some of which are intractable, in terms of the number of interacting elements, their heterogeneity, level of ambiguity and uncertainty. Hence the need for coordinative mechanisms and artefacts that help practitioners manage these interdependencies.

The notion of 'coordination mechanism' was proposed by Carla Simone and Kjeld Schmidt in the 1990s. They developed this notion from observational studies of work situations that are characterised by multiple actors and task interdependencies:

> However, task interdependencies are often of an order of complexity where the provision of facilities for mutual awareness and ad hoc interactions is insufficient. Other means are required which make task interdependencies tractable. We call such means coordination mechanisms [...]. A coordination mechanism is, simply put, a coordinative protocol with an accompanying artefact, such as, for instance, a standard operating procedure supported by a certain form (Simone and Schmidt 1998, p. 295).

So from a CSCW perspective we can think of the IoT as an evolving set of coordination mechanisms for different application areas. Of course, these coordination mechanisms do not 'just' consist of 'a coordinative protocol with an accompanying artefact' but are much more complex. Many connected objects, sensor and actuator technologies, with their associated protocols and artefacts are involved. According to Atzori et al. (2014), a decisive step forward is from 'smart objects' to objects that 'socialise' in the sense of being 'potentially able to participate in communities of objects, creating groups of interest and taking collaborative actions' (*Ibid.*, p. 100). In the case of logistics management described above this feature is based on object-to-object links that are established 'in a dynamic way and without human intervention'.

A coordination mechanism is not always connected with an artefact. But numerous studies about a broad range of coordinative artefacts and the associated techniques of writing—bug report forms, patient records, flight progress strips, whiteboards, material specifications, and the like—have shown how these artefacts, used in accordance with specific sets of rules, serve as important representations of the state of work (e.g. Schmidt et al. 2007). They provide practitioners with relatively simple and stable means to e.g. identify items and persons, prioritise, define accountability, schedule, stipulate action, and so forth. With respect to our logistics example, messages to the smartphones of the owners of chests of perishable goods may be sufficient to inform them of the results of the independent selling actions of the network of objects. But we also need to ask what kinds of coordinative artefacts could provide the owners with, for example, choices of action to select from, help with changing criteria, product information and the like. Perhaps some of the artefacts that already exist as part of people's practices of producing and selling perishable goods could be included in the network and used in a possibly enriched way. Perhaps new types of artefacts would need to be designed.

These issues are connected to the important insight from CSCW research that it is essential that users, or members of any cooperative work arrangement, can devise, manipulate and redefine these arrangements, including any associated coordination mechanisms, so as to control their daily (working) life and take account of changes in it (e.g. Schmidt 2011). Hence, one of the questions we would ask from a CSCW perspective is how—within an IoT application in which smart objects 'socialise' to retrieve information, find the provider of a service and align a protocol with those of relevant other objects—would human users (a) understand these actions and (b) configure, reconfigure or modify (temporarily or permanently) the protocols these smart objects follow?

Local Contexts and Common Information Spaces

A related question is how and to what extent might IoT based technologies take account of the specificities of local contexts and local practices. It is somehow assumed that the various objects, recruited into a network by their 'social relations' within the network structure, have access to their own local context—or indeed what actually constitutes relevant local contexts for different objects at different times or circumstances. But this assumption rests on another, that local context can be 'sensed' and 'measured' according to criteria that can be shared across multiple contexts. One of the problems here, familiar to many who use scenarios in design, is that the scenarios introduced in the IoT literature cannot capture details that are only accessible to observation in real world contexts or within participatory design workshops and similar activities. CSCW researchers have pointed out how local contexts impinge on seemingly unequivocal 'standard' measurements. An example analysed by Schuurman and Balka (2009) is emergency room waiting time, which, through close inspection, turned out to mean something else in different emergency clinics, yet was aggregated across sites into indicators that were used for comparing clinics and designing policies.

In our example, 'freshness' of a product may be less problematic to measure at first sight, although for example—as a quick search of the Internet confirmed—'milk spoilage is an indefinite term and difficult to measure with accuracy'. One consequence is that milk producers 'use overly conservative expiration dates in an effort to avoid the legal and economic consequences of consumers experiencing illness from drinking spoiled milk' (Lu et al. 2013). We can also imagine that much of the freshness of a product depends on locally variable practices of collecting and packaging and their timing. How can networks of autonomous objects systematically take account of such variations? What do they need to know and how do they find out? How can 'freshness' be made comparable across multiple sites? Within CSCW, Schmidt and Bannon (1992) used the term common information space, suggesting that 'cooperative work is not facilitated simply by the provision of a shared database, but requires the active construction by the participants of a common information space where the meanings of the shared objects are debated and resolved' (p. 27). With respect to the IoT this begs the questions of how this active construction of a common information space, by objects with each other and with people, can be supported: which ways of understanding the 'reasoning' of interconnected objects or which aspects of their specific local contexts are made available to people and how can debates and solutions found in their world be made available in the world of objects?

Awareness

Awareness is another salient, well-developed concept in CSCW research. Referring to our earlier discussion of coordination mechanisms, the key precondition for such a mechanism to be useful is that 'the provision of facilities for mutual awareness and ad hoc interactions is insufficient' (Simone and Schmidt 1998, p. 295). In our logistics example, the application needs to at least support awareness of the freshness of distributed perishable goods, their location, the location of possible buyers and the current availability of any particular chest for purchase. But the awareness of who or what is being supported here?

The literature on IoT has borrowed the term awareness, applying it to smart objects: '*Awareness* is a smart object's ability to understand (that is, sense, interpret, and react to) events and human activities occurring in the physical world' (Kortuem et al. 2010, p. 31). In order to achieve this understanding, the smart object needs computing possibilities as well as the ability to 'converse with the user in terms of input, output, control, and feedback' (*Ibid.*, p. 31). Smart objects can be designed to be aware of some activities (e.g. the timing and duration of the use of a tool and the way it is handled, such as if it is dropped on the floor); of policies (e.g. they may detect deviations from correct conduct as laid down in forms of rules or patterns); and of processes (e.g. based on a context-aware workflow model that defines timing and ordering of work activities) (*Ibid.*). So we can imagine 'smart objects' supporting and extending human awareness in multiple and useful ways. But to do this requires that the objects themselves will need their own awareness supported within the network.

Let us look at another example, which illustrates this capability

> Our early example of cooperating smart objects, the safety-aware chemical drum, is a policy-aware smart object whose application model consists of a set of rules for determining to what extent workers handle it in accordance with safety rules. When we bring multiple smart drums together in close physical proximity, they act as a collective system: drums let each other access their respective rule sets and can thus make collective assessments about their safety status as a group (for example, whether the overall volume of all drums exceeds a dangerous limit). In this example, the drums achieve cooperation via a peer-to-peer (P2P) reasoning algorithm for collocated smart objects, in which the reasoning process physically "jumps" from one smart object to the next. All drums that have been part of the collective assessment display notices for users (Kortuem et al. 2010, p. 35).

In this example objects (chemical drums) communicate about safety issues that individual workers would possibly not be aware of or may not have the time or may not care to check, displaying the results of their assessment to them. This is an example typical of distributed work settings characterised by local variations (drums have different rule sets), where establishing awareness of safety-critical conditions may be difficult for participants. A similar example, described by Atzori et al. (2010) is an application to save energy, using 'dynamically changing energy prices to influence the overall energy consumption in a way that smooths load peaks' (p. 2795). 'Awareness' within this application would apply to the networks of sensors and actuators so they could regulate the use of household devices accordingly, 'considering the specific requirements of each appliances at home (battery charger, refrigerator, ovens)' (*Ibid.*).

We could content ourselves in many situations with having chemical safety and energy saving delegated to some new and fancy kinds of 'aware' automatons. However, from a CSCW perspective we would ask, how such technology-provided and technology-focused awareness could inform, complement and support the people using these applications to be aware of relevant issues. Such awareness, as we know, 'is not the product of passively acquired "information" but is a characterization of some highly active and highly skilled practices' (Schmidt 2002, p. 292). Hence, the question to explore would be how such extended awareness could be embedded in and made relevant for a variety of practices, given that the complexity of interdependencies would make it difficult to obtain and sustain over time.

Embedding IoT in Everyday Practice

All these arguments revolve around a basic tenet of CSCW research: to study phenomena as part of people's practices. In due course we will have opportunities to study people's practices that include the everyday use of IoT technologies. In the meantime though we can recognise that looking at IoT applications as part of practice already raises additional issues, some of which are to do with the practicalities of living with complex technologies already in use. Many households and workplaces today are already equipped with sensors of all kinds and a common experience is that they often don't work or when they do work their contribution is inappropriate to current activities and requirements. Stringer et al. (2006) mention the 'issues people had with not understanding and/or not trusting the ways in which their sensors worked, as well as the practical realities of location and timing and false alarms that render them less useful' (p. 8). This resonates with the common experience that technologies often break down or don't work properly and that in many cases people with specialised knowledge are needed who know how to make them work again.

IoT applications will not design themselves, nor will they exist in 'non-places' with interconnected objects happily chatting, sensing and taking decisions. They will need people to make decisions about which sensors to use and make decisions about where these should be. Then other people need to program, install, calibrate, monitor for accurateness, clean, and repair them. And we could devote a whole paper to a discussion of the articulation work needed to embed IoT applications in everyday practice!

Conclusion

Our motivation in this paper was to explore how CSCW might be positioned in relation to the development of IoT technologies in the hope that this endeavour will benefit from what has already been learned in CSCW research. Our first step was to take seriously the cooperation between objects that underlies the visions of the IoT as cooperative work to seed our reflection on how insights from CSCW, in particular some of its key concepts, may help raise interesting and crucial questions for the design of these technologies in the future. In this exploratory paper we were able to raise just a few of these questions, answers to which will be found only through eventual in-depth studies of actual IoT applications in use. An issue of paramount importance will be negotiating the boundaries between (networks of) objects and people, making them transparent, understandable and adaptable. This also entails ethical and political questions, which we will address as part of future work. Clearly, CSCW can make important contributions to the development of IoT technologies. In the process exploring the potentials of these emerging technologies can expand the scope of CSCW's areas of interest.

References

Atzori, L., Iera, A., & Morabito, G. (2010). The internet of things: A survey. *Computer Networks, 54*, 2787–2805.
Atzori, L., Iera, A., Morabito, G., & Nitti, M. (2012). The social internet of things (SIoT)–When social networks meet the internet of things: Concept, architecture and network characterization. *Computer Networks, 56*(16), 3594–3608.

Atzori, L., Iera, A., & Morabito, G. (2014). From "smart objects" to "social objects": The next evolutionary step of the internet of things. *Communications Magazine, 52*(1), 97–105.

Bassi, A., & Horn, G. (2008). Internet of things in 2020: A roadmap for the future. *European Commission: Information Society and Media.*

Bjørn, P., Esbensen, M., Jensen, R. E., & Matthiesen, S. (2014). Does distance still matter? Revisiting the CSCW fundamentals on distributed collaboration. *ACM Transactions on Computer-Human Interaction (TOCHI), 21*(5), 27.

IoT-A (2010) *Internet of things—Architecture project (IOT-A).* http://www.iot-a.eu/public.

Kortuem, G., Kawsar, F., Fitton, D., & Sundramoorthy, V. (2010). Smart objects as building blocks for the internet of things. *Internet Computing IEEE, 14*(1), 44–51.

Lu, M., Shiau, Y., Wong, J., Lin, R., Kravis, H., Blackmon, T., & Wang, N. S. (2013). Milk spoilage: Methods and practices of detecting milk quality. *Food and Nutrition Sciences, 4*(7), 113.

Raiwani, Y. P. (2013). Internet of things: A new paradigm. *International Journal of Scientific and Research Publications, 3*(4), 323–326.

Rodden, T., Mariani, J. A., & Blair, G. (1992). Supporting cooperative applications. *Computer Supported Cooperative Work (CSCW), 1*(1–2), 41–67.

Schmidt, K. (2002). The problem with awareness: Introductory remarks on awareness in CSCW. *Computer Supported Cooperative Work (CSCW), 11*(3–4), 285–298.

Schmidt, K. (2011). The concept of 'work' in CSCW. *Computer Supported Cooperative Work (CSCW), 20*(4–5), 341–401.

Schmidt, K., & Bannon, L. (1992). Taking CSCW seriously. *Computer Supported Cooperative Work (CSCW), 1*(1–2), 7–40.

Schmidt, K., & Bannon, L. (2013). Constructing CSCW: The first quarter century. *Computer Supported Cooperative Work (CSCW), 22*(4–6), 45–372.

Schmidt, K., Wagner, I., & Tolar, M. (2007). Permutations of cooperative work practices: A study of two oncology clinics. In *Proceedings of the GROUP'07* (pp. 1–10).

Simone, C., & Schmidt, K. (1998). Taking the distributed nature of cooperative work seriously. In *16th Euromicro Conference on Parallel, Distributed and Network-Based Processing* (pp. 295–301) (PDP 2008).

Schuurman, N., & Balka, E. (2009). alt.metadata.health: Ontological context for data use and integration. *Computer Supported Cooperative Work (CSCW), 18*(1), 83–108.

Stringer, M., Fitzpatrick, G., & Harris, E. (2006). Lessons for the future: Experiences with the installation and use of today's domestic sensors and technologies. In *Proceedings of the 4th International Conference on Pervasive Computing* (pp. 383–399). Berlin, Heidelberg: Springer.

Suchman, L. (1987). *Plans and situated action.* Cambridge: Cambridge University Press.

Weiser, M. (1991). The computer for the 21st century. *Scientific American, 265*(9), 66–75.

Ageing Well with CSCW

Ann Light, Tuck W. Leong and Toni Robertson

Abstract This paper rethinks the role of technology in the life of older people by critically considering the discourses around ageing: drawing on insights from literatures on *active ageing*, findings from two studies conducted with older citizens and prevalent understandings of old age in technology design. It argues for a departure from the deficit model of old age, to an understanding that reveals older people's agency in the ageing process and the work they do to manage their capacity to age well. This reframing of ageing and the ageing population offers new insights to CSCW and suggests new goals to support when designing technology for older people—goals that are more cognizant of people's agency and their desires to manage their evolving experiences of the ageing process. We conclude with characteristics of the technologies we might develop.

Introduction

This paper critically considers design for older people, drawing on insights from the literatures on *active ageing* and presentations of old age in technology design. We explore how we might contribute to the positioning of CSCW by studying practices that constitute the work of active ageing to achieve the goals of *ageing well*. This reflection on ageing seeks to develop the field by departing from solution-focused approaches that take a deficit model of old age. Our

A. Light (✉)
University of Sussex, Falmer, UK
e-mail: ann.light@sussex.ac.uk

T.W. Leong · T. Robertson
University of Technology Sydney, Sydney, Australia
e-mail: tuckwah.leong@uts.edu.au

T. Robertson
e-mail: toni.robertson@uts.edu.au

© Springer International Publishing Switzerland 2015
N. Boulus-Rødje et al. (eds.), *ECSCW 2015: Proceedings of the 14th European Conference on Computer Supported Cooperative Work, 19–23 September 2015, Oslo, Norway*, DOI 10.1007/978-3-319-20499-4_16

aim is to broaden views about the ageing process: from the rhetoric of assistance and vulnerability to one that prioritizes the agency of older people and how this plays out in the connections and relations between people, their living environments, technologies, and artefacts. We complement our discussion with findings from two studies grounded in older peoples' own interests, priorities and everyday practices. In doing so, this paper does not present design templates or solutions, but offers a series of considerations to inform design discussion and reflection.

Background: Ageing as a Process

To capture the subtleties of ageing, with its cultural and political dynamics, we start with the World Health Organization definition of *active ageing*:

> the process of optimizing opportunities for health, participation and security in order to enhance quality of life as people age [which…] allows people to realize their potential for physical, social, and mental well being throughout the life course and to participate in society according to their needs, desires and capacities, while providing them with adequate protection, security and care when they require assistance. (www.who.int/ageing/active_ageing/en/).

From a CSCW perspective, we consider *active ageing* as the work of preparing for new life stages when interests, values, conditions and capabilities may change. In doing so, we can recognize continua in ageing (e.g. chronological, cultural, physical) and structural and emotional discontinuities (retirement, bereavement) that life as lived across many parts of the world in the 21st century introduces. Malanowski (2009) presents four phases of old age: pre-retirement; independent living as a retiree; early dependent living (with increasing limitations); dependent living up until death. We regard these as useful to think about design needs, but add the obvious point that *active ageing* can begin when young—being a lifelong condition to which different people choose to give different amounts of attention and preparation—and identify *ageing* as a process rather than a series of states.

If we regard ageing as a process, rather than old age as a state, what changes? Do we get a better model? These questions help us avoid thinking of older people as a single vulnerable group with uniform needs that remain static. Schröder-Butterfill and Marianti (2006) suggest "current research rightly criticizes blanket assumptions of older people's dependence and vulnerability" (p. 4). For instance, socio-cultural participation has been shown to positively influence older people's health (Carstairs and Keon 2008), as does reciprocity—having something to offer as well as to take—(Fyrand 2010), while even a chance to show efficacy enhances life and prolongs health (Shepherd et al. 2008). At its simplest, "the mere act of decision-making may be a way for the heavily dependent to remain engaged with life" in contrast with the negative affect associated with "giving in" (Boudiny 2013, p. 1091). Within the design literature, Brandt et al. (2010) suggest thinking in terms of 'situated elderliness' to avoid simplistic descriptions. Lindley et al. (2009) suggest that older people's communication patterns become slowly more selective and considered. And Light (2011) shows the transformative impact possible in participatory projects, reporting a participant's feelings: 'Asked what she derived from the experience [of the project, she...] spoke of regaining her identity: "We went in as old people and came out as people with our own thoughts and agendas."'. Here we see the extent to which people may be aware of their ageing and the social and structural categorization that arises from it.

However, technology design research has shown a tendency to fasten on older people's need for assistance as its principal concern, at worst treating older people as a single needy and costly demographic; at best regarding care in old age as a complex site of negotiation, but frequently ignoring the other half of the equation: what quality of life might mean and how we seek to maintain it as our capacities and priorities change. Vines et al. (2015) categorize the HCI literature on old age in four discourses: of health economics, (lack of) socialisation, homogeneity and deficit. Influential discourses reinforce this:

> The term 'assistive technology device' means any item, piece of equipment, or product system, [...] that is used to increase, maintain, or improve functional capabilities of individuals with disabilities. (US, The Assistive Technology Act of 1998 [105-394, S.2432]).

Technology is given as a solution, to make up for and even cancel out human decline. Blythe et al. (2005, p. 677) note that assistive technology is "often ugly or stigmatising", reinforcing a particular view of older people in society.

In (even notionally) adopting a deficit model, we ignore people's idiosyncratic features, as we do in many design contexts. But when we do it here, we reduce diversity of hopes, fears, needs, experiences, characteristics, interests and motivations, as well as people's own awareness of and management of ageing, to a stereotypically incompetent user, both in need of assistance to live and also to control their technology.

Boudiny (2013) warns against setting up expectations of particular types of competence in defining *active ageing*, causing the 'older old' to feel inadequate, but she devotes more of her policy critique to highlighting definitions of ageing that make *all* older people feel misunderstood, marginalized or patronized. Instead, the case is made for a rounded approach: "policies on ageing are often characterized by a dichotomy, targeting either healthy older adults by promoting active participation and self-responsibility or dependent older people by viewing them primarily as recipients of care ...In our view, however, being engaged in life and being dependent are not mutually exclusive." (Boudiny 2013, p. 1087).

As would be expected in a field such as CSCW, which places great importance on close observational studies of practice, there are already good examples in the literature focusing on the work involved in specific areas of ageing and home care, such as Procter et al. (2014), Bratteteig and Wagner (2013). We suggest a dynamic model of ageing can achieve recognition of the multidimensionality of the design space, not just to learn to design existing tools better, but to reveal new opportunities to be creative with computer-supported collaboration.

Rethinking the Ageing Process: Two Studies

In this section, we describe two studies (one Australian, one British) that sought to understand ageing from the perspective of people thinking about their present and future interests, values needs and spaces. Both were explorative, involving qualitative work with a wide range of participants in the second half of life.

Ageing Well—An Australian Study

In a project about the potential role of technology in maintaining good habits into old age, researchers conducted semi-structured interviews with Australians between the ages of 55 and 75. The demographic for the interviews was relatively narrow: white, middle-class and living in the eastern states of Australia. The first series (20 interviews) sought demographic and experiential data, including participants' definitions of ageing well, fitness and activity levels, community and social engagement, use of and attitudes to various information and communication technologies, future work and retirement plans, and current practices around keeping in touch with friends and families (Robertson et al. 2012, 2013). This group was a mix of working, semi-retired and fully retired people; some were very computer literate while others were comfortable only with (mobile) phone use and email. The second series (20 interviews) involved technology-literate participants who already used internet connections at home. These interviews linked understandings of ageing well to participants' domestic environment, the significant objects and spaces within it, and how these were used and inhabited.

Analysis reveals that participants' views of what ageing well meant to them were remarkably similar. Good health, mobility and fitness, independence, social interaction and community involvement were identified as central to maintaining current and future well-being. Maintaining good health and a level of fitness was considered central to keeping mobile and maintaining the social agency and physical independence that each of our participants valued highly. Participants all expressed their desire to maintain, for as long as possible, their capacity to experience and engage in life. They revealed themselves to be mindful of ageing and its approaching needs and interested to age in step with the networks, spaces, technologies and opportunities round them, but to keep a feeling of control.

Yet, while participants' views of ageing well were highly consistent, there was great diversity in what it would mean for each participant to maintain good health, mobility and fitness, having aged differently and responded differently to the ageing process. Everyone wanted to maintain social agency and relationships with families and friends, yet social networks and how these were experienced and managed were very different. And while all participants were already using digital technologies, again there was difference in the way technology was used.

Significantly, participants had little interest in tools designed specifically for 'the aged'. Instead they wanted to use the same technologies that 'everyone else' used. There was an expectation that tools would be designed without the negative associations of assistive, age-defined and deficit-focused technologies. But, as Lindley et al. (2009) found in their study of communication patterns, participants were selective in what they were prepared to use and how they apportioned their time, especially in learning new approaches. They were willing and able to learn and use tools they recognized as useful, particularly if they could be seen to support central aspects of ageing well, such as maintaining independence, social agency, their sense of their 'cultural self' and ability to remain in their own home. Participants had appropriated a number of communications tools into their everyday lives and were in various stages of engaging with newer social technologies. The use of word processing, email and various web services, such as online banking, was common. There were different levels of familiarity with some of the newer tangible technologies and little interest in expanding use of those currently available. In other words, the interviews provided a snapshot in the ongoing appropriation of new technologies that were not specifically age-related, but part of the general social, technological and physical infrastructure in which (ageing) people live. If there was a tendency related to age, it was that judgments on a tool's value involved different factors.

The cultural self that people seek to maintain as they age pertains to cultural origins, life histories, gender roles, and values. The interviews omitted any direct multi-cultural element, though just over a third of the participants were migrants. But a related pilot study indicates that asking questions of older people from different Australian communities would yield an even wider set of priorities and choices. A study conducted by postgraduate students interviewing elderly migrants now living in New South Wales looked at how cultural values shaped views and expectations. For instance, among the elderly Chinese interviewed (from Hong Kong or China), growing older did not mean living alone or away from their families. Instead, a lot of those interviewed lived with their children, especially if widowed. Despite diaspora, older people were in close proximity to the rest of their clan. And asking these questions of Indigenous communities would yield another set of practices that are different from the ones reported here.

FLEX—A UK Study

The *Flexible Dwellings for Extended Living* (FLEX) project worked with a broad cross-section of city-dwelling mature adults in the UK. It took a participatory look at the social factors of wellbeing as we age 'in place' to learn how neighbourhoods might tackle the promotion of sociality together within and across generations and resist trends that encourage social isolation—from erosion of meeting places to the advent of environmentally-sealed, socially-barricaded smart homes. FLEX worked specifically with the idea of *conviviality* or 'living together'; it did not specify interest in technology. We use this second study to consider further how partici-pants spoke about what they value in the social realm.

City dwellers in England and Scotland, aged 43–82, from diverse backgrounds and lifestyles (sourced through mailing lists to very different housing areas) came to talk together at tea parties about how they want to live as they age. Everyone who attended had volunteered, so they were not a typical cross-section but people with motivation to join events (see Light et al. 2013; Light and Akama 2014 for more on methodology). Invites to the discussions avoided targeting 'older people' as such, with a flier labelled 'Living Sociably as we Age' and an invitation to ask 'What might we do as we grow older to live our lives as fully and convivially as possible in our homes and domestic spaces?'. Participants reflected together in ad hoc groups, prompted by questions on the themes of 'home' and 'sharing'. They explored how social and spatial elements of their world could be configured to improve a sense of shared space or time (e.g. street-parties or co-gardening) and how these afford rela-tive strangers occasion to meet and talk. Highly prominent were discussions on (a) taking the initiative to keep social—and useful—in one's community, and (b) mixing across generations. We use these here to give specific examples of how important social agency and cultural identity are to people considering ageing.

Participants noted society's increased desire to protect vulnerable members, such as young and very old people, and how it works counter-productively by making behaviour seem risky that has traditionally strengthened social networks (neighbours involved in childcare, sharing, acts of kindness and 'popping in'). As the participants put it: 'generosity of spirit encourages people to communicate bet-ter' and, in Britain, you need 'the odd eccentric in a group to start the ball roll-ing' (tea party, Newcastle). Fired by this theme, one participant ("Jill"), a retired woman renting with her husband, became eloquent: 'I believe that if you take that first step, people will be grateful. Take the risk, because in all sorts of ways we're really becoming such a risk-averse society, aren't we?' Jill goes on to describe an occasion when she establishes contact with the student household upstairs: 'There was a mix up and we ended up with two pizzas and I just knocked on one of the flats. ...I said "Would you like this pizza? The pizzeria has given us this free because, you know ... and do you like pepperoni?" and he said "I do now.". And two days later, he said: "That was great. I really enjoyed my pizza.".'. Jill's joy at the encounter and her memory of it is palpable.

Jill is clearly taking initiative in setting up good neighbourly relations and is pleased to have done so, but we can see other factors at play. She tells the story in the context of dismay at an increasingly 'risk-averse society'. She is both engaged in an analysis of society and acting (perhaps in retrospect) to counteract the trend she dislikes. She is making herself socially useful as well as socially connected. We are not surprised that someone who values sociality should come to discuss 'social wellbeing as we age'. But we draw attention to the work that Jill is doing, first in visiting the neighbour and then in telling the story in this context. She is asserting her values, her desire to live by them and the manageable way that she can perform this in her immediate world. By 'work', here, we mean activities con-sidered 'necessary or useful in a practical way' (Schmidt 2011, p. 375).

The second theme is prefigured already: a general interest in avoiding the old people ghetto and 'that we stop separating older and younger people' (tea party, Dundee). We have heard it in the first study, where ageing Australians reject customized technology, and, in Jill's account of crossing the generation gap with pizza. Again participants saw this in broad societal terms: that youngsters would be more courteous to their elders if they knew them. But they also considered more subtle mixing, discussing the policy of council-run classes held at sheltered accommodation for the elderly that are open for anyone to attend, and which they attend because 'the teacher is good'. Photoshop classes are popular, as is dancing. 'It's a socialized intermixing of younger and older pensioners and younger people just coming up to pension age. Some of them are able to do it all, the dancing..., other ones like, say, do the cooking... and other ones just sit and watch and I think it's very good for them' (Dick, social housing).

Again, we see the self-perception as active. Attendees had various incapacities and mobility problems, but none saw themselves as part of a vulnerable group. Instead, they described concern for more aged neighbours. We see recognition of people's different needs and how they can be managed and a welcoming of policy that mixes people. We see the selectivity in joining in—because of a 'good' teacher—and note the popularity of Photoshop, a digital tool.

Reflecting, groups in both cities observed that mere recognition of issues of ageing and sociality by individuals and across neighbourhoods could make a real difference to how community reliance is formed.

To sum up, establishing social agency and cultural identity is integral to the work of coordinating with others. It is such an obvious and necessary activity that its maintenance only becomes articulated as a goal of *ageing well* during close examination. In the Australian study, people described this to researchers. In the British study, because of the different method, it was possible to see it enacted.

Discussion: CSCW for Ageing Populations

It would be easy to conclude from this argument about the diversity of older people's experience that any tool that works for the general population could be used by older people and this would avoid discrimination. That is, of course, true. We can point to older people's rich potential for informing the design of devices and networks for *all* populations, not just the old, bringing familiarity with and acceptance of change, insight into shifts in technology, felt engagement with what younger people regard as history and many other qualities. We can suggest this potential is currently undervalued worldwide (though not by all cultures).

Yet, we can go further. Not only do many people have a strong sense of what they need, witnessed in our samples, but the acts of securing it contribute to the potential for a healthier old age. We can dignify ageing—and help people live well for longer—by acknowledging ageing as a physical, mental, emotional and structural process that people work to learn to manage as part of that process, even as their capacities change. We can design with this insight in mind and design to ease tensions created by national policies (including policy on retirement age and conditions, workers' rights, power of attorney, etc.) that cannot attune to the needs of each person. Adopting this perspective, we can derive characteristics with some significance for CSCW research:

Flux: Ageing selves reflect the lives they have led. They are old enough for genetic, cultural and environmental influences to have inscribed themselves, along with experiences, such as their work, access to health care, good food and a safe environment, their communities and the kinds of social activities, cultural mores and expectations these provided, as well as various random life events and accidents. This inscription is not static, but etches more deeply as time passes. People face a continuum of small changes as well as some abrupt transitions. Day-to-day living must be managed more carefully as the effects become more pronounced. More maintenance and coordination work is needed over time to support the status quo, such as living at home, keeping up with friends, etc.

Adjustment: As Boudiny reminds us (2013), people do not make a choice between dependency and independence, but experience a gradual reevaluation of their roles relative to others and their place in their different worlds, as energy levels and capacities change. What remains is the desire to engage; what changes is what it means to engage and, gradually, the methods of engagement.

Agency: All participants in the studies desired to maintain social agency and cultural identity—to be valued as people with things to contribute and to share in. Performing these as part of social life is a transcendent but unquantifiable goal in ageing well. Being able to do the work of belonging, taking initiative and getting counted is often more meaningful than 'independence' as such.

Prioritization: As energy dwindles and the time taken to achieve tasks grows, selectivity becomes more marked. More demanding and less valued tasks and pleasures are let go, as are the more onerous aspects of their coordination.

Willingness: In the face of loss, people unfold unexpected substitute skills, collaborative relationships or creative strategies to overcome limitations (Boudiny 2013). Our studies found that, when people see a rationale for support tools to prevent them losing whatever they fear losing, they will overcome obstacles to accomplish their use. This is in balance with capacity and confidence.

Types of Tool

Working with this set of characteristics, what difference might it make to our designs? Boudiny says of offering support: "The aim is to achieve a partnership in which two destructive extremes are avoided, i.e. expert-based decision-making without reference to older adults' perspectives versus simply leaving older persons to express what they want in an unsupported way" (2013, p. 1092). The same could be said of the role of a tool or socio-technical network. We contrast the term *assistive* with *enabling* to put the emphasis on what the technologies achieve for the user (enabled), rather than what they claim by way of contribution (assisting). And we end our consideration of ageing and technology design with possible characteristics of the technologies to be built:

Enabling: Supporting the ageing person in their ever-evolving coordination of mechanisms for maintaining the status quo, so that ageing does not impinge on the execution of their goals, but allows them to keep doing more for longer.

Extending: Lengthening the period of fulfilled and self-managed living and reducing the ailing morbid phase, by making it easier to assemble, judge and grow the technical, medical and social networks of support needed.

Blurring: Helping to ease the transitions between Malanowski's (2009) first three phases of old age: pre-retirement; independent living as a retiree; early dependent living (with increasing limitations), so that personal management processes can run smoothly despite structural change.

Adapting: Following the person as they become more selective about what they do, but also helping them choose their path, thus acknowledging and supporting the work of managing ageing, as well as the ageing process.

We have seen that diversity as we age is multi-dimensional and unpredictable. The recognition of the specificity of ageing selves and the activities available to us—including appropriation of new and emerging technologies—foregrounds the further recognition that people remain embedded within their ever-changing social and cultural worlds as they age. Indeed, it is that embeddedness that we seek to maintain as we grow and continue to age.

Our aim is to help more people lead rich and fulfilling lives for longer, but we acknowledge that pressure on support systems in many countries has led to political interest in enabling people to live longer at home ('ageing in place') and promoting older people's input into 'core' (i.e. domestic, non-remunerated, societal) and financial economies. Both motivations argue for a turn to exploring the management of the ageing process in such a way people's own interest in ageing well is allowed to contribute to their wellbeing. We argue that technology can have an enabling role in this process, with insights from CSCW helping to ensure that the coordination work of ageing well is understood and incorporated.

Acknowledgments   We thank our participants, the UK's AHRC for funding *Flexible Dwellings for Extended Living* (grant AH/J007153/1) and the Leverhulme Trust for funding Light on her *Ageing and Agency* International Academic Fellowship. The Australian study was funded by Australia Research Council Discovery Grants Program. Jeannette Durick contributed to the original research in this study.

References

Blythe, M. A., Monk, A. F., & Doughty, K. (2005). Socially dependable design: The challenge of ageing population for HCI. *Interacting with Computers, 17*(6), 672–689.
Boudiny, K. (2013). Active ageing: From empty rhetoric to effective policy tool. *Ageing and society, 33*(6), 1077–1098.

Brandt, E., Binder, T., Malmborg, L., & Sokoler, T. (2010). Communities of everyday practice and situated elderliness as an approach to co-design for senior interaction. In *Proceedings of the OzCHI 2010* (pp. 400–403). New York: ACM.

Bratteteig, T., & Wagner, I. (2013). Moving healthcare to the home: The work to make homecare work. In *Proceedings of the ECSCW'13* (pp. 141–160).

Carstairs, S., & Keon, W. J. (2008). Issues and options for an aging population. *Second Interim Report, Special Senate Committee on Aging*, Ottawa.

Fyrand, L. (2010). Reciprocity: A predictor of mental health and continuity in elderly people's relationships? A review. *Current Gerontology and Geriatrics Research*.

Light, A. (2011). Democratising technology: Inspiring transformation with design, performance and props. In *Proceedings of the CHI'11* (pp. 2239–2242).

Light, A., & Akama, Y. (2014). Structuring future social relations: The politics of care in participatory practice. In *Proceedings of the PDC 2014* (pp. 151–160). New York: ACM.

Light, A., Milligan, A., Bond, L., McIntosh, L., & Botten, C. (2013). High tea at the conviviality café: Research tool or design intervention? In *Proceedings of Research through Design Conference 2013* (pp. 212–215).

Lindley, S. E., Harper, R., & Sellen, A. (2009). Desiring to be in touch in a changing communications landscape: Attitudes of older adults. In *Proceedings of the CHI'09* (pp. 1693–1702).

Malanowski, N. (2009). ICT-based applications for active ageing: Challenges and opportunities. In M. Cabrera & N. Malanowski (Eds.), *Information and communication technologies for active ageing: Opportunities and challenges for the European Union*. Amsterdam: IOS Press.

Procter, R., Greenhalgh, T., Wherton, J., Sugarhood, P., Rouncefield, M., & Hinder, S. (2014). The day-to-day co-production of ageing in place. *JCSCW, 23*, 245–267.

Robertson, T., Durick, J., Brereton, M., Vetere, F., Howard, S., & Nansen, B. (2012). Knowing our users: Scoping interviews in design research with ageing participants. In *Proceedings of the OzCHI 2012* (pp. 517–520). New York: ACM.

Robertson, T., Durick, J., Brereton, M., Vaisutis, K., Vetere, F., Howard, S., & Nansen, B. (2013). Emerging technologies and the contextual and contingent experiences of ageing well. In *Proceedings of Interact 2013* (pp. 582–589).

Schmidt, K. (2011). The concept of 'work' in CSCW. *Computer Supported Cooperative Work (CSCW), 20*(4–5), 341–401.

Schröder-Butterfill, E., & Marianti, R. (2006). Understanding vulnerabilities in old age. *Ageing and Society, 26*(1), 3–8.

Shepherd, G., Boardman, J., & Slade, M. (2008). Making recovery a reality. *Sainsbury Centre for Mental Health*.

Vines, J., Pritchard, G., Wright, P., Olivier, P., & Brittain, K. (2015). An age old problem: Examining the discourses of ageing in HCI and strategies for future research. *ToCHI, 22*(1), 2.

Collaborative Visualization for Supporting the Analysis of Mobile Device Data

Thomas Ludwig, Tino Hilbert and Volkmar Pipek

Abstract Visualizations are mainly used for providing easy access to complex information and data. Within this paper we focus on how visualization itself can serve as a collaborative aspect within distributed and asynchronous team work. In doing so, we try to uncover challenges to support a team of researchers in understanding and analyzing mobile data by collaborative visualization. Based on a review of recent literature, two workshops with participants from the academic field were conducted, which revealed use cases and major design challenges for a collaborative visualization approach. With our user-centered study, we introduce design implications for collaborative visualizations that focus on research questions instead on single visualizations, embed multiple visualizations into a discussion thread, highlight relations between research artefacts as well as include external parties in collaborative visualizations.

Introduction

In recent years, smart mobile devices have become continuously more ubiquitous in daily life. Equipped with low cost sensors such as accelerometers and gyroscopes, they allow data to be collected in situ, remotely and parallel from multiple devices (Hagen et al. 2007). Based on the increasing usage of one device for both private and professional work purposes, smart mobile devices therefore offer

T. Ludwig (✉) · T. Hilbert · V. Pipek
Institute for Information Systems, University of Siegen, Siegen, Germany
e-mail: thomas.ludwig@uni-siegen.de

T. Hilbert
e-mail: tino.hilbert@uni-siegen.de

V. Pipek
e-mail: volkmar.pipek@uni-siegen.de

© Springer International Publishing Switzerland 2015
N. Boulus-Rødje et al. (eds.), *ECSCW 2015: Proceedings of the 14th European Conference on Computer Supported Cooperative Work, 19–23 September 2015, Oslo, Norway*, DOI 10.1007/978-3-319-20499-4_17

a great opportunity to create a holistic view of the users' appropriation of such devices. Approaches already exist, which try to cover various aspects related to the mobile sensing of gathering data or mobile data mining to discover hidden usage patterns. Beyond data gathering, there are a variety of methods for analyzing mobile-gathered data. Those methods encompass mainly highly collaborative tasks including teams and multiple members with different backgrounds, located at different places and working at different times. CSCW as an interdisciplinary field influenced by various communities from computer science, social science, and psychology is conceived as 'an endeavor to understand the nature and characteristics of cooperative work with the objective of designing adequate computer-based technologies' (Bannon and Schmidt 1991). By creating an understanding of how multiple actors work in different collaborative settings, CSCW explores how groups in an organization can be supported by tools and how these tools might change the organization itself and vice versa. An elementary aspect is awareness that builds the base for exploration, evaluation and design of supportive methods/tools within work context (Bannon and Schmidt 1991).

One important field of mobile-gathered data analysis is 'information visualization', whereby visualization of data and information is not limited to explanation purposes. Instead, the visualization itself can be an independent approach to explore and analyze data based on cognitive and perceptual principles. Within this paper we try to combine the research area of CSCW with concepts of visualization and examine when and how 'collaborative visualization' can be used to support a team of different researchers in understanding and analyzing mobile-gathered data. In doing so, we review recent literature regarding collaborative visualization and its origins 'visualization' and 'CSCW'. Based on the identified design challenges, we conducted two workshops with actors from the academic field where possible use cases for collaborative visualizations and design challenges for analyzing mobile-gathered data are identified. The basis of our approach is a previously developed mobile application which utilizes the concept of participatory sensing to gather mobile data for research projects (Ludwig and Scholl 2014).

Related Work: Collaborative Visualization

Visualizations are not a modern day invention. Cartography and astronomy have been using visual representations since 200 B.C. and the 10th-century respectively. Visualizations and graphics are used for a wide range of fields even beyond research contexts: for instance in journalism, to provide a broad audience with easy access to complex information. Computer science provides various approaches and tools for gathering, processing and analyzing huge amounts of data. Chen et al. (2009) describe different processes of how interactive visualizations are created and how they can be supported by existing information. Data visualization is 'the use of computer-supported, interactive, visual representations of data to amplify cognition' (Card et al. 1999) and can be subdivided into information visualization and scientific visualization, whereby scientific visualization focuses on physically-based, scientific data and information visualization on abstract, non-physically-based data (Card et al. 1999). Collaborative visualization can be understood as "the shared use of computer supported, (interactive), visual representations of data by more than one person with the common goal of contribution to joint information processing activities" (Isenberg et al. 2011). The idea behind collaborative visualization resulted from the need to overcome the traditional design of single-user visualization systems and to allow the collective exploration and analysis of large data sets through visualization.

Current Approaches of Collaborative Visualization

First approaches of collaborative visualizations were redefined extensions of existing modular systems for collaborative use cases. These were mainly achieved by duplicating views or sharing some selected parts—or a mixture of both approaches (Wood et al. 1997). Former research has shown that visualizations are significant for collaborative work, e.g. the benefits of using visualizations compared to not using them (Bresciani and Eppler 2009); or that groups obtain better results with visualization systems in comparison to individuals (Mark et al. 2002). Isenberg et al. (2011) differentiate collaborative visualization systems into the two categories of distributed and co-located approaches. In both cases, various approaches exist (Isenberg and Carpendale 2007).

Hugin (Kim et al. 2010) is a mixed-presence tool which supports co-located as well as distributed collaboration in a synchronous working context and examines coordination mechanisms of awareness, territories and access control. For highly distributed and asynchronous settings, such as those of researcher teams, we focus on asynchronous and distributed approaches. As Willett et al. (2011) mentioned asynchronous collaboration is often based on the decomposition of work into smaller tasks which can be performed in parallel. Thus, central mechanisms of such tools are based on creating awareness and aggregating individual results. Nevertheless, for a better understanding of visualizations and their applications, knowledge about cognitive and perceptual principles is necessary.

ManyEyes (Viegas et al. 2007) is a tool which supports the asynchronous collaborative analysis of social data. ManyEyes is public and can be accessed by anyone who is interested. It maps the visualization process, beginning with the upload of data up to the discussions about the visualizations. Users can upload data sets and are able to create visualizations. ManyEyes provides various kinds of visualizations, like bubble charts or network diagrams, and supports the visualizations with collaborative features such as annotations or feedback and discussions prompted by comments. To obtain an in-depth understanding of how ManyEyes is used as a community, interviews with users and existing logs were analyzed after the public launch. It was shown that ManyEyes is not used as a dedicated community, but as a platform for other, external communities where large proportion of the communication takes place off-site (Danis et al. 2008). Heer et al. (2009) present another approach for the collaborative visual analysis of data with Sense. us. In contrast to ManyEyes users do not have the possibility to upload their own data sets. Sense.us is an analytics tool that supports view sharing, doubly linked discussions and social navigation mechanisms, e.g. listings of comments and recent activities. Heer et al. (2009) describe how central mechanisms, such as providing collaborating participants with access to the same visual environment; using graphical annotations to refer to direct conversations; or separating annotations and comments visually from the visualization, were used by participants and determined that it was especially the combination of mechanisms which allowed a deep exploration of the data. CommentSpace (Willett et al. 2011), which is partially based on the experiences previously gathered by Sense.us and ManyEyes, focuses especially on the discussions around visualizations. Willett et al. (2011) criticized that the previous approaches did not support their users in more complex analytical tasks, e.g. the gathering of evidence. CommentSpace therefore focuses on adding a small and fixed vocabulary for tagging and linking to comments. Such mechanism is especially designed to support the generation of hypothesis and the gathering of evidence. This is done by using tags like 'question', 'hypothesis' or 'to-do' and links such as 'evidence-for' or 'evidence-against'.

The presented approaches have shown that tagging and linking, if used, can have a positive impact on the collaborative analysis tasks. During deployments it was noted that tags and links were not used as often as in laboratory evaluations. Willett et al. (2011) assume motivational factors and emphasize the need for guidance and incentives to facilitate the benefits of the provided mechanisms. Based on the understanding of both fields of visualization and CSCW, as well as their implications for collaborative visualizations, critical issues for collaborative visualization designs were identified.

Design Issues

Heer and Agrawala (2008) identified important design considerations for collaborative visual analytics, which were based on prior experience of Sense.us (Heer et al. 2009) and a survey of relevant research areas including CSCW and visual analytics. In the course of their work, they identified seven areas: (1) Division and allocation of work; (2) Common ground and awareness; (3) Reference and deixis; (4) Incentives and engagement; (5) Identity, trust and reputation; (6) Group dynamics, and (7) Consensus and decision making. For these areas they went on to present 24 design implications for asynchronous collaborative visualization systems, e.g. 'Artefact histories' as part of the area 'Common ground and awareness'; or 'Personal relevance' for the area 'Incentives and engagement'.

Isenberg et al. (2008) analyzed how individuals and teams work and interact during visual information analysis tasks. Based on observations of individuals and teams, who had to solve tasks in a co-located and synchronous setting,

Isenberg et al. (2008) identified eight different processes: During the *Browse process* the team scans through the available data and artefacts to form their first impressions of the available data. The *Parse process* involves the (re-)reading of the task to create a common understanding of the problem and how to solve it. During the *Discuss Collaboration Style process* the team discusses the overall task division strategy. In the *Establish Task Strategy process*, the team figures out the best way to perform the tasks with the available data and tools. The *Clarify process* involves activities which help to understand information artefacts. The *Select process* is about finding and selecting relevant information artefacts for a particular task. The *Operate process* includes higher-level cognitive work on a specific view of the data to extract information for fulfilling a task. During the *Validate process* the team tries to confirm the solution of a task. It also involves activities which ensure that the process of the team itself is correct. Isenberg et al. (2008) mentioned that the temporal order of the process differed from team to team and one typical temporal order does not exist. For a collaborative visualization, three general implications must be addressed: It must be flexible regarding the temporal sequence of work processes: it must support changing work strategies, and it must support workspaces.

Research Approach

Currently, existing asynchronous distributed approaches for collaborative visualization like ManyEyes, Sense.us or CommentSpace are all based on design hypotheses which were previously formulated. As is usual within the discourses of Information Systems, design assumptions were derived from literature. From a CSCW and more practice-oriented perspective, we argue that there are several shortcomings stemming from the existing approaches:

1. It is questionable how the design decisions can meet the user requirements without involving the users themselves. Feedback from users which is only considered after the deployment means that it is often influenced by the capabilities and limitations of the tool.
2. None of the tools presented were designed to be used in the context of a group sharing the same goal, as it was the case regarding researcher teams. In contrast, ManyEyes in particular was designed for an unspecified and broad audience. This causes significant differences, for e.g. privacy issues or data structure.
3. None of them mapped the visualization process starting with the gathering of data and its exploration, and ending with the analysis of data. Especially within long-term studies, data explorations often start before the collection is finished. ManyEyes provides uploading final data but does not involve aspects about its source. Sense.us does not even provide the possibility to upload one's own data.

Within this paper we therefore focus on a more user-centered approach including ideas from potential users for applying collaborative visualization for analyzing mobile-gathered data. The underlying purpose is to create a comprehensive picture of relevant context of use. The resulting concept should support researchers during exploration and analysis of data gathered by mobile devices. We focus on long-term studies, where it is possible to explore data even before gathering is finished. This 'open heart empiricism' provides the option to gain first insights into the data while it is being collected, and this can then be used to adapt the ongoing research strategy.

Workshop

To gain a deeper understanding of how collaborative analysis tasks could be supported by visualizations, we conducted two workshops. The first workshop lasted three hours and consisted of six participants; one female and five male. Their age ranged from 25 to 29 years. Five of them were research associates and one was a research student. All had several years' experience an academic context. Their context of research differs and covers research fields ranging from mobility to crisis management. None of the participants had hand any previous experience with collaborative visualization. The workshop was split into two parts: The first consisting of an introduction, brainstorming and discussion of previous experiences. This served as an introduction to the topic and assisted the participants to familiarize with the context, especially the use and analysis of mobile device data within research projects. Brainstorming was divided into two phases, whereby each was led by its own central question: 'What kind of data can you gather using personal mobile devices?' and 'What kind of research questions could you answer by using the data gathered by mobile devices?' The intention was that the results should include different views from different kinds of project. The second part was intended to gather insights and design implications for possible IT support which aims at utilizing visualizations to support research teams in analyzing mobile data. It started with a presentation of ManyEyes and the participants had the opportunity to form their first impressions on 'how collaborative visualization works'. After the presentation, a Brainwriting Pool activity was conducted with the central question of 'which ideas and requirements do you have for approaches based on visualizations that support your team during a research project?' (Figs. 1 and 2). The analysis was based on the main question: 'Which design challenges need to be addressed for collaborative visualization?' The analysis revealed various design issues, which were separated into the three areas *Visualization, Collaboration* and *Sharing* (Table 1). The second workshop was used to evaluate and redefine the raised issues by other participants from academia. Seven researchers participated in the second workshop. In the following, we present mainly the results of the first workshop, which were confirmed by the participants of the second workshop.

Table 1 Design issues

Design issue	
V.1	Select relevant data
V.2	Filter and aggregate data
V.3	Link data
C.1	Merge results
C.2	Provide structure
C.3	Encourage communication
C.4	Reveal relations
S.1	Build commitment
S.2	Allow participation

Fig. 1 Participant reviewing Brainwriting cards

Fig. 2 All Brainwriting cards

Visualization

Visualization includes design issues which are directly related to the visualization of the data mobile-gathered by researchers. Thus related questions are: 'How can one visualize the data?' or 'Which capabilities and features regarding data and visualization need to be provided?' In respect of this, three issues have been identified and outlined below.

The design issue 'Select relevant data' appears in various notes and comments. The question behind this issue is: 'Which relevant data does the researcher need to visualize gaining the best possible insights into his/her research interests?' The initial note was "*I would like to visualize relevant locations*". 'Select relevant data' was mainly discussed in context of the dimension 'location'. That may have been caused by the participants' research focus, but beyond this, the same questions can be transferred to most other categories of data. As implied by the participants, relevance depends on various aspects and differs due to individual factors. Supporting researchers in this issue may help during the selection of data for the visualization. However it should also provide an opportunity to focus on important elements of the resulting visualization.

The second design issue is 'Filter and aggregate data'. The participants continually mentioned filtering and aggregation of data as being important capabilities which IT support should provide in context of research projects. Aggregation affords different levels of abstraction and enables researchers to explore a research problem from different angles. This was highlighted by one participant during the prioritization of the Brainwriting Pool: "*What are relevant places? What are relevant buildings? Or what may be relevant... well, that has got different levels, different levels of abstraction, which are based on the same data*". Advantages of the data filtering are mentioned as they offer support in the context of exploring visualizations and their meaning by experimenting with different filters as well as using them as bookmarks and, therefore, providing options to share a current visualization.

The last design issue is 'Link data'. The participants had several ideas regarding the linkage or enrichment of the mobile-gathered data. Notably, the opportunity to link visualizations with other data sources which provide additional information about the context of use was one reoccurring aspect for the participants: "*I would like to be able to extend data visualizations with qualitative data, e.g. questionnaires*" or "*How can I combine sensors with qualitative or other quantitative data? How can I get feedback from the users about their context?*" Remarkably, the participants focused mostly on capabilities related to the underlying data and possible operations based on them. Various aspects of the issues 'Filter and aggregate data' and 'Link data' were often mentioned and prioritized during the Brainwriting Pool. According to this, these two issues and their implications must be considered particularly when designing a possible IT support.

Collaboration

Collaboration includes issues related to features regarding team work. The central question is: 'How can possible IT support be designed and structured to support the work of a research term beyond the process of visualization?' Here our specific focus is on the actual research team; external stakeholders such as study participants who contribute their mobile data, or other involved stakeholders are covered in the section 'Sharing'.

The first design issue is 'Merge results'. It became clear that it is important to be able to combine or to merge visualizations and (interim) results with each other. It was stated that these combinations may be difficult to implement, but regarding the merging of multiple data analysis, one of the participants said: *"Nevertheless, [merging multiple data analysis] does have great potential, as one is just able to reproduce several, more complex scenarios"*. As a solution, the participants suggested switchable layers.

The 'Provide structure' is another important design aspect: *"I need a good underlying workflow which structures the collaboration"*. Based on this comment, several suggestions were added, e.g.: *"One should be able to filter the workflow based on time or data"*. Additionally, related questions were raised: *"How can cooperation be structured? How can rights be managed?"* Furthermore, version control and change history were often mentioned as necessary functionalities. Keeping the history of visualization changes also provides other advantages: *"It helps team members to stay up-to-date, to prove validity and reliability of the former process and its results"* and it could also be used to support new team members to become acquainted with the project; or to learn by reviewing the previous work of other team members: *"... if you integrate new people at a later stage, the data changes are visible. Thus, s/he can image how the project evolved"*.

The design issue 'Encourage communication' includes the thoughts and ideas which refer to the capabilities related to the question: How can people be made aware of each other and their work; and how can communication be stimulated and supported by adequate features? The need to encourage communication was noted: *"The stimulation of discourses and group discussions (forums) for specific topics, their aims [and] the implementation of aims"*. Regarding this issue and especially the associated aspect of awareness, it was suggested that team members should be visible during shared editing, to provide user profiles and also to visualize the relationships involved in the cooperation. One of the participants suggested *"the creation of filters and data sets that can be shared"*. The motivation behind this idea was that if s/he is stuck in a vast amount of data, s/he could share the current filter and a team member could try to help. Additionally, this provides another opportunity for learning, as exemplified: *"This should allow me [to support other people] who work with similar data sets; telling them: 'I performed an analysis, which might fit [your case]. Just have a look how I did it'"*.

The last design issue is 'Reveal relations'. In the workshop, the participants several times highlighted relations between different entities of possible IT support: *"Filters can and should be added to certain research questions"* or *"Goals should be added to visualizations, if applicable, to make the collaboration more efficient"*. Additionally, they proposed linking related visualizations with similar goals as well as research questions respectively, to allow the addition of qualitative codes for visualizations. Regarding goals and visualizations, one participant stated: *"I think mostly [goals] are mostly defined by the project. But when I think of our group, goals change every six month. You keep getting new insights the whole time and you build [your future research] on them. You develop new goals and directions that must be addressed"*.

The issues presented by 'Collaboration' show that, in addition to capabilities for the visualization itself, IT support has to incorporate adequate capabilities for supporting collaborative work into its design. Both the issues 'Provide structure' and 'Encourage communication' have been considered, but in particular both revealed ideas and thoughts with a slightly different focus compared to the existing systems, e.g. Hugin or ManyEyes. The collaborative analysis and exploration of data is less focused on visualization and the discussion based on them. The considerations to highlight relations between projects, visualizations and goals provide an interesting new approach. The thoughts behind 'Merge results' point out that the participants do not consider that a single visualization provides the basis for visual analysis. In contrast, the visual analysis is understood to be a process that includes the merging and combination of multiple data analyses and results.

Sharing

The third area, 'Sharing', includes design issues which address the sharing of information and results with external stakeholders as well as their involvement in the collaborative analysis. External actors can be, for instance, participants, who contribute mobile data.

The first design issue, 'Build commitment', pertains to the considerations necessary to ensure the participants commitment to the study. One participant asked: *"How can I integrate people who supply the data so that sustained success is ensured?"* Because: *"If someone provides data, you have to give him something in return"*. Besides providing incentives like *"I would like to send visualized results to the participants"*, the researchers suggest allowing the participants to perform all data analyses themselves.

'Allow participation' is the second design issue. The participants suggested: *"The integration of feedback possibilities for participants"* and *"the creation of participation possibilities, so that participants are able to create visual analyses themselves"*. As shown, it is related to the previously mentioned design issue which utilizes participation as a possibility to promote commitment. The notes showed that feedback can also be used by the researchers to involve participants later on in the study or project phases. For instance, one participant explained: *"In context of research data sensing and analysis, one has to give the user something in return. So that they know progress has been made and, based on that, new goals can be developed collaboratively with the user"*. Notably, prior to the workshop, the importance of those issues were not expected to be as high. However, with regard to our approach, sharing and participation are not directly linked to visualization itself, but, in fact, crucial to a lasting success in the context of this work.

Conclusion

Due to the workshops we gained insights into the needs and thoughts of researchers regarding the design issues pertaining to the support of the analysis of mobile-gathered data through collaborative visualization. The identification of the three areas outlined underlines the variety of issues which have to be considered when designing possible IT research infrastructures. An approach based on these insights might provide a valuable basis for computer-supported cooperative work in the context of visual analytics as further steps towards eScience. As expected, the participants provided new insights and ideas which had not previously been considered in literature. Related to the gathering of mobile data within long-term studies with participants, the issues 'Build commitment' and 'Allow participation' were highlighted as they not only state which requirements have to be met for lasting success; they also show which synergies can be created through the involvement and participation of data suppliers. Beyond that, further ideas were revealed. We found that, instead of focusing on groups that are formally defined as an organization, a tool of collaborative visualization within the academic context must focus on informally defined teams grouped by their interest in shared research questions and common goals. For example, some of the participants' thoughts shifted the focus of collaborative analysis to underlying research questions and the relations between the different artefacts of such an approach. This has only been lightly addressed by existing approaches like CommentSpace (Willett et al. 2011), but not as deeply as the participants mentioned. This paper contributes first steps of using a CSCW lens towards existing approaches of collaborative visualization; and, based on the two workshops, we derived user-centered design issues for visualizations that encompass a collaborative analysis of mobile-gathered data and therefore contribute to eScience. As our next step we are currently implementing a web-based application building upon our uncovered issues for providing a tool to analyze mobile-gathered data aiming at fostering the collaboration between academic project teams and external stakeholders by simple visualizations.

References

Bannon, L. J., & Schmidt, K. (1991). *Studies in computer supported cooperative work* (pp. 3–16). Amsterdam: North-Holland Publishing Co.

Bresciani, S., & Eppler, M. (2009). The benefits of synchronous collaborative information visualization: Evidence from an experimental evaluation. *IEEE Transactions on Visualization and Computer Graphics, 15*(6), 1073–1080.

Card, S. K., Mackinlay, J. D., & Shneiderman, B. (Eds.). (1999). *Readings in information visualization: Using vision to think.* Burlington: Morgan Kaufmann.

Chen, M., Ebert, D., Hagen, H., Laramee, R., Van Liere, R., Ma, K.-L., et al. (2009). Data, information, and knowledge in visualization. *Computer Graphics and Applications, 29*(1), 12–19.

Danis, C. M., Viegas, F. B., Wattenberg, M., & Kriss, J. (2008). Your place or mine: Visualization as a community component. In *Proceedings Human Factors in Computing Systems* (pp. 275–284).

Hagen, P., Robertson, T., & Sadler, K. (2007). Accessing data: methods for understanding mobile technology use. *Australasian Journal of Information Systems, 13*(2), 135–149.

Heer, J., & Agrawala, M. (2008). Design considerations for collaborative visual analytics. *Information Visualization, 7*(1), 49–62.

Heer, J., Viegas, F. B., & Wattenberg, M. (2009). Voyagers and voyeurs: Supporting asynchronous collaborative visualization. *Communications ACM, 52*(1), 87–97.

Isenberg, P., & Carpendale, S. (2007). Interactive tree comparison for co- located collaborative information visualization. *IEEE Transactions on Visualization and Computer Graphics, 13*(6), 1232–1239.

Isenberg, P., Elmqvist, N., Scholtz, J., Cernea, D., Ma, K.-L., & Hagen, H. (2011). Collaborative visualization: definition, challenges, and research agenda. *Information Visualization, 10*(4), 310–326.

Isenberg, P., Tang, A., & Carpendale, S. (2008). An exploratory study of visual information analysis. In *Proceedings of Human Factors in Computing Systems* (pp. 1217–1226).

Kim, K., Javed, W., Williams, C., Elmqvist, N., & Irani, P. (2010). Hugin: A framework for awareness and coordination in mixed-presence collaborative information visualization. In *Proceedings of Interactive Tabletops and Surfaces* (pp. 231–240). New York: ACM.

Ludwig, T., & Scholl, S. (2014). Participatory sensing im Rahmen empirischer Forschung. In Mensch und Computer 2014—Tagungsband: Interaktiv unterwegs—Freiräume gestalten, Hrsg. v. Butz, Andreas; Koch, Michael; Schlichter, Johann, München, Oldenbourg-Verlag, pp. 145–154.

Mark, G., Kobsa, A., & Gonzalez, V. (2002). Do four eyes see better than two? Collaborative versus individual discovery in data visualization systems. In *Proceedings of Information visualization* (pp. 249–255).

Viegas, F., Wattenberg, M., van Ham, F., Kriss, J., & McKeon, M. (2007). Manyeyes: A site for visualization at internet scale. *Transactions on Visualization and Computer Graphics, 13*(6), 1121–1128.

Willett, W., Heer, J., Hellerstein, J., & Agrawala, M. (2011). Commentspace: Structured support for collaborative visual analysis. In *Proceedings of Human Factors in Computing Systems* (pp. 3131–3140).

Wood, J., Wright, H., & Brodie, K. (1997). Collaborative visualization. In *Proceedings of Visualization* (p. 253–259).